Speak So I
Shall Know Tl

C000025159

EDITED BY WILLIAM J. WALSH

*David Bottoms: Critical Essays
and Interviews* (McFarland, 2010)

Speak So I Shall Know Thee

Interviews with Southern Writers

WILLIAM J. WALSH

McFarland & Company, Inc., Publishers

Jefferson, North Carolina, and London

The present work is a reprint of the library bound edition of Speak
So I Shall Know Thee: Interviews with Southern Writers,
first published in 1990 by McFarland.

Acknowledgments: Some of the interviews have been previously
published in whole or in part in the following: *The Albany Review, The Chattahoochee
Review, Cotton Boll/Atlanta Review, Earthwise, Georgia State University Review, High
Plains Literary Journal, Michigan Quarterly Review, Negative Capability, Other Voices,
Pembroke, Southern Humanities Review, Southern Quarterly, Verse,* and *Webster Review.*
The author thanks the editors of these magazines for their permission to reprint
these interviews.

I am grateful to each writer for his or her cooperation in granting the
interview and for taking an interest in my work. They were a source of great
encouragement.

Most especially, I would like to thank my wife, Amy, who had the insight
to buy me a new tape recorder after the first interview and somehow sensed
what I needed to do.

LIBRARY OF CONGRESS CATALOGUING-IN-PUBLICATION DATA

Walsh, William, 1961–
    Speak so I shall know thee : interviews with Southern writers /
by William Walsh.
       p.   cm.
    Includes index.
    ISBN 978-0-7864-6749-5
    softcover : acid free paper ∞

    1. Authors, American—Southern States—Interviews. 2. American
literature—Southern States—History and criticism. 3. Authors,
American—20th century—Interviews. 4. Southern States—
Intellectual life—1865– 5. Southern States in literature. I. Title.
PS261.W27 2012   810.9'975—dc20   [B]   89-43689

BRITISH LIBRARY CATALOGUING DATA ARE AVAILABLE

Front cover image © 2012 Shutterstock.

Manufactured in the United States of America

*McFarland & Company, Inc., Publishers
  Box 611, Jefferson, North Carolina 28640
  www.mcfarlandpub.com*

To my grandfathers:
Arthur Card,
who taught me to fish,
and William J. Walsh, Sr.,
who taught me to play baseball

Contents

Preface

When I decided to become a writer I had no idea where to begin. This was frustrating; there did not appear to be a clear-cut answer to achieve my goal. I had to discover, by exploration, through raising questions and listening to answers, how one becomes a writer—how one goes from thinking about being a writer to getting to whatever place there is so you can write. Many people want to write, but have no idea where to begin. I have done so by interviewing those who are ahead of me, writers who have made the journey to that place.

I was fortunate, when I began interviewing writers, to be living in the South, a region rich in literary tradition. Therefore, much of the discussion revolves around the Southern literary scene. Who is the Southern writer? What defines the Southern writer? Why is the South recognized as a unique area? These are just a few of the questions that were of interest to me.

To define the Southern writer, one must first define the South. The first Southern newspaper, *The Maryland Gazette,* was founded in Baltimore in 1727, but scarcely will you find a person, today, who will consider Baltimore part of the South. Today the South is changing geographically, just as it was when *The Maryland Gazette* was first published. The editors and writers of that newspaper may have never imagined the sweeping changes that would occur, and just as sweeping are the current economic changes unearthed in the resources of the Southern states today.

The South is growing at a vigorous rate. There is no question about this. But where is the South today? Is the South limited to the enclaves of rural areas outside the metropolitan cities: Atlanta, Birmingham, Columbia, Jackson, Little Rock, Memphis, Nashville, New Orleans, Richmond, Winston-Salem, and the other dozen or so homogenized cities with an influx of inhabitants from all over the country? Can Florida still be considered a Southern state in any respect except geography? How much of Texas is Southern, and where is the line drawn where its Western influences begin? Can the expanding metropolitan areas still be considered Southern when their influences are New York, London, Paris, California, and the television/pop culture? These are questions for great debate, and out of this debate more questions are raised: How does a writer deal with the changes, are the changes beneficial, what are the concerns of the writer, is the Southern voice fading...? And so on. For each question there are tenfold answers. In addition, because most writers agree that the Southern writer is "Southern" because of early childhood experience, many of the questions are geared toward the writer's life, not biographical conversations, but conversations exploring the writer's early childhood background, early interests in writing, education, influences, their writing, and other concerns and aspects of writing that ultimately shape the writer's work. These interviews attempt to discuss writing — all aspects applicable to the writers and try to capture the answers of the changing South.

To the writer from the South, the term Southern writer is a connotation for a regional writer, sometimes a local colorist, and often one restricted by the boundaries of the South. However, even though these writers are proud of the South, they are quick to point out, and heavily defend, the idea that while they may have been born and raised in the South and often chose to live there, their work transcends *all geographical boundaries,* and their concerns, professional and otherwise, do not begin and end in the South. Their concerns, sometimes local, are the same as writers in New York, Chicago, Vermont, Colorado, Montana, California, or elsewhere in the country and the world.

What distinguishes the South from the rest of the country and how does this interconnect with writing? William Price Fox recalled, in relation to the Southern idiom, a friend who wrote a song about a woman leaving her husband, "I've gone and told the children you were dead. I've even had a funeral for your side of the bed." And his description of the redneck at Burger King who wants a croissant, "I'll have a hamburger, a side of fries, a milk shake, and honey, put my hamburger on one of those curved biscuits." These distinctions go beyond verbal idioms into attitudes developed from the early Southern experience. Someone growing up in Boston for the first 12 years of their life, even if they lived in the South for the next 30 years, would never call a croissant a curved biscuit. Each writer has his or her own South, their definition of what makes up the Southern writer, and how the South has influenced their writing. When discussing with these writers how they made the journey to become writers, it is of great interest to reflect upon their development. If there is a common denominator of an answer from these conversations it is the *early Southern experience,* the early childhood experience, or what is more commonly known as "roots."

"As long as there is the land," Scarlett said in *Gone with the Wind,* the South will survive. But the loss of the land is changing the face of the South, and with that may go many of the traditions. As Madison Jones said about the buying up of land for commercial uses, "It's as if your whole family has been raped twenty times — you don't think much about it anymore." Is this changing the face of the South? Where there once was a loyalty to the land, to a person's roots, today the number of people on the land has substantially decreased, propelling the landowner into a minority status.

The writers in this collection of interviews are poets, short story writers, and novelists; many have won awards such as the Pulitzer Price, the National Book Award, the Bollingen Prize, the Prix de Rome, Guggenheim fellowships, the Walt Whitman Award, the O. Henry Awards, the Lamont Poetry Selection, the James Baldwin Award, the Thomas Wolfe Memorial Award, the Townsend Prize, National Endowment for the Arts grants, numerous state awards, and grants from the National Institute of Arts and Letters and the Rockefeller Foundation. The collection embodies firmly established writers side by side with newly emerging talent. I strove for a balanced representation of writers in the contemporary South, and spent many hours driving in the wee hours of the night to Mississippi, Florida, North and South Carolina, Alabama, Louisiana, Arkansas, and throughout Georgia, through rain and snow storms, in a car without heat or air conditioning, and at one time looking like an aquarium of blue smoke rolling down the highway as it filled up with exhaust. Even so, the writers I interviewed are those whose work I had previously enjoyed and whose work I discovered in the course of my research. Writers and friends often suggested the work of other writers, too.

It has been the goal of these conversations to adhere to the craft of writing and to discover how one becomes a writer, while at the same time defining the modern Southern writer. Everyone becomes a writer differently — some know they want to write from early childhood, others come to it by accident, or through friends. I have found a rich variety of answers.

How does one become a writer? Where do you begin? How do you publish what you've written? What is the current state of writing? Can writing be taught, and if so, where does one go to study? What kind of advice do writers have for new writers? Over the course of three and a half years I have eagerly listened to these writers. Now, I'll let the writers tell you.

William J. Walsh, III

Betty Adcock

Betty Adcock grew up in East Texas and now lives in
Raleigh, North Carolina, where she is Kenan Writer in
Residence at Meredith College. Her collections of poetry include *Walking Out, Nettles,* and *Beholdings.* This interview
was conducted April 14, 1988, at my house in Stone Mountain, Georgia, as she and her husband made their way to
East Texas on vacation.

Could you discuss your background?

I grew up in East Texas in a little town called San Augustine, population
2500, then and now! It was a very old town . . . for Texas. The place calls
itself the Oldest Anglo-Saxon Town in Texas. That is, the first one settled
entirely by immigrants from the then—United States, as opposed to those
from Spain or Mexico. My family was there from about 1819 or '20. So it was
a very rooted town in the county, and because of this it was the county seat.
We were pretty isolated, really in the woods, though we were within thirty-
five miles of college in Nacogdoches. Because my town was then utterly
dependent on agriculture, and so isolated that it did not change, and did not
wish to change, I saw life very nearly as it must have been lived in the nineteenth century. I am too young to have seen the things I saw, but I saw them
. . . the big cotton gin belching out lint, the icehouse with its wet black floors,
farmers bringing mules and wagons, as well as those who brought pick-up
trucks, into town on Saturday when the stores stayed open until 10 o'clock.
Life in other places, for other children, must have been very different at the
same time. I find it a marvelous resource to have lived almost in a past time
for awhile. It gives me a perspective I couldn't have had otherwise, that most
people cannot have. I must say I can't quite imagine what it would be like
to grow up in suburbia. That I can't imagine.

Your first book Walking Out *is extremely different from your second collection* Nettles. *Two different poets could have written each book. It's the same kind of material,
but the style is completely different—short poems verses the longer meditative, narrative
poems. In fact,* Nettles *is a prelude to* Beholdings.

That's very true. *Walking Out* was a beginning, a kind of apprentice work, as I guess all first books are to some extent. I wasn't thinking of a book. I was just writing one poem after another, until one day there were enough to send out somewhere and see what might happen. A number of those poems are probably imitations of poets I liked. I was at the age when you say "well, I can do that, maybe," when you see something interesting by someone else. The so-called "deep image" poem was around and I was trying that out, and other things. I heard Robert Bly read the other night, which was interesting . . . sort of a trip back. But he's rather different himself these days. I had some poems that tried out the *stones* and *bones* and *dark.* It was never really my voice. But I didn't know what my voice was. I tell my students to imitate, try something. How else do you learn what is or is not going to be your own voice? At the time I wrote *Walking Out,* I didn't have hold of my material, partly because I was running away from East Texas. I was living in the South, North Carolina, but Raleigh felt as if it might be New York, it was so different. So I was running away from my subject in some of the poems in *Walking Out,* but in some poems in that book I was groping toward it. It's a process of exploration after all.

In searching for your voice it appears that you have circled back around to your origins and have incorporated it into your poetry.

Well, the first part of my new book, *Beholdings,* is East Texas folklore and history. Even prehistory. It's narrative. I even got ambitious enough to work with the story of how the soils were built. Because that particular part of the world is fascinating, especially the Big Thicket. Botanically it is unlike any other place. It was more or less unknown until recently, when the tiny bit of it that is left was made into a national Wilderness Preserve. Now you need a guide to go in there. But it was a wilderness with a small "w" when I was a child, not yet so completely cut by timber companies. My father hunted all over that area. He'd come in with stories about wild orchids and other strange flowers, about enormous trees, and the animals: wildcats, cougars, red wolves, foxes. He brought me baby skunks and raccoons. He knew the names of the waterbirds and hawks. Even where I lived one could sometimes hear cougars at night, and I lived fairly close to town. Our town was on the far northern edge of where the original Big Thicket had been, but those mysterious places were still deeply wild. The place resonated with stories . . . Terrible feuds, strange hunts, murderous incidents and brave ones, and funny ones. When I heard these stories as a child, I felt I was seeing them, sensing them.

On the other hand, it is not all interesting stories. When I left it was to try to become something other than what my role was to have been had I stayed. I was obviously not going to take to that role. Already I wanted to be a poet. At nineteen I married and moved to North Carolina. I had always wanted to be a poet, and I had always read poems. I don't know where that came from, but I wanted to be a poet of the world, a "sophisticated" poet, smart. But you could only do that in the city, right? It took me a long time to come to terms with, and to accept what was to be much of my material.

I don't mind using the term "regionalist." It has been felt to be a negative term. I have felt it so. And, of course, work that doesn't rise above the "local colorist" variety is not what one wants to go after. But it seems to me that everyone is a regionalist. One has to be somewhere, after all. John Ashbery could only have come out of New York, William Stafford only out of Kansas. People write out of a place whether or not they mention it. So, yes, in much of my work I am writing out of this place, East Texas. I see no reason for critics to be disdainful of the term "regionalist." Richard Hugo has a wonderful essay on place in which he says something like, "If you're in Chicago, you can get to Rome, but if you ain't nowhere you can't go no place." (*Laughing.*) So if you are in, say, East Texas, you can get to that Rome of the imagination, the place in your head where poetry is made.

You can see the settling down in the first and second books into your voice and the material that is important to you leading up to Beholdings. Beholdings *begins with "Clearing Out, 1974," which is about your father's death.*

My father's death had a fierce impact on me, and somehow on my work. He died an unusual death, and the poem that is really about that is in *Nettles,* "To my Father, Killed in a Hunting Accident." The poem you mentioned that opens *Beholdings* is about going through his desk after his death, a metaphor I suppose for coming to terms — what we do in sorting out what is left behind. But then the whole first section of this book is about what is left behind, what happens when the obscure tribe of Indians vanishes, when the wilderness is irrevocably changed, when a family leaves. What do you do with the bits and pieces that are left? So I used the process of going through my father's ancient rolltop desk as my frame for that, for the whole book really. In a sense my father's desk contained the land, the tribe, the forest, and it's animals. It doesn't matter that it happens to be true, but it is... That desk was full of feathers, snakeskins, turtle shells, boar's teeth, stones, arrowheads — all this instead of business papers desks are used for. The items I found there, including the bloodstained checkbook, all became images for this work, turning up in other poems, etc.

The first section of Beholdings *is about the clearing of the land and the building up of a civilization. It's a historical piece that is captivating. But, one of the biggest disappointments for me was when I began the second section and the history of the area did not continue. Now, the second section is good and it holds its own, but the history ends in 1950, and as you said that is when you left East Texas. I was wondering why you did not continue with the first section all the way through?*

Well, I didn't leave until 1957, but I suppose I left in spirit when I went away early to school in 1954. Around 1950 feels like the time I stopped having personal memories that are of a piece with the place. But there were poems set in the nineteenth and early twentieth century that I wanted to include, to add to that part of *Beholdings*. I had other poems about various people, but I did not finish them. Also, I did not want to make it a whole book about that area. Some poems will go into a later book. I might have been nervous about finishing so many in that narrative mode as I have been mostly a lyric poet. I love the intensity of the lyric. I wanted this book to have poems of that kind also. I was a little nervous about putting my foot into water of that kind of writing. The narrative is new to me, at least in the way I've used it in this book. Some of the history is oral, common knowledge to natives like me—some I stored up with material from the written versions in some folklore collections from the University of Texas Press. Some required digging into old newspapers and ethnologist's reports. It doesn't really matter that it is all true, that is, taken to be true, known by memory to be true by real people. That interests me. Rather than making things up, I have always worked with the imagination playing over an external event.

How would you describe your poetic style?

I don't know how I would describe it. I think I know a good deal less about my reasons for writing than many poets seem to know about their own work. I don't really care. I'm not interested in analyzing it. I haven't any neat little theories. I usually like a fairly long line, but not always. Line breaks are very important to me. I work with internal slant rhyme a lot. Some of my poems are sort of plain . . . as in "plain style," but most aren't. I do work slowly and judge myself harshly, as far as my capacities allow. I almost never let a poem go until I've had it at least a year. As to style, well, I know I write at least two kinds of poems. They feel different.

Is it important to get your work published?

I don't think it's the most important thing, and isn't for a poet to be published right away. I've had poems published I was sorry about. It's relatively easy to publish after all. What does it matter if a magazine takes it if you aren't satisfied? Or even a book editor. I have a trick I use. I tell myself that nothing I'm writing will ever be published, that no one will ever see it. And of course that is indeed always a possibility. But it is a trick I play on myself. That way I am free. I don't worry about it.

What writers have influenced you?

It's not easy for me to know what sorts of influences may show in my poems. There have been certain poets whose work was deeply important to me, whose work kept me writing. And there's no pattern to it, I think. Dylan Thomas early on—instead of Eliot. Walt Whitman instead of Pound. I say that because Eliot and Pound were the poets I was told to read, as everyone was. I discovered Robinson Jeffers right away. (This is because I didn't go to school in the usual ways, and so *could* find Robinson Jeffers!) He was the first poet I read entirely . . . Everything he wrote and everything I could find about him, books, reviews, everything. His vision was kin to something in myself.

And I loved the sheer power in his work. People used to say Jeffers hated women. I never saw that. His female characters have tremendous force. Whereas the women, when there were any, say, in Eliot, or the work of the other moderns, were pretty dippy, shadowlike. James Dickey's early work was important to me. He brought certain kinds of experiences into poetry that were familiar to me, experiences of a South I knew. And I loved the motion and transformative power of the language in those poems. I've loved some of Yeats, much of Thomas Hardy. I'm mixing up times, but William Stafford's work is important to me, has been since I first saw his work. Is there anybody steadier? I loved Hopkins with both ears. Keats, Robert Penn Warren later, and one particular period in the work of the Greek poet Yannis Ritsos whom I found much later. I could go on — the list is long. Nothing consistent about it.

Who are you reading now?

I reread a good bit of Jeffers recently to do a little piece about him. I reread Stevens with more interest recently. Right now? I'm reading a book called *What Is a Poet?* which is an account of a gathering of poets and critics. So far it seems the critics think they are the poets and the poets are fighting back. We'll see how it comes out. I'm usually reading a lot of new work. Richard Kenney recently, and the last two volumes of Thomas McGrath's *Letter to an Imaginary Friend,* a poet too many people seem not to know about. Richard Wilbur. I poke in and out of books.

You haven't mentioned any women poets.

That's true. Well, women poets didn't influence me much. Sylvia Plath is a wonderful poet. I admired tremendously what she could make language do, but because I'm naive enough to read poetry for content, I never got past the fact that she wanted to die. I didn't connect well with what she said. She wanted to die. I didn't. One can want to die very beautifully, but that won't make me follow you.

Oddly, a reviewer said that *Walking Out* showed Anne Sexton's influence. I thought that was a mistaken statement. But who knows. Anyhow, you have to remember that when I began there weren't many women poets available, and those that were most available I didn't find all that interesting. And because I lived and worked outside the academic world, my reading was sort of hit or miss. Now everything is different. Young women poets have older mentors who are women all around them, all kinds, books left and right, new ways into the work of women in the past. I loved Emily Dickinson, but from a distance. Elizabeth Bishop, too, whom I discovered late. Today I read as many women poets as men, though not just at this moment it seems. Mary Oliver is wonderful. Maxine Kumin, and Adrienne Stoutenburg — who's been dead for years and whose work I didn't know until a few years ago. Levertov right along, Pattiann Rogers. I admire and envy all of these. Margaret Gibson, too. I didn't think about gender when I was starting out.

I still don't. I hate that kind of agenda, that insistence on being always aware that one is female, or Southern, or any particular thing. My poems could only have been written by a woman. I'm pretty sure of that! But it isn't often my subject.

Here's a digression that may be interesting. Recently I gave a reading at a large university. I was told that the faculty's feminist contingent, that is, the women's studies, theorists, and so on, a rather large group, had deliberately not shown up at my reading — because I don't follow some party line or other I suppose. This surprised me but I guess it shouldn't have. I have never been where the party line was. I didn't write anti-Vietnam poetry in the sixties, though I was indeed marching against that war and working actively in organizations. My poems aren't *about* a particular place *or* the fact that I am a woman. They come at what they're about *through* those things, through place overtly, perhaps not so obviously through the angle of vision a woman can have. Some of my subjects are rooted in observations of a vastly flawed and vanished time, and it seems to me that since we have now decided to see to it that there may well not be a future, we have no choice but to look back in the light of that to see what is behind us, what has led to this, and why the future we may have seems, in Jeffers' words, "an iron consistency." But this is digressing. Yes, the poets whose work was important to me when I began were men. This was cultural coercion perhaps, but I learned and wrote, or so I think, *my* way. Young women poets have things much better now.

It may be changing, but there are relatively few women poets in the South. Some years ago I gave a talk at Auburn with novelist Doris Betts. She spoke about Southern women novelists and I spoke about Southern women poets. Doris, of course, had a tremendous amount of material. I had four poets of the past, Julia Randall and Eleanor Ross Taylor and a couple of others, and a few younger poets. Now there are more. But I simply hadn't thought about it before preparing that speech, that there were so few. I posed the question to the audience. Why? My speculation was that poetry in the South centered around the Fugitives during the energetic beginnings, and the Fugitives were completely in and of the university, the academic world, at a time when women were not much tolerated in that world. But the truth is I have no idea why. Certainly there is no dearth of women fiction writers here, nor was there in the past. There are more women poets now in the South. In North Carolina, Kathryn Byer, Ann Deagon, Susan Ludvigson, and others. But still there are not so many as in other regions, but scores of fiction writers! I'd love to write a novel but I don't seem to be built that way.

When you're not writing what do you like to do?

Walk in the woods. We still have some real woods around Raleigh. I read all the time: poetry, criticism, fiction, everything. I love old movies. I do not jog, play tennis, or otherwise overexert! I like to do readings when

I can. And my husband and I travel when we can. We've made several trips to Greece — always in the spring. We stay for months at a time in a tiny village in the mountains on an island in the Cyclades. It is emphatically not a tourist island. We rent a farmhouse from a Greek family, the same house every year. The last poem in *Beholdings* is about that place at Easter. Life there isn't easy, but is very beautiful. Few conveniences. No K-Marts.

You grew up in East Texas which is in the middle of several geographical areas. On one hand you could call yourself Southern, but then you could call yourself Midwestern. How do you make that distinction to call yourself Southern?

My part of East Texas was a border, the last stand of pine belt and big hardwood forests. Early immigrants went that far and stopped at the last stand of what was familiar to them. They brought their cotton and their slave economy, all that wouldn't work farther West. My hometown was as much deep south as Mississippi or Louisiana. It's only a few miles from the Louisiana state line. On the other hand, people there were very conscious of having fought a revolution and became a separate nation for awhile. I have my great-grandfather's Civil War letters, but I also have old editorials earlier advocating that Texas remain its own nation. That independence is pretty Western. There is definitely a mix there on that edge, and edges are where one moves toward mystery in two directions, wouldn't you say? There was something Western in the place, something open and openly wild — even to early day shoot-outs, street killings in broad daylight as late as the thirties — nineteenth century Western style. It has interested me to catch this mix, but I don't think I've done it. My work is called Southern, and that's right enough I suppose.

With the homogenization of the South do you feel that the Southerner may be using that voice?

Yes. In the small towns people still *don't* sound like the man on the six o'clock new, but the small towns are dying, or becoming extensions of cities. Around Raleigh people sound like the six o'clock news. If you mean the Southern writer, well, of course, he or she is changing with everything else, as it must be.

You know, one thing I loved about Greece was that there are no chains, no McDonald's or Kentucky Fried Chicken, or even any Greek chains outside Athens or the big tourist areas. When we used to drive from North Carolina to Texas, years ago, we'd stay in funny little motels and eat in the local restaurants in small towns. I still like to travel back roads when possible, where every place has its slight difference, some imprint of a human personality. Like Elizabeth Bishop's gas station... The "changing of America" changed all that. My hometown hasn't gone that way yet, too off the beaten path. There is one small supermarket and one Dairy Queen, and the rest of the businesses are mom and pop. No chains.

There is a book, Class, *and other books, too, which discuss how this is the classification of America — how no matter where you are in the United States you will not feel intimidated by obscure surroundings. This places you in your class surroundings. You know that K-Mart in Florida or North Carolina is the same as the one in Seattle. When you walk in you know where the automotive department is, where sports and clothing is. When you're at Burger King, Wendy's, or McDonald's you know exactly what is on the menu. You don't have to worry about ordering something you've never heard of before, something you may have to send back because it wasn't cooked to your taste. That is intimidating to a person when they are out of their class surroundings. If you're intimidated by your surroundings you're less likely to stay as long in a place where you are uncomfortable, thus spending less money.*

In other words, the destruction of the regions from which comes regionalist, which used to be a bad word. But do we really want to think it is? Well, money is finally what things are about in this mass technological culture, and the destruction of localities is part of this. Money now is an abstraction, and what is taking the place of real localities is abstraction. K-Marts, shopping malls — all abstractions. Certainly I'm not going to speak against getting rid of the class structure . . . But we are indeed losing the sense that any place has character and customs of its own. Perhaps this is why I have become rather defiant about the poems of mine that deal with a particular region. It is vanishing; it is mine and there is not another one like it in the world — it has story — it holds my personal memories connected to those of generations before me. It is a place where a dead man's desk could contain pieces of the land and its destruction from the beginning. What has been brought to extinction, clear-cut, bulldozed over, made profitable, often for people who live far away is not a situation confined to the region I happen to have written about.

I'm not blind. I know there were no golden ages, especially not in the South. For a huge number of people there weren't even any reasonably-good old days. I rebelled early against the racial horrors of my part of the country. And the child in that poem you had me read, "Remembering Brushing My Grandmother's Hair," senses the wrong in her grandmother's lifelong stasis, "the land sown deep with salt." But we may be sowing the land with worse than salt. The South, and the rest of the country, still has to overcome the worst in itself, but it won't help to exchange one poison for another. Instead of a global village, imagine a global K-Mart, with homeless multitudes on the street outside, the whole thing sitting on a radioactive chemical dump.

In what direction do you see your poetry moving?

Right now, still toward using personal and historical material. I'm working on a long piece about my mother's life. She died when I was quite small, and I am trying, I suppose to recreate her for myself. The poem I'm working on is based on the sacred harp songs, also called fasola or shape-note songs that she and her sisters sang in church in their crossroads town through their young lives. They were very poor, hardworking farm people with a few acres. This early music died out in New England where it began, but held on in a few places in the South. Wonderful songs.

I've used phrases from the songs and borrowed the fugal structure of the music, very complicated. In *Beholdings*, the historical section deals with men, primarily — my father's world. This next book will have a section that centers more on the female experience. At least I think that is what I'm doing. That may change completely. Nothing is finished yet. My poems take form from one another, I work with them together, striking off one another, at least in the historical pieces. But I do know that this one poem about my mother will be there. She was the oldest of nine children in a dirt poor family, and she somehow managed to educate herself, to go through college without any help, even into graduate work. She became a teacher of Latin and English, beginning in a one-room school in the middle of a woods. I saw what is left of that school recently — not quite fallen down. She was one hell of a strong woman. I want to find her. She kept journals, and filled them with bits of poems she liked. Poetry may have been her way of finding things, too. I have written about her death, about losing her, missing her, but I have not written about her life, which I have had to search out. So this poem takes that direction. After that, I don't know what.

One of your poems that I enjoyed a great deal from Nettles *is "The Swan Story." The first stanza says, "If you take my hand/ and what you hold is instead/ the prickle and broken/ knuckles of feathers, dismantled/ fingers,/ stay with me anyway/ where we walk in the year's last snow./ If I tell you only a child's tale,/ its fragment of singing, its unkempt puzzle not worth it,/ stay." It seems to be a matrimonial love poem to your husband who it is dedicated to.*

That's right. That poem grew from a fragment of four lines at the end of another poem — which is why I tell my students never throw anything away! The plot of poem parallels the Hans Christian Andersen story, "The Wild Swans." It begins with the middle-aged speaker addressing her husband as they walk in snow, the part you quoted. She tells him a story, and it is the story of her growing up — that is, of growing into flesh, mortality, life, from the half-spirit existence of childhood. The elements of the Andersen story are all *inside* this child in her journey. She is the daughter of the dead mother, as in the Andersen story. She is the sister, and she is the eleven brothers and the swans they become. The original story elements become something else, something in the psyche. She is the penance, the silence, the gathering of nettles to make the shirts to break the spell. She is the youngest brother whose shirt is never finished, the one who is left with a swan's wing instead of an arm. I loved that part of the story when I was a child. I felt that having a swan's wing would not be a punishment, but rather a grand thing. As I wrote the poem, I knew I was thinking of that wing dragging the ground as poetry, part of an incomplete disenchantment. The poem ends with the speaker finishing her tale and speaking of present things to her husband as they walk together on a snowy evening.

Interesting things kept turning up as I wrote this poem. I picked up along the way that swan's quills were often used for writing. And of course, poets were sometimes called swans at one time. That *Bird-Loose-Feather* is the translation word for snow from another language—I forgot now which—but those kinds of things turn up to help you, to twine the poem tighter. I played with this poem and got furious with it and wanted to tear it up, but finally finished it. It was ten years from first draft to last. Like a number of my poems, this one came to me before I was able to write it.

You worked on the editorial staff of the Southern Poetry Review *for eight years. Obviously you received quite a few manuscripts.*

Yes, we did. I once coedited a woman's issue with Heather Ross Miller. Guy Owens, the editor, had placed ads in all the magazines—"Special woman's issue, send poems." At one point I had twelve A&P sacks stuffed and overflowing in my study. Then Heather got a grant to England, and there I was working full-time in the business world, 9 to 5, and coming home to those sacks of manuscripts. I've never forgotten that. There were some preliminary readers, of course, but I still had to read a lot. We got a lot of manuscripts for regular issues of the magazine, too, though not so many as that! It brought to me how many people are writing poetry in this country. And that was years ago.

What did you see as being a major mistake for writers with sending out manuscripts?

Two things maybe. One, they don't have enough ambition for their poems. They want the poems published but they haven't bothered to look closely enough to see that the work is what it should be. Their ambition is in the wrong place. The second thing is part of that too... Poets often don't keep their poems long enough, don't revise them, or think about them enough. We'd get poems that were dated as to the time of composition, and the day would be last month's, or last week's. I can't speak for every poet, of course, but I think it is rare that a poem comes whole, without needing time and work. It happens, even to me, but rarely. People want it to be easy. Actually, it is publication that's pretty easy. The best you can possibly write is what is hard.

Out of your childhood do you have a favorite memory?

I have wonderful memories of one particular summer. I spent lovely hours in the porch swing reading a book about Spanish galleons. We had a big old rambling house with porches all around it. But perhaps better than that, I remember taking the trail through the woods behind our house with my grandfather. I was very young when we'd do this. We'd build a twigfire and roast little canned sausages on a stick. As it would begin to get dark, my grandfather would call the owls—and they'd answer.

I also have a least favorite. I don't like to speak of it, but I guess it is the memory of the night after my mother died. I was barely six years old. In those days the dead were placed in the parlor of the house, rather than a funeral home. Family and friends sat up with the body all night, right there. I woke up that night crying. Someone, an aunt by marriage who thought she was doing the right thing because I was asking for my mother, took me into the room and lifted me up to see into the coffin. I screamed. I have never forgotten it. Terribly, that is the clearest memory I have of my mother's face. Except for the artificial memory supplied by photographs, whenever I try to see my mother's face, in my mind, it is the dead face I see looking like someone who is not real in a box in her own house. It is the clearest memory in the world, that moment. I remember the colors, the flowers, the faces. And the one face that was and was not my mother's. It's a memory I've written about, but not well. Some things are too powerful to write, too unspeakable.

I remember my first memory really clear; it's of a fall, of falling down the back steps. I was two or so and playing dress up or something. I had on a necklace of my mother's, long, with a large black pendant, a cross I think, and I was jumping down the steps, flat-footed, one at a time. The necklace flew up into my face and I thought the pendant was a big bug or something. I fell all the way down these high steps, and at the bottom our big black dog came and licked me all over. It's very clear, every detail. Is that a crazy memory? There's a certain balance there, isn't there? Black cross, black dog. Anyway, before that I remember nothing of being in the world. (*Laughing.*)

Is there anything I haven't asked you that you would like to add?

Yeah. When are people going to start saying "Man Poet" as often as they say "Woman Poet"? And when are they going to write in reviews, "This book is rooted strongly in the New Jersey suburbs, and the poet is a regionalist familiar with divorce, green lawns, commutes, and the folk tales of the local tavern, though he rises above this with etc., etc." That'll be the day, huh?

A.R. Ammons

A.R. Ammons has published 17 volumes of poetry, including *Collected Poems: 1951-1971* (winner of the National
Book Award for Poetry, 1973), *Sphere: The Form of a Motion*
(winner of the 1973-1974 Bollingen Prize in Poetry), *A Coast
of Trees* (winner of the National Book Critics Circle Award
for Poetry, 1981), *The Snow Poems, Corson's Inlet, Diversifica-
tions,* and most recently, *Sumerian Vistas.* This interview was
conducted on March 6, 1988, in Winston-Salem, North
Carolina, at the house where Ammons and his wife were
staying while on sabbatical from Cornell.

*I read an interview the other day where the guest was asked if there had been a ques-
tion he had always wanted to answer, but had never been asked.*
Most of the questions I have been asked have had to do with something
apart from what I considered largely the nature of poetry — investigating what
poetry is and how it works — in what way is it an action or a symbolic action,
in what way does poetry answer the question what kind of behavior is this
poem recommending? Questions like that are an absorbing interest to me.
What Robert Bly or somebody else is doing is of no interest to me whatsoever.
I've written my poetry more or less in isolation without any living day-to-day
contact with the South. Though I have read tidbits in anthologies of other
people and so on, I've made no study of anybody else's work, except in school
where I read Shelley, Keats, Chaucer, and so on. I like questions that address, if they can, the central dynamics of this medium we work with, not that
any answer is possible, but that we meditate the many ways in which it
represents not only our verbal behavior but other representative forms of
behavior, and how action and poetry resemble other actions such as ice
skating or football. That is to say, I think poetry is extremely important
because it's central to other actions, and it should not be pushed far to the side
as a strictly academic study or a technical investigation, but that it is important because it is an action in common with so many other kinds of action.
Do you think poetry is pushed aside into an academic field only?

To the extent that it becomes a form of study, yes. I worry about that, because that means the action of the poem and the mind, the action of the body of the poem itself, is going to be paraphrased into discursiveness — something is going to be said about it, which will be different from the original action. And while I don't know how classes can be conducted any other way, that's not why poems are written. They are not written in order to be read or studied or discussed, but to be encountered, and to become standing points that we can come to and try to feel out, impressionistically, what this poem is recommending. Is it recommending a loud voice, extreme action, or is its action small, does it think we should look closely at things, should we forget the little things and look at some big inner problem, should we understate our stances toward the world, or does hyperbole work better, is this a shallow poem, or is there some profound way that it achieves something it didn't even mean to achieve? In other words, we're trying to live our lives and we go to these representative, symbolic actions, to test out what values seem to have precedence over others. If human beings everywhere could approach poetry more in that way rather than an historical or strictly theoretical form of study, then they might feel the ball of strength in poetry and come to it because it would inform them the way Madonna does or punk rock does. Of course, I'm not insisting that poetry become a popular medium. It requires the attention that few people are willing to give it. I kind of wish that weren't so.

Many of the people who I have come in contact with that don't read poetry say it's because they don't understand it. But, is it that we have alienated poetry into an academic field to the extent that they "think" poetry is too difficult to understand or that they shouldn't be able to understand it?

"Understanding something" has been defined for them as a certain system of statements made about something. They don't get a very good statement about the poems which means they haven't opened themselves to the rhythm, pacing, sounds of words, colors, and images that they are supposed to move into — not understand. Who understands his own body? I mean the gorillas have been walking around for two hundred and fifty thousand years with extremely complicated enzymic and other kinds of operations going on in their blood streams that they know nothing about, which prevented them not at all from being gorillas. We're the same case. What are we supposed to understand about poetry? I've studied and worked with poetry since I was eighteen. Poetry astonishes me day after day. I see something else that is somehow implicated in that. I never expect to understand it. You see, there's where the problem is. The kind of understanding that was defined for these people, most people, has been trivial and largely misses the poem. How could it have been interesting?

You spent the first seventeen years of your life in the South, in Whiteville, North Carolina. Could you discuss your background and leading up to when you took an interest in writing?

It covers the period people like to cover in ten years of psychotherapy and don't give up and walk away from until they have an answer. (*Laughing.*) I was born in 1926, which you probably already know—just toward the end of the good times—the twenties into the Depression. Our family had a pretty rough time on the farm. We had a small farm of fifty acres, which was caught in between another type of change—one of a subsistence farm, which my grandfather had had where he raised thirteen children, and which in my father's hands became a cash crop farm that was not large enough to raise enough cash. Yet, we didn't do the dozens of things that would have continued it as a subsistence farm. Apparently, my grandfather had done very well. So we were caught in that kind of bind, aggravated by the Depression, about which you've heard endless rumors. All true. (*Laughing.*) It was a rather desperate time until the beginning of the war provided jobs for people, and changes—radical changes. Do you realize that when I was a born in 1926 something like eighty-five percent of the people in the country were rural, lived on a farm, and now it's about three percent? So the most incredible silent revolution has taken place just in my lifetime.

After I graduated from high school in 1943 I worked for a shipbuilding company in Wilmington, then entered the Navy when I was eighteen. I was in the South Pacific for nineteen months, came back and entered Wake Forest College in the summer of 1946 on the G.I. Bill. Nobody in my family had gone to college before. It was a truly daunting experience for me. My major was premed and I did most of the premed work. I minored in English, and then everything sort of collapsed into a kind of general science degree.

Prior to studying English in college had you written very much?

The first poem I wrote was in the tenth grade, where you have to write a poem in class. It was on Pocahontas. Then I didn't write anymore until I was in the South Pacific and discovered a poetry anthology when I was on the ship. Then I began to write experimentally and imitatively. There was a man on ship who had a master's degree in languages and I began to study Spanish with him. We didn't have a text; he just made it up as he went along. It somehow gave me a smattering of grammar—you know how helpful it is with your own grammar to study another language. Pretty soon I was writing. Then I came to Wake Forest where there were no creative writing classes, but I continued to write for four years. About a month before I left Wake Forest I had finally gotten the nerve to show some of my poems to the professors and they were very encouraging to me. From then on, my mind, my energies were focused on poetry even though I had to do what everyone else does—try to figure out some way to make a living.

You didn't begin by sending your poems to small magazines, did you?

I didn't even know they existed. I was just totally ignorant of the literary scene. What a load that is on the mind not to know what the configuration, the landscape, or to know where the literary world is. I got married the year

I was the principal of the elementary school in Cape Hatteras. From there we went to Berkeley, California, where I did further study in English, working towards a master's degree. I took my poems to Josephine Miles, of whom you may not have heard, but she was very famous. She died a couple years ago. She consented to read my poems and said I should send them out. That's where I first heard about literary magazines.

You don't categorize yourself as particularly Southern, a Southern writer.

I think the first seventeen years finalizes the situation, but I haven't lived in the South for years. However, I feel my verbal and spiritual home is still the South. When I sit down and play hymns on the piano my belly tells me I'm home no matter where I am. So, yes, I am Southern, but as I said I have so long been away from the immediate concerns of the South. I guess we should define Southerner. Who are Southerners? Are they white, black? Does a black Southerner want to be separated from a Northerner? Does he feel the same boundary in the North as the Southerner often does? Also, as you suggested, the South has changed so much demographically, that it's difficult to know.

How does a poet deal with this change?

I wonder. I don't think it has very much to do with me as I feel the sources of poetry, by the time you are as old as I am, sixty-two, have taken all kinds of perspectives, and while it may be changed in tone and mood by recent events, it's changed only slightly. Curvature of the narrative, by that time, becomes fairly well established, and while it can change, it won't change much.

You never dreamed of becoming a poet in the sense of receiving recognition for your work. You sort of thought of yourself as being an amateur poet and not a "Poet." Once you began publishing, when did you think of yourself as a "Poet"?

When I said amateur poet, I meant that I didn't want to professionalize it. It seems to have more spontaneity, immediacy and meaning to me when I think of it as just something I do. I worry when poetry is professionalized. I think maybe I am a poet. I keep getting letters from all over the world from people who say they are moved by this and that. Whatever it was that they were moved by is in the past for me. I just wrote a poem this morning. That's where I'm at. I try to live each day as I can. If I write a poem, fine. If I don't, that's fine. I think life ought to come first. Don't you? One is alive in the world with other people. I write poetry. Other people collect insects or rocks. I don't think I have answered this question very well, but you know how at some point in your life you have meditated deeply on a subject—you remember that you have meditated on it, you file it, and the next time you try to remember it you can't access it. You have to take thirty minutes to work your way there, then you might have something to say, or you might not. That's what just happened. (*Laughing.*)

Do you think there are writers, poets, who take poetry too seriously, that they feel poetry is almost more important than life, thus ignoring the interaction of life?

The solemn, the pompous, the terribly earnest are all boring.

You started in a premed program with hopes of becoming a doctor.

Yes, I had. I think it came out of a general interest in things and people and feelings. To be a doctor would have been to get completely out of the mess I was in as a farmer. It was a different social and economic level. I didn't pursue it beyond my undergraduate degree. I had wanted to stay a farmer, but my father sold the farm. So, that option was eliminated. I love the land and the terrible dependency on the weather and the rain and the wind. It betrays many a farmer, but makes the interests of the farmer's life tie in very immediately with everything that's going wrong meteorologically. I miss that. That's where I got my closeness and attention to the soil, weeds, plants, insects, and trees.

You've taught at Cornell since 1964.

Yes, that's right. Denise Levertov was poetry editor of *The Nation* and she wanted to take off for six months and she asked me to fill in for her. During that period I accepted a poem by David Ray. I didn't know who he was, but I published his poem. Some months later I was asked to read at Cornell, and it turned out that David Ray was a teacher there. I guess he was glad I published his poem and wanted to meet me. I went to read and they asked me why I wasn't teaching and I said because no one had ever asked me. They proceeded to ask me. I became a full professor in seven years. Some years later Yale made me an offer, so Cornell countered their offer and gave me an endowed chair. They have just honored me beyond all dreams. I teach part-time . . . One course that meets once a week. It's like having your life free. I go over everyday and talk to students and go to meetings, but I don't have to.

Is it stimulating for your work to meet with the students everyday?

Not much any more. I need human contact, but it needn't be profound. To see someone and have a cup of coffee really restores me. See, I don't like to live alone. I see people and I do enjoy that. I don't think that I'm much of a teacher, but that's not what the students tell me. I never feel very competent. I don't think anyone who teaches poetry can feel very competent, because the subject is so overwhelming and it's easy to miss the center of it. Can you imagine in a creative writing class the interplay of the relationship between the teacher and the student—how complex that is on both sides? Superficial, no matter how profound. It's so superficial and so mixed, "Help me, don't help me. Criticize this poem but only say good things. Don't tell me what my next move is. Tell me, but don't let me know that you told me what my next move is, so it will seem that I discovered it for myself. When I owe you something please be the first one to say I owe nothing." That is to say it is extremely complex and draining on that account. You would have to be superhuman to know what to do in that situation. I am, as it turns out, not superhuman. But they say I'm a good teacher, nevertheless.

I do the best I can. I must say that I have a pretty quick eye on a poem. I can tell what it is likely to amount to or not amount to rather quickly. It's just a wonderful job, but I'm tired of it, only because of something they call "burnout." After having done something for twenty-five years I don't know what happens. I guess you begin hearing yourself say the same thing, repeating yourself.

When I first began to teach, Bill, I would go into the classroom and see eighteen or twenty individuals and I believed they were individuals. After about five years of teaching six courses per year, I would come into a writing class knowing full well that there were three or four basic problems: diction — there is always too much poetic diction. There's the problem of shape, or the lack of it — some contact with an ideal form. There's the problem with consistency. It's not just fine to have a good line and a good image, but can you write a whole poem. Then, as a teacher, you have to begin to nudge yourself and say this person sitting in front of you is not an example of one of these problems, he's a person. After awhile, if you have to nudge yourself too much, then it's time to quit.

If the burnout begins to weigh too heavily upon you, is there something that you would prefer doing instead of teaching?

I would like to, now, be designated, more than anything in this world, POET. Not teacher, not professor, not farmer, but one who writes poems. What I would like to do now, since I have not allowed myself to do it in twenty years is to go out and meet the people who read my poems. I have been giving poetry readings lately which I did not do for a long, long time. I would like to stay home when I go back to Ithaca and write my poems, send them to magazines, go see people, because I don't know how to tell somebody else how to write.

Do you plan on retiring from Cornell?

Yes. I'm sixty-two now and I'm eligible for social security, but I'm on sabbatical and one must teach a year after sabbatical. And at the end of that point I will consider whether it will be beneficial to retire. You do get old. Your eyes get tired, your teeth fall out, your knees hurt. It's just the natural process of aging, and perhaps you become irritable to hear the same questions a million times. You're no longer in the best position and you no longer believe in the illusions of this world that that young man or woman is setting out to realize those things also. You've already been through that. You've seen those illusions disintegrate. As an older person you're looking for that abiding value that may be there and probably isn't.

Your first book of poetry, Ommateum, *failed terribly . . .*

I believe the publisher knew it wouldn't sell and so they only bound one hundred copies of the three hundred sheets pressed. It sold sixteen copies the first five years. Five libraries bought it — Princeton, Harvard, Yale, Berkeley, and Chapel Hill, only because they bought everything. My father-in-law sent forty copies to people he knew in South America. I bought back thirty copies for thirty cents each. So I guess you could say it failed miserably. One review in *Poetry* magazine, my first review, was favorable. But now *Ommateum* goes for about thirteen hundred dollars a copy.

The reason I brought this up is because you did not publish another collection of poetry for nine years. What transpired in those nine years, between the time you wrote Ommateum *and* Expressions of Sea Level *that produced a resounding critical change in your work?*

We cannot imagine, sitting here, how long nine years is. I just kept writing, resubmitting manuscripts, tearing them apart, putting them back together, getting rejected, trying again, and so on until I was finally rejected by everybody. I took my work to a vanity publisher in New York City and I was turned down by them, too. I went to Bread Loaf in 1961 and met Milton Kessler, who at that time was teaching at Ohio State University. He said their press was starting a poetry series and I should send my poems early on before the hundreds of manuscripts began to arrive. I did and they took it. It was favorably reviewed, but it took ten years for them to sell eight hundred copies. I used to get monthly statements from them saying this month we've sold three copies, this month we sold four. For ten years this happened, and I'm not sure they ever sold all one thousand copies. It is amazing how favorably it was reviewed. I just saw *The Oxford Companion to American Literature* which has an article on me saying from the day *Expressions of Sea Level* was published, A.R. Ammons was a major poet... Nobody told me I was a major poet. Now, as to what happened to the poetry itself, that's a story so long I wouldn't know how to tell you. I'd have to go back over the stages, the failures, the rebeginnings, and so on. It isn't easy to be a poet. I think if the young poets could realize *that* they would be doing something else. It takes a long time. It took me a long time. I do believe there are poets who begin right at the top of their form, and usually, are exhausted in five years. In a way I wasn't bad either early on. *Ommateum* remains a very powerful influence with me.

Who do you see as starting at the top of their form?

I just happen to think of James Tate, who won the National Prize when he was twenty-two. I don't mean to say he burned out. There are poets who seem to be at their best right away. I'm a slow person to develop and change. The good side of that is that it leaves me so much more to do.

When you look back at the poems in Ommateum *as a whole what is your reaction? Do you still feel the same way?*

It's a very strong book. It may be my best book. *Expressions of Sea Level,* though more widely welcomed, more obviously ingratiates itself to an easier kind of excellence. The *Ommateum* poems are sometimes very rigid and ritualistic, formal and off-putting, but very strong. The review I got said, these poems don't care whether they are listened to or not. Which is exactly true. I had no idea there was such a thing as an audience; didn't care if there was. I was involved in the poem that was taking place in my head and on the page and that was all I cared about. If I had known there were millions of people out there wanting to buy my book, which of course was not the case, it would have been nice. But an audience meant nothing to me. Someone else said that I was a poet who had not yet renounced his early poems. I never intend to renounce those poems. (*Laughing.*) I can assure you. I have published some inferior poems in each volume—that's inevitable. But as Jarrell said, if you are lucky enough to write a half a dozen good poems in your life, you would be lucky indeed.

Critics have traced your creative genealogy to several noted influences: Whitman, Thoreau, Emerson, Pound, Stevens, Frost. One critic stated, "Ammons' poetry is founded on the implied Emersonian division of experience into Nature and the Soul." Would you agree with their findings?

First of all, one has been influenced by everything in one's life, poetic and otherwise. There have been predominant influences, such as Robert Browning, whom I imitated at great length as an undergraduate, writing soliloquies and dramatic monologues, trying to get anywhere near the marvelous poems he wrote. I failed miserably. Whitman was a tremendous liberation to me. Emerson was there in the background, though I am said to be strongly Emersonian—I sort of learned that myself. I haven't read him that much. When I read Emerson I see a man far wiser and more intelligent, and a better writer than myself, saying exactly what I would say if I could. That's scary in a way. We're still different in so many ways. But then I do believe I hear, at times, in my poems, distant echoes from every poet, not in terms of his own words, but as a presence. Frost is there, also Stevens. I have read very little Stevens, and basically he's not one of my favorite poets, though I think he's a good poet. They do say of me, even though the influences are there, that my voice remains my own, which is a mystery to me, but apparently it's true. I believe I assimilate from any number of others and other areas. I'm that kind of person—one who is looking for the integrated narrative. That's where my voice finds it's capability of movement. It is my voice, but it is an integrated one. Does that sound right?

Oh, yes.

I just made it up. (*Laughing.*)

How, then, would you describe your poetry?

It's a variable poet that tries to test out to the limit the situation of unity and diversity—how variable and diverse can a landscape of poetry be and at the same time hold a growing center. I have written some very skinny poems you might call minimalist and I've written some very long-lined poems, such as "Sphere." In my early poems I was contemplating the philosophical issue of the One and the Many. Wyatt Prunty wrote an article about Creeley and me, saying we were emaciated, that we wrote emaciated poetry. Obviously, this man has read only one of my poems, and that one not very well.

Your poetry deals heavily with man in nature, the phenomena of landscape — earth's nature. I've wondered, because of your scientific background, if you have ever thought about taking man off the earth into space? I don't mean to say science fiction poetry, but into the nature of space.

I don't believe I have, though I've thought a great deal about it — billions and billions of galaxies and billions and billions of stars in each one. Who was it that said if you stick out your arm at the end of space what does it stick into? If space is limited, what happens?

In about ninety percent of your poetry the reader is brought into the poem to witness the solitude of the speaker. Is this solitude your poetic vision of loneliness?

Yes.

Is it your loneliness you're writing about?

Yes it is. I really don't write to an audience. I never imagined an audience. I imagine other lonely people, such as myself. I don't know who they are or where they are, and I don't care, but they're the people whom I want to reach. It seems to me that the people who are capable of forming themselves into groups and audiences have something else to go on besides poetry. So let them go ahead. It could be political, sociological, mystical, or whatever. They're welcome to it and I hope they do a good job, but I am not part of that. I'm really an isolationist. And I know there are others like me. Not necessarily entirely, but there is some element of ultimate loneliness in each person. In some people it's a crisis. Those are the pieces of loneliness I would like to share at this distance.

What are you working on now?

Some new poems. I've only been in Winston-Salem for two months and I'm going back home next Sunday, but I've written a few poems down here and they are slightly different from others. I don't think I'll publish anymore. I've published so many books it just tires my mind to go through that again. I've been sending poems out to magazines, and most of my poems get accepted now, which scares the pants off me, because I wonder if they are read more now than when they were all rejected. (*Laughing.*)

I'm having a good time writing the poems. Of course, I have no more confidence, no more assurance that they are any good now than I did twenty years ago. But that should never be the reason. Once you do something, if you are interested in it because it gives you vitality, life, engagement, and if somebody else reads it fine, but if they don't, that's fine, too. On the other hand, if you don't do it because you are interested in it deeply and personally, nobody else is going to be interested in it either, no matter how much you try to press it upon them. So I do whatever I please and the world can do likewise. (*Laughing.*)

Donald Justice said at one time, and he and I discussed this when I was in Gainesville . . . He said the United States has not produced a major poet in the last thirty years. Do you agree with this?

I agree with that. The possibility is that Ashbery is a major writer, but other than that I don't know any major writers, except possibly myself. The great poets of the first half of the century are not as great as we thought they were, but they are greater than anything since. I think Eliot was a great poet. I like Ransom a lot. I don't believe Lowell and Berryman are going to prove to be as strong as was thought. I hope I'm wrong about that. The poetry in the country has become sort of a company affair where support for the arts has just about ruined the arts and the system of bureaucrats managing the funds that are being developed here and there, is turning into trade unionism, which may be the best way to write poetry, but it is unfamiliar to me. I don't know if trade unionism would tend to even things out, but it seems to me that there are a million poets that write interesting verse, but I can't think of a single one that I would think of getting up in the morning and going to to find my life profoundly changed and enlightened and deepened by. Not a single one. Isn't that amazing? Or do I just not know about them? I don't mean an answer to life, I mean an encounter of intelligence, sensibility, feeling, vision. Where do I go for a verbal encounter that will be sufficient to cause me to feel that I should come back the next day and the next day to drink from that fountain again?

Do you think we will see a major poet evolve out of the last eleven or twelve years of the century or has the well dried up?

I think not. This century has had it. It's been long thought that we've been replaying the seventeenth century in which there was a great deal of poetic energy in the first part of the century drying up into Dryden and Pope. Dryden at the end of the seventeenth and Pope at the beginning of the eighteenth. And we have started to take on a formalist cast now. We may be replaying that, and I think it's drying up energy that was long since spent and maybe we're going to need a century or two before we get back on line. It has a lot to do with the scientific beginning of Donne and others — Eliot's awaking of our interest in Donne and Marvell sort of parallels the seventeenth century.

You published three major collections in a row: Collected Poems 1951-71, Sphere: The Form of a Motion, *and* The Snow Poems. *How does this affect a writer in the sense that what you're doing is working? Can you become held back thinking this has worked before so let's write this way again?*

Yes, but I can't get stuck in a pattern, because I don't believe in patterns. I believe in process and progression. I believe in centralizing integration, that kind of ongoing narrative more than I believe in the boxes of identification and completion. That's just the way I am structured as a human being. *Collected Poems* contains two or three other previously unpublished books. I just dumped them in there. I had them, but didn't want to bother sending them out to magazines.

But *Sphere,* finally, was the place where I was able to deal with the problem of the One and the Many to my own satisfaction. It was a time when we were first beginning to see an image of the earth from outer space on the television screen, at a time when it was inevitable to think about that as the central image of our lives—that sphere. With *Sphere,* I had particularized and unified what I knew about things as well as I could. It didn't take long for me to fall apart or for that to fall apart, too. Thinking of the anger and disappointment that comes from such things. . . I wrote *The Snow Poems,* where I had meant to write a book of a thousand pages. I don't know why I didn't go ahead and do it, because I wanted to say here is a thousand pages of trash that nevertheless indicates that every image and every event on the planet and everywhere else is significant and could be great poetry, sometimes in passages and lines. But I stopped at three hundred pages. I had worn myself and everybody else out. But I went on long enough to give the idea that we really are in a poetically inexhaustible world, inside and out.

Your work has been anthologized in many publications over the years. They usually publish "Corson's Inlet," "This Is," "Bridge," and "Visit." Of all your poems which do you think is your best work and what will most likely survive?

I have always liked two poems of mine that are always twins "Conserving the Magnitude of Uselessness" and "If Anything Will Level with You Water Will" from the *Collected Poems.* I think those are fine poems, but other people don't reprint them. I think anthologists tend to imitate each other. If they find a poem anthologized, they put it in their anthology. I have a great many poems, to tell you the truth, that could just as well have been chosen for an anthology as the others.

Have you written your best poem?

I hope not. (*Laughing.*) You never know.

We touched upon your childhood earlier and I'd like to ask if you have a favorite childhood memory?

I remember one Christmas when I got a little tin wagon with milk cans drawn by a mule or a horse. I must have been five or six. I remember getting back into bed and playing with that on top of the quilt, thinking it was absolutely marvelous.

The most powerful image of my emotional life is something I had repressed and one of my sisters lately reminded me of. It was when my little brother, who was two and a half years younger than I, died at eighteen months. My mother some days later found his footprint in the yard and tried to build something over it to keep the wind from blowing it away. That's the most powerful image I've ever known.

There is a sense of structural change in your latest book, Sumerian Vistas.

It's changed consistently as every individual life changes color and tone.

You are using much more punctuation than previously. It appears to be a more pronounced structure.

Yes, that's true, and I also think the lines have become more structured. For a long time I had a meandering left-hand margin, which has become stiff and straight. That all means something, but who has time to analyze it? I mean, poetry comes close to being nearly a total revelation, if people will only read it.

Throughout your career you've professed formlessness and boundlessness. Have you found either?

I guess the other side of that question is, is there anything, in fact, in our world and perception that isn't formal in one way or the other? I guess not. The air between me and that oak tree is invisible and formless. I can't see the air. So I see nothing but form out the window. I know the air is there because I see it work on the trees, and so I begin to think there is an invisible behind the visible, and a formlessness, an ongoing energy that moves in and out of a discrete formation. It remains constant and comes and goes and operates from a world of residual formlessness. That space, at some point, develops what we perceive. In a way I have experienced the idea of formlessness and boundlessness, but these are imperceptible thanks to our senses.

For the last three or four months I have been just profoundly occupied with the conceptual aspect of poetry — poetry that has some thought behind it. But also, the poem is a verbal construct that we encounter, learn from, make value judgments with, and go to, to sort out possibilities in relation to our own lives in order to try to learn how to live. I'm sick and tired of reading poets who have beautiful images that don't have a damn thing to say. I want somebody who can think and tell me something. You reintegrate that into a larger thing where you realize that thought and loss are certainly not the beginning and end to things, but are just one element in the larger effort we are making, which is to try to learn how to live our lives.

Raymond Andrews

Raymond Andrews was born in 1934 in Madison, Georgia, the son of a sharecropper and the fourth of ten children. His books include *Appalachee Red, Rosiebelle Lee Wildcat Tennessee,* and *Baby Sweet's.* He lives outside of Athens, Georgia. His work has been called "a blacker, funkier version of life down South than [Faulkner's] famed Yoknapatawpha County." This interview was conducted on March 10, 1986, at his home.

You came from a large family, ten children. Could you tell me about your childhood?
I was born in the country, but not on a farm. We moved to one as sharecroppers when I was eight years old. My family always read a lot, but there weren't many books available, mostly magazines. Most people didn't know how to read where I came from let alone think about writing. Going to school was hard during that time, because sharecroppers weren't allowed to send their children to school during the time of picking and planting cotton. But my mother insisted upon us going, which we children didn't object to because if we didn't go to school we had to work in the fields. All of us finished school. I left Madison when I was fifteen, because at that time the cotton picking machine was coming in, sending the sharecroppers and small farmers on their way out. Growing up, we Andrews children were also big movies fans, especially me and my brother, Benny, who's now an artist. As kids, he would draw and I'd write stories. I told him when we grew up I would write the books and he could draw the pictures in them. At fifteen my parents sent me to Atlanta to work while I attended high school at night and worked during the day at a hospital. I also worked as a bartender and as a dishwasher in the employee's cafeteria at Rich's. Upon finishing high school I joined the Air Force.
How did your brother Benny and yourself start working the stories and the pictures which ultimately ended up in your books?
I used to draw as a child, but wasn't that interested in doing it. I was such a perfectionist and my drawings didn't look like I wanted them too. They

24

didn't look exactly like the magazines or the comic strips I copied from, so I always destroyed them. Eventually, I stopped drawing. Benny kept on. His didn't look exactly like the magazines or comic strips either, but I didn't tell him. I became more interested in stories and reading. When I finally published my first book I was fortunate my editor liked my brother's drawings. Not many books have illustrations.

That's something I enjoyed about the books. It breaks things up a little bit.

With today's readers I think it's important, because we live in a visual society with kids brought up on television. They are accustomed to seeing things. When I grew up everything was imagination with reading books and listening to radio. You pictured everything in your mind, but today the mind has nothing to do, the picture, someone else's imagination, is presented to you.

When you were growing up, what did you want to do?

Oh, first I wanted to be a pilot, then a private detective. You name it and I wanted to be it for awhile. I grew up during World War II and as a kid I was thinking the war would just go on forever. I figured when I grew up I would join the war as a pilot. But then the war ended and Benny and I were the two saddest people in the world in 1945. My dad said not to worry they'll have one for you. But what do parents know, we thought. So, low and behold along came Korea. But I didn't become a pilot. I was too young to become one when I joined the Air Force at nineteen and a half. Besides, you had to be very good at math which I was terrible at. I wasn't sure then if I really wanted to write or not. But looking back, beneath I did. I also wanted to be a movie star. I wanted to be so many things that it took years to finally get around to being a writer.

Did you start writing when you were young?

I dabbled, daydreamed, stole some ideas. But I really didn't start until I was thirty-two years old.

Did you start with the short story, poetry or the novel?

I quit my job with the airlines on my thirty-second birthday. I said, after walking out on the job, I've always wanted to write so I may as well start now. I remembered having just earlier read a story in *Sports Illustrated* written by a Canadian about when he was a youth, the Montreal Canadian hockey team came to his home town and what a big thrill it had been for him and the town. Hell, I thought, I could do something like that. So I wrote a story and sent it to *Sports Illustrated* telling about the time Benny and I introduced football to our rural community. We didn't have a high school football team at that time and knew nothing about the game except what we saw in the movies and the newsreels. We never saw a complete game. We didn't know how they got the ball, we just knew they ran and threw it all the time. We didn't see the plays where they gained nothing, just the highlights. Nor did we have a football, only a baseball or a tennis ball. I sent that story to *Sports Illustrated* and they bought it for two hundred and fifty dollars. I said my God there's nothing to this writing game, I should have been doing this all along. My next story sold twelve years later. That $250.00 had to stretch a long way.

From tracing your life it seems to have a romantic, nomadic texture to it, from leaving home at age fifteen to finish high school, to joining the Air Force in the early fifties. It seems to be almost a movie script of a young farm boy who seeks out adventure. Was that the case?

I always wanted to travel, to go places. I didn't want to stay home. I wanted to leave, especially the rural area of Madison. I wanted to eventually get to New York and from there to Europe. I got to Atlanta, which was all right at the time, but to me it wasn't the top. I wanted to, had to, get to the top. As my brother says—go for the jugular. Then I joined the Air Force where I went to Texas and California and ended up in Korea. Then on to Tokyo. I saw much of the Far East. I loved traveling. When I got out of the Air Force I went to school up in Michigan and worked the summers in Chicago. After that it was on to New York where I got a job with a European airlines, permitting me to travel everywhere. From New York I lived in Switzerland and Holland. When I finally decided to return to Georgia I came back to write five books by 1990. Traveling still interests me, but not as much as it once did.

Then you always had this kind of a restlessness?

Yeah, I wanted to see things, to go everywhere and do everything. Of course, that was impossible.

You attended Michigan State University then moved to New York City. New York seems an unlikely place for a farm boy from Madison to end up. Was New York part of your training for writing? Did you go there with that idea in mind?

Oh no. I didn't go anywhere to train for writing. You can write anywhere. I just wanted to travel. In New York I wrote about this area. I do think you can write better from a distance, it's easier to write about New York here then it was while I was there. I had to see and live in New York. But following my divorce I didn't do much work. For four years I did practically nothing. So I came back to get started again. True, I get restless at times down here, but I have no car so I have to stay and work. I planned it that way.

Appalachee Red received the James Baldwin Prize in 1978. How well has your writing been received critically?

Critically very good. I've gotten very good reviews, but haven't sold that much—mainly because I never got paperback. My books weren't that popular in New York. Throughout most of the country they were popular, but New York publishers believe there is no life beyond the Hudson River, except in California. My books sold very well in Europe, but were considered too "regional" for any area outside the South, and because of this I never got a big New York promotional or killing paperback rights. But now that has changed. *Appalachee Red* has just come out in paperback. *Rosiebelle Lee Wildcat Tennessee* will be out in the spring of 1988 and *Baby Sweet's* will be out in the fall of 1988. All three are out in paperback by The Georgia Press.

Your writing has been described as having an angry view of life for blacks in Georgia which is completely opposite of you. You are not an angry person, but your writing tends to be that way.

Yes? (*Laughing.*) I didn't know that.

I didn't think it was anger, I thought it was a very detailed description, an accurately painted picture of life in Georgia in the black community. It is historically accurate, not racially negative or bigoted as other books have suggested. How do you feel about the subject matter and the way people have interpreted it?

Anytime people read anything about the South, black, white, or whatever, usually they go into it with their minds made up about what it's going to be. Most of the time, I suppose, if a white person reads it, he would be on the defensive, and if a black person reads it, he'd be ready to go out and get Mister Charlie. I tried to write where some people were mad and some people weren't mad, or *so* mad. I know in *Appalachee Red,* during that time, the only whites blacks came in contact with were the landowners and the law, and so continually you had this uneven confrontation. People didn't go to school together, they didn't go to church together, so they didn't have any contact in the community sense.

I think the worst thing of all at that time was that the children didn't get to know one another. We didn't get to know whites, or they us, as children. You didn't ever get to know one another. I remember as a child we occasionally played with white children on the sly. We weren't supposed to. We would play just like anybody else, but once the adults came around the whole scene changed. That's what I like now, the children are getting to know each other. The worst thing about the past was the adults passing along these false racial myths to their children, forming their minds forever.

There were some angry times in my life, but in my writing I try to present things as they were. As a writer, if you let your emotions take you away you end up not writing anything well, and I am always interested in writing a good story, yet presenting things that did happen. I'll always do that.

There's a great deal of prejudice in the world because people don't understand one another. Your books reveal a bond between people, which is that people suffer, whether they are black or white or as in Bernard Malamud books the Jewish suffer or in other books, the Irish or the English. Everyone suffers, and I don't think people realize this anymore.

No one has a monopoly on suffering, but I think it's important to make people aware of your particular suffering, as well as your being aware of theirs. In the South, blacks have to try to keep in the past what happened and just go on and take every advantage of that which is available to us now. We don't want to dwell on the past, but at the same time must be knowledgeable of our history. I'm interested in all nationalities and histories. I'm interested in the South as a whole. When I grew up I could see how whites were victims too, "po' white trash" they were called. It wasn't just the blacks, but we blacks were always the low man on the totem pole, both South and North. The South, Georgia, didn't want Erskine Caldwell to write about his poor whites in *Tobacco Road*. He was banned. This is because Georgians wanted everyone to think of Georgia like Margaret Mitchell's *Gone with the Wind*. Georgia ate it up. *Gone with the Wind* could be the worst thing that ever happened to Georgia.

Your work has been described as a blacker, funkier version of life down South than Faulkner's Yoknapatawpha County. How do you feel about the comparison?

Anytime you're compared to another writer like Faulkner it feels great. It's like a young baseball player being compared to Ted Williams. I don't mind it at all. But I don't write like Faulkner. I don't think I write like anybody else. I really don't. The closest writer that I think I might write like is another Southern writer, one of my favorites, William Price Fox. I love his writing.

Your books work on a historical progression to the present day, under certain conditions until the characters' lives become, maybe not better than, but parallel to the white community. The characters go through a great deal to survive. Did you try to make a statement about the struggle of blacks against whites?

No, I wasn't trying to make a statement. I don't know how to. Like I don't know how to write symbols. I was trying to present what happened. This is what happened, take a look at it. This did happen whether it was good or bad. As a writer, that's all I try to do. This is what happened and this is the story I'm telling. I'm a storyteller. I enjoy telling stories. I get involved in a good story and enjoy presenting it. I like getting people caught up in wanting to know what's going to happen. I love characters. Sometimes I get accused of not having a plot. Well, I don't know how to make a plot; I just tell a story. I say hell, life's got no plot, but it's sure full of characters. I think people make the story. You write about what a person does then it leads to a story. This is how I look at it.

There's a large amount of Georgia regional history involved in your books. Do you do a lot of research?

I do a fair amount. I didn't have to do too much with *Red,* just about all of it I knew. For the most part I can remember most of it. People talk. Southerners always talk about things like that. Places and names are passed down from one generation to another.

I read your article in the Atlanta Constitution *defending* The Color Purple. *Could you clarify what the problem was with the movie and why everyone was upset?*

Most people thought that the black males were being stereotyped as being negative. The protest was that most males came off as negative and few were shown as strong. I'm not thinking in terms of any other film, just in terms of *The Color Purple,* but I don't think it makes the men weak just because of what they were doing. Alice Walker was writing about a period at the turn of the century where a lot of black males were frustrated and turned to fighting their own, especially their wives. There are only two or three males in the film, so I don't think of it as being typical of the black males as a whole. If they had shown several areas or several cities where all the black males were that way, that would've been different. There were in the book, correct me if I'm wrong, a couple of good males, the minister and and one of the sons. But when it comes down to making a movie or writing a book, it's difficult to make anything interesting about people who are too good. People want to see something about a person that comes off being bad. Is Rambo typical of all white males? I don't think he is. There have been so few black films made that when something like this comes out everybody wants to comment about it, which is all right. But just let as many films be made as possible, because I wouldn't want to scare anybody off. Spielberg might be scared off so not to make another black film. I sure wouldn't want that to happen.

I thought they were nit-picking. Look at Danny Glover, a good actor who's been in Silverado, Places in the Heart, *and other films. He was passed right over — very few people commented on his performance.*

He's a top rate actor. But blacks over the years have not been depicted very well in film, especially in the old days. So it is a very touchy subject. Like I said in that article, during the time when they were making all of these "super spade" films, they weren't right either, yet I didn't hear anybody complaining about them. The macho black men, Jim Brown and others, they weren't typical of black males. I thought three or four these males in *The Color Purple,* at that time in history, were more typical than all these Shaft-type guys of black males today. What I don't want to happen is where directors, Spielberg or whoever, are frightened off from making black films, because of the uproar over *The Color Purple.* But on the other hand, I don't want blacks to think they can't say anything about what's being made about them. I would like for it to get to the point where there are so many black films being shown that people stop talking about them as "black films." Most people, black and white, enjoyed *The Color Purple,* even though there are some things in there that are far from real. Towards the end where the local juke joint and local church come together, that was a bit much. In the first place, the church and the juke joint don't get together no matter what. It seemed like something out of the *Wizard of Oz.* Sort of like a MGM musical, not real at all. But for the most part I enjoyed the film. It wasn't a great film. But I enjoyed it. I liked Shug. I think she should have been named best supporting actress.

What are you working on now?

I just finished one book last spring and I'm doing another one now. It should be finished soon. The one I just finished is called *Ninety Nine Years and a Dark Day.* It's about the South, again in Mushkogean County, a black family, but not a poor family. For the area they're considerably well off. At that time you had a few black families with money, but you didn't hear much of them. This is about one of those families. Briefly it starts around 1800 and comes up to the current day. They have to fight both the blacks and the whites, because they have money. Neither side likes the idea of this family having money. The one I'm working on now is a novel about one hundred and twenty or thirty pages. I'll have two written and three to go.

Do you ever write short stories or poetry?

No. My short stories turn out to be novels. I'm too wordy. Actually *Appalachee Red* was going to be a poem. A best-selling poem. Take a week to write it, some publisher buys it, I get the money and get on the best-seller list. *Red* became too long, so I thought I would make it a short story. But it was still too long. A novella? Too long. I took the easy way out and made it a novel.

James Applewhite

James Applewhite was born in 1935 in Wilson County, North Carolina, and grew up in between the Southern tradition of his ancestors and the newly emerging technology brought about by the second world war. His five collections of poetry include *Statues of the Grass, Following Gravity, Foreseeing the Journey, Ode to the Chinaberry Tree,* and *River Writing: An Eno Journal.* He is associate professor of English and founding director of the Institute of the Arts at Duke University, and in addition to his collections of poetry he is the author of *Seas and Inland Journeys: Landscape and Consciousness from Wordsworth to Roethke.* This interview was conducted on April 15, 1988, at his house in Durham, North Carolina. He and his family live on Seven-Mile Creek, adjacent to the Eno River State Park.

I asked you to read "Stopping for Gas," because it displays your Southern voice.

It is Southern. There is a personal history behind the Esso Station as well as the rest of the poem. When I was growing up my father ran a station and garage in a small town of a thousand people in the eastern part of North Carolina, Stantonsburg. My grandfather had a tobacco farm, which is still in the family, though at the time my father wasn't tending to that. He ran the Esso station and I worked there, too. It seems to be getting into my poems still. (*Laughing.*)

In fact, that is one of the things I was going to ask you about. You have what could be considered your gas station poems. "The Station," "Rooster's Station, and in Ode to the Chinaberry Tree and Other Poems *you have "The Advisors," all of which seem to play into your early childhood.*

That town of a thousand people held a lot of interest, a lot of tensions. My parents were Methodist on both sides—my mother was the daughter of a Methodist minister who had been a district superintendent and the president of a small college in Maxton—my father was a strong and fierce man as well as religious. He was a wrestler at Duke. He was short of stature, but powerful of build, so he ran the service station with a good deal of authority.

One of my uncles was a minister and another was a schoolteacher who used
to tell me stories I thought were wonderful. Turned out they were taken from
Homer. (*Laughing.*)

There was a kind of post–World War II atmosphere to it all. One forgets
how much that war influenced the tonality of life. In the early part of the war
it was feared that enemy planes would come in at a low level, so there were
civilian watchtowers installed. We lived seventeen miles from the Seymour-
Johnson Air Force Base in Goldsboro. P-47's practiced flying overhead. Occasionally one would crash. I remember being taken to the sight of a crash
and seeing the plane broken in two. It had a huge radial engine that went
through a pine grove like a loose boulder. The pilot's seat was jellied with
blood. It was a terrible image for me at an impressionable age, and it made
the war very real. After the war, two men who worked at my father's station,
Ralph, a Marine, and Bill Davis who had been in the Army, were out there
on the wash pit and grease racks firing high pressure hoses and grease guns.
So the gas station had a sort of war tonality. (*Laughing.*) It was kind of fun,
too.

I tend to conceptualize the town between polarities. My father's gas station had a portico—almost like a Greek temple in my childish imagination,
rimmed with bulbs, so that when dusk gathered the moths would orbit and
the sign would seem to rise slightly against the rich humid night. I associated
all kinds of learning and precision and made things with that service station.
In a service station you have these books, parts catalogs, like vast Bibles of
the machine age. The fittings are numbered and referenced. It was kind of
the axis point to technology, to the modern world.

You have an affinity with nature.

Very much so. The other day I was talking with a colleague who is into
this new style of analysis where he sees everything as constructed—
everything is a human artifice. I told him that he grew up in Manhattan and
I grew up in a town of a thousand people so I knew where the water pump
and the sewage plant was. I saw where the transformer substation was. People
knew where the water came out of the ground and went through town. We
knew nature was there and we saw how we were plugged into it. In a way
it was very simple. It was also comprehendible. A plan. A simple outline. A
stick figure of a town. Here's the bank, there's the barber shop, grocery store,
gas station, church, and school. A connection with reality was forged for me
quite early. In Manhattan you don't have that. That is one aspect of the
Southern background.

The other is such a cliché, but it's true—the Southern gift of speech and
the sense of time—to sit on the front porch. My uncle, who lived with us in
the summer when he was not teaching would sit out on the porch with my
mother, who was shelling butter beans, and he would tell me about Odysseus
in the cave with the cyclops and the great boulder at the door, with no way

out. So Odysseus blinded the cyclops and rode out under the great sheep, holding on to its fleece. If you're a kid that's a great story. The story-telling trait is rich in the South.

So, you must then consider yourself a Southern writer?

Yes, but I have complex feelings about the term. I think it is undeniable and it is something I am proud of, but I'm a little uneasy with the cliché and the stock tendency of Southern literature. One doesn't choose to be Southern—one is or one isn't. I'm uneasy talking about Southern literature as though it was a profession one went into, like law. Within that is the implication that you *elected* to be a Southern writer. You can't be a Southern writer without having the experience at a relatively early age. If someone has the early experience then they can't avoid being a Southern writer unless they take great pains not to be.

Many Southern writers write about their early experiences in the South and in some respects that can be a difficulty, because often, it has the effect of condemning the writer *only* to write about their earlier life. Most Southern poets are not living in anything like the circumstances of their childhoods. They're mostly living in "yuppie" situations, whether in Raleigh, Charlotte, or academic communities.

There are ways of dealing with the Southern experience—Robert Penn Warren, for example, grew up Southern and took on Southern history as in *Brother to Dragons* or in *Audubon.* When Warren was at LSU in the spatial proximity to the lake where Audubon did a lot of his work, he became fascinated with the naturalist who shot birds to paint them. There's a case of a writer who has taken the personal Southern experience as a way toward dealing with the larger issues of Southern history and identity.

The majority of the poems in Ode to the Chinaberry Tree *are about your youth.*

The big issue for me is dealing with contemporary life. I've dealt with the past in the earlier books. I don't primarily want to keep writing about the past, but I want to see ways of relating the life I'm living to the past. That's more evident in the new book, *River Writing: An Eno Journal.* Previously, in *Ode to the Chinaberry Tree,* I was using measures, rhymed stanzas, the ode form, a sestina, or a variety of blank verse as in the poem "For W.H. Applewhite," which also has a great deal of pastoral elegy involved. The poem "Greene County Pastoral" is a pastoral elegy in its major conventions. I was trying to unify my Southern subject matter with my formal immersion as a result of studying English literature. The title poem has a deliberate reference to Wordsworth's, "Ode: Intimations of Immortality." The structure of the poem is my rewriting of the structure of Wordsworth's "Intimations," but in my own terms. It's much more psychological. The poem had its genesis when I was at the beach reading Freud's *Totem and Taboo.* I saw a way of recasting the oedipal complex in the ode form.

In *River Writing* I wrote the poems on foot while running. Originally, I had figured it was going to be a prose journal. Since I was running along the river I was going to write a little record of each day's run. When I started writing, it went to verse instead of prose—free verse with a lot of internal rhyme and wordplay. Basically whatever happened in the run would be part of the poem. If I saw a beaver or an ice storm I would use it. There were some power company cables across the river—a lower and an upper cable so I could inch my way across to the other side. The landscape along the river had been farmed in places, where I could see the old rows of the last farmed season— some with big trees on them. There is a place up the ridge where a homesite once stood. There's a pile of rocks where the chimney fell. Down the hill there is the wreckage of a Model-T. It's very much a kind of inscribed landscape. That evidence of an agricultural past, for me, ties in back home to eastern North Carolina. I found a way of mediating between my past life and my present life. I was able to carry my concerns into a contemporary meditation in my present moment, in my own voice, which included, among other things, theoretical issues about language. It also involved my own current tensions about my career and getting axed out of the arts directorship I had put a lot of effort into—kind of mid-life crisis poems. Also, I used whatever was on my mind. I'd be working at the office, get home with just barely enough time to get a run in. Sometimes it would be night when I'd get back. Sometimes I'd feel pretty low. But somehow, confronting your demons in all weathers is very restorative. I don't run great distances, but I'm kind of a running addict. It's more for psychological relief.

After a long day the running revived you.

Running provided such a cleaned "state of mind," so I could function poetically after a day of work without having to wind down all the way to bedtime. Halfway through the run it was like waking up fresh in the morning. It cleaned the slate so anything could come in.

In that River Writing *is a bridge between your past and present, two completely different worlds, though not many miles from the original childhood, and though it is a time span of between forty and fifty years, what does it mean to be a Southern writer today as opposed to the era of your childhood when the agrarians were writing?*

That's a very difficult question. I can only speak of someone in my generation. I was born in 1935 in eastern North Carolina, which is still more agrarian than here in Durham. There is a sufficient continuity, there, of that culture we call the South. There wasn't any question of getting immersed in that. I grew up and was formed before the television age. World War II was crackling in the news reports and inserting itself into the static of the radio, into the lightning of the thunderstorms of summer. In some ways I think World War II was almost a continuation of the Civil War. That's a partial statement, but somehow the South has had in its collective mind a war ever since the Civil War. Southerners are more warlike because they didn't win that war and they've been wanting to fight a war and win it. They're more patriotic. For instance, in David Bottoms' poem "Shooting Rats at the Bibb County Dump" you have these guys shooting rats — these kind of pathetic warriors — the kind of guys who ride around in a pick-up truck with the guns on the rack with the Confederate flags on the bumper. They didn't get to fight that war so they're looking for one, and they'll beat the Hell out of you if you give them a chance. (*Laughing.*) The Civil War was the past, but World War II was a current war — so there was a WAR. It was still the South and we were on the right side. The Japs were bad. The Germans were bad. We were good. Things were clean and simple. You put in tobacco like you were fighting a war and you fixed the engines of your tobacco harvester like you were fighting a war. Ralph and Bill told us about shooting Japs or carrying a BAR [Browning Automatic Rifle]. (*Laughing.*) You had a flaming good time out there.

Then what happened? Part of what happened to the South happened to the whole country. We had Vietnam. It was a bad war and the country decided it was wrong. The country experienced a kind of fall. That gets complicated, because, in a sense, the South had had its fall one hundred years earlier. One of the distinguishing features of the South is that it is the one area of the nation, before Vietnam, that had experienced military defeat and a complex burden of shame. We had had slavery and military defeat. The nation, as a whole, hadn't had anything like that until Vietnam — napalming children and losing the war.

In a way, the South and the nation experienced a kind of rapprochement. The rest of the country had not been like the South, but now was going though an analogous experience. So that the isolation and the uniqueness of the South were being changed by those and other forces, mainly television. So today the issue of whether there is a unique Southern culture weighs on people's minds. The South will always be there. Certainly it will always be in me. It's changing, but it's hard for me to believe it will ever be totally changed.

Though you pointed out earlier that the change is beneficial?

Oh, yes. In some respects the change is very good. We so quickly forget just how hideous the racial situation, particularly the repression against the civil rights movement, was in the South, how badly parts of the South behaved during that time. Now that's changed, and changed for the better. Only the worst conceivable bigot could regret that these changes for the better occurred. The races, the blacks, the whites, and the Indians in the South are not necessarily going ring-around-a-rosy in perfect harmony, but at least those very worst features of oppression and separation have been done away with. That and the development away from poverty are very good changes in the South. I don't see why any change in the South has to be lamented. It's not, after all, a kind antebellum mansion in a paperweight. It's a place where people live.

With the homogenization of the South, with the melding of cultures, is the Southerner going to lose his or her particular voice?

In a way the South is influencing the rest of the country. Country music, for example, is now a national phenomenon. Movies are being made in the South. *The Big Chill* was shot in South Carolina. The Southern dialect is not going to go away. Oral communication, that sort of narration of lineage between the generations, will perhaps persist. What is most in danger is that quality of explaining ourselves to ourselves and our offspring.

One of the great acquisitions of the South is its sense of history. The Civil War was a great event in that it is the sort of thing from which one traces history. In a sense the Civil War was the loss of paradise to the Southerner — the myth is that the antebellum plantation was paradise, and that then there was the fall, the expulsion from Eden, the war, and living in a kind of ruined world. That story is handled by Milton and other writers in the foundation — myth of Western history. History comes from the fall, this expulsion from the garden into the world of events. So the Southerner has had this regionalized version of history. The narrative, the voice, in my case the uncle, the grandfather, or the mother spinning out this tale of the earlier days, was the medium of the transmission of history and identity. The literary critic makes it sound as if the poem or story is only a product of its literary sources, and other critics make it sound as if Southern writing is only a product of the Southern experience. Neither of these propositions are true. Southern writing is an interaction between Southern experience and a particularly favored set of literary sources, part of them in earlier Southern writers. But I think it is important that other writers, other than just Southern, are entered into the equation, too.

In a sense history escapes us. But in another way it is there. It's mysterious, the way in which anybody can know another time. My own grandfather was the closest history I had, and yet the world of my grandfather and grandmother was very different from mine and not easy to know. They moved into town in the 1920's, built a white house, raised chickens, and had a garden. He killed himself plowing the garden just like I say in "My Grandfather's Funeral." They killed hogs on the farm and would render the lard and give me cracklings out of the pot. That was a slice of an earlier world, there across the street from my father's house and his modern involvement with the service station. Even so, it's very problematic to know the past, especially in America. But there's a sense in which the soil and its places may retain the potency of the past, as with a Civil War battlefield. It's as if you stepped into a different era. Time stops, for that spot of ground within the markers. I am utterly fascinated by that kind of memorial presence: something in the ground or something cut in stone, or names cut in a tree.

How would you describe your poetic style?

I once rather ambitiously and half humorously decided I would like to write a kind of "symbolist Whitman." (*Laughing.*) I like the pungent, innate musicality of Whitman — the cadences, as opposed to the iambs. The poetry I wanted to write was much more slender, more symmetrical and compressed, but still, that was not a bad ambition. Musicality is very important to me. In a way I am an abstract poet. In "Barbecue Service" it is the essence of pig — here's the blue smoke which is the soul of the pig and the soul of North Carolina. It isn't just the narrative of one barbecuing day, it is the smoke, the flavor, it is many barbecuing days, autumns, and all kinds of smoke from Southern cooking distilled into one poem. And it is an abstract poem in the way that art is abstract. So I suppose I am an art poet in a way — I studied piano and I like music and the visual arts very much.

The novel I'm writing involves the love affair between a Southern descendant of a tobacco farming family who is teaching at Chapel Hill, and a soprano. I am fascinated by the *idea* of art. And yet, I guess there is a kind of rough and ready particularity in my poems. There are also a lot of thoughts about formal matters. I'm influenced by writers like Randall Jarrell, Allen Tate, Robert Lowell, and Theodore Roethke, as well as Yeats, Stevens, and Plath. I often write stanzaic poems, but my rhymes are deliberately slant rather than full. I rhyme between stanzas as well as within stanzas. I'm rather drawn to poems with occasional rhyme. The stanzas in the English ode vary in rhyme scheme — the poet makes them up as he goes along, and that English ode gives the form to the title poem of *Ode to the Chinaberry Tree.*

You mentioned your novel. I was going to ask you about that.

It's about the issue of Southern identity, about characters trying to reconcile small town Southern roots with living in the North Carolina triangle region, in a life of literature, art, and thought. There are considerable family complications — including the issue of carrying on the tobacco farm, or not. The narrator hates the idea of smoking, but honors his family's past.

It sounds extremely autobiographical.

There is a good bit of autobiography in it, but strangely enough one of the things that propelled me into writing the novel was reviewing the collected letters of Randall Jarrell. I knew him at UNC–Greensboro back when it was a woman's college. His kind of artiness and literariness clicked and helped me conceive this narrator who is not me. He's a projection of a side of myself, but a different side. It's more true to say that the narrator is much more of a persona in the way that J. Alfred Prufrock is a persona — considerably distanced from me. But the experiences and the places are extremely close to the real me.

What was your childhood like?

I made up stories, perhaps as an imitation of the stories my uncle told me. I first told them to my younger brother, and to my cousin (who was like a sister), and then when I went back to school the teacher allowed me to stand up in front of the class to make up stories, in which my classmates took part.

I guess that was my first writing so to speak. My childhood was in many ways very pleasant, once I got over the trauma of the rheumatic fever scare. I remember being frightened to death by the doctors and the tests. When they let me go back to school, I got back into things and enjoyed it. Our town was so small that about four years before I was old enough to play football they brought in six-man football. It was like basketball with tackling. The strategy was not very well worked out. But I had been reading these books on eleven-man football, and how to run the single wing. When I was old enough, I worked out a single-wing offense, and our little undermanned squad went to the eastern finals my senior year, until we were overwhelmed by this great squad from Southern Pines.

From early on I loved the memory of lard being rendered in my grand-parents' backyard and the cracklings out of that pot. They are some of the best things ever eaten. I remember the visual image of when my father turned me over in the creek in that red speedboat and I looked down, down, down, forever down into this brown water. Later, my grandfather's funeral was very vivid in my mind. I had been in graduate school a year or so and I had lost contact with the town and the people. At eighty-seven his mind was kind of going, though he loved to be driven around to see the crops. He had heart trouble, yet, he got out his hand plow and plowed two rows in the garden, then he came inside and died. They told me about it. I didn't actually see that, but it was vivid.

At the funeral, seeing the townspeople come across the winter-bleached grass, remembering their names and their particularities—I guess that is ac-tually the moment when I reexperienced my continuity with Stantonsburg and the people. That's really the first time I wrote about the town and the people—the first serious poem I had published.

I have a least favorite memory that would probably be in the hospital pediatric ward with babies screaming in the distance, the doctors looking grave and dubious about my condition. There are plenty of bad memories. The downside of the war. The broken P-47 with the pilot's blood on the seat and feeling just for a tiny moment the real terror that underlined that preteen triumph that I tended to feel in the air war. Seeing the P-47's zooming overhead had seemed like ultimate power—the antithesis of my earthbound position. Once the tide turned and we were winning it was such an ego trip for our side, but yet, that crashed plane reminded me of the darker side.

Your poetry, especially, Ode to the Chinaberry Tree, *is concerned with the past and how it relates to the present and how it reflects your childhood.*

That's right. The new collection will be concerned with the past in a more challenging way, the way you would in psychoanalysis or politics. It will confront the past and not replicate it, not talk about it in a nostalgic way, but challenge the past and ascertain its relation with the present, so as to energize the present by reexperiencing the past, but in a way that deepens

understanding, so that it overcomes some of the hesitancy about conformation that is one Southern attribute. I wrestle with racism, sexism, and the bad
male image that I hated. I'm able to let my anger be more constructive, which
also allows me to love a little better.

In fact you unleashed that anger in Ode to the Chinaberry Tree *with "The
Morning After."*

True. That's a more societal, generally political poem. I will unleash
more on Southern topics in the new book. Being unable to face one's anger
is a great limitation. In a way my poetry strikes some people as being
idealistic and goody-two-shoeish, but in fact, the idealizing of an idea often
springs from the inability to face things as they are, or especially if glossing
over anger. The more you wrestle with your aversions, and the more you see
through them so that they are no longer intolerable, and forgive the people
or forgive yourself for hating them, or express your anger so that it's no longer
so venomous within you, the more you can deal with problem of over-
idealization. It's like trying to reach the adult stage of transactional analysis—
you don't want to be a parent and you don't want to be a child—you want
to be an adult. I want to live in the South the way it is, and that's one reason
I wrote that book of poems.

I need to incorporate the past, it's part of my identity, but I also need
to carry it on in a form that represents me and my wife and my children now,
and that project has to incorporate new knowledge and broader perspectives
than one would find from the stereotypical South. Many Southerners and
Southern writers leave the South. I don't want to leave the South. I want to
construct (by God and good grace) a livable South, or a livable place in the
South. I don't want to leave because I like it too much.

In what direction do you see your poetry moving?

I've described the newest things I've done, but what it will be next is very
hard to say. My ecological interests are becoming more important as are my
social interests. My newest poem is about the two Americas—white houses
and picket fences and an America with F-16's blasting straight upward like
hypodermic needles carrying a chemical fix for some teenage kid whose getting it all through rock music. The dangers our nation faces from our trash
culture are coming to be incorporated.

More political?

Maybe, but it's hard to perceive. Eliot said that you only know how to
write the poem you have already written, that the new poem is always a raid
on the inarticulate. I know how to prepare myself to write poetry, but I don't
know what the poems are going to be.

Doris Betts

Doris Betts was born in 1932 in Iredell County, North Carolina. Her books of short stories and novels include *The Gentle Insurrection, Tall Houses in Winter, The Scarlet Thread, The Astronomer & Other Stories, The River to Pickle Beach, Beasts of the Southern Wild,* and *Heading West.* She was a finalist for the National Book award for *Beasts of the Southern Wild,* and has also received the John Dos Passos award and a Guggenheim Fellowship. She is currently completing a novel, *Souls Raised from the Dead.* This interview was conducted on April 16, 1988, in her office at the University of North Carolina at Chapel Hill.

Could you discuss your early background?

I was born on a farm outside Statesville, North Carolina, in a house which has finally been torn down—the same house my mother was born in. Everybody else my age was born in a hospital. I come from a rural background. Both my parents grew up on farms and they were the first in their family to move to town to work in the mills. It's such a classic Southern story. (*Laughing.*) They did live very much on the edge of the mill village in Statesville where my father was a cotton mill weaver. We lived there until I was fourteen when we were finally able to afford to buy a house. They did not own a car until after I was married. When I look back I realize we were poor, but it did not seem so to me at the time. I was very fortunate as mine was a very loving family—with double sets of grandparents and going out for big Sunday dinners. I didn't have brothers or sisters, so I confess I was sort of the apple of my parents' eyes—a blessing I did not appreciate until years later. Being an only child you learn to read, to play by yourself—all those good things. It wasn't until I went away to college that I realized people existed who grew up with much less love than I had. I thought everybody lived like me. I don't think I fully appreciated my parents until adulthood.

I felt very different from most Statesville children in that books were my world. My parents wanted me to be very well educated, but they wanted it the way you have great respect for an opportunity you have not had yourself. As a result I passed through a rather dreadful teenage phase when I had wished they could have been professors or artists on the Left Bank. I went away to Women's College — what is now the University of North Carolina at Greensboro, married before I finished school, had children before I had intended also, before I finished school, and then ended up teaching.

Do you consider yourself a Southern writer?

One hates these terms. You hate them because they are more useful to literary scholars than writers. I agree with Eudora Welty: everyone is a regional writer. One trouble with being a Southern writer, especially if you are a woman writer (which is an even smaller Chinese box) is that the category becomes the de facto minor league of letters in some people's minds. It becomes the stereotyping like that on the *Dukes of Hazard.* Sometimes, because Southerners have a sense of humor, our temptation is to play to that, but other times the temptation is to rebel violently. So the term produces a general falsification of writers from the South. I am my definition of a Southern writer, but I always want the other person to tell me what is meant by the term. Also, there is not just one South to come from, though you'd think so if you came from New York. I have little in common with Tennessee Williams — with writers who lived in the low country, delta, or Appalachian South. The South I come from, the piedmont mill town area of North Carolina, is where, historically, you had industrialization and people owned few slaves. That region had a different history — poor folks, yeoman farmers, lower-class and lower middle-class Scotch-Irish or German strugglers.

When I published *Tall Houses in Winter,* my first novel, it came out in Italy and the cover had an enormous Southern mansion, Spanish moss hanging from the trees, and a woman in a ball gown looking like Scarlett O'Hara. Of course, the picture had nothing to do with the content. That moss won't even grow where I lived near the cotton mill, and nobody in my story ever owned a ball gown. So that's the kind of stereotyping you get.

Since it needs definition, how would you define the Southern writer today?

It has become difficult. At one time there was a long list of traits of a Southern writer — beginning with where you were born, grew up, and what you wrote about. They say Southerners like to write about the seasons. Southerners usually have a religious background, a sense of history, and are affected by defeat in the Civil War and by being isolated nationally. In the low country South, gentlemen talked about chivalry, and so on. I can't find these traits anymore. In fact, younger Southern writers who are doing very well are contemporary and urban, and the Dixie itself has become all K-Marts and trailer camps. You can't draw a line at the Mason-Dixon. It would have to be drawn at the city limits. I represent small town/rural ideas. I believe small-town Indiana people would probably be more like small-town Southerners than like Chicago residents, certainly more so than fifty years ago. Atlanta is more like Detroit than like the little town of Pittsboro I live in. You can argue that, but I see a distinctive South fading very quickly.

In the South, the "writing" South, are we experiencing a renaissance?

It seems to me, yes. Not the traditional renaissance, not like the one we had in the fifties and into the early sixties. They say if you throw a rock in Chapel Hill you'll hit a writer. The liveliness now is in Southern women writers. Black writers also are on the upsurge, but less so in North Carolina than some states; that's still coming for us. There are so many gifted young women writers: Lee Smith, Bobbie Ann Mason, Jill McCorkle, Kaye Gibbons. Mary Hood of Georgia is a wonderful story writer.

In fact, I wanted to ask you about the short story writer. I read an interview you did twenty years ago with George Wolfe where you said you write novels so you can write short stories. Since then there has been a renaissance in the short story.

Yes. (*Laughing.*) And with my ill luck I have changed to writing novels. It used to be you couldn't sell a volume of short stories, except as sandwich fillings between thick novels. And the story form was certainly not the way for a new writer to make his or her name. That has changed. I can't decide how good to feel about that. The American short story forms a very strong strand in our literature. Americans have always been appreciated for it, but not by the reading public of popular books. Some of our best writers have been short story writers. During the last twenty years we may be appreciating the story form less for artistic merit and more because stories are short and TV has shortened our attention span, though the stories also happen to be good. Today's crop of stories may be better than the reading public deserves. I do feel sad about the decline of reading, now that many people will pick up a book to read fifteen or twenty pages and a unit, as opposed to immersing themselves in the long, complex novel you'd carry with you on a six-month visit to a country house in the nineteenth century. So the short story as a literary form may not be as healthy as it looks. Minimalism reinforces my feeling that brevity alone sometimes seems a virtue in itself. It's not always that readers absorb three words and get ten words worth of value, which is how good readers read; some are just getting three words worth of value. Period. Or writing three, for that matter.

It's been my perception that it is the woman writer who is handling the short fiction more so than men. You mentioned Bobbie Ann Mason, Mary Hood, and yourself. It just appears that the strongest group is women.

One area I think that has not been fully analyzed is the effect creative writing classes have had on American literature. Critics have commented on how during the fifties writers were finding the academy to be the twentieth century patron. Since then the trend has proliferated into two-hundred and fifty writing programs in the country. People in England have never heard of this. They think we're crazy—it's so American. I've been teaching at Chapel Hill for twenty years and have seen an enormous change in student writers. At one time more than half were male, which paralleled the whole UNC student population; now women make up two-thirds to three-fourths of the writing classes, but they are not the same women writing about the same 1968 things. I used to get the prom story, the horse story, and in most situations women characters were waiting: for somebody — the father, a boyfriend — or just to grow up. But ten years ago on the first day of one freshman writing class, a new student read her first piece about her first menstrual period. The prose was graphic and blew the men away. I thought then that the tide had changed. One reason we teach the short story in college is not because it is an easier form to produce, but because pragmatically you can teach it — you can get a whole unit out and work on an overall revision. I think we have bred a generation of writers who have practiced the short story form, and second, many others now do know how to read it, though they didn't go on to write; they learned to love it as a form. These balance out my short-attention-span readers. I hope. When I went to college in the fifties I realized that I had read few short stories in high school, "The Necklace"... all those surprise ending stories. I didn't even know how to define a literary short story. Katherine Ann Porter, Welty, Mansfield, Joyce, etc., were all brand new to me. That is not true for student writers today.

That is another aspect of the short story that was not true in the recent past — the growing audience. There is a tremendous upsurge in the short story audience.

And yet the market has disappeared from mass magazines.

In the past the pulp magazines published short stories, but now, even though something like 30,000 different magazines are published, all specialized, most do not publish short fiction.

Even the areas that popularized the short story in the thirties and forties like the *Saturday Evening Post,* places where Fitzgerald published.... We have nothing equivalent now. It's hard for me to tell students with good stories to send them out. They say where? I list five or six major markets in New York City knowing, of course, the competition. Then you move to little and literary magazines where quality is outstanding. This confuses me — you have a mass audience for books of stories, but you don't have a mass audience for the short fiction periodical.

Editors of literary magazines are starving to death just as they did twenty years ago. The little magazines are as bombarded with stories as *Good Housekeeping* used to be. I like to quote what Max Steele said to my class once, "The pulp magazine is gone, and most of the mass fiction publications are gone. In fact, the kind of slick story that used to appear in so-called "women's" magazines can now be seen on television between one and five everyday. So without much market for pulp or slick manuscripts, you may as well write the good, the true, and the beautiful."

In discussing Southern women writers, you have to take into consideration the changing South. Is the old South disintegrating?

It would be more interesting to ask a writer in Mississippi or Alabama where they've always had more "Old South." North Carolina was never as Confederate, as traditional, except down east; and yes, it is changing. I say that with mixed feelings. I hate the homogenization of our culture—a generalized America is not good for writers. Specificity is much better. But young writers are resisting broad oversimplification, still trying to use local settings as well as mock qualities in American life that have become generic. Chapel Hill is, of course, an enclave; that's one reason I live in Pittsboro that has resisted change though it's just about to explode with progress this next decade.

I see two things happening with young women writers. The Southern woman, almost the Southern belle (and Lee Smith comes to mind as one who could have played that role to the hilt had she chose), has come down off the pedestal. The young black woman is long out of the cotton field and kitchen and on the way up. These two groups of Southern women are meeting halfway. It's almost enough to give sisterhood a good name. As writers and scholars, escaping stereotype, they are beginning to review each other. Though their experiences are different, racially, they have gender in common. I'm not sure what South tomorrow's changed Black and white women writers will be writing about. The change has resulted in a democratization of material so that much student fiction relies almost exclusively on voice, which, again, is a national trend. In my classes it's not a streetwise voice, but it's a small townwise voice, often female, and its owner is between the ages of twelve and twenty-two. We're also beginning to get female parallels of genres that have been male, the female bildungsroman, for instance, but we're also getting female picturesque heroines in little Moll Flanders books.

Voice as your chief literary device can easily become a real dead end. You love it the first time you read it, then with a second novel you think, well, I've had and admired the voice; now what is this voice going to say? As the pages mount you begin to miss some of the other niceties of prose such as beauty and rhythm. Intellect, depth. The narrator's strong voice carries many Southern novels. The Southern woman writer is also very strong on character, in novels often told in first person with more personal insight than plot—though that's a general modern phenomena. The standard charges about women's writing being more personal and concrete and less abstract are still being made. However, I think with greater skill and perception many women writers are getting a hell of a lot more out of even personal material than they once did—that their experience has become metaphoric and not just a restriction.

Which writers have influenced you?

I doubt if any writer knows. Other books have just been in there so long and I read so much and change so often that at any given time there is some writer I am enjoying a great deal; next week it may be someone else. I tend to take a writer and read everything — including a lot of criticism about that writer — exhaust his biography and work for awhile and then spit out the seeds. There are writers I go back to, usually quite different from me. Over Christmas holidays I was as starved for plot as you would be for potato chips, so all I read were detective novels by women: P.D. James, Martha Grimes, Amanda Cross. For awhile I was very deep into South American writers and taught Garçia Marquez, Borges, and others. I like European writers, too.

When did you first take an interest in writing?

I learned to read when I was four and from then on, even though I couldn't have articulated it, I was hooked. I wrote poems back then which my mother saved. They are no good at all; not one of them reveals a gifted child. In grade school I don't think I even knew an ordinary person could be a writer. I didn't even understand fully where books came from. But somewhere in there you get your first library card and you check out a book, open it up and smell the pages, and you can't wait for the summer to lie underneath the apple tree and read. From love of reading I thought that would be the best thing in the world to do — to make books.

You've always been a short story writer, but then about twenty years ago you changed to the novel form. You didn't consider yourself a novelist at the time. . . .

And I still don't. I'm still learning how to write a novel — hoping the last one was better than the one before. Some forward progress may be all that keeps me writing. The reason I changed to the novel is that I got older. I associate the short story with the lyric poem, similar in form, suiting the usually youthful person who creates them. It's a certain vision they have. At the end of the day writers and poets lie in bed thinking about what happened during the day — that's a short story writer's mood. One day, one focus, one significant change. The older you get the more you think about what happened this year, this decade. Your scope changes, your scale of measurement enlarges. The short story becomes too small. There's a moment in most short stories where an insight gets locked into the prose. When you get older you think: I've had a million insights and I'm still the confused person I always was. You grow more interested in attrition and cumulative knowledge; you mistrust the easy answers the short story can offer. If you had an affinity for and a skill at the short story, you realize it wouldn't be hard to keep knocking off short stories, once you've grasped the form. Story content may decline, though, as you get older knocking off ten smooth stories per year with not much wrong with them. You would know they were weaker stories though, and eventually everyone else would know it. I was writing short stories people were willing to publish, but then I ceased to learn anything from them — they were not difficult. I'm always afraid the short story will become artificial, the way rhymed poetry can, where it turns into not a device that disciplines you but restricts you, a form too neat for what the years have been telling you.

The short story, just because of brevity, almost always falsifies emotion. If you put sentiment in a short story the risk is very great that it will exaggerate itself and turn sentimental or melodramatic, that the effect will outweigh your intention. Hyperbole rules, characters flatten. Everything serves a central effect. If you spread out in a novel you're often more able to control sentiment, or violence, or eccentricity, not by discipline as a story writer would, but simply by scale. If you put a virtue in a short story you may get Pollyanna oversimplified. But if you put virtue in a novel along with vice and weakness, then you may have a chance to do the hardest thing literature can, and that is to write well about a *good* person. Charity, kindness, the cardinal virtues require a novel. A good person in a short story sounds smart ass, or pious or insufferable. The great fear of all us women writers is sentimentally — that's been the easy stereotype — that we may become Valentine writers.

The Bible has had a large influence on your writing. . . .

Yes, it has. When I started writing I assumed Bible allusion was universal — a background everybody had, and in Iredell County at that time it was. I did not know how local or time bound that vision was. Bible references are not common in my students' work now unless they are rather strong fundamentalists. But I continue to use Christianity and Bible stories because that's what I know. Religion has become again important to me, also. I don't want to turn into a writer whose fiction is intended to convert or to prove theological points. That seems to me death to aesthetic success, at least in our culture.

Do your students appear to be more secular?

Almost entirely. The love for other people is there, but God is not behind it, and the whole leaf of ritual has dropped out. That seems a general pattern, but then college is when everybody gives up religion. I certainly did. There are also entirely respectable and serious Christians, Jews and Hindus on the campus who pursue their faith, but with decorum, perhaps even anxiety. In Chapel Hill I feel differently than at home in Pittsboro. At the university it would be in rather bad taste to mention a spiritual view of life. If everyone talked about general religion with a lower case "r" and no specific religion that would be more acceptable.

You have been compared to Eudora Welty and Flannery O'Connor, but you had not read O'Connor before you started writing, it was only after the comparison was made.

Everybody loves what Flannery O'Connor said when she was compared to William Faulkner, "Nobody likes to be caught on the tracks when the Dixie Special comes through." The first time I was compared to O'Connor I thought Flannery was a man's name. That's how ignorant I was. The comparison simply reflects the fact that we both came from the Piedmont South, which is much the same in Georgia and North Carolina. Essentially our experiences and outlooks are similar though she was Catholic and I was Protestant, and

I came from the kind of family she would have satirized. I'm one of the millions who read her letters in *The Habit of Being* and asked: why did she write to A? If she wanted an earnest and sympathetic correspondent, she could have written to *me!* I would have very much liked to have known Flannery O'Connor. She and I had one good friend in common, Louise Hardeman Abbot.

Your characters, in a sort of odd, awkward way, are looking for love. They do find love, but often in a grotesque manner, though not specifically physical — it's more often emotional.

I'm probably not conscious of that much anymore. Nowadays I'm more interested in love in a larger context, as a part of what Christ had to say — not what Oral Roberts or Jimmy Swaggart say, and certainly not the sweet simplicity of Robert Schuller. "I have come that you might have life and have it more abundantly." To live fully, which always means to love fully. Recklessly? Jung says that after thirty-five his patients didn't have the standard problems of sexuality or parents or career — they wanted their lives to have some meaning. Love has by far the best chance of counting in that search, that's all. What we are here for is to live abundantly, to "redeem the time," as T.S. Eliot said, though Paul said it in his letter to the Ephesians first. The capacity to love, the great need to be loved. Many of us female writers come back down to that as our theme, but to say it out loud puts love in the category of sentimentality. We don't want to write lacey valentines. I think C.S. Lewis was the one who said love was both more fierce and more significant than that. A loveless life would be the closest thing I would understand to Hell, and self-love is one of the traditional downhill roads.

You've been called one of America's finest women writers, but yet, you have not received the recognition that many critics say you deserve.

I'm very lucky. Especially since I live in America. I have the same feeling as Rainer Maria Rilke's *Letters to a Young Poet:* Just be grateful you have not been discovered. Now you have the freedom to get on with your work. What we do to American writers in this country, because we are celebrity conscious, is pester them to death. You can be a big frog in this small pond forever giving speeches and judging literary contests and meeting writers, and on a small scale it's burdensome, too; but what's it like to be Toni Morrison this year? What's it like constantly having your private life interrupted? My private life is very important. It's not accidental that we are talking in my office, not in my living room.

You go to great lengths to separate the two.

Very carefully. Lately, I've concentrated on the private life and the last several years I have not gotten much published. I don't care much about publishing, wouldn't want to be famous. What I want is to write something wonderful. You will know. Even when you're not writing something wonderful you'll write a good page now and then; that's what keeps you writing. But

I would have liked to have more money. Money buys freedom; freedom is time to write.

Once you've finished a story do you continue to revise and when do you let it go?

There is a moment to let it go because if you go over it too long it will congeal. Part of what I want to learn from the novel form is less congealing, more fluidity of style. Short story writing tightens you, turns you into the kind of person who never colored outside the lines. A novel can have a loose end or two. It almost needs some. Someone once said, "A great novel is a good novel that has something wrong with it." You can put all kinds of critical holes through the novels that are durable.

Something I would like to talk about that your work has continued to utilize, that a lot of fiction does not, is comedy. Lee Smith uses comedy, but there isn't much else out there that is truly funny, or at least I haven't found it. You have an underlying comic mode in your work and I want to discuss the nature of that comedy.

I hope I have comedy. The novel I have been trying to finish is sad, and that's why it has been hard to finish. The story needs a foil or balance. Comedy may be an outgrowth of maturity. Many young women writers who are breaking out still have grievances to tend to; let them get those grievances out of the way. One of my earliest reviews said it would be interesting to see what kind of books I would write when I got older and "cheerfulness breaks in." I now understand exactly what was meant. Young writers believe only tragedy is serious. Your grandmother was quite right when she said: you may as well laugh as cry. I'd like to write a comic novel. I have not been able to. I've started comic stories, but about half way they break over to tragic. With me there's always going to be a mix. Comedy is not so much funny as life affirming. That's its real function. When I'm comic, the reader may smile but he rarely laughs. And I incline to the character who is sarcastic. Women today say what they think. In my generation you didn't say aloud everything you thought, but your thoughts were quite wry. Comedy is healthier than the victim routine. It is life affirming—a response that involves laughing at oneself as well as at others. It redeems the time.

Is there any one thing that can make a situation funny—a device that you can employ for a humorous effect? Humor is actually tragedy inverted. So what is it that makes a situation funny and not tragic?

That's an excellent question and I haven't thought about it. Humor, like tragedy, begins with the great gap between how things are and how they ought to be. The situation statement is that there are two ways to react, that the world is a tragedy to those who feel and a comedy to those who think. Comedy is more rational. You have reminded me of Arthur Kessler's book on creativity, *Act of Creation*—he actually draws that diagram tracing the pattern of a joke to how it functions in *Oedipus Rex,* and says what happens in both cases is that the equilibrium of what you expected has been rudely disturbed. Pratfall or Jocasta. I use humor with women characters to contrast what is on the inside and outside. When your inside and outside are the same you can pass beyond the need for humor and into sincerity. There has to be some discrepancy either in the person or the situation at which you will either laugh or be grieved.

One type of humor I enjoyed in your novel Heading West *was when the main character, Nancy Finch, was lost out West and they were looking for her, and the police officer can't remember her name, but keeps saying it has something to do with birds. He rattled off all the bird possibilities like sparrow, jay, and on and on. It was a dry humor that worked well.*

That got in for the wrong reason. Originally, I didn't have a title. I thought of Nancy as sort of a bird in a gilded cage — that's where Finch came from, a subliminal message to the reader. But then I realized nobody would think of that but me — I might as well italicize it and add other birds. And she did fly the coop. The name Nancy came from Nancy Drew — somebody who goes to solve the mystery. The Nancy Drew series was one of the few girls could read in which there was a female heroine.

I went back and read the interview you did with George Wolfe twenty years ago, and it is funny how some of the questions are quite dated, especially when he asked you if you had ever dropped acid. And of course your answer was no.

(*Laughing.*) I thought that was funny at the time. Can you imagine that people even cared or thought drugs were artistic? It was a time when artists were into experiments — like Coleridge and believed L.S.D. might alter their perspective for all time. It was trendy. I was then reading material from students who had done drugs and thought they had some revelation — and the exact opposite was true. They began to write things like, "Wow! I see all these colors. Boy, are they beautiful." They didn't communicate anything.

Since then, in the last twenty years, what has been the biggest change in your work?

I'm writing about people more my own age, which is inevitable. I suspect the content is becoming more theological for good or ill. The novel underway, the sad one, is about theodicy. I am more self-conscious about my writing so maybe I need to get away from the university. Sometimes I look at sentences the way a schoolteacher does, and that's not good.

I'd like to ask if you have a favorite childhood memory?

I have a great many, especially those when I spent my summers on my grandparents' farm in the woods and pastures. And to some degree I have recaptured rural life now, living where I do. One memory in *Heading West* that is almost literally mine is given to Nancy Finch. She is crossing the stream and the grandfather wants her to learn to walk the log but she is afraid of falling into the creek, so she climbs down. Though my grandfather never would have thrown stones at me as he does in the novel, he did go off and leave me because I was too frightened to walk the log. My reaction was essentially the same as Nancy Finch's — that he was one of the rare adults who had taken the time to try to teach her something difficult. I had a good childhood. Now I'm a new grandmother and I hope that my grandson has as good a childhood.

Turning this around, do you have a least favorite childhood memory?

I went to a very old fashioned grammar school at the edge of the mill village. It was a tough school, which you would expect, and there was a lot of serious physical fighting. I was a tomboy and I did fight. I didn't win them all, but I fought boys and girls, and there were a lot of bloody noses. All of those memories of fighting, even the ones I won, are to some degree unpleasant. Maybe my worst memory is when I did something cruel. We had a boy in my class who was a sissy, though he and I had been reasonably good friends. One day we got into a fight, I forget why; and I was enjoying being the stronger of the two. He was wearing an army cap. I snatched it off his head and popped him with it, not once but harder and then harder. I had no idea it had a metal button on the edge. The button cut his head. And as you know a scalp wound that isn't even deep will just bleed and bleed. I thought I had fractured his skull, that I had maybe killed him. I was sent to the principal and was spanked. It is the horror I remember because I was being downright vicious—and at that time I was enjoying hitting him and then shocked by the results.

I remember my first childhood memory—I was about seventeen or eighteen months old and we lived in what is now called a concrete block house, divided into two apartments. My best friend lived in the next downstairs apartment; we lived upstairs. The pantries of the two kitchens joined and for some reason the adjoining wall had been left open in each pantry about halfway down. In the mornings when I and Mary Elizabeth, the little girl next door, got up we would run down to our pantry and simply stand there and look at one another's feet and pajamas. We were very good friends and played together, but I don't remember playing. I only remember running down there to look at her feet. There wasn't a "Good morning" or a "How are you?" We just stood there looking at each other's feet. I had ducks on my pajamas and she had little pink flowers. She and I have become reacquainted during our fifties—she's a minister's wife in Virginia—and I've enjoyed rehashing our later childhood. But she's younger and doesn't remember the ducks and flowers.

Do you still receive letters from people who say, "Dear Mrs. Betts, I have just read your novel and my unpublished novel is on the way under a separate cover"?

Do you see that package up on the shelf? There they all are. I receive a lot of them. Very often they just come. I send them back or just hold onto them since many don't provide return postage. Some write notes like, "Enclosed is my novel. I would like to have your opinion and I admire your work. I would like to have it back by April 3." What must Toni Morrison receive? I am sympathetic towards these people who believe (falsely) there is something I can do for them. I have a letter that tries to explain to them that they are asking me to do the job of an agent or a Knopf editor. I, too, write things that don't get published. I don't say to them what I long to say, "Would you say to your doctor that you have an interesting disease that you want him to treat on Sunday for free?" This is what they are asking, that I teach them free, on Sunday, what I am paid to teach full-time. But they don't mean to be irritating, so there's no real advantage to being quick-tempered with them.

David Bottoms

David Bottoms, born in Canton, Georgia, in 1949, is an assistant professor of English at Georgia State University and the author of *In a U-Haul North of Damascus, Under the Vulture Tree,* and *Shooting Rats at the Bibb County Dump,* chosen by Robert Penn Warren as the 1979 winner of the Walt Whitman Award. He is coeditor of *The Morrow Anthology of Younger American Poets* and his novels include *Any Cold Jordan* and *Easter Weekend.* He has been the recipient of the Levinson Prize of Poetry 1985, NEA Fellowship, the Ingram Merrill Award, and the Award in Literature from the American Academy & Institute of Arts and Letters. This interview was divided into two sessions — on March 10, 1986, at Livingston's Library, a bar across the street from Georgia State University, and on April 7, 1987, at Bottoms' home in Marietta, Georgia.

What inspires you to write?

I don't know. Do you mean what did at one time or what does? I don't really know. That's one of those deep metaphysical questions. I'm not trying to give a short answer. I have always been interested in words. I always read a lot when I was a kid and I just sort of got the notion about being a writer that you somehow knew more than anybody else. Which is not true, of course, but that's the kind of romantic idea you have when you're a kid. You want to write and express yourself, investigate the mysteries of the cosmos. I came to it that way, and I just enjoy it. I like to work on poems and it's very frustrating when I'm not writing anything or when I'm in between things. I do it because I enjoy it. I enjoy reading and writing poems. That's kind of the bottom line. If I didn't, I wouldn't be involved.

Who are some of the writers whose work you admire and have influenced your work?

James Dickey. Robert Penn Warren, who has been writing for so long and has such a variety of things. I like Warren's poetry and Dickey's poetry. If you want to be a writer you have to be very well read, so those two poets for sure. They would have to be my big guns. The others I admire are Elizabeth Bishop and Theodore Roethke. Roethke is certainly one of my heroes. I like Robert Lowell. Those folks in contemporary American poetry. In fiction— the biggies like Hemingway. I like his short stories and what he does with the power of concentration, the economy of his statements. Faulkner is okay, too.

Do you have any advice for aspiring writers?

Advice? No. Just determination, I suppose. It's the big one. It takes a very long time to develop a particular voice, a voice that makes you unique. Before you do that you have to go through an agonizing sort of apprenticeship. I went through that when I was in college and several years after. It's necessary that you believe that your work is good, but it's also necessary that you continue to learn. There's a hard leap to make from being a competent student to a competent graduate student poet. There's a big leap from that particular kind of competence you find all over the place to one that takes you into a voice where you have something unique to say. Not everybody makes that leap, but you sure don't make it unless you're tremendously determined. You have to say so what, another rejection, what do these people know? Keep pushing it. Half of it is pure determination.

As a child you loved baseball and fishing. What else did you do? Did you ever have any rebellious trouble or anything like that as your poetry might tend to suggest?

Well, not anything very serious. I grew up in the country. Not in the country, but not in the town either. As I think about it now, I had a very sane and happy childhood, which seems incredible in this day and time. We weren't rich, we were very far from it. My family grew up in the same area, in the same town. I had cousins. My grandma and granddad lived about one hundred yards down the road. My granddad ran a little country grocery store, so I grew up around that. It was very nice. I couldn't imagine growing up in a better atmosphere. He had walking horses and dogs. It was an incredibly stable period in my life, but by the time I was a senior in high school I was ready to leave, do something else, go somewhere. I left home and didn't come back here to live until 1982. I left when I was eighteen and didn't come back until I was thirty-two. I had a pretty good upbringing. My folks were concerned that I get a good education, and they sacrificed a lot so I could go away to school. You can't ask for much more than that.

Your poems deal with people searching for personal identification. Do you feel that people have lost their personal identity and in doing so must look toward specialized groups, whether it be the Shriners, Women's League, KKK, a bowling league or a political party in order to fill that void of not belonging?

That's one crisis of the twentieth century—the problem of establishing your identity. Existentially that's what we do all our lives—we continue establishing our identity. Who are you? Who am I? One thing about our lives is that the older we get our possibilities keep running out. When you're young, like you, you keep thinking the world's out there in front of you; you can do anything you want to. The older you get, the more your life narrows — your possibilities become less and less. That's one of the tragedies about aging. Dickey said to me one time, "One of the most frightening things is going into middle age without being good at something, without accomplishing something." Nobody wants to be just another guy. It's kind of scary being just another guy. There's that horrible sense of being anonymous.

Your poems also deal with the hidden conflicts that plague people's lives, mainly attributed to the changing values of their culture. These changes are especially true in the Southern area. Because of this, mainly the influx of business, how do you feel this is affecting the South and the Southern way of life?

Well, that's a good question. It's having a negative effect in a way — positive and negative effects. What's happening is that the South is becoming "Americanized." It has been over the last several years. There are scholars who will argue that there is no longer a Southern literature, that the South has become like television, and everybody talks like the guy on the six o'clock news. I don't think that's true. I think what you will find reflected in southern literature, now, are people dealing with the changes. Look at those great stories in Bobbie Ann Mason's *Shiloh*. She deals essentially with the clash between generations, the power of generations and the way the values of our generation clash with the generation of our parents, how TV, radio, pop culture, and the California culture have influenced us and changed our values. You see this more in the South than any other region in the country, because we held out for so long. We had such a special culture for so very long and we still do. We are pained to change it all. Either you, as a writer, take all that into consideration or you fall behind and become archaic rather quickly. It would be impossible, it seems to me now, for a young writer to write like the Fugitives. It would be ludicrous. We don't have the same concerns, though some of them are the same. Our South is very different from the South of the 1920s and '30s. As a writer, you are in touch with your culture, you take all that in, distill it, and see what you come up with.

In your poems, life is portrayed as a ruthless procession of bum deals, hard bargains, meaningless jobs and clumsy marriages. That's a pretty distressing synthesis.

It's because trouble is more interesting. Everybody wants to live the fairy tale where you grow up, get married, have two kids, and live happily ever after... — then you die. It's not very interesting. You don't want to read about that. Everyone would like to live that story, maybe, but it doesn't make very interesting reading. In poetry, as well as fiction, nothing is more interesting than trouble. Conflict is the name of the game. My interests have always leaned toward the darker element anyway. Those are the sort of poems I like to read.

On winning the Walt Whitman Award for Shooting Rats at the Bibb County

Dump, *you seem to feel lucky and grateful that you won considering there were 1300 other participants, but many of your characters in your poetry life went the other direction. They didn't win the award or find the glory. Do you think, much like your characters, that success could have gone in the other direction for you?*

Oh, absolutely. I might still be selling guitars at Bibb Music. That's what's so incredible about this game. That's what I tell writers — you can work all your life and be published here and there, getting very little recognition, then suddenly you get a break and it all comes together. Look at William Kennedy, who wrote three or four novels that didn't do very well. Nobody had heard of William Kennedy before he wrote *Ironweed,* which was rejected by sixteen or seventeen publishers. Saul Bellow had to get it published for him, then he wins a Pulitzer Prize and they bring all his books back into print. Now, nobody is more well respected than William Kennedy. That's why I say determination is really what separates the professionals from the others. Being ready for it. Eventually it will happen. You have to be ready. You have to be waiting for it.

You have previously written some poems about rats and snakes, but in your most recent collection of poems, Under the Vulture Tree, *you seem to be changing animals. How do animals play a role in your poetry?*

Vultures ... changing animals ... I sort of wore rats and snakes out? I like animals. There's something about nature and animals that speak to the things in us that are most elemental, most primal. The best thing poetry can do is put us in touch with that part of ourself which is most elemental. This isn't anything new, it's extremely old. If you know your Wordsworth, you know that he talks about the innocence of the child and that original happy state of innocence, and as he grows older society corrupts him and his innocence is lost. In terms of what's most natural in man, it's that element of animal. I sympathize with the animal. Most poets do. There's an extremely romantic notion that we can learn something from animals, that animals know more about the real world than we do.

It's like the wilderness movies that come to town where the people are lost and they learn from the animals, not only how to survive, but how to be humanitarians once again. The animals, of course, always survive because they have that knowledge.

Could we do that? It's something we lost. That's attractive to writers.

This is a quote from D. E. Murray, "Your characters are light years away from the American Dream, characters whose hopes have been broken down like so many old farm tractors." It's like in Miller's Death of a Salesman, *the American dream which is sold to us everyday. Do you find this hypocritical of our society?*

I don't think so. It's inevitable. One of the most painful human emotions is disappointment. Everyone is disappointed to some degree. You always dream just beyond your ability to realize what that dream is, just beyond your reach, otherwise it's not a dream, it's reality. As you live your life, your life is a continual dream and redream. When your dreams fail in certain areas you reevaluate and choose alternatives. Unfortunately, sometimes a disappointment is so tragic that it's difficult to rebound. As long as you still have those other viable possibilities you're okay.

There's also the preoccupation with life and death in your poems, and with that I can't help tying this into the contrasting occupations of your parents. Your father was a funeral director and your mother was a nurse.

That's interesting, but I don't think it really had much to do with it. It wasn't always so in my life. My mother was always a nurse, but she didn't work at all when I was growing up and my father had other jobs. So that really didn't play into it. I think it's kind of ironic.

You were raised in a fairly religious background, but you no longer have a religious stand?

You read that in the Rick Lott piece. I don't know if I entirely agree. I don't go to church anymore. I used to when I was a kid. I tend to think of myself as religious in a way. Things in my poetry seem to be antireligious, almost sacrilegious. I don't think that's quite true. I believe in God.

The afterlife?

I could probably believe in it if I thought about it hard enough. I could convince myself of that. Every writer works inside a myth, and to me that's most attractive. I'm not a fatalist, though some of my poems have a bleak vision, but I'd hate to think that's been my life. I believe in something beyond myself, a higher intelligence that hopefully has more control over things.

*   *   *

It's been a year since we last talked, and since then a lot has happened.

Well, just the novel and the new collection of poems.

That's quite a lot, isn't it?

It's something.

Didn't you also read at the Library of Congress?

Oh yeah, I did a reading at the Library of Congress with John Ashbery in February. It was just Ashbery and I. Robert Penn Warren wrote an introduction, but he wasn't there to read it. I thought he was going to be there, but he had arthritis and the weather was bad, so he sent the introduction. It was nice. My editor came down from New York. I was there three days and had a real good time. It snowed ten inches the first day, so I didn't get to see much of Washington. I got to talk with Senator Sam Nunn for awhile. He invited me to stop by his office, but it snowed some more and I didn't get to go.

Had you ever met Ashbery before?

No, I hadn't. He was pretty good. We don't have much in common as far as poetry, but he was very nice. And I liked him.

You just had Any Cold Jordan *published. Could you discuss it?*

I worked on it for about two or three years and had a lot of insecurities about it. It's a really different thing than writing poetry. I was a little worried about letting Peachtree Publishers handle it, and not a New York publisher. I thought they might be publishing it because I'm a hometown boy. But I know that's not true. So, when I got a good paperback offer I felt better. The whole thing with Peachtree is my own insecurities. They're smart enough to know whether a book is good, and I'm sure it wasn't because of anything else other than that. It's just one of my insecurities. You always have those deep down. If I had tried to, and sold it in New York, I would have felt more secure.

More confident of the work itself?

Yeah. I wouldn't feel that way about the poems, because I've been writing poetry long enough. But having never published any fiction I didn't have anything to gauge it by.

Did you send it to any publisher other than Peachtree?

I sent a very early version to Morrow, but they weren't interested — that's normal. They've never been interested in any ideas I've had for fiction. They've always been interested in the poems, which is understandable. Editors tend to pigeonhole you. They think you're either a poet or a fiction writer, so it's really hard to cross over into a different medium. It's hard for a fiction writer to cross over into poetry, and for anyone to take them seriously. It's probably even harder for a poet. It's a dangerous thing. It's odd that editors think that way.

Chuck Perry, the executive editor of Peachtree, was really good. A couple years ago he had heard I was writing a novel and asked if he could see it — just to read. This was a long time before I would let anyone see it. He read it, and liked it, but said it needed a few things. I worked on it some more. After this I sent it to Morrow, but they weren't hardly as encouraging as Chuck, so I didn't even send it back to Morrow. He read it a second time, and was very enthusiastic about. So he called my agent, made her an offer, though I didn't think the book was finished then. I didn't even think it was finished when I gave him a manuscript copy. But he was so eager to do it and had been so good that I thought Peachtree would do a good job all around.

Did they do much editing?

He did a little. He gave it one complete reading where he made suggestions, but he didn't say I had to change anything. A copy editor went through and put semicolons all over it. I say Chuck didn't do a lot of editing — maybe the reason I say that is because he was so good about the way he handled it that I took every suggestion he made. So, it didn't seem like he was trying to tell me what to do. I think you're a pretty dumb writer if you don't listen to your editor. As a writer, you lose perspective about your work, it's only natural. You can't see it as clearly as they can.

I don't know if this was intended, but Any Cold Jordan *appears to be very autobiographical.*

Not really. Just traces. The music is.

What about the setting being at Florida State where you received your Ph.D.?

The geography is autobiographical.

I have found a lot of little things in the novel that appear to be autobiographical. For instance, I found your backyard described in one scene.

Well, yeah. You have to describe something. I think that particular house and backyard are in Tallahassee. Probably a lot of writers work that way—from geography. It's difficult to create a whole world, so you just describe the one you have, I suppose.

There's also all the fishing, hunting and guns, which you have a great interest in. Also, Billy Parker drinks Bass Ale, and anytime I've been somewhere with you that's what you order. I just pulled all of this together and felt it wasn't just coincidental.

I guess a lot of my prejudices are about music and art, that's what the book is really about—about a guy who's trying to be an artist in a culture that doesn't really appreciate his art, and how he has to come to terms with the popular taste. He's not good enough to be a real artist, a classical guitarist. He's not even the best at what he does, but he's an appreciator. Fred Chappell wrote me a letter about the book and said that Billy Parker was an appreciator of the pure music. He wasn't as good as other musicians, but he was an appreciator. I think the book is about coming to terms with yourself and not succumbing to the public taste, which is not very good in most instances.

You mentioned that after Any Cold Jordan *you wanted to get back to poetry. Are you going to write any more fiction, short fiction?*

I've never written any short stories. Warren published one book of short stories when he was very young. Later when asked why he didn't write more short stories, his said if he could get a good short story he could get a poem. I guess that's the same with me. I'd rather have the poem.

Writing fiction is totally different. I had to work on fiction every day. Sometimes I'd work twelve hours a day. It's real work. You can sit down and plan it, but it takes a long time to execute. With poems, I just work on them sporadically, when an idea comes. I don't work on poems every day, sometimes months will go by without writing a poem, then they just come to me. But, if you don't have the idea you don't have a poem, and you can't force the idea. It's something you have to be sensitive to. When it comes to you—you can work on it, but you can't force it.

How much revision do you do?

An incredible amount. I might write it in one or two days, but it takes weeks to revise it. I might work on it for a few days at a time, then put it down for a couple days, then pick it up every day for awhile, then every few days, maybe in the afternoon. It might not be anything more than working on one little phrase, one line, one word. It's just something you pick at.

When writing Any Cold Jordan *did you encounter any problems you had not anticipated?*

There were hundreds of them. Just keeping the story straight was difficult. It's such a massive undertaking that if you change one thing, if you decide you don't want the guy to be right-handed, then you have to go back though a hundred pages and change every reference from right-handed to left. It's incredibly complex with such little nit-picky stuff. There were all sorts of things to concentrate on, like pacing the story, developing the character . . . — it was hard. It's totally different than writing poems. I guess it's more logical, though it's not nearly as intense as poetry, but it's grueling work.

You have a logical sequence of events in the novel that are more intense than poetry.

Yeah, you're right. I guess it's more logical, though it's not nearly as intense as poetry, but it's grueling work. Having written poems for so long that I found myself having to have every paragraph of the novel perfected before I'd go on to the next. I'd work on a paragraph, work on a paragraph, work on a paragraph, one at a time. I'm not the kind of guy who can sit down and write twenty-five pages a day. On a good day I might have gotten five pages, but they had to be perfect before I could go on to anything else.

Was that frustrating?

Yes, because you don't see much progress.

The character Billy Parker seemed to be doomed from the onset.

I can't remember at what point his fate was set. He loses big, but kind of wins, too. In the end he gets out of music, and that's what he wanted.

But at a big price. He loses his arm.

Yes. I don't exactly remember what happened in the early versions. The ending was different. The early versions were different, but I can't remember whether or not he got killed. Originally, his wrist got broken, and I had to change that for some reason. I changed it to his fingers being broken, and taped up in a particular way. Another thing about writing novels is that you have to have so much specific and particular information about different things. You have to know about everything. I knew all the stuff about music, but I didn't know anything about the medical aspects or the ambush. I didn't know nearly enough about all the weaponry that's used in the end. So, what I did was send the last third of the book to a friend who is a colonel in the Special Forces and an expert in guerrilla warfare. He went through and straightened it out; he set up all the ambushing techniques, the explosives . . . What I'm trying to say is that a novelist has to verify everything. So, with the medicine what you do is call a doctor. It just so happens that my agent's husband is a psychiatrist in New York, a very nice fellow who had been in Vietnam as a medic. I sent that part of the book to him. He and I sat down and went over things. In Vietnam he had done any number of field amputations, so he told me step by step how it would have been done. All that stuff, at least for the layman, is all right on the money, because two experts rode along.

I found when writing fiction that you have to make yourself an expert, and if you can't do that you'd better find someone who is, because nothing is worse than a glaring mistake. And that's what I was really afraid of—a glaring error. If you're going to write about jockeys, you'd better know a lot about horses.

What do you think having a novel will do for you?

I don't know, I haven't the slightest. You never can tell, it might do nothing. (*Laughing.*) I can think of a number of people it did nothing for. You hope you will get a few more readers, and if it brings a more readers to the poems, that will be what pleases me. I hope people will enjoy it enough to read the poems. That would be best. That's what I would like it to do.

Olive Ann Burns

Olive Ann Burns was born in 1924 on a farm in Banks County, Georgia, and went to school in Commerce. She attended Mercer University in Macon, Georgia, and received a journalism degree from the University of North Carolina at Chapel Hill. For ten years she was on the Sunday magazine staff of the *Atlanta Journal and Constitution. Cold Sassy Tree,* her first novel, roots itself in stories told by her parents and relatives. She began writing *Cold Sassy Tree* while undergoing chemotherapy. This interview was conducted at her home in Atlanta on June 20, 1986. Olive Ann Burns died July 4, 1990, in Atlanta. She was 65.

What inspired you to write Cold Sassy Tree?

Well, I had written a family history, in which I think I was just writing out grief over my parents' deaths. My mother died and ten months later my father died. She had cancer and I knew she wasn't going to live. I had always wanted to interview my parents and get all their stories that I had heard all my life. You think you can remember, but you don't remember all the details and you don't remember it in their words, which is what brings their personality alive.

A cousin of mine became interested in the family name. He was a genealogy nut looking for royalty, because all our ancestors were dirt farmers, but with twenty-nine first cousins, he wanted to find out their names and where they were living. In the process he got interested in tracing the family tree. But a few years later he was murdered — my cousin was, and we got his material. Putting it together was something we could do with my mother while she was sick. When you get to those ancestors who are remembered in the mind of somebody still alive, you can write a lot. But even if all you know is that he was short and she was tall, you can see them — they're not just names on a tombstone. Anyway, I wrote elaborate biographies of my maternal great-grandparents, my grandparents and my mother, and after she died I started interviewing my father. He was a great storyteller. One of

his favorite stories was about his grandfather, who, as in the first chapter of
Cold Sassy Tree, married three weeks after his wife died. My aunt finally looked
it up in the Bible and it said seven weeks, which she thought made it a lot
better. My father always said three, and I always thought that story would
make a good first chapter for a novel. I never thought I would write it. I never
thought about writing a book at all, but I had assumed that if I ever did write
a book, it would be nonfiction.

Then, in 1975 I went to the doctor for a routine physical and he found
a blood abnormality. He said I would probably develop leukemia or lym-
phoma. Maybe in two years, maybe in two months—or maybe it would go
away. I think I was grabbing at something to lessen the shock when I decided
right there in the doctor's office to write a novel. I wasn't going to sit around
waiting to see if and when I would have cancer. See, I had all this material,
it was all right there in the family history. So I just started writing. It was two
years before I had to start chemotherapy. The white count went so low that
the doctor told me to stay home; he was afraid I might catch something.
Several years before, a rheumatologist said I couldn't vacuum because of a
little arthritis in my back. If you can't vacuum and can't go anywhere, there's
more time than you know existed. One thing I found out about being sick,
you need work to do. You can watch television and read books, but at some
point you need to be producing something. So writing worked out very well.

Were you still writing while undergoing therapy?

Yes, I was well into the novel by the time I started running a high fever.
I ran a fever for ten months, but I could still write in bed. I didn't have near
the problems a lot of cancer patients have. For example, I didn't have to go
through any surgery, which in itself is debilitating. Still the novel was more
like a pastime. I didn't work at it eight hours a day and I didn't write every
day. I just wrote when I wanted to.

Was the book, in itself, a form of therapy?

It was an occupation, as I said, and that's therapy. A lot of sick people
knit or do needlework, or they paint pictures. If you can get a good cold, you
can read for two or three days, and that's wonderful. But ten months, that's
too long. The book actually made my being sick a happy time. I was doing
something new, it was a new challenge, and it was fun getting down all those
people, inventing them.

What was your childhood like?

I lived on a farm until I was in the second grade, then we moved to Commerce, Georgia. My family spent a year at my grandmother's house, then we
moved back to the farm for a year.

In the novel, Will Tweedy hopes to study agriculture at the university,
which my father did. But that didn't make a bit of difference to the boll
weevils. They didn't care about his degree. He lost his land and eventually
went to work for a farmer's cooperative. We moved to Dawson, Georgia, in

1935, then to Macon in '37, then to Atlanta in 1945 — just before my senior year in college. I don't remember it as being a particularly happy or unhappy childhood. There were four of us. I was the youngest — less than five years between the oldest and me, and two in between. Children that close together do a lot of fussing. And the Depression was a very hard time, but we never went hungry. In Dawson, there were gentlemen farmers — they lived in town. They couldn't sell their meat, so if they butchered a calf or hog for their own use, they just gave it around to everybody. There was no such thing as a freezer. Everybody in Dawson grew asparagus. Neighbors might bring a dishpan full of asparagus to us. In Dawson nobody had much money, but they had food. I never went hungry, but we had a right lean year in Commerce the year before we moved to Dawson. We had a cow in the backyard, so we always had milk, but I remember many nights in Commerce my mother would cook just streak-of-lean and cream gravy on toast for supper. I thought it was wonderful. My favorite meal. But it wasn't a well-balanced meal. The Depression was very hard on parents with children. They didn't go to doctors, because they couldn't pay the bills. They didn't get eyeglasses and they didn't go to the dentist unless they had a toothache so bad they couldn't stand it. My mother said we left Commerce owing everybody in town. Honorable people can't stand to live that way. We were happy as a family, but in a way the family was a victim of the Depression.

My next novel is going to start in World War I with Will's marriage to a woman somewhat like my mother. It's not a World War I or Depression book, that's just the setting. It will reveal the strains put on a middle-class family by poverty that there was no way out of.

You have said Will Tweedy was fashioned after your father. Was he run over by a train as Will was in the book?

No. The train scene came from a three-inch newspaper article I saw after I started the novel, about a little ten-year-old girl who saved herself by falling between the tracks. I wouldn't go on a trestle for anything. I couldn't have imagined anybody doing it. But I had the clipping in a box. Writers think in terms of keeping a notebook, but when you get home at night you may not have time to write in a notebook. Anytime I read or hear something that interests me, I write it down and put it in this box. About four hundred pages into the novel, I sat down one day with my box. I'd pick up a piece of paper and think, "How can I use this?" Some of my notes were anecdotes, some just colloquialisms. One might end up as a dependent clause, another might give me an idea for a whole scene. I stuck each note in the manuscript where I thought I might be able to use it, then went back later and wrote it in.

There's a Southern flavor to your book that can be narrowed down to a Georgia flavor that's still seen in small towns.

Yes. You'd expect old people in the South to identify with *Cold Sassy,* but I have letters from upstate New York, from all over the country — some of them are from young people — saying, "This is just like the small town I grew up in." So apparently the atmosphere of today's small town is not that different from 1906. I tried to figure out what it was, why a small town in 1906 would be like a small town now. I decided, and this was something I had not expected, that it was the way people are involved with one another in a small town. They may see their friends every day. In Atlanta, I may see even close friends only three or four times a year. Small-town people do tend to each other's business. They want to know why Mr. So-and-So wouldn't let his wife go on the cruise, or what Mrs. X said when she found out her daughter was expecting and not married. But there's another side of the coin: in a small town people are very aware when somebody is in trouble, or having trouble, and their arms go around that person. One reviewer started off his review with "Cold Sassy is a nasty town, with nasty people harping at each other and tending to each other's business." That's all he said. He didn't sense the love. I don't believe he had ever lived in a small town.

When did you begin taking an interest in writing?

When I was in the ninth grade I had an English teacher who put a long list of words on the blackboard and said pick out several and write similes. I wrote, "A violin sounds like a refined sawmill." She got so excited about that, and the result shows what praise can do. She thought my simile was just wonderful and read it to the class. She called the woman who was the adviser to the school paper and told her to get me to write for the paper. It was the kind of school newspaper that always won awards, so it was a real good beginning. I think my newspaper background has made a big difference in the novel. Newspaper editors stress that you must write clearly enough to communicate, and that anytime a story gets tedious, the reader will quit reading. Editors want you to stay aware of your audience. By contrast, people who write abstract poetry seem unaware of the reader — not even interested in whether the reader understands the meaning. A poem like that might as well be in a foreign language. In fiction, too, some writers get lost in their words. I think many novels are written for the satisfaction of the novelist, and I got that personal satisfaction, but all the time I never lost sight of communicating with the reader. If I read a chapter from my book ten times and it got more and more boring, I knew it wouldn't communicate anything. If I got goose bumps every time, I knew the reader would get goose bumps, too.

But to answer your question, when I was a sophomore at Mercer University I became editor of the school literary magazine. That's when I caught on fire about writing. I even took a typing course that year. When I went to the University of North Carolina and presented myself to the journalism department, the only thing the dean asked was could I type. I said "Yes." He said, "Good, because if somebody comes to me who can't type, I know they're not really interested."

With your writing experience, why did you wait till you were fifty-one to start a novel?

Because I didn't want to write a novel before that.

You just didn't have an interest in it?

Well, I'd always read a lot of fiction, but I was more interested in writing nonfiction. I used to think if I ever wrote a book, it would be nonfiction. It takes a lot of energy to interview, as you know, and I figured if I were going to get sick, as the doctor predicted, I wouldn't feel like interviewing. So fiction just seemed like the thing to do.

One of my favorite passages in Cold Sassy Tree *is on page seventeen: "Jesus said take up your cross and follow Me, but He didn't ast [sic] us to go out and nail ourselves to a board." I almost fell on the floor laughing. That's a great line.*

It is and I wish I could say I made it up. But all I did was use it. On the newspaper I was trained to listen to people, not just to what they said, but to how they said it; the exact words that give flavor, that make one person's speech different from another's. Too often a writer tends to paraphrase everything, and all the quotes end up sounding the way he would say it. That way the facts may be true, but the quotes don't have the person's style and flavor. The reporter may describe a personality at length, whereas if he would use the person's dialogue, personality and character would be revealed. That's also true in fiction, and one thing I really tried for in my book. I like dialogue. It's revealing, it's easy to read and there's more action in speech than in a a long passage narrated by the author. Even if it's merely one character telling another what happened, direct quotes have an aliveness.

Another of my many favorites is on page 137 where Miss Love is being kissed by Clayton McAllister, ". . . he put his arms around her and kissed her. Right on the mouth! Kissed her like he was starved and she was something to eat."

You like that? I like it too. Well, that one I made up.

Being that the narrator, Will Tweedy, is a fourteen-year-old boy, did you have any trouble putting yourself into his mind?

I thought I couldn't do it. I said to my husband, "I don't know how boys think." He said they think just like girls, but they think about different things than girls. I proceeded on that theory, and young men, boys and old men say I've written just like a boy. Later I asked Andy how he knew this. He'd never been a girl. He said he made it up.

One reason I wrote as the boy was because I was tired of books and movies that make exhibitionists out of the characters and Peeping Toms out of us. I decided that anybody can write a page-turner if they put in enough sex. I thought it a challenge to see if I could do it without that. There's just more to life than sex. I have a lot of respect for sex and I feel most books don't. Most writers don't. It's one thing if it has something to do with the story, it's another if it's used to manipulate the reader. I don't want to be a manipulator. After I decided to close the bedroom doors, I thought if this is written by the boy instead of by me, I won't have any temptation to be explicit. There's a great deal of excitement and tension when two people yearn for each other, whether they're in love or not. That can last a whole book. But if they just hop in bed, it's over and done with. There's no more suspense about that part of the relationship.

Are we going to find out what happens to Miss Love and Rucker Blakeslee's baby in the next book?

Yes. I was signing books at Oxford Bookstore when the clerk came back and said, "There's a lady on the phone who wants to know whether it was a boy or a girl." Somebody else got real annoyed with me when I said I don't know yet. She said, "Will Tweedy wrote this book eight years after it happened and he knew what it was by then." I said, "Yeah, but he chose to stop the story before the baby was born." The child will be nine years old at the start of the next book and will be important to the story.

Do you know yet if it's a girl or boy?

I know, but I'm not telling.

I was quite disappointed when Rucker Blakeslee died.

It nearly killed me. I cried, even though I had planned for him to die from the beginning. I had heard about a real funny funeral that would just fit him. Anybody who would marry three weeks after his wife died wasn't going to worry too much about shocking people at his own funeral. When I was writing the burial, it was very upsetting to me—a really terrible scene. However, it added dimension to the kind of person Grandpa was. I remember seeing graffiti in the women's restroom over at North Fulton High School: "Die young and be forever beautiful." Well, his and Miss Love's relationship was perhaps more romantically beautiful when he died at sixty than it might have been by the time she was sixty and him eighty-five.

I heard it's going to be made into a movie?

I don't think about that until somebody mentions it. I know a man whose daughter is a good friend of Faye Dunaway's brother's wife (*laughing*) and the brother and the wife say that anything Faye says she's going to do, she does. I've seen several interviews in which Faye is talking about something else, but she says she's bought a book called *Cold Sassy Tree* by Olive Ann Burns and she's going to make a movie of it in Florida. So, apparently, she means to. But just as I didn't assume the book would be published, I don't assume it'll ever be a movie.

Have you actually sold the movie rights?

Yes, she has bought the rights. Having a novel published is very exciting, especially if it keeps going on and on like this. I was sixty-one when it came out, an age when a lot of people's lives are winding down. It's been like a whole new career. It has put the possibility of everyday surprises into my life. When the phone rings, it may be an invitation to speak in New York or at Queen's College, or it may be my agent saying that a German publisher has bought the novel for a hardback translation, or that he hasn't been able to sell it in England — British publishers think their readers wouldn't understand the Georgia dialect. I said I would be glad to Yankeefy the dialect. Did you find any symbolism in the book?

I have a lot of things underlined and dog-eared, so I probably did. But I can't recall anything offhand.

I ask you that because fiction readers typically see symbolism that wasn't intended by the author. The death of the grandfather and the cutting down of the last huge sassafras tree, at the end, was my only conscious symbolism.

I saw that and also the circular movement of the death of the grandmother back to the death of her husband, Rucker Blakeslee.

That's interesting. Incidentally, *People* magazine said that like many Southern writers, I was obviously obsessed with illness, death, and burials. But if you write a book set in 1906, you have to have deaths. Folks died a lot back then.

There are technical problems to fiction that you don't think about until you start writing. I can read a novel now and see how it's structured in a way I never could before. I used to read for the story — I didn't pay attention to how it was done. I had an author friend who said if she could write a novel I could write one. I said I don't even know what the word *plot* means. She said, "Don't worry about it, a plot is when you get people into trouble, then get them out." I wrote *Cold Sassy Tree* by getting the characters into one trouble after another.

What's the title of the book you're working on?

The title is *Time, Dirt and Money.* Those are the things people worry about the most. At least women do. I don't know about men.

I think we worry about time and money.

It is a sequel to *Cold Sassy Tree.* It starts ten years later, at the start of World War I, and goes until 1934 — unless I change my mind. It's mostly Will Tweedy's life with the girl he marries. But Loma ain't gonna stop making trouble.

Fred Chappell

Fred Chappell was born in 1936 in Canton, North Carolina, and grew up in the mountains of Haywood County.
He received both his undergraduate and graduate degrees
from Duke University, and is now professor of English at
the University of North Carolina at Greensboro. His
writing includes novels, short stories, and poetry: *Moments
of Light, The Inkling, Dagon, The Gaudy Place, I Am One of You
Forever, The World Between the Eyes, River: A Poem, Castle
Tzingal, It Is Time, Lord,* and *Midquest,* which is comprised
of *River, Bloodfire, Wind Mountain,* and *Earthsleep.* This interview took place at his house on November 6, 1987.

Could you discuss your background?

I was born in 1936 in a small mill town in the western part of North
Carolina called Canton, and I grew up on a farm in the mountains. Both my
mother and father were schoolteachers and farmers, because then as now,
you couldn't make a living farming or in teaching school. So they tried both
at the same time. After awhile they got tired of starving and my father opened
a retail furniture business. Later on my mother followed him in that. So I
grew up on a farm and worked in the furniture store in my off-hours. My
family was middle class. I was blessed among the children of the world...
Of course, I thought I was mostly suffering. That's children for you.

Much of your writing, and especially with your most recent novel, I Am One of
You Forever, *has an agrarian texture to it. Is this autobiographical in nature?*

Only in a very distant way with some small autobiographical instances
that triggered the stories in the book. But no, they're not really autobiographical. The first book I published, *It Is Time, Lord,* is autobiographical
probably more than the other books, but still it's not very autobiographical.
If I wanted to write autobiographical material, I would rather write essays.
I have no reason to turn my life into fiction.

*You've written five novels and six books of poetry. Which do you consider yourself,
a poet or a novelist?*

I flatter myself by thinking of myself as a poet. I don't know if that is true or not. I never think of myself as a novelist because it's bad luck. (*Laughing.*) You never know whether or not you're going to get the novel written. I try not to think in those terms. The hardest form I've worked in is the short story. It's something I'd really like to succeed in most, but it is so difficult. Poetry, of course, is the noblest art form, and the one I habitually think in, even when trying other forms.

Are you working on any type of short story collection?

I have kind of a stillborn collection that I keep taking pieces out of and adding to. It'll be a few years yet before it sees the light of day. I'm a novel man right now. The novel you mentioned, *I Am One of You Forever,* is projected as the first of four novels about this family. I'm working on the second novel now called *Brighten the Corner Where You Are.* That's about three-quarters finished.

I first read your work in several anthologies then discovered you had written several novels. I really enjoyed I Am One of You Forever. *The coming of age of the child, the humor, and fantastical things that occur has made it one of my favorite novels.*

That's sweet of you to say. Actually, that book's more about the coming of age of the father, the beginning of age of the father. The second novel is about the father actually "having" to come of age because of various pressures. The child is just there to tell the story. It's not really centered on him, he just observes. The child, Jess, tells the second novel too, except he's not present in any of the events. He's asleep throughout the whole novel. I don't know how he knows to tell it, but he tells the story anyway. (*Laughing.*) I really didn't want to write another story about coming of age in the mountains or anywhere else, I mean, about a child coming of age. I wanted to write about adults coming of age. It's been my experience that most of my friends grow up about age forty. I'm serious. (*Laughing.*) At that time it's too late to do any good.

What signified their growing up?

They began to take on some responsibilities. They quit driving around drunk, hollering at night, carrying on. They always looked after their children and that sort of stuff, but they really didn't have any dignity or seriousness about themselves until they realized they were going to die. (*Laughing.*) That's been my experience, too.

In a large sense, that's what you were saying in your four volume tetralogy, Midquest, *which you began writing at age thirty-five. You said to yourself I am growing up, I am contemplating what it means to be thirty-five.*

I was trying very hard to grow up. I had hoped to be grown up by the time I finish this poem, by the time I tell the story. That book is semiautobiographical, too. And by the time I did finish it I was grown up. I started it at age thirty-five and I finished it at age forty-five. You should probably grow up by the time you're fifty.

One of the things I enjoyed about I Am One of You Forever *are the shenanigans, just the absolutely hilarious things the father does. Like switching the gum with a laxative gum to keep Johnson from marrying the girl.*

That's an experience that's not autobiographical, that is a folktale, the old switch of the chewing gum. It's a folktale that is collected by Vance Randolph in one of his books. I'd heard it in other forms. A lot of folktales are cruel in nature. I said there's a problem of giving a cruel folktale some humanity, but if I could give a cruel folktale humanity, at some point, then it could work. I thought it would be challenging to see if I could give dumb practical jokes some meaning, context. I discovered in writing that practical jokes, when they take place inside a family, are actually a pretty good thing because they imply a great deal of trust. If the family didn't trust the father, he wouldn't be able to get away with anything at all. If they didn't trust him he wouldn't have been able to play any practical jokes. But it's because they trust him to do silly, but harmless things, he is able to do them. It's interesting, but I hadn't realized how jokes work until I had to write them.

The folklore tales occur again in the Halloween scene with Jess and the veterinarian where the practical joke comes back on the boy, Jess.

Yes, as a matter of fact, I like to do that, to turn the joke around because you have to have some surprises in a book. But also, until the joke is turned around on the practical joker he learns nothing about himself.

In fact, Jess learns quite a bit, because, like the things children believe about adults are not always true. Jess knows or believes deep down that the doctor, whom he views as wicked, killed his dog. Kids are like that. They'll think an old woman must be a witch or wicked just because she's old. When the joke was turned against him he learned the truth about the doctor.

That's right. A few blocks away from here there's a house the children for years have called the witch house simply because it was a big house and the lady who lived in it was old and reclusive. Even after she died and someone else moved in, the new generation of kids still called it the witch house.

Between writing novels and poetry, which do you feel most comfortable with?

I enjoy writing poetry more. I don't feel comfortable writing anything, but I enjoy writing poetry more because it is such a concentrated form. A good day of writing poetry is to scratch out the two lines you wrote the day before. But you enjoy the intensity of it. Fiction is fine and I enjoy it, but the thing I hate about fiction is all the housecleaning. You're all the time putting clothes on characters, taking their clothes off, emptying ashtrays, opening doors, getting people in and out of rooms, thinking about what houses they live in, when they pay taxes, a lot of just dirty work, which is boring. But it's absolutely necessary. Which tells you I'm not a real novelist like Dreiser. That's the first thing he thinks of. He thinks of these first before he thinks of anything else. I think of the character first, then try to fill in the details. I do it kind of backwards. Which do you like to read best?

It depends on the writer, but generally, I read more poetry than anything else. I like a poet's poetry more than their novels, most of the time, and the same goes for the novelist. I liked David Bottoms' novel, Any Cold Jordan. *The last twenty-five pages in the woods with the ambush had me on edge.*

That was the only part of the book I didn't like. I liked it all but the last twenty-five pages. (*Laughing.*) I wrote David a long letter telling him I didn't think the last twenty-five pages were quite convincing somehow. I finally didn't believe the protagonist, Billy Parker, had got himself into this fix. He didn't seem dumb enough to finally let it go this far. So, I knew something awful was going to happen to him and I felt he knew, too. But I really love that book—the music. I loved the talk about music. I like David; he's a very interesting person, a very straight person, straightforward. He's also a good ol' boy. That helps. (*Laughing.*)

Well, how would you describe your poetic style?

Kind of a main strength—and awkwardness—is about the best I can do. I don't think I really have a fixed poetic style. If you picked up a poem by Wallace Stevens you'd recognize it immediately by Stevens. If you pick up a poem by Albert Goldbarth you'd probably think it's a poem by Albert Goldbarth, but if you picked up one of my poems you might think well, this could be Frost or Dave Smith or David Bottoms, Jim Applewhite or any number of people, because I'm not interested in creating a fixed poetic style for myself, but matching each separate poem to the subject matter. I deliberately try to be as fluid as possible. I've noticed that each of my books seems to have a style the book settles into, and if one knew the poems better, he could then identify a particular poem with the book. Again, that is because very early on I begin to think of the poems as a book instead of separate poems. When I have six or seven poems that don't seem to be going anywhere I'll look to see what's happening and if they suggest themes, then I'll try to build a book around them.

Midquest, particularly, I wanted to draw the interior of the world and the exterior of the world—to balance them almost equally. That was deliberate. With the other books, I didn't know what the hell I was doing. (*Laughing.*)

One of your poems that I've enjoyed the most, not only as a poem, but, because it has a never-ending story quality that just takes you away is "My Father's Hurricane" from Wind Mountain. *The central focus for all your poetry is extremely imaginative in that they can go anywhere, and in fact, that poem does.*

Poems like that, and some other works, are practical jokes on the readers. First you convince the reader that these people exist and live in this place, and you go on. Pretty soon you've got them strung way out. (*Laughing.*) Then you saw the limb off once they're out there. That's part of the fun. And if you do it so that they don't object to it, then it's okay.

That poem in particular had me going and going, then it drops just like you said. So, I guess I fell for it.

When I used to read "My Father's Hurricane" at readings people would say, "You know the end of that poem just really makes me mad."

You may have guessed how the novel *I Am One of You Forever* came about. It's from material left over from the books of poems. It's the same family. I had some material I wanted to put into the poems and this material didn't fit the poems, so I thought, why not ditch them and write fiction? That's how that novel started. I had planned to write a novel once I finished the poems. I wanted to write a historical novel, eighteenth century, about colonial America, specifically about Benjamin Franklin. But I couldn't get back into it. I had to deal with this first so I started writing prose. I started in on this material and it just kept on, and now I'm really tired of this material, but I'm stuck with it for awhile.

You're working on the second book and have two more to go. Will you have a break in between writing them?

The first one is about the loss the family sustains. The second one is simply about the father who has had to take up teaching school while the mother, who was injured, recovers. It's about one day of the father teaching school which he doesn't like to do. It's a rather long, complicated day. It's a short novel, but a long, complicated day. The third novel will take place in the intertwined minds, the stream of consciousness of the mother and the grandmother. The fourth novel — I haven't quite decided on the design yet, but it will have something to do with the Vietnam War, but it's hard to see that far ahead.

Do you see yourself taking a break between, say, the second and third novel to do something else?

Yes, I certainly do. As a matter of fact the next book I have coming out is a book of poems called *First and Last Words* which will be out in the fall of 1988 . . .

Earlier you mentioned that you got a hold of Lee Smith on a Friday night. Well, good for you. She's a busy girl. She's the most charming person in the world. I ought to tell you about the first time I met Lee. I think she was a sophomore or junior at Hollins College and I was there for a reading and a party afterwards. I think I was thirty. Anyway I kept staring at this girl, which turned out to be Lee Smith, because she was so pretty. I kept thinking — what a pretty girl, but I didn't say anything, didn't make any terrible moves on her or anything. I just kept staring at her. In a few minutes she came walking over and said, "Hello, Mr. Chappell," and she punched me just as hard as she could right in the stomach! I tried to be macho, you know and showed that I didn't feel a thing. We had never met. I didn't know who she was. I think my face turned bright red and steam came out of my ears. I said, "Hi, how are you doing?" For twenty years I thought she was teaching me a lesson not to stare at people. It's bad manners. The year before last I asked her about it. Turned out George Garrett and Richard Dillard had put her up to it as a practical joke. (*Laughing.*) For twenty years I thought she was just a good ol' girl who wasn't going to take a lot of nonsense.

Your poetry utilizes many different conventions and forms. "My Grandfather's Church Goes Up" rolls with alliteration, and your other poems are concerned with rhyme scheme and meter and so on.

I enjoy using all kinds of different forms. They're not just a lot of fancy things people made up in order to make poetry hard. They're there for very good reasons. Almost all of them developed from dance. Almost all the old poetry forms are dance forms except for the narrative forms. Almost all of them are dance forms that are directly connected with the functions of the body. They're very physical, and that's why I use them. They're challenging and expressive. I write as much free verse as I do formal verse. I admire the forms more than free verse. Free verse is a very different discipline; it takes a very musical ear, and either you have it or you don't. Sometimes you think you have it and you don't have it. Some days you're on, some days you're off. That's true with formal poetry, too, but when you're off with formal poetry you know it immediately. You know it's horrible. With free verse, you begin to say, I don't know what it is. There seems be a lot more interest in formal verse than there was five or six years ago. Whether that means anything, I don't know.

Could you discuss the idea behind Midquest *and using the four elements of the earth?*

I had in mind a vague analogue to Dante's *Divine Comedy* that would take place on someone's thirty-fifth birthday. He would look over his life, his autobiography, and he would discover that at the same point of time at the end of his life it was no different than when he started out, and it would have many different stories about different people, different characters and their interests. It would have different formal schemes, poetic schemes just for the fun of it. And then I thought how am I going to organize it? It seemed to me that some of the poems I wrote without knowing what I was quite doing. They seemed to center about the imagery of water. So I thought I'd use the four elements, it doesn't mean much, but it's a way to organize four volumes to come out even, and give it some kind of a point. And also it adds themes and motifs to the poems so they can fit together. I thought perhaps when it was all finished I'd have a little Pythagorean universe made up of the four elements comprised by one person. All that sounds very highfalutin, but what that means is that when you're writing you hope you get the commas in the right places and if you've got this line down another one will occur to you at some future date. But first you start out with a grandiose scheme.

Each volume has eleven poems dealing with specific characters. It's all very symmetrical. In the old Pythagorean mysticism, numbers stood for things, and number four stood for world, number three was man. I've forgotten them now, but there are lots of books on the subject. I find out that when

I'm working on a book and need to know things, I know them, but as soon as I finish the book I forget them. I used those numbers to some extent. If it wasn't constant with what was interesting and the poetry itself, I just threw it out and wrote the poem. Because that has to come first. Where I could use the numbers and get away with it, I did. Partly, because Dante did with the triad, number thirty-three. But also, because the more challenges you can give yourself the more games you can play. The more you can sustain your interests with the work at hand, the more you're able to put into it.

Was it difficult to sustain your interests?

I began to get a little weary toward the end of the third volume, and after the third was finished I thought this might be the last volume. I didn't know if I would finish this or not. But I knew I had to do it. I had to finish it. It would be horrible not to finish. So to make myself complete the fourth volume I left the last line in the third volume unfinished and the first line in the fourth volume picks it up and finishes off the sentence. Otherwise I'm not sure I would have finished. I did get tired of it, because I got weary of the material. There's something a little circumscribed about going over the same Appalachian material so many times, and I think people who read all four volumes straight through might get a little tired of the same old stuff.

Midquest has a central theme of earth's four elements: water, earth, wind, and fire, and your other volumes also stay within the guidelines of a specific subject matter, they have a central theme.

Yes, except the first book which is kind of pre–*Midquest* narrative poems that were attempts at writing *Midquest* when I didn't know what I was doing. They didn't turn out; they fell apart. I suppose there isn't a theme to the first book, but the others do have a theme: *Source, Castle Tzingal, Bloodfire, Wind Mountain, Earthsleep* and *River*. So they all have central themes except that first dreadful book of poems. (*Laughing.*) I hate that book. The worst part of it is that I thought I liked it.

How old were you when The World Between the Eyes *came out?*

Hell, I was old enough to know better. It came out in 1971. I was thirty-five.

By that time you had already published several books.

I had published three novels.

What didn't you like about The World Between the Eyes?

The lousy poems.

The central image, the reoccurring theme you use, is it something that has resulted from the form you work in or do you sit down and say I am going to write about wind or fire?

In the case of *Midquest*, which you're referring to, I had the material. It was simply the material of the characters. It was their autobiography.

You call each book a poem. It's not a book of poems, it is a poem. With that single theme, do you abandon a poem regardless of its merit if the poem does not fit the theme?

You may have written a very good poem, but because the poem doesn't fit the theme of the book that poem is excluded?

That's correct. I did a lot of that with *Midquest*. If a poem doesn't fit, you shouldn't put it in no matter how good it is. The poet can't really just sit there and say, "Hey! This is a damn good poem. I'm going to put it in." He's got no reason to say it's a damn good poem in the first place. There are certain things that don't fit. Baudelaire said if you have twenty-four poems, the order of the poems makes up the twenty-fifth poem; that is, the design of the whole book is a poem itself. I agree with that. It seems to me that a book should be a poem. Books of poems are so small anyway that they should be well designed.

So then, you must have a number of poems you've written that are as good or better than the other poems but do not fit into a central theme?

I've got a whole pot of poems I've never put into books. I don't know if they're any good or not. It seems to me some of them are as good as the poems in the books.

Do you see putting them together?

Maybe sometime in the future. I have enough projects on hand now to last me for awhile.

Castle Tzingal *is a very imaginative fairy tale.*

Weird, you mean. (*Laughing.*)

Could you talk about the history behind it and how it came about?

That's one of those books that you don't have a whole lot of control over. The first poem came to me almost just as it is. It's a long poem, almost a hundred lines. I woke up at three o'clock in the morning and there it was — the whole thing. I got up and wrote it down. I didn't know what it was about or what it meant, who these people were, or anything, but I knew it meant something. So I waited. I didn't look at it for six months, then went back to read it, made a few minor changes and had the whole story. The second poem came to mind (all the characters), then after that all I had to do was write the poems. That took a long time to do. It took three years of off-and-on labor, very intensive labor in the last six months. I wanted to make the story more complicated and I probably should have done so, but I was afraid of getting lost in the material, it was so exotic. So by the time I was three-quarters of the way through I realized I should have invented more characters for this. But then I would have had to go back and rework the whole story. I had too much invested and I didn't know how to do it.

I went back and read an interview you did with John Carr in 1969. Since then, what has been the most significant change in your writing?

What'd I tell John? (*Laughing.*) I don't remember what I said. The largest thing that has happened is that my son Heath has grown up and is now a young man living in Chicago. He's married now. That's the major thing that has happened. I still have the same wife I started with. I haven't changed much. I quit smoking. That was hard. I travel around a fair amount. There was a turning point for me when I finished the novel *Dagon,* which was a very hard, horrible novel and not a lot of fun to read or write. I got rid of some things that were troubling me. That's one of those books you have to write whether you want to or not. I didn't want to, but having got past that novel my writing lightened up a lot. I changed my ideas. I had taken the downer about as far as I could have taken it.

What was it that forced you to write this out?

Probably some personal compulsion. At the time I thought it was a tragic vision, but I don't think so now. I think it's just some sort of weird personal compulsion I didn't understand. I'm not interested in finding out. I'm not interested in understanding to tell the truth. I thought by faithfully pursuing the tragic vision you could peel back the layers of hypocrisy and sham that clutter our lives. Now I see that that's not really true and it's the comic vision that tells more about us than anything else. The wonderful thing about tragedy is that it winds up in a neat little bundle. People die — that's the end. Fortunately, most of us don't die when horrible things happen to us. We have to go on living. The fact that we do have horrible things happen to us and still survive means it is a comic mode.

When you look at comedy in it's purest form it's actually tragedy inverted at the end.

It's extremely sad when you think that the subjects of comedy, which are the follies, the stupidities of mankind, have not changed since the first man wrote the first comic work. That's sad. And we're still doing the same things. (*Laughing.*) We haven't learned a damn thing.

Could you discuss what it means to be a Southern writer today?

It means that on the one hand you get some respect because our twentieth century tradition is so rich in fine writers. But on the other hand, you're expected to write about a certain kind of subject matter only. That's vexing.

Do you see the South disintegrating as a culture?

The south hasn't been a separate *culture* since the Reconstruction. As a regional facet of the larger American culture, it changes continually. It is not disintegrating, except in the way that the whole world is. Everything gets trashier in a trashy era.

What about as a specific region for writers to draw from?

It's as interesting now as it ever was. The processes of change leave writers with plenty of subject matter.

What are you working on now?

The novel I mentioned, *Brighten the Corner Where You Are.* A three-act play, a comedy, currently called *MOONJOX.* Many poems and essays. Some stories. And I'm taking notes for the third novel in the series.

You used to write science fiction, and had published under a pseudonym. Could you discuss this area of your writing and what name did you write under?

I no longer write what is recognized as science fiction, though I think that some of the stories still are. "Moments of Light," for example. I wouldn't mind writing more science fiction, but there's no time. I published a small amount of science fiction in the pulps in the fifties under a pen name, actually a house name. It is lost in the miasmas of pulp time.

Where do you see your work heading in the next ten years?

Over the next five or six years my poetry will probably change a great deal. Probably no one will notice. I simply want to keep on writing. There's a way in which every piece of writing is an experiment for me, since I really don't know what I'm doing.

Pat Conroy

Pat Conroy was born in South Carolina, grew up throughout the South, and is a 1967 graduate of The Citadel, the basis of his novel *The Lords of Discipline*. His other books include *The Great Santini, The Water Is Wide, The Boo,* and *The Prince of Tides.* He lives in Atlanta with his wife and children. This interview was conducted at his home on May 2, 1988.

I like to begin an interview with the writer's background, but I found that a difficult place to start with you because a large amount of your fiction is based on your childhood. I almost feel as though I know you from your work. Does that happen a lot with people you meet?

It does, and it's my fault. When you first start writing you have a decision to make — whether or not you're going to write autobiographically. When I began to write I decided to disguise everything. If I made my father an Air Force officer it's a very different than a Marine Corps officer. I knew a great deal more about Marine Corps officers. Also, if I made him a ground officer that's very different than a pilot. But, I kept coming back to why don't I just write about a Marine Corps fighter pilot from Chicago who married a woman like my mother? Writing fiction is difficult enough without putting additional problems in your way. So when I wrote *The Great Santini* I was writing out of real autobiographical territory. People do feel they know me, and it's a natural product of that first decision I made when I started writing fiction.

How much of your fiction is based on your life and your family?

Certainly the sensibility of the narrator is always mine, so far. Even when characters do things that I or my family have never done, I am operating as though someone like me is telling the story. You start making myths within that. There are times when I invent a new sensibility for myself, or as my sister says, "What kind of wonderful guy are you going to be in this novel, Pat? What kind of fabulous sensitive human being are you going to make yourself when you dump on the rest of the family?"

When I began writing I was trying to explain the world to myself, and explain the kind of person I was to myself, the kind of life I had led. It was natural. I came out of a background so nonliterary that I can't even invent this as I go along. Please explain to me how I ended up at The Citadel. In my wildest dream I can not reinvent why I chose that school. So many things happened by accident.

Do you find that when you meet your readers they almost feel they know you?

I have had so many surprises when people read a book and take it literally. They say things like, "It was awful what happened to your brother Luke." I'll say, "I don't have a brother Luke." They argue with me about this brother Luke. I've had people meet my father and gasp. They'll say, "But you're dead. I read it in *The Great Santini.* I saw the movie. I saw the burial." They identify so strongly that the aspects of fictionalizing get lost in the confusion when I said I write autobiographically.

Can you as a writer draw on the autobiographical too much?

I guess. Other writers get extremely angry at me. They don't like autobiographical writing. Some other writers, too, don't like Southern writing. I would like to write differently, but I have discovered to my astonishment and sometimes dismay, that I write the only way I can. I would choose to be Norman Mailer, if I could. I'd choose to be John Updike, Anne Tyler, or Joyce Carol Oates, but I can't. I find myself imprisoned in the sensibilities I was given. I don't know about trapping myself with the autobiographical material, because there are many things I have invented. I've stolen the lives of other people. One thing I do when people tell me wonderful stories about their life is incorporate them into the life of a character. You told me about you and your wife eloping to Ringgold, Georgia. Ten years from now I could use something like that because it is a beautiful story. It's stuff like that that will always come back to me when I am writing. So if my autobiography were to disappear tomorrow, there are still enough stories in the world that I would be able to write.

I know with what I am working on now that a tiny fragment from your childhood can become something much larger than what it actually was; it can become an entire fictitious scene based on a microscopic fact.

That's right. Something happened to me in Atlanta ten years ago — my grandmother wanted me to help her buy a coffin. I said, "Jesus Christ. I'd rather die than go out and buy a coffin." She said I had to help her because she didn't want to buy one too expensive. Here's this whole scene of going down to the funeral home on Spring Street with my grandmother shopping for her casket, actually trying it out. I helped her into it. This tickled me so much that later with *The Prince of Tides* I wrote this scene into Tom Wingo's childhood. But that could have happened to someone else. A neighbor could have told me that story. It does not have to be part of my life for me to use it.

That was a hilarious situation.

I thought it was ridiculous. Here I am, I'm not a kid, I'm thirty-six, telling her to get out of the goddamn casket. She was trying it out like it was a mattress. Then someone walked into the place and I almost died. My grandmother loved it because I was embarrassed. I always look for those stories or the turn of a phrase, or the revealing aspect of a personality.

When did you start writing?

My mother wanted me to be a writer. I remember starting at what seemed to be fairly early. In our family being a writer was as rare as being a pearl diver. It simply did not exist. My mother was a great reader—loved *Gone With the Wind.* She seriously identified with Scarlett O'Hara as someone she was like. We were raised by this woman who wanted one of us to be a Southern writer. My mother encouraged me to write my first poem and stories. Dad could not have cared less. He thought it was a questionable and defeatist activity at best. But mom wanted it and encouraged it. I started writing poetry when I was in high school and short stories in college. I looked great being a writer at The Citadel. The field was almost mine alone.

Did you try to publish those short stories?

No. That's another thing—I didn't know any writers. There was a woman who taught me creative writing in high school who had published novels and lived in Beaufort, South Carolina. She wrote me all through college, but she died the year I got out of college. My one connection with publishing was gone. So I simply wrote in a vacuum while I was teaching. It was all terrible stuff, but at least it was a beginning—trying to shape a style, which is all part of the process.

I read where you can go months without writing a word, then lock yourself in a room to write nonstop.

I write in great spurts. I may not write anything for years, but I'll spend that time taking notes and figuring out where a novel is going. Then somehow it will catch fire, and I'll go to the beach or a cabin in the mountains to get away from the telephone and simply write and read. That's basically all I do during those months. Then I'll come back to civilization and family until something strikes me again. I try to write everyday, but sometimes I feel the need to get away from it weeks at a time to empty myself out.

What do you do when you're not writing?

I read. And usually I take notes. I try to keep a journal. Journals have helped me a great deal because I write details—things in my life that I would normally forget.

You mentioned getting away to the mountains to write. What conditions are best for you?

I write best in absolute silence, but this makes it hard when you have a family. It's always a great difficulty to balance the two. I've generally done this when I've run out of money and there is a desperation. My wife gets as desperate as I do, then she's grateful that I go away, because she knows I'll come back having produced something. I've always written, then run out of money!

When I am writing I try to keep it like a workday. I get up, read the paper, work from nine to twelve, break for lunch. After lunch I read or take a nap, then from two to five I work some more. I try to keep a schedule like a normal human being. Sometimes it works wonderfully well, sometimes it doesn't. There are writers who can write four pages a day—I've never been able to do that.

Do you labor over each page, or do you throw everything down on the page then edit to what you want?

Generally, especially when I'm in the middle of the book, I try to write well the first time, then I'll rewrite that better, then I'll rewrite that even better. Rewriting becomes a large part of the process. I overwrite by nature, then there is the gradual moving toward something tighter and tighter.

You've been back in Atlanta now for awhile after having been in Rome for some time.

We were back and forth between Atlanta and Rome for three of the last five years. I liked Rome very much. I have always wanted to live in a foreign country. I wanted my children to have that experience of seeing different countries, hearing different languages, and knowing there were different kinds of people. Living in the South it is easy to think that everybody is exactly the same. But, that's how you become provincial. I worry about becoming provincial—the Southern point of view that overwhelms all other points of view where you don't know about different parts of the world. Also, I like expanding the things I can write about—learning about Italian, French, and European writers. It seems naturally a good part of that education. I always worry about stagnation. I like to think of things in a new way—think of the world in a new way.

Will Rome be incorporated into your next book?

I think so. I love Italy. There were wonderful things about Italy. I could walk into a church and see a priest walk to the back where something was going on. I'd walk back there and there was a whole convent hidden behind the church—nuns that never appear in the light of day. There are all these secret cities within the city. I found out a lot of things I would not have known had I stayed in Atlanta. Every four or five years I hope I can go to another country.

Did you do any work while over there?

Yes, I did. And it's fun writing about the South from that vantage point. I think about the South as being old, but in Italy they think of it as the newest place in the world. There was a landlord from Yugoslavia who I asked if the house we were renting was old? He said, "Ah, you Americans love the old. The Americans have a soft spot for the old. In Italy this house is not old, it's not even five hundred years old." I told him it's older than my country. He replied, "You must understand. In Rome, she's a baby." This is the sort of thing I would never have learned had I not lived there. I stayed in the country long enough to learn little secrets — things that they know in their blood, but don't think to tell you. They completely take the age of their country for granted. You almost end up taking it for granted yourself. At the second place we lived we could look out from our window and see a building Michelangelo designed, but, because I saw it every day I would forget about it. It was simply thrilling to me. We walked down streets where saints were killed and people were burned to death. In Rome we walked over cities, down streets with cities underneath, ruins.

In the preface of The Boo *you quote the Boo, "It has to be a fun book, Bubba, and it can't hurt The Citadel in any way." In fact, you didn't hurt The Citadel in* The Boo, *you waited until the* The Lords of Discipline. *Had you always had it in mind to write* The Lords of Discipline *even while writing* The Boo?

I always thought The Citadel provided marvelous material the way I felt my father provided marvelous material. When I wrote *The Boo* I was still at that stage, that trivial, vulnerable state when you are first trying to be a writer. It took me years to get up enough courage to call myself a writer. I published three books before I felt comfortable saying I'm a writer. I felt pretentious. I had not paid my dues to call myself a writer. So at the time of *The Boo* I thought, sure, someday I would like to write about The Citadel, but that was like saying I would like to go on a photographic expedition of Kenya. It was a dream I had, but I did not have the confidence to pull it off. I didn't think I could write *The Boo*. I'm real glad I did, because I learned if I kept at it, eventually, a book would come. It also taught me a great lesson about craft, and if I did not want to be humiliated when a book came out I had to work a lot harder then I did with *The Boo*. I had to rewrite. I once wrote fifty pages in one night. It was just ridiculous. Now this mortifies me. Originally, I used people's real names, but the lawyer said to change all the real names. One night I stayed up making up names — the stupidest names I've ever read are in that book. I can just blush with embarrassment with how silly the names are. *The Boo* taught me that I had to work a lot harder if I was going to take myself seriously as writer, or for anyone else to take me seriously.

So even while you were writing The Boo *you had the implication in the back of your mind to write* The Lords of Discipline?

I was ready to write *The Lords of Discipline*.

Without any reservations?

Yes, none whatsoever. Also, The Citadel was obnoxious and repulsive about the publication of *The Boo*. They thought it was a document of great savagery against the school. They banned *The Boo*. I thought, "Hey boys, just wait." There was not one single thing I thought would hurt The Citadel in

The Boo. But they were so paranoid, so stupid to think *The Boo* a dangerous document, something that could harm the school grievously. When I sat down two books later to write *The Lords of Discipline* I was ready to tell The Citadel story I knew that if they thought *The Boo* was bad, they would think *The Lords of Discipline* was out of this world.

No doubt The Lords of Discipline *was banned.*

It didn't have a chance.

Also, they didn't allow the movie to be filmed there.

Yeah. It's amazing we win any wars. The lucky thing about the military mind is that it is the same all over the world. The Russians must have stupid soldiers just as Americans do. They must just bumble at each other. One military mind gets together with another military mind until one bumbles in a greater way and loses the war. I have not been impressed with the military in the way I have seen it.

I was in Charleston for a book signing and they wouldn't let me on The Citadel campus to sign books. They let me use the alumni house which is off campus because some cadets wanted me to sign books. It was so ridiculous. There are not a lot of us from The Citadel writing books. The Citadel has a very schizophrenic relationship with me — we don't get along. It's impossible for me to feel that The Citadel graduate must always be dealing with the Vatican. It's too difficult for me, because it's too mean-spirited a place. I always run my mouth and piss them off.

Were you ever threatened?

I got some telegrams and letters from ex-cadets. But most cadets loved the book. The alumni loved the book. The book sold forty thousand copies, and I'll bet ten thousand went to people at The Citadel. When I went for an autographing, there were Citadel people just lined up. I wrote about the plebe system the way it seemed to be to me. What The Citadel doesn't understand is that people love cruelty. When my dad was upset over *The Great Santini* and how he knocked around his family, I said, "Dad, they love a Nazi in America. You'll never have to worry about it, because you beat your wife and kids. In America, you're a hero. Everyone will think, there goes the old type of America when America was great and we had men like this — men of iron." I told The Citadel the same thing — people are going to love this school. The applications to the school went up like 150 percent after *The Lords of Discipline* came out. If I hurt the school so badly what do they attribute the increase in applications to — the improvement to the athletic facility? Kids love this like they are attracted to the Marine Corps. America has always doubted its manhood and it has always looked for ways to prove it. The kids were attracted to the incredible brutality of the plebe system as if they'll try to prove their manhood.

Could you give an example of how you take autobiographical material and create the story, such as with the rape scene in The Prince of Tides?

The rape did not actually happen. At one time my grandmother lived behind Callonwolde in Atlanta where Rosedale Road runs behind Callonwolde — there were these incredible woods, which are no longer there. Like I wrote in the book, we used to sneak over to Callonwolde to see the people who invented Coca-Cola. Whenever they were not at home the staff would let us ride the horses and swim. They even had a zoo back there. My dad went overseas during the war and told me I was the man of the house. So there I was five years old when this huge giant came after my mother. The cops couldn't believe his size, almost seven feet tall and he had a beard. My mother was very pretty and this guy kept coming out of the woods. The cops couldn't surround the whole woods, and he'd come out in different spots. He became a great symbol for the defenselessness of my childhood.

Somebody in my neighborhood raised black widow spiders and I remember my mother taking me to see these spiders. So these instances converge with another story of a relative who was raped. It was the brutality of these situations that intermit one way or another. I had also heard about some kid in prison who had been raped. Also, I was in Atlanta when the Alday family murders occurred (the defenselessness of a family in modern life when intruders come though your door and break into your house). What do you do? When I'm writing everything converges and things from my past, present, all culminated into the rape of that family. And as a child there are stories I fell in love with — like the moving of Ellington, South Carolina. My mother said you shouldn't be allowed to move a town, the town is a place with a reason. We saw a house going down the road on a trailer. It was just the idea of a town being moved for a nuclear power plant.

None of this story would have come about had it not been for the tiger. There was a tiger named Happy the Tiger that lived in an Esso gas station/car wash in Columbia, South Carolina. This was the only station in the country who had a tiger. You know, "Put a tiger in your tank." I saw this tiger in high school or college. When you got your car filled up with gas the kids got to go over and watch Happy the Tiger. Getting your car filled up is pretty boring unless there's a tiger. So I followed the tiger's history, because eventually the society for the prevention of cruelty to animals went ape shit when they discovered this tiger lived in a cage in one hundred degree heat by a car wash. They built the Columbia Zoo to give Happy a home. The Columbia Zoo is one of the nicest zoos in the country, state of the art, all because of Happy the Tiger. When they put Happy in with the other tigers, they beat Happy up. They mauled Happy. Happy was a car wash tiger and the other tigers knew it. So they had to separate him, and he was miserable. Not knowing what to do, they finally put Happy in a cage the size of the one at the car wash. It still didn't work — he was still miserable. Finally they figured it out. They recorded the sound of a car wash that played twenty-four hours a day. Happy the Tiger was finally able to stay at the zoo fairly comfortably. I always loved that story. I could not help it. So in *Tides* I figured I'd have the father buy this tiger. It took me years to figure out how to throw the story of that tiger in.

Now the story of the tiger has absolutely nothing to do with the book. My agent said, "What the hell is this tiger doing in this book? You got a god-damn tiger and a porpoise. What is this a zoo book?" (*Laughing.*) He's pissed off at me because I'm really stretching the limits of credibility. I was living in Italy I when wrote the rape scene, and I had all the components with the nightmarish Callonwolde figure. He knew where the mother was and he waited to come back. So now I was in Italy and I was stuck. How the fuck do I get the Wingo family out of the scene. What would happen to them is what happened to the Alday family. They would all be killed. First I had to get Luke out of the house, because originally he was inside. I couldn't have him hunting because it wasn't the season. Luke may have been strong, but he was still a boy and couldn't take on these armed men. I just didn't know how to do it.

Well, we were eating in a piazza in Italy and the woman I was sitting next to was missing an arm. She was beautifully dressed, but she did not have an arm. While we were eating she asked me, "You are probably wondering about my arm?" I said, "Yes, yes indeed." She said, "I'm a naturalist and I work with animals, big cats, in Africa and Asia. At one point I saw a tiger being abused at the zoo, so I went over to the man who was abusing the tiger to say something to him. I was not watching the tiger and he reached out and tore my arm off with his paw."

I didn't think a tiger was that strong. Then it hit me. I had a tiger in the backyard. I had written that scene years before and had sort of left the tiger in the cage. It wasn't until I had talked with this woman that it hit me. It's moments like that that I always trust when I'm writing a book. Why else would God have you meet a woman who had lost her arm to a tiger if she wasn't to remind you of something? That's how all of that material came together. I instantly knew what could happen. I had it. All I had to do was make it plausible.

I have discovered in modern fiction that there is a certain kind of fiction where nothing happens, where people are embarrassed if there is any action at all. It also seems that the novelist has given up a great deal to the nonfiction writer. Have you noticed that nonfiction is so interesting? Nonfiction produces Charles Manson. But if you wrote about that it would embarrass the novelist to come up with a figure that interesting. But I don't like to give anything away to nonfiction. I won't let them have the most fascinating characters, or will I let the most extraordinary human behavior take place in nonfiction. I like to have some of that, too.

Was your childhood as terrible as you have written?

I think so. Dad was here at the house this morning being interviewed by a guy from North Carolina, and when he talks about my childhood he presents himself as a Bambi-like figure. It's possible he has repressed this and just doesn't remember, but he was a tough father. He knocked us around. Unfortunately for him he was knocking around a kid who would grow up to have a terrific memory. I remember each incident; he remembers none. He says it didn't happen; I say it did. We have a problem with witnessing. Unfortunately for him my six brothers and sisters back me up.

That leads to a question I wanted to ask. In The Prince of Tides *Tom Wingo remembers these instances, but his sister, Savannah, either does not remember them or remembers them in her own way. Out of your memories, do your brothers and sisters remember them the same way you do?*

They don't remember them the same way I do, and certainly time has softened them. They're much more forgiving than I am. Carol, who is the basis for Savannah, did not remember anything for years, and she was in therapy and mental hospitals for years. It took her a long time to fight her way back to these memories, but generally, her memory of our childhood and mine are very similar. The other kids — the loyalty factor always came in. Family loyalty was the most important thing — exactly like the Wingo family. When *The Great Santini* came out, Dad wrote, "Don't talk to reporters. This is distorted. We must concentrate on the happy memories." I think my family is typical of most families.

Since The Prince of Tides *was published your sister has not talked to you.*

Not a word. She has not only not talked to me, she has ruled out people close to me. She is not talking to my first or second wives or my children.

Does it bother you?

Yeah, it bothers me. You pay a price for writing, and this is the price I paid for *Tides.* I certainly paid the price with Mom and Dad when *Santini* came out. As a writer you have to be prepared. You cannot be completely loved for the things you say about the world. You must be prepared for all consequences. The loss of my sister is what I paid for *Tides,* and it is a heavy price.

On page 160 of The Prince of Tides *Tom Wingo says to Susan Lowenstein, "There's only one crime a woman cannot be forgiven for. No husband will ever forgive her for marrying him. The American male is a quivering mass of insecurities. If a woman makes the mistake of loving him, he will make her suffer terribly for her utter lack of taste. I don't think men can ever forgive women for loving them to the exclusion of all others." How true is that?*

I was speaking for myself. An amazing number of women write to me about stuff like that in the book. My surprise in writing is that I think I'm writing about myself as "The Lone Ranger" and not about every man. The men in my family can barely stand human touch. We actually recoil from it. When I see my brother I hug him like I'm a boa constrictor, and he reels back in horror. The wives touch us and we just curl away. I don't know if it's because

Dad hit us, if touch was pain, but there is something so damaged about maleness in our family, our inability to love, to say we feel something. There's something so emotionally tainted with all of us that there is nothing we can do with this generation. It's simply gone. It must be that way with other families — the boys — touching is like putting a cattle prod to them. But what is amazing is that I get letters saying, "Jesus Christ, my husband is just like that." "My boyfriend or father is just like that."

I don't know where it comes from, but it has to come from women, too. I mean, what they do to us! It has to come from our mothers, because Dad was never around. He certainly never hugged or kissed us or whatever you do to make a little boy comfortable with this. Something about touch is poisonous to males and it's infectious.

Out of your childhood do you have a favorite memory?

I loved Christmas. Christmas was Dad's best time of the year. I loved my Aunt Helen and Uncle Russ — two relatives who seemed like a portrait of normality to me. They were like mothers and fathers on television, and they lived in one house their whole life. I can go back to their house in Orlando, Florida, but because we lived in fifty houses I can't go back to my own house. They and my grandmother gave me whatever stability I had in my life. I'm going next week to their house to visit my grandmother and I know how to get there. Uncle Russ was a hunter and a fisherman and was part of that South I didn't know from Dad. It makes me happy every time I think of central Florida and going to the beach. Their kids grew up in the same place and had what I thought of as a normal life. I always aspired to be like that.

I have such a fear of moving, of being rootless. I have pretended in all the books that I am strongly rooted in the South, but I'm not rooted anywhere. I belong to no place. Here I was in the South, a place you could find roots, but we moved every year. We didn't live in our own houses. We grew up on federal property, houses owned by the federal government. I didn't have friends because I moved to new towns — I was always a stranger. Then we were Catholic which makes us strangers once removed.

Do you have a least favorite childhood memory?

I didn't like it when Dad knocked me around. There were different times that were bad, but all the bad childhood memories were when Dad was hitting me. There was a time in high school in Washington, D.C., when we were receiving our athletic letters, and some boy sitting next to me played a practical joke on another boy. He pinned a number on him as he walked up, so that this number hung off his sports coat. Everyone laughed and it made the priest, who was handing out the letters, mad. It was nothing. But afterwards I walked up to Dad and he knocked me to the ground — backhanded me. I wasn't expecting it. Then he beat me up in the car. My thoughts were very clear, "I'll never talk to him again. I'll never speak to him again. And I'll never be like him." That was a recurring theme of my childhood, "I'll never be like him." Of course, the way nature gets you back is that you become exactly like your father as you grow older.

You've mentioned that when you were young your mother wanted you to be a writer, but what did you want to grow up to be?

When I was at The Citadel I wanted to be a Marine pilot. I wanted to be better than Dad. I wanted to fly with him. I wanted to become a better pilot than him, then quit. But the writer—that's the dream I always had, the one thing I wanted to be. I have this disease, Bill, like you would not believe, an incredible desire to succeed in writing, because if I succeed it will mean I have existed, and they cannot take that away from me.

The first time we met was at an awards banquet for Georgia writers and afterwards you were talking with some people and several members of a literary group cornered you and asked if you could speak at one of their monthly meetings. You nicely declined, but they persisted. Their persistence became irritating, not to you, but to others standing around you.

You did well to remind me, because now I remember. The problem is that I remember exactly what it felt like to be in their position. I really do. Because I still feel that way. The thing with writing is that I have to go to a room alone, and until I go out to a banquet I have no particular feeling for being read. It still scares me to write or send something off. What if they don't like it? What if it's junk? Who am I fooling? I have this fear of the "imposter syndrome" where someone will find out that I have been fooling the world. They will expose Conroy. Bill, it could be you with this interview realizing that I am a fraud and I have been pulling something over on people for years. Somebody will find out and this will all disappear. So, I don't believe in being abrupt with people like that. It would be a sin.

This is what I'm getting at. There are hundreds of writing groups in the United States, and you must meet thousands of people from these groups when you tour with your books. I imagine they must ask you to speak to their groups?

You can't believe it. You cannot believe it! This has been one of the shocks of my life. I can speak to a group every night and every day for the rest of my life. I can speak to any high school group in the country I want to. People ask me if I can speak to their daughter's high school class. I could speak to every library. Do you realize how many book clubs there are in Atlanta? Hundreds! Ten, fifteen people get together once a month to discuss a book. I've spoken to a lot of them, especially in my early career, but I've had to cut that out. I'm either a speaker or a writer. Which do I want to be? I've had to attach an absorbantly price to speaking. Lenore has to negotiate it for me, because I can't do it. It's gotten to the point where I feel badly about it. I don't know how else not to quit my writing career. One thing the price does is cut out all book clubs. Now if something happens like I get drunk and say I'll speak to them, then I tell Lenore I screwed up and that I'll hold true to my word.

What is the price?

It's five thousand dollars. Several years ago it started out as a hundred dollars. I had to increase it beyond people's ability to pay with the purpose being so I wouldn't have to do it. What astonishes me is that people come up with the money. Now, the speaking money puts our kids through college. I have three kids in college and next year four. I can't believe how much college costs. One thing I forgot to do is ask the kids where they were applying—I tell them I'll have to start writing pornography to pay for their college.

Throughout The Prince of Tides *you mentioned the worst possible things for Tom Wingo was being born a white, Southern male in the twentieth century. Is the Southern male misunderstood?*

No. I think he is perfectly understood. The Southern male has been a pain in the ass in the twentieth century. Generally he has gotten what he has deserved and what he's asked for. I was born one.

What are you working on now?

A new novel that I don't quite know everything that's going to be in it. It's going to cover the Vietnam era and my teaching during the sixties, my first marriage, and certainly it's going to cover the death of my mother. Mom died four years ago and nothing has affected me quite like that. I was in a state of shock. I knew this happened to people, but Mom was only fifty-nine. I was not prepared. It's affected the family. I'm sure it's going to be a centerpiece for the book one way or another. My mother had a thousand different faces, so I might use her. The father might be a sheriff or a lawyer. I'm messing around with different concepts. I'm thinking of using Italy and Atlanta. I haven't written an Atlanta novel, but I'm certain that will come sooner or later. I've started writing the new book, but I'm still in the note-taking process. I've been interviewing people who were holocaust survivors, and that will play a part in the book, especially the children. I don't quite know where it all fits. There's a large Jewish aspect to the book, also, South Carolina, European, and a great mother aspect, but how they interact—I don't know, yet. I have confidence that eventually it will come out. If there's a narrator, it will come out. For some reason the narrator is six foot six, and I can't figure out why. I don't have a title.

Do you have any advice for the young writer?

Yes, I encourage the young writer to acquire every possible experience that they can and to make it as unusual an experience of anybody of their generation. A summer job seems to be a great place for experience, especially if it is away from the family. It needs to be a place where you can learn. They should also have deep and varied reading. Read everything, and copy and imitate a writer until you know the secrets of their style.

We mentioned García Márquez's *One Hundred Years of Solitude,* and one reason that book appealed to me so much was because of the first sentence. When I read that sentence I realized I knew nothing about writing. The sentence is so complex and has such an amazing relationship with time. The line is, "Many years later, as he faced the firing squad, Colonel Aureliano Buendiá was to remember that distant afternoon when his father took him to discover ice." I've copied that sentence and I've tried to write sentences like that using time the way he did—"Many years ago..." and "Years from now..." trying to write differently so I knew the secret of that one sentence. A writer needs to read broadly and as critically and as joyously as he can. The other thing—travel. I've never known writers who have traveled enough. I wish I had gone everywhere when I was young.

What can we expect from you in the future?

I imagine I will write five more novels before I die. I would like to write some nonfiction, and probably some screenplays. That interests me more than other forms of writing. I like movies. If I could get one great theme for a nonfiction book I would like to do that. I found out when I was in James Dickey's class that I wasn't a poet. I did not have that intensity poets have. I found myself too far-ranging. I was not able to focus like poets.

In The Prince of Tides *you have poems written by Tom Wingo's sister, Savannah, which you wrote yourself.*

This is another secret of that book. Originally, I was going to use my sister Carol's poems. Unfortunately, for her own reasons she decided she didn't want to have anything to do with the book, so she told the publishing company they could not use those poems that we had mutually agreed on. I had a week to write three poems. It was a time of great dread for me trying to write poems like that. I had to sit down under pressure of a deadline to write three poems by a woman living in New York in a fictional book. That was a great moment of self-definition that came into the writing of those poems. It scared me very badly.

How did the short story within the book come about?

I dreamt that short story—these three girls—my daughters. It was during the time of my divorce. I rarely have dreams of one piece, but that simply came out. I wrote it in my journal because I wondered where it came from, and what it meant. I tried to work it into the book in some form and it became the children's story. My editor wanted to cut the story, and that is the only great fight we had, but I had to cut out some other chapter to save that one.

Critics have called you the Faulkner of the "New" South. How do you feel that about that designation?

I come to this question you have just asked having grown up being me, and not being able to relate myself to a writer like Faulkner. If I had my family around here they would tease me for ever entertaining the question. In my family I have to pretend I am not smart, nor can I ever mention the fact that I am a writer when my family is sitting around. There is such a fear of intellect and achievement, a fear of making it, that I have to play this game. So it terrifies me even when the question is asked. Because I came from a family without art, that question doesn't even make sense to me. Do you realize that my answer has not even responded to the question — it makes me feel very uncomfortable for reasons in my novel I try to explain. It's simply an overwhelming question.

Faulkner is so much better than me. Faulkner is such an icon to me. He represents so much, but he's not my favorite writer by any means. I don't feel the passion and response I like to feel when I'm reading him. There's something cold and remote about Faulkner that has never touched me. I don't fall in love with the characters in his novels like I did with Sophie in *Sophie's Choice*. Novels that move me change my life — none of Faulkner's novels have ever changed my life. Yet, when one is reading him, one knows it is greatness.

Harry Crews

Harry Crews has a reputation of being a hard-driving, hard-drinking, bar-fighting writer. The horror stories of his harsh life run rampant in the literary circles; half of them are true and the other half might as well be. To sit down and talk with him is a powerful experience; he stares you in the eye, cusses, gulps his coffee, puts out his cigarette butts on the table edge, sits broad-shouldered, and asks why anyone would drive all night from Atlanta to Gainesville to talk with him. He has published a dozen novels, including *Gospel Singer, Naked in Garden Hills, Karate Is a Thing of the Spirit, Car, The Hawk Is Dying, The Gypsy's Curse, A Childhood, All We Need of Hell,* and most recently *The Knockout Artist.* He is straightforward and to the point, and I couldn't help but believe he could be any one of his characters from the meanest to the nicest. He was born in 1935 in Bacon County, Georgia. This interview was conducted on January 10, 1988, at his office at the University of Florida.

After serving in the Marines you attended the University of Florida where you met Andrew Lytle.

Right. I didn't meet him for a good long time. As a matter of fact, I was at the school two years, left on a motorcycle for a year riding all over the country and Mexico, then I met him when I got back. I always knew he was on campus, but I didn't go to any kind of writing classes. I think it's generally true the more serious a young man or woman is about writing the more steadfastly they refuse to go to anything called a writing class. Primarily because they have the wrong notion of what goes on in the class. No, they probably know what goes on in there and they stay away for good reason. But if you can go to a writing class in which the writer, the person holding the class, understands that writing cannot be taught, but can only be coached, and if the teacher is really undertaking to do for you what a good editor would do for you, if you had a good editor, then it's worth going to. Anybody who really is out to "teach" writing; you want to stay away from that son-of-a-bitch.

Anyways, when I got back I lived with some veteran friends in a place called Twelve Oaks Bath and Tennis Club. They were apprentice writers and they knew about Lytle, and finally they got me to sit in on a class. After one class I knew that's where I ought to be. That was the first glimmer, the first notion I had of how truly ignorant I was of what I was trying to do and how much I had to learn if I was ever to write. I was with him for a couple of years — a good long time. The game was — I wrote and he read, and sometimes he talked to me about what I wrote, sometimes he didn't, which was precisely right. Much of what I wrote wasn't worth talking about.

In mentioning editing and workshopping a writer's work, do you agree that in a workshop the students are editing work they are incapable of editing? How do you feel about the workshop?

No. No. It's up to the person running that thing to try to give the class direction, to cut off long monologues that aren't going anywhere and have no point. But it's all part of the process, having everybody talk about everybody's work. It always seems like wasted motion to the person whose work is being considered. They want to know what the writer thinks and not what their peers think. Not only are you trying to coach what the people write in the workshop, but you are trying to develop in them editorial skills only because they're going to have to edit their own work. If they don't edit it, no one will. We don't have any editors at publishing houses much anymore. I don't know what they pay editors for at houses anymore — like Random House, Knopf, Morrow, or Viking. They don't have editors in the sense that Maxwell Perkins was an editor — people who really did edit work. Editors think that if they quarrel about a fact or two, or an image that they are editing manuscripts — that's not editing at all. While apprentice writers may object to other apprentice writers talking about their work, that's all part of the process, part of the pain of it, but just as long as it is understood in the workshop that the writer is under no obligation to do anything anyone tells him. If you hear something you can use — use it. If you don't hear anything you can use, then just disregard the whole goddamn evening and go do what you want to do.

How much editing do your editors do, say on your latest novel, All We Need of Hell?

I can't speak for what may have happened to other writers' manuscripts, but my editor goes through the manuscript and quarrels with language. They say this is too fast, this is too slow, I don't believe this — all that stuff — most of which can be disregarded. I believe that if a good reader has trouble with something you've written, the least you owe to yourself is to take a good hard look at it. As far as I'm concerned editors are a goddamn nuisance and an obstacle to get over. I've had two editors that were good — Jim Landis and Chuck Corn. Landis edited my first five books. He's a good reader, a very conscious worker, and he was fine. Charles Corn, a boy from Macon,

Georgia, helped me a lot with *A Childhood.* He was a good editor, but I only worked with him on one book. So with six books I've had good editors, and maybe I'll run into another good editor.

When you first began writing you dissected Graham Greene's The End of the Affair, *where you broke it down it to numbers — the number of characters, scenes, rooms, etc. Could you discuss how and why you went about doing that?*

Desperation! I wasn't getting anywhere. I kept writing stuff I couldn't publish, and I was aware of how ignorant I was of what I was trying to do. It was just an exercise in thrashing around, struggling to see if I could find something that would help me. What it did was make me read a book very, very closely, and that can only help. Looking back now and trying to use those numbers to write a novel myself, I could have saved myself that year. But I didn't know that then, and I don't know it now. Maybe it was a good thing to do. I don't know. If I hadn't done it I don't know what I would have done otherwise. As the logicians say, it's reasoning contrary to fact. I don't know what I would have done if I didn't do what I had done.

How long did it take to break Greene's book down into numbers like you did?

It took about three or four months. I really did have that sucker cut apart neatly. No, it wasn't neat at all — it was about as butchered as it could be butchered to get it into its parts. By then the book was dead, and that's what happens when you analyze anything like that — you kill it. It isn't necessary for everyone to fool with literature that way, but it is for writers at some point in their lives to do something like that, and that point being when they are young. I still believe it was a good learning tool for me. I haven't told anyone else to do it. I have no way of knowing if it was a good thing, but that's just how it feels.

Why Graham Greene and not Faulkner or Hemingway?

Because I had read everything Greene had written up to that time, and still have read him right along over the years. I honor the man's name. I do. I hold him in high esteem. Graham Greene is a very fine workman, a fine craftsman, and whatever else Greene does, he tells you a story. In every one of his novels there is a very strong narrative line, which is a thing I like in fiction. If you look at my work, my strong suit is the narrative line, the story, and everything else works off of that. The action of the fiction determines what is admissible to the work and what is not.

Why not Faulkner? At the time I was doing this I probably wasn't a good enough reader, and I had not read as much Faulkner as I should have read. Reading Faulkner isn't going to make you a better writer, because he was such a one-of-a-kind writer that much of what he does is very useless to the rest of us. Faulkner, when Faulkner is bad, is as bad as it gets. There are similes and metaphors and language in Faulkner that are absolutely terrible. There's a story called "Wash" where Faulkner is writing about a shack and it's built down by a stream, and the shack is tumbling down. He says the shack looks like some ancient primeval beast that has dragged itself there to the stream to slake its thirst and die. Terrible, dreadful. And all that doom is terrible.

Don't misunderstand me, because I concur with a great many other people that Faulkner is a genius, but whether or not he is a great place for a young writer to go to emulate... I have problems with that. You sure as hell can't take any of his things as a design that you're going to use as a model. That won't do. Of course, you have to understand I'm talking about very young writers. I'm not talking about guys as old as I am. With luck there comes a time when you're not trying to model yourself after anybody. You're trying to discover whatever is in you, which you were doing from the beginning, to release as dramatically and compellingly as you possibly can. But in the beginning, you are trying to find your voice, your subject, whatever you do well, what you don't do well — all those things, then you're subject to do anything. There's nothing wrong with modeling your story on someone else's.

The bottom line on this for me is — you do whatever you have to do to get where you need to go. You dig that? You do whatever you have to do to get where you need to go. And no two writers do it the same way. If whatever it is you feel is necessary for you to do, and if other people make fun of that, well, my feeling is — to hell with them. If you find that it's a good thing to do, go do it. Because the world is full of bad advice. As a matter of fact, the world doesn't want you to do anything. The world wants you to work the lawn or walk the dog or paint the house — anything but write, just so you bleed whatever energy you have away from writing, and if you're not careful that's exactly what you're going to end up doing. There are writers who manage to be good husbands, good fathers who paint the house, water the lawn, and do their writing, too. If that's the case, wonderful. There's nothing wrong with that. I've never been able to do that.

You have to hoard that energy and keep it for the work and not spill it willy-nilly here and there. Obviously, you have obligations to husbands and wives and children and to a job to keep bread on the table. I know that and I accept that, but we have too many examples before us of writers who simply wasted their energy and talent by using it up in other things. There are a number of people who would point to me as an example of one of those writers who has used up his talent and energy doing things he should not have been doing instead of writing.

Much of your writing generates out of those experiences you've had while not writing.

Exactly. If I had not done the things I had done I would not have written the books I've written.

In reference to your work, Allen Shepard wrote in the Dictionary of Literary Biography, *"It is not something one wants to [read] too much of at a single sitting. The intensity of his vision is unsettling." How do you feel about that description of your work?*

I resigned myself a long time ago to not have very many readers, because I have enough sense to know that not many people are going to want to read or are capable of reading what I write. There simply aren't many readers of fiction anyway. Unfortunately, fiction, if it is equated with anything, it is the movies and television—that is to say as entertainment. There's nothing wrong with being entertaining. Fiction ought to be entertaining in the sense that it takes you out of your own skin for awhile and puts you in someone else's skin. But over and above that, good fiction, unlike most of the other forms of entertainment that fiction competes with, ultimately, ought to turn you back upon yourself and force you to make judgments about your own life and the rightness and wrongness of your life. This should happen to your particular reader. He should see your particular vision of the world. It should force him to make judgments and most people don't want to do that.

Your books are funny. Some of the passages had me rolling on the floor, but that's not what drew me to your books initially. Essentially, it was the craft of storytelling, especially in the understatement of your descriptions. In Car *specifically, there is a scene where a family of four is killed, and instead of going into the bloody gore like you could have, which a lesser writer might have, you described the little boy, who, instead of going through the windshield or being cut up . . . —you said there was a spot in the glass where someone's head had stopped. Reading that scene was a startling experience. That understatement is seen throughout your books, and it's very powerful.*

Very often the horror and the terror of the thing becomes magnified by simply drawing back and understating.

Let's discuss the grotesqueness of your work.

People have brought it up and reviewers talk about it—they use words like Gothic and grotesque, and if that's what I am then that's what I am. That's alright. I take no offense at it. You've got to understand that I think of myself as a storyteller. I tell stories. That's what I do. All of my stories have a certain flavor, smell, taste, texture—whatever you want to say, as do most writers' stories. If a reader finds what I write distasteful, then I'd be a fool to argue with him. I'd say don't read it. And many people do find what I write distasteful. It's more than that—they're absolutely outraged. The first review I saw of *All We Need of Hell* I was in a little cabin in Louisiana and a boy brought me a *USA Today* and the review was just terrible. Initially, I wondered why the guy went on as long as he did. If you think something is absolutely dreadful, without any merit, why the hell go on at great length about it. Just say it's terrible and stop. That fellow simply doesn't need to read any more of my fiction. I hope he doesn't upset himself that way. Life's too short for him to read something that's going to put him off so badly.

The grotesqueness is brought about by the character's actions, but, also, to a large extent by the character's physical features—like the boy, Marvin, with no legs in The Gypsy's Curse. *There isn't any of that physical grotesqueness in* All We Need of Hell.

Right, and there isn't any in my new book coming out in the spring called *The Knockout Artist*. Except there is in a way. The kid can knock himself out. That's his claim to fame—he can knock himself out... I've been asked time out of mind why the boy in *The Gypsy's Curse* walks on his hands, can't talk and he can't hear, and so on. I have no ready answer to that. I've been asked that nine million times, and I guess the quickest and best answer to that is that I can write better about the "normal" world by writing about the "abnormal" world. It seems to me that this is in no way unique to me. All we have to do is look at *Gulliver's Travels*. Why write about little tiny people? Why write it the way he did? Obviously, it's saying something about you and me or it wouldn't have stood up for this long a time. But from the number of times I'd been asked about it you'd think it was unique to me.

The reason I brought it up was because you have been heavily criticized for it. I mean, who wants to read about normalcy. Many of your characters border a fine line between normal and abnormal.

Fiction always deals with extremes. Fiction is always about someone whose ass is on the line. He has to jump left or jump right, he can't stay where he is. And the reason for it is very simple—it is in a crisis, conflicts, in what I think of as "blood moments" that you find out who the hell you are, what you really are, what you really believe, what you're really capable of—that's where you find it out. You don't find it out otherwise. Would you sell your sister for a Baby Ruth candy bar? And of course the answer is no, no, no, no. Men have done it. You may need the Baby Ruth to feed your starving mother, and so the sister volunteers her body or you volunteer it for her to keep your mother alive. Most of us are never caught in those circumstances, so we won't know. Are you a coward or are you able to control your fear and behave with what the world calls courage? Most people won't know, because they've never been tested. In fiction, if the fiction turns you back upon yourself, then despite the fact that you've never been caught in those circumstances, you have to deal with those issues. That gets to the heart of why I write as I do, and why all other writers write the way they do. If you look at a really good novel, like Norman Mailer's *An American Dream*, most of us aren't going to kill our wife and leave her by the bed, dead, and then go down the hall and screw the maid, and then come back and throw our dead wife out the window. I suspect none of us are going to do that. But, Mailer forces us to consider it in his novels. If we read the novel we are forced to psychologically and emotionally (spiritually, if you will) deal with those circumstances.

In A Childhood *you state, "There wasn't enough money to close up a dead man's eyes." You grew up on biscuits made of flour, lard, and water. You would eat dirt to get the minerals you needed. Was this the hardest part about your childhood?*

We didn't have to eat the dirt, but we did. That's not too unusual for kids to do. They don't know why they're doing it but their body knows why. The lack of money wasn't the hardest part, but it didn't make my childhood particularly pleasant. Not to have food, clothes, and to not have a place with any permanence was hard. There were all sorts of problems: my father dying, a mother who was uneducated having to raise two small children, getting involved with a second husband whom I loved very much, but unfortunately was locked into an alcoholic mist, and my brother and I were thrown back upon our mother's resources that were nonexistent, except for courage and determination. I think the worst part of my childhood was the absence of a father. But again, I'm reasoning contrary to fact. I don't know what it would have been like if my daddy had lived. I never knew him. I don't know him now. I know him insofar as I wrote about him in that book, and whatever I know about him is what people have told me. And since memory is always suspect, I don't know if what I know about my father is true or not, or if my notion of him is true or not. It's just the one I'm stuck with.

On page 14 of A Childhood *you wrote, "And more marvelous still, to be able to return to that place of your childhood and see it through the eyes of a man, with everything set against that long-ago, little boy's memory of how things used to be."*

Place is very important to me. What I was writing about there was about my part of the county, the land I was raised on, the house I was raised in, and to come back and see it as a grown man. As a kid we moved a lot, so we never were in one place for too long. I never had a lot of things. I still don't have many things. I don't want a lot of things. I never buy myself anything. I did not buy these shoes I have on. I didn't buy these trousers. This vest was sent to me from New Orleans as was the shirt by Maggie Powell. She bought them and sent them to me. I don't think having things is a great plus. I don't know if I'm making any connection necessarily with my childhood. Am I this way as an adult because I was that way as a child? That's too simplistic to reason that way. It may very well be a natural extension of my childhood, but I don't know. I don't own many things. I don't have many things. Whether they be books, clothes, or furniture I think of them as an encumbrance. I could pack up everything I own and put it in the back of my truck along with my dog and I could leave town today.

A Childhood *was beautifully portrayed from making up stories from the* Sears Catalog *to the neighbor raiding your smokehouse. Out of that do you have a favorite childhood memory?*

Yes, it's sitting around the house telling stories. But it's got to be cold outside and it's got to be dark and you're tired and you have the foot tub in front of the fireplace and everybody's washed their feet—that's about the only thing we washed. We told stories. Tobacco-selling time was always a favorite time of the year because strange things came into the house. Tobacco was a money crop and you got new overalls, new shoes, and weenies, which you never saw—store-bought goods—sliced bread and all that good stuff. So that was a great time. Hog-killing time was a great thing.

What was the worst part of your childhood?

Probably the episode when my legs drew up so that my heels were against my buttocks. I couldn't walk for a year. Whether it was infantile paralysis or polio I don't know. Some doctors said it wasn't either one of them, but that it was an hysterical symptom, and that there was nothing wrong with me. Maybe I just retreated to the bed because I couldn't deal with what was outside the bed.

Why was writing about your childhood a difficult book to write?

I wrote it for my son so that he would know some things in greater detail than he otherwise would. I thought writing about it would help me get through all this stuff, put it to rest.

Did that occur?

No. I don't think there was much purging or catharsis in the experience.

Your novels are set in Gainesville, Florida, and in Georgia, and yet you don't claim to be a Southern writer.

I write about the South because I'm stuck with it. I can't very well put my stories in New York. I don't know anything about New York City.

You were born and raised here and you do write about this area.

If somebody wants to call me a Southern writer it doesn't offend me, but you probably have reference to the fact that I have told people or have written that I don't think any novelist wants an adjective placed in front of the word novelist. I don't think you have to be a Southerner to read my fiction. I hope not. That would mean I failed utterly. Is Tom Wolfe or Walker Percy a Southern writer? Is Faulkner a Southern writer? One of the things you have to resign yourself to as a writer is this business of people labeling you, labeling your work... Putting stickers on it. That's just the way of the world and that's alright. You don't have to like it, you just have to live with it.

That's one of the things I'm getting at. On page five of All We Need of Hell *it says, "The rest of the country may have been homogenized, but the South held onto their Marvellas and their Roids and their way of talking...," which may be the only thing the South will be able to hold onto when they're done. This is very characteristic of your writing in that you may not be writing of the South as a region but you're pinpointing a microscopic area and you're extracting its characteristics and writing about it.*

The name of the game in writing is that you write about something specific and concrete and nailed down in place, in time and in circumstance. Always! That's the first order of business. If you nail down an action then it will translate for anybody. For me to read about an Australia aborigine father trying to feed his child, somebody must know the circumstances. If somebody wrote and knew the particulars about an Australia aborigine, then I would be moved, despite the fact that I've never been to Australia, and with any luck I'll never go. I don't know from Jump Street about aborigines, but because I know about children and food and hunger, then if it's written well and truthfully, then obviously, it's going to connect with my life.

Could you discuss The Knockout Artist, *your new book coming out this spring?*

No, it's complicated and too complex. I like the book a lot and the publisher likes the book a lot. I don't have the foggiest notion what reviewers, the public, or anybody else will think of it, and I don't care. It's done now, and whatever reception it has that's the reception it will have. I'm working on a play, now. I will say that it's about a twenty-year-old boy, a fighter, and he's had thirteen fights. His manager abandons him in New Orleans after a fight where he was knocked out. That boy comes from where I come from — Bacon County, Georgia — right off a farm as I came off a farm. He has to make do as best he can in what for him is a foreign land. I went to New Orleans to write the novel. I'd been there many times before, but I'd never written a novel set in that city. Since he comes from a farm the way I did, why not let the boy have my sensibilities and feelings — I mean, I know how a person from Bacon County, Georgia, would react to New Orleans. Said more specifically, I know how I would react to New Orleans. So that boy very much has my own knowledge, sensibilities, and prejudices. I probably identify with the boy in that book more than any other character I've written.

You would say that this is you under the circumstances that you could have put yourself in?

Yeah. Pretty much the way he reacts is the way I would react when I was his age given who he is, had I been who he is. And at the same time I am, I'm not.

The thing I found with your books is that you have never trampled the same ground twice, you never backtrack. You must have a wide range of interests and knowledge as you cover so many different things, from manning a hawk, to putting headliners in cars, to karate.

I've trapped and trained hawks like the guy in *The Hawk Is Dying* at a place called Payne's Prairie. I caught two hawks out there; I manned them and flew them. I didn't do that to write a novel. After I manned them I just happened to write the novel. I studied karate with a guy named Dirk Mosie here in town, and I never would have written *Karate Is a Thing of the Spirit* if I hadn't studied karate. I never would have written *The Knockout Artist* if I hadn't spent a good bit of my young manhood around a fight gymnasium with boxers, managers, or if my brother hadn't been a fighter. In *The Gypsy's Curse*, the guy's name is Al Molarski. Well, I knew a guy named Al Berkowitz who owned a gym. He own the *Firemen's Gym* in Jacksonville — I just moved the gym to Clearwater when I wrote the novel. There was in that gym a guy who walked on his hands and was a deaf-mute, and he had been raised by Al Berkowitz. But I never knew the guy. I saw him. I saw him running up the stairs on his hands to the gym. I saw him hand-balancing, but I never knew a deaf-mute in my life. I didn't know him; I just saw him. This was thirty-five years before I wrote about it.

Every one of my books has that sort of point of departure. *Car* would have been a better book if I had not hated cars as much as I do. *Car* was written out of my hatred for the automobile and what it has done to this country and the world. Not only should automobiles not be allowed in Manhattan, they should not be allowed in downtown Gainesville, the little town we're sitting in right now. What we ought to have is a rapid transit system everyone can afford, then get these goddamn monsters off the road. What sense does it make for a one hundred and thirteen pound housewife to get into four thousand pounds of machinery and drive two blocks for a thirteen ounce loaf of bread? What kind of goddamn sense does that make? If that's not madness, then I don't know what madness is. What sense does it make for there to be a filling station on all four corners of an intersection in a city as small as the one we are sitting in? And yet, I can show you that intersection here in Gainesville, Florida. The emotional violence out of which *Car* was written is simply that everybody in this country has his car to eat, and we will, by God, eat it, because the whole economy and social fabric of the country is set up to force us to eat it whether we like it or not. That book is a metaphor for much of what I feel about the place where I happen to have found myself living for the last fifty years... — my life.

Most of us have no idea where our bank has its money invested. If you've got fifty thousand dollars in a bank's savings account you can bet your ass your bank is not leaving that fifty thousand dollars just sitting there. They're paying you whatever interest, but they've got to make more on that money. So, does the bank you do business with own any slum real estate? Probably! Because it is so tremendously profitable. Sure. You might be a slumlord. You might be contributing to the circumstances in which some child somewhere is eating the plaster off the wall or being bitten by rats at night. Our lives have been so abstracted from us, taken from us by our being intertwined with so many things that we have no control over it. It doesn't hurt to be aware of what we have done to ourselves and what we are busily doing to ourselves. My fiction would probably be better if it were not written out of such a sense of anger and outrage. Because it is. Inevitably. All of it. Every last fucking line of it.

My fiction is a visceral response to the world I live in. I guess to some extent it is an intellectual response, too, but it's a gut response to the world I live in, much in the way that some people, because of certain body chemistries, can walk through the woods and break out in a rash because they are allergic to certain plants. Artists are people who walk through the world, and because of a certain psychic chemistry they break out into novels, poetry, paintings, and music.

James Dickey

James Dickey, born in Atlanta, Georgia, in 1923, has long since established himself as a major American poet publishing 11 volumes including *Puella, The Zodiac, The Strength of Fields, Poems 1957–1967,* and *Buckdancer's Choice,* winner of the National Book Award in 1966. In total, he has written more than 20 volumes of fiction, prose, children's poetry, criticism, and belles lettres, including his 1970 novel, *Deliverance.* Most recently, he has published his second novel, *Alnilam.* He is poet-in-residence at the University of South Carolina in Columbia, where he lives with his wife and daughter. This interview was conducted at his home on October 14, 1987.

Alnilam *went through many stages of development. What was the original idea behind it?*

I work from images. For example, *Deliverance* had a mental picture of a man standing on top of a cliff above a river, then it became a matter of interest to me as to what he was doing there, how he got there, did he come out of the woods to the cliff or did he climb up the cliff? What happens I don't know. It developed just about out of that image. With *Alnilam,* it was something I had heard in the Air Force forty-five years ago. The service is full of mythology. Someone said there had been someone who was looking through a turning propeller and on the other side was another aircraft with the propeller also going. As he looked through both of them at the same time, they formed the image of man, the human figure — sort of like the shadow created by the spinning blades. That's where *Alnilam* got started. The idea of the ghost and the machine began to spark something in my imagination, and it just gradually built up from there.

I thought about it so much that it began to be obsessive enough to spend that much time on it. I'm working on two other novels now that have that same quantity. The reason I don't write a lot of novels, say, like John Updike, is because I'm a writer in a different sense from him. It's something he works at like a job. I don't have that orientation at all. It's got to come out of some deep inner disturbance that won't be put to rest until that is done. I'm all for writers sticking to the typewriter or word processor and working on it a lot, but I don't keep any kind of schedule like that. I write in long spurts and stay on for long hours at a time, for a long time, then I don't write anything for a long time. I think one of the hardest things to do is to preserve the sense of excitement about what you are doing. If you turn it into drudgery the excitement will leave you.

You started Alnilam *thirty-seven years ago.*

I started in 1950; I wrote down the first idea of it, just sketched it out. Again, that's a little misleading because it seems to imply that I wrote nothing but that for thirty-seven years which is not the case. For many years I didn't even think about it. During the interim I wrote twenty-five other books of various sorts. But *Alnilam* was always gestating. I would add to it, turn it around. About eight or ten years ago I found I had such a huge mass of notes on various incidents and people that it was practically already written. All I had to do was form it up and give it a shape that could utilize the material that had the central narrative running through it, instead of a lot of incidental things I had been experimenting with—most of which had to go out.

When you weren't working on the book were you always thinking about it in the back of you mind?

Well, yes, but unconsciously also. That's where the real work gets done.

Alnilam *is seven hundred pages long, and as you just mentioned you had a large stack of notes. When you actually had the finished manuscript, did you have to cut it down or did the publisher cut it down?*

No, the publisher liked it like it was. Again, at Doubleday I had nine different editors, all of which wanted something different—change this and change that. But I never changed anything, and I still wouldn't. I wouldn't change a word of it. It's exactly like I want. (*Laughing.*) It's worth waiting for when you can say that, because a lot of writers, and some of my work, I can say, I could have done better than the final product. If I had known more or if I had done this or that. I can't say that about *Alnilam*. If *Alnilam* is not a masterpiece, and I think it maybe is, then it's not anybody else's fault—it's my fault.

Throughout the book I made the comparisons between Joel Cahill, who we never see, we only hear what others say about him, and Jesus Christ.

You just see that brief picture of him on the screen when they show the movie of the parade.

Yes, that's true. I made the comparison between Jesus Christ and Joel, who we never see, except for that one instance which is a technological image, not a physical image. Like Christ, Joel Cahill is worshiped by these young men, and we've never really seen a picture of Christ, just hearsay and what people have preached about to mankind for centuries.

What we see with Joel is the same thing we have seen with Jesus Christ — technologically produced images of one person's rendition of what he should look like.

This is right, but I wouldn't insist on it. Some people have pointed out that there is some kind of parallel, but it truly is not intentional, except in some ways I suppose it could be construed as intentional on my part — the business about the possibility of Joel coming back, and his followers think he is going to reappear at a key time. That's obviously connected with some kind of resurrection situation.

I also drew a parallel between Joel and Christ when he was in the farmer's house and they threw a quilt over him. Well, I saw this as a shroud.

Yes, in a way, but I wouldn't insist too much on that myself. I really haven't thought too much about it. I remember what Hemingway said about *The Old Man and the Sea,* which is pretty good Hemingway, although not as good as what is made of it. Somebody asked him about all the parallels between the old man and Christ: "I didn't think about any of that. That's for other people to find. My job was to make a real old man and a real sea and real sharks and a real big fish, and endow that with as much reality and interest as I could, then let the other people make whatever parallels they want." Well, this is the way I feel.

The reason I asked that is because you've been called a religious writer.

Again, it's not in any orthodox sense, I'm sure of that, because I don't belong to any church. Technically, I'm an Episcopalian, but I almost never go to church. I think the feeling I have is largely some kind of personal sacramentalism, but not orthodox.

I think Alnilam *was a perfectly-timed book about the cult admiration we have in this country, and really in the world, as demonstrated by the cult-type admiration the young pilots have for Joel Cahill. We have cults going on all over the place and being exposed. Most recently, Jim and Tammy Bakker, and everyone caught up in that organization.*

There are a lot of cults around. The novel is probably about the growth of a cult and the mystique of leaders. There a lots of examples: The John Birch Society is one. Nobody knows who John Birch is; you'd have to look it up in the records to find out who he was. But the society honored in his name is very evident. There are lots of examples in history, some of them good — like Jesus, some of them bad — like Hitler. People have a hunger for this sort of thing, especially if there is a mystery in it or supernaturalism, don't you feel?

I agree. I think it's the loss of personal identity. People latch on to whatever will give to them a method of belonging. Frank Cahill, the main character in Alnilam, *is blind from diabetes. You're a diabetic, right?*

Well, no. Just borderline. I have the conditions of the diabetic. My family is full of diabetics. I had a first cousin by marriage who went blind from it, and died. I've been hearing talk about diabetes and diabetic procedures all my life, so I know the scene pretty well.

Do you think if you had sat down for two or three years and worked on nothing else that you could have written Alnilam?

It wouldn't have been the same. It might have been better or worse, I don't know. It wouldn't have been the same. As I say, the accumulation of notes for a novel, at least the way I write them, and the passage of time is important. You can't do them all at once, because your moods change. You can take some notes on one aspect of the story when you're feeling a certain way, because of some external conditions, that you wouldn't be able to do with that orientation at another time. No, I like the slow accumulation of things. I like to live with the material, because different things, different vectors, different angles of attack on the material will occur to you at different times. Sometimes you can hit one very early on that seems to be the answer, but I don't even trust that one. I want to give everything a chance that wants to come in and announce itself as a possibility. It's like when you have a stick in a glass of salt water and as it evaporates it accumulates crystals, and after a few days or weeks when you take it out it's covered with crystals. Things accumulate around a central stem or central theme, and they all sort of reinforce one another all glittered together.

Crux *is the second book of* Alnilam.

That's a way off, but I got a lot of notes.

How long have you been working on it?

Well, I haven't really been working on it. I have to generalize about what's going to happen in it. This is a sequel to *Alnilam,* which is a Northern Hemisphere constellation in the center of Orion. The *Crux* is the Southern Cross, that's not the most prominent, but the most famous in the Southern Hemisphere. This is about the *Alnilam* plot and the ideas under the influence of Joel Cahill taking over the whole Southwest Pacific night air war. The actual clash will be between the invested authorities of the service and the Alnilam people.

So, instead of fighting the enemy, they'll be fighting themselves.

No, they'll be fighting the enemy, but they'll be fighting them in their own way, and the orders are coming from Alnilam instead of the Air Force.

So, Joel Cahill is alive?

No, but people keep saying he is, that they've seen him, that he's over there with them somewhere, that he comes out.

But he's actually dead?

Yeah, I think so. Think! (*Laughing.*) If I could find a way to resurrect him spectacularly enough, believe me I would do it, but I think it will remain a matter of hints and conjectures— like the second coming of Jesus, maybe.

What will actually take place in Crux?

I'm really not sure, and I probably ought not talk it up too much until I do it. I think it will center on the character of Harbelis. He was one of the cadets and he's a decent fellow, but even decent people can be swept up into a cult with a charismatic leader. It will turn on his final decision. Most of the young men of Alnilam will be killed, and it will be made plain to him that he's the leader now.

He'll have to make a final decision about "Alnilam."

Yes, and he does. He walks away from it. He lets it die. I'll have him walk—let it die. Harbelis is the one that can keep it alive, but after the war he won't. It's too extreme. It's really antihuman. It's asking too much of humanity to be that extreme to have those particular ideas.

You said you first heard about "Alnilam" when you were in the service. How realistic is the internal cult of "Alnilam" in a regimented organization like the Air Force. I don't think a group could actually go up against and control the service, could it?

No, but you can be very subversive. This kind of paramilitary outfit within the military is quite possible. It is quite possible! Of course, there would be all sorts of investigations. But the more underground something is, and the more widespread it is, the harder it is to kill it out. Someone asked why these boys would follow a leader no matter how good a pilot he was or how charismatic he was if they weren't given any more of an ultimate goal than Joel does. That's why I think they would follow him, because the goal is something that will be revealed. I had a whole Utopia mapped out with a blueprint for a whole new society that he was going to institute, but that would have weakened the structure and taken the mystery out of it. All he talks about is the enormous purple field and the existence of nihilism and music.

It's essentially like a religion, there's really nothing you can grab or hold onto.

That's right. And that's part of the mystique. It's like the argument on religion in the Middle Ages where it is said in regard to Christianity, "I don't believe in it despite the fact that it's absurd, I believe in it because it is absurd." The cadets believe in "Alnilam" because it's not definitely stated.

Alnilam *actually had two other titles:* A Minor Constellation *and* Death's Baby Machine. *Did each title represent what the book was about at that time?*

As I say, it's gone through a lot of evolution, metamorphosis, and at the time, yes. Again, when you look back over these things some parts of it look as though somebody else had written it. You change from year to year, and you look back at some impulse that had hold of you that you no longer understand.

When you went back to read over parts, did you ask yourself if you really wrote it?

Yes, you do think that (*laughing*), especially with the good parts. And really you didn't write them. I think there's a sense in which you can say with those parts of a novel, poems or anything else, you don't just say I wrote that, but I was written. Something wrote me. It's some sort of visitation. This is what Plato and the ancients meant when they talked about inspiration, though that was not their word — that came later. Their word was something like seizure. Possession. It possesses you, comes through you and takes you over. You've got to do it. The American poet Winfield Scott said, "The good poems are the ones you get out of bed to work on." You can't leave them alone, you don't want to sleep, you want to get close to it. You want to get it. It's the idea that it takes hold of you and uses you. I very much believe in that.

When I heard that Alnilam *was written over a period of thirty-seven years, and when I read it, I looked to see if I could spot the stages of development of the writer, the different time periods. But they're really not there. You don't see thirty-seven years here, then twenty-five and fifteen and five. The book is very smooth and unified.*

I was aware of exactly what you're describing, and I rewrote it after I had the whole thing. It was twice as long as it is now. It was very, very long. It was about three thousand pages, and I went back and rewrote it to get the sense of unity and style. I rewrote it twice, then it came down to the length it is now. Someone asked if I realized my book was only thirty pages shorter than *The Magic Mountain*. Recently, I had read *The Magic Mountain* for some reason. I hadn't read it since I was in college. This commentator asked with a book as long as *Alnilam* how could I avoid certain boring stretches. I said I don't know that I haven't done that, but I can tell you, categorically, that there's nothing in *Alnilam* that's as boring as the seventy-eight pages in the middle of *The Magic Mountain* where Settembrini and Naphta debate the true meaning of free masonry. (*Laughing.*) They're like two graduate students who don't get around to taking the final exam.

You've said that you thought Deliverance *was a poet's novel...*

Did I say that? No, I think someone else said that.

That's true, someone else did, but you agreed with them.

Well, I guess so. I suppose you could call it a poet's novel. But the deliberate poetic novel, so-called, is usually not very interesting as a novel, and I wanted to write a novel that was interesting, so I tried to keep the obvious poetry out and in context with the qualities of the characters. That's why I made Ed Gentry an art director who has a certain amount of sensibility which is a cut above that of the other fellows he's with, but not much. He's still pretty much an average fellow like they are. Except for Lewis who is a deliberate self-willed "Superman" of the suburbs.

He's the only one with the vision?

Yes, well, he doesn't have a vision so much as he wants to have one.

But the other characters have knowledge, an organized knowledge, whereas Lewis doesn't necessarily have that, but he's the only one who can see what's going to happen to the river, and it upsets him more than the others.

Yes. When I wrote some of those scenes and the dialogue in *Deliverance* I had no idea what I was actually talking about, especially when Lewis says, "The machines are going to fail. The system is going to fail." I thought now what could I mean — the machines are going to fail? How can a machine fail? But that was before the gas crisis. And the machines did fail, and could fail again — to say nothing of the oil situation in the Persian Gulf.

Well, we've established that Deliverance *was considered by some to be a poet's novel.*

I really don't know what they meant by that.

How do you see Alnilam?

A different person could have written that from *Deliverance*. It doesn't have a definitive et al. with the other book, which is fine with me because I don't like to repeat myself. I could have made a lot of money and notoriety if I had wanted to follow up *Deliverance* with a sequel. I don't believe in that sort of thing. I believe it is the business of the artist to move out into new territories. Always! Try things you haven't done before. You should be willing to fail. You should not play it safe like so many American writers do. I can name you fifty of them. They started off pretty well and have been terrified to change their direction because they'll lose the little inch they've already gained. So they end up sterile, artistically dead because they won't take a chance.

Throughout your career that is something you've done constantly — changed, and never looked back.

That's right. This is a great lesson of Picasso's. He never allowed himself to be trapped in a single style. A man who started cubism along with Picasso is Georges Braque, a good painter, maybe even a great painter, but cubism had all he ever needed. And he just developed that and refined that. I've always liked him and he's a very fine artist, but he's not Picasso. He's not the fountain, the demiurgic fountain of creativity, not pure creativity like Picasso.

You are a Southerner, but there is such a strong changing force reshaping "The South" now....

Yes. That aspect of the Southern scene is going to make some great novelist possible. I'm not the recorder of the social scene in the sense that Dos Passos, Fitzgerald, John O'Hara, or Updike are, but the person who writes this novel will have to be someone who has an interest in changing social patterns that they have. There are changes in the South that alter the way people see things and take things and experience and evaluate things — those changes are a subject of a very great interest. I suspect this will be done by a woman rather than a man. The upheaval that was caused in the South by slavery, the Civil War, and the Reconstruction, that is a very great tragic theme, and we had a writer who rose to the occasion of dealing with material that large: Faulkner. As seriously flawed as he is in some ways, he intuitively sensed, I think, though he didn't strike me as being a man of much real intelligence, that these changes could be recorded by him in his own way. That's really all the material he had and he worked it to death. But out of it came the really only big epic literature the South has produced. It could have been better, but it's pretty good as it is. The theme now is going to be the social change; it's not going to have any big upheaval like the war or any tragic time of the Reconstruction. The changes will be just as far-reaching. They have to look at the industrialization and the urbanization of the South, which until recently has been predominately rural, and the moving of people (who've been farmers) to the North to work in industry or work in the mills in their own area where they farmed the land instead of working in the factories. So all those are very strong possibilities.

There are people who think the South eventually will win the war in some way. I don't think we will have slavery again. I don't think we would have had it very long anyway if there hadn't been a war. But the issue of human enslavement is so basic and is fraught with so much horror and drama that people can't leave that alone. It did exist and it was one of the causes of the war, though some historians say no. There's not anything in the "new" change that is that dramatic, but the individual stories will have plenty of drama, too.

Do see yourself as the "old" South or the "new" South?

My sympathies are all with the "old" South. The "new" South is too much like the North. I remember what French writer Julliard Greene said, "The moment when the South truly lost the Civil War was when it consented to follow the lead of the North." They're begging for industry to come in down here to start a plant for Mack trucks. They want it bad.

I went to school at Vanderbilt, the home of the Fugitives: John Crowe Ransom, Robert Penn Warren, Allen Tate, Donald Davidson and others who were very eloquent in defense of the old Southern values and wanted to do whatever they could to prevent the industrialism on the Southern scene. They lost that. That's another war they lost, because the South is becoming less and less agrarian. They wanted a Jeffersonian situation. Jefferson wanted a nation of small farmers, what he called yeoman. He thought that would be best for us. Maybe it would. I don't know. There's no way to know now, because it's gone the other way. We have consented to follow the lead of the North, therefore, the traits we think of as Southern are dying out. The true Southern culture we think of now is way off in enclaves in the Appalachians. Some of those places have changed very little. The masses of the population are not really very Southern anymore in the sense they were even when I was growing up. The accent is still here with us. The further out in the country you move the more you can recognize certain traits from the old ways. All those will disappear, and everything will be homogenized. The idea of heaven will be for us all to meet in that great Rexall in the sky—you know, some chain drugstore or K-Mart.

But again, I'm a little divided of mind about what should have happened. I don't know what might have happened had the South refused to

industrialize. If you refuse to industrialize you don't have hospitals, you don't
have adequate medical care or very good schools. God knows what you don't
have, but you don't have a lot that we do have. Some of it is desirable, and
I suppose some people will say indispensable. If the extremist of the Fugitive
group, like Donald Davidson and Andrew Lytle had had their way, there
wouldn't be any automobiles. There would be just mules and horses and
animals. It would be hard for us to imagine living that way. All the folkways
would be preserved, the songs, and also the varieties of life presumably would
still exist. Southern businessmen and real estate operations wouldn't be trying
to cheat each other—there wouldn't be so many crooked Southern lawyers.
(*Laughing.*) I guess there are plenty of crooked lawyers everywhere, but the
Southern variety of them is particularity disgusting.

You were born in Atlanta, near Buckhead. Could you discuss your early background
as a child?

I had a happy childhood, and though it was in the Depression we weren't
deprived any more than anyone else. My mother owned some shares in a
medicine company that came down through her family, and we lived on that.
SSS is like *Geritol,* and you'd buy it at the grocery stores. The Depression
times were very good for medicine sales, because people couldn't afford doctors and they tended to do a lot of self-medication and home remedies. So,
that's where we came in. The Depression was not real hard on us. I had a
very happy childhood.

I think the happiest time of my childhood was when I was in the sixth
grade. I had just discovered sports then, playing football at every recess and
after school. My father was an ex-athlete and he encouraged that. My brother
was two years younger and he was also interested in sports. Sixth grade was
the best. The sixth grade was the last time when sandlot football was fun.
After that I was playing on teams where everything was organized. I thought
it was sacrilegious to have plays where you were supposed to carry out an
assignment on the play instead of just running out there and catching the
ball—you know, for the passer to throw the ball to whoever was open. The
regimentation of football killed it for me, and the fun of sports never came
back after the sixth grade. I played one year of football at Clemson, and then
everybody went into the service—I along with the others. When I came out
of the service I didn't go back to Clemson. I had the GI Bill and could go
anywhere I wanted. My interests had changed and I went to Vanderbilt, and
started over again as a first-term freshman.

I remember once my father had been out playing golf and we were sitting
around the fire at my grandmother's house. I was young. I couldn't even
walk. I remember there were some sticks of sugar cane that my father had
brought in from the country. The sugar canes were standing next to the golf
sticks, and they cut off a piece of sugar cane and gave it to me to suck on.
I thought my father had cut the sugar cane fragment from one of the golf

sticks. And still today I cannot look at golf sticks without getting the taste of sweetness in my mouth.

Do you play golf?

No (*laughing*), that's the closest I ever got to it.

Well, you have your favorite memory, do you have a least favorite?

Most of the bad ones are things that moved me badly that I couldn't get out of. The service, like baseball, is another form of organized tedium. Being in those huge army camps — there's just that military desolation in every direction. You think you're trapped in this thing along with hundreds of thousands of other people, and yet, some of the military was very good. You meet a lot of good people in the service. The overseas and combat time was really the best. All the training and mass action and mass response, and mass this and mass that — the regimentation was very tiresome. But overseas there was very little of that. It was free and easy. It was like belonging to a country club where the members kept getting killed instead of moving out and being transferred in their business. Then I came out and my values, I found, were mainly formed by the military. I came out of the service with two convictions: that too much regimentation from the outside is bad for people, and that responsibility is good for them.

In your poetry you like to draw on the unknown as a myth. As you get older and technology opens up those myths . . .

No. The more technology we have the more mysterious the universe becomes. We actually develop more myths through technology. That goes farther down into the human psyche than anything that technological advancements can count on. That's a matter of reasoning, the other is a matter of psyche, or what used to be called the soul. There are a lot of questions that science and inductive investigation can answer, provisional answers. They can answer the "what" in many areas, but what they will never be able to answer is the "why." Why is there anything? Why does anything exist? What is the meaning of it, if there is one? Everyone's trying to figure it out, but there's never going to be an answer to it, unless every man comes up with his own solution. Whatever this universe is, whether it's a chemist's universe or a physicist's universe or a mathematician's universe — it may be those things, and in part is in some ways — but it indubitably is a poet's universe. You could not make a set of conditions that would be better than this one. If God is anything, He's a poet. And what promoted any of this, if there was a conscious or subconscious motivation to God's creating any of this, is that He wanted it like the poet would want it. Because He Himself is the greatest of us.

Does the poetic vision grow as you get older?

It does in my case. I can do things easily now that took me the greatest labors to do before. Sometimes they're so easy I don't even want to do them. I'm still after the hard things. Those are the best.

What would that be?

I don't know. Something unsayable—to get the closest I can to the unsayable.

You have typewriters all around the house. When you walk by, do you just stop and type whatever strikes you?

I do. I have different projects in each one of them at various stages of completion. I'll look at something and say this was okay yesterday, but what I should have done is this. Then I sit down and try to do it.

You've said that writers are too self-protective, that they are afraid to work at ordinary jobs. Why is this?

I had an ordinary job for a long time working in the advertising business. If a writer is good they are so obsessed with what they are doing that they can't think that anything else could possibly be as important as that. And it's true. There isn't anything as important to them—since it's their work and their life there should be some credence in the matter. The main problem is having your mind taken away from what you consider your real concerns by doing someone else's bidding in something you don't really care anything about. I would far rather write poetry than sell Coca-Cola. Coca-Cola and these other soft drink companies like Pepsi—when you sign up with one of them and take your paycheck, you sign up in a war that's going to go on long after you're dead. (*Laughing.*) There will never be a resolution to it. And it's your life that's going down the drain. You can't let that happen.

I guess you could say that when you sign up you become a mercenary for a soft drink company.

That's right. I used to write at home at night and on weekends, write on airplanes, on vacations, mainly at night after work. I was selling my soul to the devil all day and trying to buy it back at night. That's a frantic type of an existence to go on for too many years. Wallace Stevens was an insurance lawyer and vice president of an insurance company, but it didn't seem to bother him any. It bothered me after awhile. I worked in advertising for six years in Atlanta, then received a fellowship and moved to Italy.

The story I find interesting is when you taught freshman composition at the University of Florida and you read "The Father's Body," which upset some people, so instead of being fired you left in the middle of the night.

It was a tactical error on my part. But it led to the other things that eventually led to this room right here, so I can't think it was all bad. It was "The Father's Body," a poem about a son noting the difference between his own body and his father's. It was not really sexually explicit, not really. I was Andrew Lytle's assistant at the University of Florida, but really I got the same salary as the rest of the freshman English teachers. My main commitment was to teach freshman English just like the rest of the guys were doing. A more thankless job never existed—teaching freshman English at the University of Florida. The students are so crooked; they're not allowed to write their themes on their own because they will buy one from someone else and turn it in. The fraternity houses had a whole bag of these things you could buy or rent to turn in. So they had what's called "writing labs" where the students had to sit and write their themes under the supervision of the teacher. Surely, this is a failure of something or another. I don't know—integrity. I was never so happy to get out of a place in my life. I left in the middle of the night for Jacksonville and flew to New York. I was with an ad agency the next day. I didn't know anything at all about writing advertising copy. They showed me some copy for Coca-Cola. . . "How do you like that?" they asked. "You think you can do that?" I said, "Yeah, I can do it. Asking me to write this stuff is like asking Rembrandt to draw Dick Tracy."

I don't regret it. I had some pretty good times in the ad business. I couldn't believe the money that was available. There was nothing like that in the teaching profession. They said, "You want an apartment, we'll get you an apartment. We'll get you what you want. Here's an expense account. How much do you want as a salary?" I said, "I'll take twice as much as I got as a teacher." "That's no problem." I had never been in a situation that had this set of circumstances. It was a very pleasant kind of shock that they would do this for you just as a matter of course. The only thing I've seen equal to it is Hollywood. Which is even more wasteful and extravagant than the commercial world. You never saw anything like it in your life. They're prepared to waste untold amounts of money to get some tiny thing to suit them.

When I played the part of the sheriff in *Deliverance* I got the call from wardrobe to be fitted. They had a whole closet of sheriff's uniforms. There must have been twenty-five of them. They fooled around and finally found one that fit, and I asked them what they were going to do with the rest. They said they would give them away.

How did you like acting the role of the sheriff?

I can't claim any great distinction. I liked it all right. I didn't really want to do it—we were kind of in a bind as far as the shooting schedule was concerned. They didn't have time to go get someone who knew what he was doing. It was mainly Burt Reynolds who wanted me to do it. It was his idea. The director picked up on it and I went down to see him. He said, "You have to play the sheriff. This is your story Jim. We need you to play it." I said, "I don't know anything about acting. Are you sure you want me to do this?" He said, "Yes, I do." Then I said, "Well, okay. Give me back the script and let me build up the sheriff's part." (*Laughing.*) So consequently, I was only in two scenes.

In the past you've never consented to having a favorite poem of your own — one poem you've written that you know is your best.

(*Lengthy pause.*) I think maybe some of the longer ones will outlast anything that I've done. Probably "The May Day Sermon" is the best I've ever done.

The poem you're most pleased with?

The one I tried to bring off the most and came closest to doing.

Anthologies publish what they consider your best work, which is usually "Cherry Log Road," "The Performance," "Armor," "The Heaven of Animals," which I have enjoyed, but the poem of yours that I have enjoyed reading time and again is "For the Last Wolverine."

That's good. I like that one, too. The wolverine is kind of the ultimate wild animal. I'm glad you like that one. I'm very fond of it, too. The wolverine will take on a pack of wolves; there's not anything in the north woods that will fool with him. The Indians think the wolverine is endowed with such a powerful spirit that they're afraid to kill him, because it'll come back and get after them. They won't kill him, instead they put his eyes out and turn it loose. There are strong spirits in the wolverine.

Is there anything in your writing career that you see as a mistake?

Plenty. There are millions of mistakes. I've taken wrong turns, but I've always learned from them. Most of the time I did, anyway. One of the mistakes I made was in procedure that cost me an awful lot of time and it took me a long time to learn from it. I thought, in choice of subject matter, that I could take anything and by sure verbal ledger make it valuable. I wasted a lot of time trying to salvage poems that never could have worked. Some sections and lines of the poems are very good, but the whole poem was an unviable and unworkable idea. Nobody could have made it work. I thought I could, but I couldn't. We're all amateurs, we don't live long enough to be anything else.

With the volumes that have been written about you is there anything that has been misconstrued?

Oh, lots of things. I've been pictured as being things that I am not. They're probably partly my fault. I continue to be portrayed as some Hemingway-type of a macho, outdoors man — the hunter and that sort of thing. I'm not anything like that at all. I would never want to be pulled into an orbit of that sort. That's what destroyed Hemingway. He encouraged it too much. Hemingway became much more interesting as a man than as a writer, and that's death for a person who is a writer, and whose only posterity will be in his work. When you have all the emphasis on your lifestyle and personality . . . I don't want that, I don't need that, I don't encourage it, and I'm not comfortable with it. But journalists want to do that sort of thing, and they will pick up on any opportunity to do it that they can.

Have you written your best poem?

No. You always want to write the ultimate poem.

Is there something we don't know about James Dickey?

Yes, but there's a lot that I don't know about him, too. I don't know, but if there were something like that it would have to be very dark and uncommunicable.

Clyde Edgerton

Clyde Edgerton was born in Bethesda, North Carolina, in 1944 and raised in the Durham area. He was in the United States Air Force from 1966–1971, serving as a pilot in Southeast Asia from 1970–1971. He is the author of *Raney, Walking Across Egypt,* and *The Floatplane Notebooks.* He teaches at St. Andrews Presbyterian College in Laurinburg, North Carolina. This interview was conducted at his house on December 2, 1988.

I would like to begin with your background.

I was an only child with twenty-three aunts and uncles, most of them living close to me. Two of my mother's sisters had no children, and the three of them spent a good bit of time together, so in some ways I grew up with three mothers. I was around those three women right much — still am — and they liked to talk about family and the past and their own growing up, which was around the turn of the century, so their talk influenced me in ways I didn't realize until I became a writer.

The intense drama in my life when I was growing up revolved around the alcoholism of an uncle, and also my health. The uncle lived with us off and on, my mother's brother, and would go on binge drinking sprees. I was around that and I was frightened by it. I also had a condition — urethral strictures — such that there were times when I couldn't urinate and I'd be rushed to the hospital. This happened off and on throughout my childhood until I was thirteen or fourteen when the problem simply went away. Those times when I was rushed to the hospital were dramatic. I liked baseball and hunting. My father was a bird hunter so we always had bird dogs, and there was a tradition on both sides of the family for a male to have a shotgun at age twelve.

The Baptist church was an influence in my life. I had strong feelings about good and evil, sin and redemption — had doses of all that while I was growing up. The people in the church were important to me in that they were a kind of extended family.

I was a better than average student, not exceptional. I decided to go to college after receiving an application in the mail from the University of North Carolina. I liked the color of their stationary so I decided to apply, and was accepted.

Those two things you have mentioned — the shotguns and the alcoholic uncle — play into your novels. The uncle in Raney *and the young boys buying shotguns in* The Floatplane Notebooks.

Yes. The uncle in *Raney* is similar in ways to my real uncle, although the personalities of the two characters are different. I make distinctions between real fictional characters and real life people — just as there are distinctions among real life people. A fictional person could no more be a real person than one real person could be another. My fictional characters are different from real people in ways I know and don't know about. So when someone comes to me and says my uncle is in this book, or my mother's in another, I usually try to explain about distinctions among people — real and/or fictional. Fortunately, members of my family understand this.

When did your interest in writing begin?

In high school I enjoyed reading Emerson and Thoreau for some reason. Before that, in the seventh or eighth grade I became interested in reading fiction. I remember reading sports books, *The Red Car, The Kid Fights Back.* I remember reading *Old Yeller* in school in one day. It's one of the few books I've ever read in one day. I finished it on the playground at the last recess and cried at the end of the book. That book was important to me in that it was the first to strike me so powerfully. In high school I decided I wanted to fly jets — I wanted to be a fighter pilot. I got into ROTC at Chapel Hill, and held to that ambition. But I knew I didn't want to be a military "lifer." I also wanted to teach English, and I probably unconsciously wanted to become a writer. I was a junior in college when I read *Farewell to Arms.* The narrative style led me to read all of Hemingway. I tried writing an answer to an essay question in Hemingway's style, and the comment at the end was, "C-. Short choppy sentences are not very effective."

Once I was in the Air Force my dream of flying came true, but, of course, I hadn't dreamt about a war. While I was in the Air Force I read more Hemingway, Mark Twain, and Stephen Crane. After the Air Force I went back to Chapel Hill to get a Master's of Arts in Education, taught for a year in high school, remedial students, and then went back to graduate school as a graduate assistant. I stayed in school for four years to work on a doctorate in English Education. I got out of the Air Force in 1971; finished the doctorate in 1977. This is all between 1971–77. I fiddled a little bit with short stories and novels in there somewhere, but I never could finish anything.

In 1975 I married Susan Kitchin. She brought to me, among other things, her love for traditional American music and Southern writers, particularly Flannery O'Connor and Eudora Welty. In 1977 I got a job, and Susan and

I moved into an old house. There was a soft spot in the kitchen floor, and that Christmas I crawled under the kitchen to see what the problem was. There was an old well under there. I had some time on my hands during the holidays and I decided to write a short story about someone falling through the floor into the well. I finished that short story and was a little bit amazed. About that time I had discovered Eudora Welty's work, and on May 14, 1978, I saw her read "Why I Live at the P.O." on PBS. I decided that the next morning I would start writing short stories, seriously. That's what I wanted to do. And I did it.

The first short story about the hidden well is from your recent novel, The Floatplane Notebooks.

That first short story served as the core for *The Floatplane Notebooks.* The characters wouldn't leave my mind. The novel was finished ten years — to the day almost — after I wrote that first story.

How much of The Floatplane Notebooks *did you write before you stopped to begin the next book,* Raney?

I didn't know I had anything other than a short story or two at the time I discovered *Raney.* That summer of 1978 — my first summer of writing — I wrote four fresh stories and I tried to write each from a different point of view, because I felt I needed the practice of trying something different with each story. One of those stories became "The Club Oasis" in *The Floatplane Notebooks.* One was called "Roy Rogers," which was about a little boy who broke his finger and had to go to the hospital. That story ended up in *Raney,* completely rewritten. Then at some point I wrote a short story about Raney and Charles. I started sending the stories out in February 1979, and between Christmas 1977 and September 1981 I had finished thirteen short stories. Realizing I had enough stories about Raney to start making a book, I did, and I initially sent the stories to the major magazines until someone finally suggested I try little magazines. I continued to send short stories to little magazines, and between 1979 and 1983 I had two hundred and two rejections and six acceptances. Of the six, three were by friends. So that was my apprenticeship.

I had bits and pieces of both *Raney* and *The Floatplane Notebooks* by 1981. I had one hundred and twenty-five pages of Raney and Charles material and sent it to a friend of mine, Syliva Wilkinson. She wrote back saying it was good — to double the length. So I did. Later, Algonquin Books of Chapel Hill bought a first option, and then accepted it for publication.

Now that your books are selling very well, have you thought about a big New York publisher?

I haven't thought about a big New York publisher because what I need from a publisher is good editing and I can't imagine it could be any better than it already is. I would only go to someone else if I thought it would make my fiction better than it is. I can't imagine better editing than I get at

Algonquin. They are also small enough and close enough that I can drive over and pick up any leftover sandwiches lying around the office. Early on there was a dog at the office and I knew his name. I guess he knew mine, too.

The administrators at Campbell University, where you previously taught, provided a little trouble for you over the publication of Raney. *Could you discuss what happened and why?*

Three administrators at the college read the book — or parts of it — and called me into a meeting to tell me, among other things, that they were withholding my yearly contract. They felt the novel "caricatured part of the body of Christ," which meant make fun of Freewill Baptists. Number two: they said the book "showed a clash between the new and the old with the new replacing the old." Number three: the book depicted "alcohol as a catalyst." Those were their problems with the book. Then they followed a statement of those problems up with a question: How does the book further the purpose of the university? At that initial meeting I refused to answer the question. I asked if my answer had anything to do with the granting of my teaching contract? They said it did. Over the next few weeks I did several newspaper interviews about the book — which had just been published, but I did not say anything about this problem I was having with the university administrators. After three weeks I was asked in an interview how the college had reacted to the book, and I said my contract had been withheld and was still being withheld. For the next two months it was big press in North Carolina.

I felt my academic freedom had been abridged, but I wanted to have an impartial hearing into whether or not that was true. I found out Campbell University did not have a grievance procedure for nontenured faculty members. This added insult to injury. I went to the dean, provost, and president asking for an impartial hearing. It was denied at all levels, and I resigned.

You had taught there eight years. Did you have tenure?

I didn't have tenure. I had been promoted before my time, had nothing against me, and everything was positive in terms of evaluation. But tenure was granted on a percentage basis, and too many people in my department had tenure according to the administration. My wife was without a job, because her five-year instructor position at North Carolina State University had been completed. I had a two-year-old child, and was confronting administrators who were holding back my contract. I didn't know if I would be able to keep my job, and if I did, I did not know what the contract would say, because of a book I had written. I was very upset. Then when I was told I *would* get a contract, I was told it would be with an attached letter. I didn't know what that meant. I thought it was unfair. I thought it could have been handled in a fair way and it wasn't. Louis Rubin wrote fifty letters and sent them along with fifty copies of *Raney* to fifty heads of English departments in the Southeast, and out of that I got a job at St. Andrews College. Of course

the administrators at Campbell never asked anybody in the English department what they thought of my novel. I imagine that's because the answers
would have been irrelevant to the administration.

What's your relationship with the administrators now?

There is no relationship, except occasionally in the press. Most recently,
in a negative article about Campbell, the college president was interviewed
and my name was brought up. He said, "I understand he's coming out with
a new book. I don't want to help him sell it." Odd thing to say. I've never
minded his opinions of my books — the problem is the way he and his two colleagues acted as *representatives of a university.* I was in the military for five years,
and believe me, I can smell the similarities.

*You were a pilot in the U.S. Air Force during the Vietnam War, which is one sub-
ject of* The Floatplane Notebooks.

That was a very difficult book to finish so that in the end it wouldn't look
difficult to write. As a writer I wanted to write a book that was easy to read,
though maybe not easily thought about, and get all the stories and angles into
one book. That was not easy. It took many large drafts over quite a few
years.

At one point, Susan and I saw a fellow in a homebuilt floatplane. It was
similar to the one in the book with a lawn chair bolted into it. The guy — Tom
Purcell, I later found out — wore waders and a blue motorcycle helmet. He
cranked the aircraft with a lawn mower rope — almost too good to be true —
almost too far-out to work in fiction. This along with needing to write about
the Vietnam War, a family, and a family graveyard, seemed to be important
to me. I had eighty pages towards the end of the book about the air war, pilots
talking . . . and it turned out to be extraneous for the reader, so I took about
seventy pages out. I might use it later, but right now it's dead wood.

*Your novels are set in small towns. How important is the small town for you and
for the characters in relation to their motives, actions, thoughts . . . ?*

The small town is what I know better than the big town or no town, so
that's what I have to write about mostly. If I have a character in my mind
he's probably going to live in a small town without me having much to say
about it. I don't consciously decide that a character is going to live in a small
town or a big town or no town. That's secondary. Location is a tool which
helps me tell the story of my characters. A small community is what I know
about, where I grew up. But in a sense there are small communities in all big
towns, I suppose.

*Do you think your characters could live in a small town in New England or
California — transcending those established boundaries?*

I think my characters could live anywhere, however, they would be
changed by where they lived. Some of the deeper fears and hopes would be
similar anywhere. But they would surely speak and move differently and tend
to see things differently. I've received letters from people in Canada, New

Jersey, California, and Brazil saying that my characters remind them of people they know. That's reassuring. This is tricky and dangerous to say, but if there are three levels to a novel the top level has to do with customs, norms, mores of a particular culture or group. The middle level has to do with hope, and the lower level has to do with fear. You could say that the bottom two levels are more easily transferable than the upper level.

What was your childhood like?

I played baseball, organized baseball, from age nine through my freshman year at Chapel Hill. Though I had no brothers and sisters, I had plenty of friends in the neighborhood. We spent right much time in the woods playing Robin Hood. I now realize it was dangerous. We would find water reeds and put nails in the ends for arrows, then we'd make a bow and shoot the arrows at trees and things.

At one another?

No. (*Laughing.*) But for a short while we had BB gunfights. Some Yankees moved into the neighborhood with that idea. I spent a lot of time playing basketball, sandlot baseball, outside running, and as soon as I was fourteen I was out hunting by myself and with friends in the woods, quail hunting. I had a bird dog. I didn't read much as a child. My mother read Bible stories to me. Starting in the seventh or eight grade I remember enjoying reading, as I mentioned earlier. I didn't consider being a writer. I wanted to be a fireman early on, later a doctor, and finally a jet pilot. I first liked fire trucks, then white clothes, then jets.

Of the characters in your books which one do you think you are most like and why?

I'd say I'm most like a combination of four characters: Raney, Charles, Mark and Meredith. That's a hard question. None of them may think they're at all like me.

I would have fallen out of the chair laughing if you had said Wesley.

My new book, *Bottleneck,* is about Wesley, and when I finish I might choose him. It appears that Wesley wants to become a preacher and he's reading the Bible for the first time, and each time he reads something he preaches about it and he's recording it on a cassette recorder. He's in love with a woman who weighs over three hundred pounds. He meets an evangelist named Markham Thorpe at the local grill; he's in an interracial band that plays four kinds of music: rhythm and blues, country club music, white gospel music, and black gospel music. Mattie will be in a rest home, but Wesley visits her. She got him involved in the church through her care and love and through her discussions of Jesus. This was a profound experience for Wesley who had no family. So he becomes attached to the church, but then he becomes a little bit disenchanted with the Baptist church, and starts to read the Bible on his own, drawing his own conclusions. He's enthusiastic enough about what he reads to want to become a preacher.

What has the success of your novels done for you?

Fogged up my time. There's a lot of phone and mail stuff. Traveling to promote the books has become more difficult, and partly as a consequence of that I became sick this fall with something like mononucleosis. I was sick for four months of the last two years, in two and three week spells. I cancelled all my fall promotions and appearances. So the success of my books brought all that, but it has also brought in letters from readers which are meaningful and encouraging. Recently, it's allowed me to make enough money to put some more time into my writing. It's a risky business to depend on the money, because it means you have to write a book that sells very well every two years or so. A study of the lives of authors will probably demonstrate that not too many have done that. It's given me some time to write. I won't be teaching this year. I'm still on the faculty at St. Andrews, I just won't be teaching. They're very good about things. They let me write when I need to and travel when I need to, and teach when I want to.

How grueling is a book tour?

For me it's quite grueling. There is the problem of being before an audience on a Thursday afternoon at four o'clock in a store signing books, then at another signing at seven o'clock along with a reading. I put a lot of energy into readings. I read and then sometimes play my banjo. The next morning I get up to go to a junior college or university to talk to a class for an hour, then a reception, then that night another reading. You're going to sleep somewhere, but not very well. You've flown there and now you have to fly back, and you're supposed to do it all again the next week. It's the kind of thing four years ago I would have thought would be easy. You just travel somewhere, sign books, and read. No big deal. But somehow it gets tiring. I also receive a lot of requests from book clubs and groups, but I have to say no to most of them. I get several every week. At this point in my career for a short time I could quit being a writer and become a full-time traveling author. I could make a living doing that. I never understood why Mark Twain dreaded going on his last tour to pay off all his debts. He hated to go on tour, but he had all these debts and he needed to lecture to pay them off. It once sounded like a fun trip to me. I couldn't understand his reluctance, but now I understand.

Between 1966 and 1971 you were in the Air Force, and therefore you were not in the United States much during the majority of the Beatles' musical domination, as well as the rest of the British invasion, a time when the war was being protested and the LOVE generation emerged hand in hand with the psychedelic movement. Here you were in 1964 and '65 with songs like "She Loves You," "Love Me Do," and "I Want to Hold Your Hand," pretty mild, innocent songs, then six years later you return to an almost completely different social and musical presence—post-love generation gravitating into the "Me" generation of the seventies. The innocence of the fifties and early sixties had vanished. What did you think when you returned after being in the war?

I enjoyed the Beatles for the first couple of years, but their big impact was while I was out of the states, and at that time I was listening to jazz. Those things you mentioned, the love generation and the psychedelic subculture seeped in when I would return to the states, so it was not lost on me. When I was in Japan in 1968 and '69 my refrigerator had a big peace sign on it. In my quarters there was a large picture of Snoopy dancing with beads with "GROOVY" written underneath. I had graffiti on my refrigerator which reflected sentiments of the hippie movement. There was kind of an underground feeling among my pilot friends of empathy with all this, though at the same time we were flying jet fighters and wearing uniforms and had short hair, very short hair.

One example of a kind of tongue-in-cheek embracing of the movement happened in Clovis, New Mexico, in 1970 among a group of pilots in gunnery training. Along with some friends, I masterminded a hippie dance where we dressed up like hippies. I filmed it in my quarters. People were wearing wigs, beads, and all kinds of things. We had a great time, and it wasn't a put-down, it was almost as if we were saying, "We missed this, but we don't want to have missed it, so we will pretend that we're hippies." I don't suppose there were many groups of hippies dressing up like fighter pilots. Actually, I'm not sure what all of that meant. I'm sure there were hippy-haters as well as hippy-sympathizers at the dance. It was a strange time. And the moral implication of flying in a war in Southeast Asia seeped in, in spite of this physical involvement of flying a fast machine.

The voice in your novels has a great deal of compassion, but here you were fighting a war in which the citizens of the United States were opposed to and rebelling against. You mentioned the moral implication. Was there a conflict for you?

Sure, there was an internal conflict. I wasn't dropping napalm, but I was involved in directing bombers to bomb trucks on the Ho Chi Minh Trail. That's what I was doing specifically. I was a very comfortable distance away. I'm up there in the sky away from the action, firing a smoke rocket to mark a target and directing the dive bombers to bomb it. You don't see any people. Up until I went to Southeast Asia I could avoid Vietnam physically, emotionally, spiritually, and mentally by choosing my assignments. When I became involved in ROTC in 1962, Vietnam was not an issue, so I didn't have to make a moral decision. In 1966, the war was not generally unpopular, and that's when I went into intensive flight training in Texas, so I was able to avoid the issue until I got to Vietnam. Then I couldn't avoid it, and there was internal conflict and I wrote it down in journals and other places, which was some of the material taken out of *The Floatplane Notebooks* in revision. It was difficult, and there was internal conflict in other pilots. We wouldn't talk about it directly, but indirectly. We gave a great deal of credit to the enemy. When someone left Thailand to go back to the states, it was not unusual for that person during his going-away party to propose a toast to the truck drivers we were bombing. That doesn't seem kosher when you think about it from the military perspective. There were also places pilots wouldn't fly for fear of being shot down. There was an underlying sentiment that we were involved in a losing cause. When I left in 1971, I wrote down a prediction that by 1973 the war would be over and we would have lost. It was obvious that it was a no-win situation. Plus, the moral question of whether or not we should be there came on quickly after arrival.

You're involved in this day-to-day routine, which is not without pleasure, the pleasure of flying, which was the seductive aspect of the war for many pilots. The most exciting thing I've ever done in terms of physical charge is flying these aircraft. It was easy to disengage that physical charge from any kind of moral or ethical conflicts. But I did feel uneasy about, not only the big question, but a lot of small questions like: Why is it not being explained to me why I am here? And underlining this is the belief of youth that you won't be the one who is killed or shot down.

What type of restrictions were you under?

We couldn't bomb North Vietnam. So we'd watch these trucks line up at the North Vietnam-Laotian border in broad daylight. At night they'd zip across the border and then we'd try to find them during darkness or the next day.

Did you believe you would not be killed or shot down?

I didn't believe it would be me. If I had, I don't know what I would have done. No, I figured people *around* me would be shot down. And they were.

Since you didn't think it would be you, did you think it would be the guy standing on your left or right?

I said, "It's not going to be me, but unless I go out here and stop these munitions from going down the trail, or unless I'm a part of that, it might be my friend who's there in Da Nang. I could justify my actions by saying I was protecting my friend. It was an odd situation. Also, I was twenty-seven years old, coming off a childhood in which war was glorified, to be sought out. I now see proud ROTC boys, and see the never-ending cycle.

You mentioned the power of flying, and so there you were flying this great machine, enjoying directing the bombers, and you're getting a rush, a high from flying, but here are bullets and rockets that could come blazing past you and in an instant you could be dead. . . You have to think about that while you're up there flying. How did you sort out these thoughts?

I knew I *could* get hit, I just didn't think I *would*. It's a kind of anesthesia. What was so enjoyable about it at night was looking back on the day and knowing that I could have gotten hit and didn't. I got away with something. I cheated death. It was a cockiness which comes in part from being young. It's the same as when you were a child. The reason you enjoyed playing cowboys and Indians was because you just missed getting shot, and you lived and you told about it. Or if you were shot, you eventually came back to life.

When I came back from a mission after being shot at without being hit, when I could have been shot down, the drinks tasted just a little better.

Would you do it again?

No. I have no desire to do that again. But I would if I felt it was for a good cause. It's sad to have done it for a misguided cause. I've learned that there is a cemetery in North Vietnam for those who died on the Ho Chi Minh Trail.

What was the closest you ever came to being killed?

As far as I know, the closest was in training at Fort Walton Beach, Texas, at Hulbert Field in 1970. I was training in the OV-10 which was the aircraft I flew in Southeast Asia. This plane is a twin-turbo prop, a relatively small, fast aircraft, and I was flying solo one day out of the traffic pattern toward a practice range, and suddenly, probably one hundred yards in front of me across my nose, directly from left to right, flew a fighter. Instantly, I knew there was another one, because they flew in pairs all the time. I knew the other plane was behind and either to the right or to the left of the first jet. And just then he filled up my windscreen. He came so close across the nose of my plane that my whole aircraft lifted up and slammed back down in the air of his wake. When he landed he wrote down in his debriefing log that he thought he had hit me.

The drinks tasted good that day?

Yeah, they sure did. The food, too.

Any future plans?

Buy an airplane. Keep writing novels. Spend time in my home with my family. Learn to cook cornbread like Belinda McFee cooked the other night for our families.

Is there anything I haven't asked you that you would like to discuss?

This is good because we touched on things I don't normally talk about. I'm always asked why I write about women, and I end up saying it's because I grew up around a lot of women who talked and a lot of men who didn't talk much.

William Price Fox

William Price Fox was born in Waukegan, Illinois, in 1926 and lived most of his life in the South. In 1962, he began to receive national attention with his first book, *Southern Fried,* a 40-cent paperback. His other novels include *Moonshine Light, Moonshine Bright, Doctor Golf, Ruby Red, Dixiana Moon,* and *Chitlin Strut and Other Madrigals.* He also wrote the screenplay for *Cold Turkey,* a movie starring Dick Van Dyke. In 1968, he became a teacher at the Writer's Workshop at the University of Iowa, then returned to Columbia, South Carolina in 1975 as writer-in-residence at the University of South Carolina. He lives in Columbia with his wife and two children. This interview was conducted at his house on September 18, 1987.

You were born in Columbia, South Carolina. Could you discuss your background?
I went to school. (*Laughing.*) Dad's from Columbia, and Mother's from Chicago. They used to argue and separate every now and then, and then I'd go to Chicago to live a couple years, but I'd come back. I went to junior high in Illinois, came back, and went to Columbia High. I worked as a Western Union boy after Dad had left us — he joined the navy in the old Pearl Harbor days. I failed the ninth grade. The following year I passed. I quit school in the tenth grade and joined the service when I was sixteen. I took a Naval ROTC exam and passed it, but they found out I was only sixteen and wouldn't let me in. So, I took the Army test and they let me in. All of a sudden I was an aviation cadet. I was nineteen or twenty when I went back to the tenth grade. When I came back as a lieutenant after a year and a half later — they thought I was impersonating an officer and tried to put me in jail. I was a bad actor in high school. (*Laughing.*) I'd been in the service where I had money, an airplane, a chauffeur and all that stuff, and I had to go back to the tenth grade. That was pretty humiliating. But I took a test and skipped tenth, eleventh, and twelfth. From there I went on to college. I took no English. Studied engineering and didn't do very well at that. Gradually, I got

over to medieval history. I liked history very much, and majored in that—some psychology and philosophy. I got out in 1951 and went to Miami where I taught school at the Miami Military Academy. Back then you had to do everything. I taught four grades in one room, all subjects—a real thorough education there, right!? I coached all sports. It kept me busy from six in the morning until midnight—nonstop. There was no work back then so I had to do something. I quit that and went into bellhopping where I made a lot of money.

I hitchhiked to New York in 1954, and I got a job in insurance only to quit a month later. I took a test in sales, and scored pretty high. I've always tested very high, though I never did anything in school. I got a job in sales, and stayed there about nine years, selling packaging, cellophane, paper wraps, flexible packaging—*Planters Peanuts* is a perfect example. We designed the package and sold the material. It was very complicated and very competitive. I played golf for the company, and did very well. I got bored with it and began writing.

At the time you began publishing you couldn't give up the money you made selling so you kept up with that.

Yes. I didn't write until I was thirty-two or thirty-three, nothing except letters and expense reports. Now that's real fiction there. That's the greatest stuff I'll ever do. After I began writing I would visit one of my accounts—Beech Nut Chewing Gum. I never sold them anything, but I called on them a lot. The reason I went there was I could always get snowed in. I'd stay three or four days at a motel drinking beer and writing. I didn't drink much, but I could live like a king, and they'd think I was snowbound. What a loyal salesman I was.

Your relatives were bootleggers?

They were all bootleggers from way back when bootlegging was bootlegging—until the thirties. A moonshiner makes it, a bootlegger sells it. Dad was one of the real big guns down here, he and his brothers—he had eleven brothers, all in bootlegging. They ran the whole place down here. They'd make a lot of money, drink champagne, then be broke and in jail. A typical example would be that dad would get a sheriff of some small county and pay him off for a month, then build these big storage containers like DuPont has, the big eighteen-feet high containers, like a thousand gallons a day... Big, big time. This was in the thirties and forties, especially the thirties. They'd ship the whisky north, packed it in Vat 69 bottles with Vat 69 stamps on them. So, it was a big industry down here. There are a lot of politicians down here who got their money out of that.

They pretended it came from Canada. They faked all the water marks and the cartons. It was one of the biggest rackets around. It was connected with the mafia and everything else. Columbia was one of the centers for it, right down in here, because they knew how to build the big stills, they had the room, and the water nearby for cooling and refuge. Dad built a lot of the big stills, then he got caught and did a year at the state pen. While he was there he learned refrigeration mechanics, and he did that for the last twenty years of his life. It's a little like building moonshine stills with gases and plumbing. Bootlegging is a very elaborate field cause it takes in everything. Not only is it illegal, it's very complicated to make the good stuff, and package it.

So, by the time you were of age their bootlegging operations were more or less out of commission?

Pretty much, but it was still on a small scale. We sold it from our house. We had a shot house where we sold shots for twenty cents an ounce. We had a jukebox and a band in the front room.

When you first started writing you didn't really write for smaller literary magazines, did you?

No. I was working full time as a salesman living in the village in New York City. One night Bill Manville and I were drinking, and I always did a lot of jokes, and he said I should write his column. So I did a *Village Voice* thing. It was called "Tourists." They printed it on page one. The next week I must have gotten calls from five magazines to do stuff. That was it.

Having not published in smaller magazines, what kind of effect did this have? Was it beneficial or did it really make any difference?

In my case it was better, because had I gone through college and taken a lot of grammar I probably would not have written. I never had any English. I read a lot, but never got involved with tenses. (*Laughing.*) I knew the basic stuff so I was never afraid of it. I took a course under Caroline Gordon about that time. She was very good. She said not to take any college courses, just do it naturally. And when I teach I try to teach kids to write the way they speak. When you start phonying it up with fancy words it becomes too clumsy and the lines don't run the way they should. Caroline Gordon asked us to do a short story, and I did "The Pit Fight," a story my dad had told me. That came about under a weird set of circumstances that I never really talked about with anybody. It was a short story reading class, where she read Joyce, Andrew Lytle, and we'd discuss them. We read Faulkner's "The Bear." I remember very clearly how I read that story closely and realized Faulkner had never seen a bear fight a dog. He faked all that, because all of a sudden there was a confrontation, then he goes into a metaphor, and then the fight's over. It struck me that if you're going to write about a bear fighting a dog, you should damn well do it. This was naive, of course. I said, hell anyone can write like that. He doesn't know about Paris and dogs. So I wrote that story and made it very literal and exacting. And I've been looking for things like that. I began reading the writers she gave us. We read very competitively at a certain point, saying, this writer can't do this. If you look closely at any kind of action it's usually faked. Something happens on the page and action is never as active as it should be. I've read a few things. Caroline liked my story, got me an agent, and started from there.

When did you study with her?

That was 1964. I was going to dedicate the book to her but she said not to. She hated the title *Southern Fried*. It's a great commercial title, but I hate it, too. When the book came out it had a Jack Davis drawing on the front, with the hound with his ribs sticking out, chickens, and all. Fawcett published it and sent all the copies down South to the Greyhound bus stations. When they got the late reviews in the *Tribune* and the *Times* there weren't any books in New York City. We got a lot of flack because of that. The books had to be sent back to New York. We got a lot of publicity because of that, too, and I did all the talk shows. Then the book got real hot.

How many copies did you end up selling the first year?

A half million that first year, I guess. It was real cheap back then, a half dollar.

It must have taken you by surprise.

Um... yes. I got a lot of offers out of that. Then I did *Dr. Golf.* I wrote that because I wanted to get away from that Southern image.

What was Caroline Gordon's method of instruction?

She was a good reader. She had a great voice and a great way of phrasing, of extracting rhythms from a work. She picked up on that. That was probably her strongest point. She read us Flannery O'Connor before it came out, because at the time she was editing and working with her on some short stories.

Caroline's strongest thing was her point of view and voice. She always believed in some moral being there, too. At first, the class was just a reading class with short stories, then three or four of us began writing and it became a workshop.

Was she the foundation of your work after she read your short stories?

I guess so. I guess Knox Burger was more than she. He discovered Kurt Vonnegut and John D. McDonald. He was the editor of Gold Medal Books, a division of Fawcett. They did a new book every month, anything he wanted to do, so he'd try all kinds of weird things. Caroline Gordon was instrumental in getting me to read the right things, and knowing how to shape an ending on a story. She was very good with that, especially with Joyce, that "dead story," where the lines increase and roll back.

You were a Southerner living in New York City studying from a well known Southern writer. Did she effect you in that way, that Southern genre?

I don't know. I'm not sure. That may be overstated a bit. If you had some medium in your story that was Southern she wouldn't miss it. She did help in that way. If a New York writer wrote a bad article with a Bronx quality she'd pick it up right away and react against it.

When Southern Fried *came out the dust jacket had a hayseed, redneck, the dog with his ribs showing, the typical Southern stereotype. You didn't care too much for that, did you?*

No, I didn't care for that, but it sold a lot, so I didn't mind. I was so mixed up I didn't know what was going on. I thought it was kind of a joke, it came so easily. I thought someone was going to arrest me for being an imposter. It was so easy to write those stories. I didn't think the book would be reviewed at all. Matter of fact, we didn't think it would be reviewed because it came out in softcover. But it got good reviews and started selling. Still, I couldn't take it very seriously. I did *Dr. Golf* kind of tongue-in-cheek, too. I figured I was going to be a salesman the rest of my life, so I kept my job for three or four more years. In *Dixie Anna Moon* there is a little auto-biographical stuff in the first twenty pages. In New York, my office was on 250 Park Avenue and the sun would go down and cast a shadow. They were building the Banker's Trust across the street, and the higher up the building went, the more the shadow increased. I announced that when the shadow hit my building I was going to Hollywood. I had had offers to go out there, but it's hard to leave. I made a lot of money in New York, had a company car, country club... Everything was set up. I hated like hell to leave all that and start over. But I left when the shadow hit. I went to Hollywood where I had a contract for about a year with *The Beverly Hillbillies*.

Could you tell me about that?

Paul Henney wanted to do a Broadway play with *Southern Fried*. He owned *Green Acres, Petticoat Junction* and *The Beverly Hillbillies,* and he hired me to come out there as what they called a "doctor." I'd look over scripts and change things. I didn't get any credit for any of that. But while I was there I got involved with MGM and some others doing rewrites. I did some original pilots based on *Southern Fried* with Paramount and Fox. I did a movie called *Cold Turkey*. I was out in California four or five years.

Jack Davis also did the cover for Chitlin Strut, *and from what I've read you didn't like your work being lumped into that stereotyped category. I'm curious to know since* Chitlin Strut *is accompanied with those drawings, how did you feel about that?*

Well, the book is just a collection of articles anyway. I really didn't care that much about it. These are articles from magazine where I had kept the originals. They're all fairly good articles. It's just that I never believed in a book of articles — I think they're always a joke. There are two or three very good stories in *Chitlin Strut* that I like very much. I'm glad they're out there. I really didn't care for the drawings, but they didn't bother that much. If it had sold it'd have been alright, but it didn't sell.

You said in a previous interview that when you were first writing back in 1962 the country was very touchy about everything, that we were defined and had distinct regions in regards to, not only literature, but our way of life. Has this changed since then, and is the South more accessible?

It's more accessible now. I have never thought that out as much as I should have. I write about Southern things a lot, but I don't know if I'm a Southern writer. I'm not sure. I write about other things, too. I guess the fact that you live someplace means you're going to use the idiom around you. I don't necessarily subscribe to all the loss of the confederacy, all that crap. That's no longer around, I don't think. Not with me it isn't at least. Most of my friends who write are from the Midwest. TV has broken a lot of that stuff down a great deal.

So, the Southern writer, that genre is dissolving?

You don't want it to dissolve, because you like it the way it is. It's very attractive to have an area that's different than anyplace else. As long as you like that you're going to protect it. If I go up North or to Europe I become very defensive about the South. Right now I couldn't care less. That's the way it is. Certainly, writers like Welty, O'Connor, and Lee Smith — they're very Southern. You can't set a book in an area you don't know. But once you start faking an area, everything fakes, because you got to know the words, the specifics.

There are some kitchen scenes I wrote where I have a guy pour salt on the duckboards to keep from slipping. You have to know that kind of information to write it. If you use information like that the reader knows you're in the kitchen without saying, "Hey, I'm in the kitchen. This is the proof." You have to feel the scene taking place. The things you need to make that scene take place are those kinds of literal details. You can't do that if you're from Des Moines and living in Gainesville. You can't fake that. There has to be a literal gauze between you and the material.

A perfect example is your bellhop story where they set up a system to teach the new kid how to make the most tips, who to look for for the biggest tips, and who not to waste their time with. You could never have faked that had you not bellhopped.

That's right. It takes awhile to realize that everyone is stealing, and with bellhopping the person who is not stealing gets fired, because it screws up the system. Everyone is taking from someone else. It's a circle. Once some honest Jehovah Witness-type comes in and starts raising his hand to the stealing, it's all over, so they get rid of him. It's a murderous field, because there's no salary. You have to make it on your own.

What I thought was absolutely great was when the young, naive man went down and became corrupted.

(*Laughing.*) Totally corrupted! Which I think everyone is very capable of very quickly, if the price is right. Most businesses are like that, too, if people look at them closely enough. They're able to hide behind legal setups.

Where do you think the Southern writer is headed?

God, I don't know. I have no way of knowing that at all. I don't think anyone is writing that big pageant-type book anymore like Margaret Mitchell. Maybe Pat Conroy is doing it, but it seems to me writers are doing quick books. All this minimal crap has messed up things. We were getting through with that right now. There will always be a real strong Southern story, because the idiom is so strong here. You can't get away from it, and it's attractive, too, because you can say so much so quickly. I'll give you an example: I have a friend in town who writes music, though nothing is published, and he has a song about a redneck woman telling her husband it's all over and his clothes are on the back porch in a paper sack. In the middle of the song she says, "I've gone and told the children you were dead. I've even had a funeral for your side of the bed." Well, that is Southern. That could not be written in New York City. No way in the world. I was doing a show a few years ago, when someone asked me what was new in Columbia. I said, what's new in Columbia is that Burger King has introduced the croissant. He asked what does that mean? I said, "We hang around to see what the blacks are going to call it. The blacks will call it something, but the real fun is when a redneck says, 'I'll have a hamburger, a side of fries, a milk shake, and honey, put my hamburger on one of those curved biscuits.'" That's very Southern, but that changes every few years. Another thing my friend wrote was, "If you don't leave me alone I'll find someone who will." We do rhythms down here that they can't do up North, long run-on sentences with flopovers. The South will change a lot, but it will change using it's own form and specifics, which are only specific to this area.

Who do you think is the best Southern writer today?

García Márquez. (*Laughing.*)

That's a little too far South, though I enjoyed One Hundred Years of Solitude.

It's a great book. He's my favorite writer right now.

He was ten years ago.

Yeah, yeah, still is. I read it again. Lee Smith is very good.

What is it about Márquez that interests you?

Just the wildness, the tremendous imagination. He takes enormous chances, but chances you can understand. Some people take chances and then lose you; you don't know what the hell they're doing. But I can follow García Márquez, and I like the way his mind works. I don't think you can learn from any writer, I really don't. You're either in awe of them or you're bored by them. Usually, you're bored because their rhythms don't hold up. García Márquez is different, his rhythms do hold up, and he has this great pace. I'd be hard-pressed to say why he's so good, but I'm a lot better off having read him I know that. He holds up after the second and third reading. I like Davies and Márquez. I read so much student stuff, too. I also like Jane Austin a lot. I'd probably put her up there with Márquez and Davies. Flannery O'Connor, Fitzgerald, Hemingway. I don't care for Faulkner that much—he's too hard to read.

Who do you think is overrated?

Everybody probably. García Márquez and Austin have lasted. O'Connor

may last. I don't know. See, most writers are friends, so you see... I love
Catch 22. It could have been cut some, but it's a great book. I know Heller
very well, and Vonnegut. You wait ten years and see what happens. Erich
Segal's no longer around, is he?

*You've been teaching at the University of South Carolina for eleven years now, and
previously you taught at the University of Iowa. Which did you prefer?*

There are better writers out in Iowa, of course, because they're all from
all over the country. No one is from Iowa. No one! I had MacPherson and
Tracy Kidder in one class—two Pulitzer Prize winners in one group. There
are better writers in Iowa, but this is nicer for me because I like the people
more. I take off a lot, and my kid's a big little league star. It's much easier
down here.

Was it difficult in Iowa having potential Pulitzer Prize winners in your class?

Oh yeah, because they're better writers than you are and you know it.
All you do, kind of, is do what you can.

*You've said that the voice is the main idea you try to get across to your students. Why
do you feel this is most important as opposed to the characterization or point of view?*

Well, if it doesn't sound good there's no compatible reason to read except
for the character, and then you might as well read nonfiction. I think fiction
has to have a voice. Flannery O'Connor has a great voice, Fitzgerald does,
Joyce does in some things. And it has to be different, like in music. Barbra
Streisand is different than Liza Minnelli—there's that difference, and you
have to have that difference. It's got to be very distinct. You should be able
to take a paragraph of somebody's work and without their name being on it
be able to recognize it. It should be that recognizable, and it should be able
to withstand that test, otherwise it looks like Sidney Sheldon or James
Minscher, or people who make a lot of money, but are basically hack writers.
They all sound the same. Stephen King sounds like everyone else. But
O'Connor sounds like O'Connor. If a writer writes the way they talk, then
they have a chance of getting at it. If they start copying somebody or using
a thesaurus to plug in the correct word when often the wrong word is what
you want, well, then it won't work.

So, if the writer can conquer the voice than everything else will fall into place?

If you can get through that, then you know that no matter how shallow
your ideas are, they are going to come through in a much better way, and
whatever compassion you've got is going to come through. Your voice will
allow everything good in you to come through. If you force your voice then
it's like planning a novel—I'll be this far on April 2. You can see those kinds
of seams in a novel. You want it to be open.

*You've had a great deal of success with your students going on to be published. Why
have certain students succeeded?*

The ones that have been successful are the ones with tremendous energy
more than anything else, not as much talent as the ones who didn't make it

necessarily. If you have two writers, one with a lot of energy and a little talent, and the other has a lot of talent and no energy, the energy is going to pay off because they'll give that extra mile, they'll hustle. They'll become a pain in the ass to someone on the west coast or in New York until they get it published. You need that energy. You need to have the guts to send out your manuscripts in a shotgun blast. Just send it to six people at once and take a chance. I believe in that. In screenplays and dramatic plays you can submit simultaneously, but for some reason they say you can't do that with short stories — the novel is the same way. I tell my students to get the damn thing out there, send four copies out. If you get in trouble I'll take care of it. I'll say I did it or the dog did it. I mean, *Esquire* will take six months to reply sometimes. You can't afford six months every time you do an article. You've got to break all the rules, every damn one of them. It's a game.

Which way do you see writing going?

I see a lot of screenplays being written. I get the feeling there are a lot of bad movies coming out right now. God there are a lot of bad movies, and I try to see most of them. The Australians are good. I liked *Breaker Morant* and *Lonely Hearts*. Everyone's watching the VCR now, and there may be a reaction against it. People are going through the film titles pretty quickly and they won't last unless someone goes over to the Bruce Lee pile or *Porky's Revenge*. There may be a demand out of this for real good novels — there always is. The demand may be even more so, because people are getting tired of the VCR. It's amazing how quickly a movie dates itself now, especially the black and whites. You just can't watch them anymore. There will always be a big, big place for the novel.

You used to work for Western Union as a messenger boy.

That was in 1941 or '42. I was living here in Columbia. I had a little uniform, a cap and a bicycle, and I worked from four in the afternoon until two in the morning and went to school and tried to play football. That's why I failed. I've always had a job since I was eight, always doing something. It's good for you.

You've previously said that you always had jobs as a child, and that you'd do anything to get out of the bottom. What did you mean by this?

We were living in the bottom of Columbia — it was all black, near the penitentiary and the cotton mill. I didn't want to live by either one of those places. I was determined to get out of there. It wasn't a horrible way of life, it's just that I didn't want to wind up down there. I played a lot of ball and worked. I had three younger brothers I was trying to take care of. Dad was gone a lot. I had a lot of responsibility which I didn't take. I didn't do well in school, just did fair. I read a lot. I used to sit on the front porch and watch for the police for my uncle. I was small and scrawny, and I got into fights. I caddied at the golf course, sold whisky bottles to the bootleggers — when you couldn't sell whisky over the counter. We'd go in the back allies, pick up bottles, and resell them to the bootleggers. It was pretty colorful, but pretty grim.

Do you have a favorite childhood memory?

Yeah! When I was ten I was a curb hop out at the Pig Trail Inn on Broad River Road. Eventually, I got fired from there for trying to organize the curb hops into a union to get more money. Anyway, we had a fellow named Vaughn who hung around the jukebox who used to wear these gas station whites with his name on the front of his shirt, "Vaughn." He had an eighty IQ — just barely there, a real dim bulb, but he was a very pleasant guy. He used to stand next to the jukebox and sing along with the songs. The big song then was "Racing with the Moon." He would come in every night and order a Miller's High Life, because he loved to say "Miller's Hiiiigh Liiiife." He loved to say it more than anything else. He'd drink his beer and listen to the juke. Well, the PA system is right by the cash register, and the guy behind the counter would call us in for our orders. One night, Al, the cashier went to the back to break up a fight and the PA system was open. I couldn't resist it. I took the microphone and said, "Ladies and gentlemen, direct to you from Hollywood, California, Mr. Vaughn Monroe." I put him on and he sang, "Racing with the Moon." He only knew one or two lines, so he sang real muffled, "Racing with the moon, roo-roo-roo-roo-roo." I had him on for about two minutes. God, it was great. Then they came in and fired my ass. I knew right then I was destined for higher things. But they hired me back a month later.

Well, do you have a least favorite childhood memory?

We lived down in the section that was all black, and I would never let kids know I lived down there. So, I was always getting off in mysterious places. I'd say I lived over here or over there. They'd drop me off, then I'd go home the long way. No one knew where I lived. We lived in a three room house in the middle of the black section. I wasn't very happy there. That's about it.

What are you working on now?

I'm finishing a book. It's a little like the delivery in the "Chinese Baker" story — the *National Enquirer* reporter type. It's called *Coed Drinks Blood from Skull of Murdered Lover.*

That's a line from the "Chinese Baker" story.

Yeah, it's a wild damn book. It's so wild I'm afraid of it. This guy drops out of a Ph.D. program within about three pages and gets a job writing for the Midnight Enquirer.

Talk about falling off the edge.

Right off the end of the world. (*Laughing.*) The first thing he does is spend a week on the 800 leaper line. They talk to people they call leapers. That's the bottom, then it gets very complicated. And very wild. I'm finished now, but I've got to go back for a few things.

Shirley Ann Grau

Shirley Ann Grau was born in New Orleans in 1929 and raised in Montgomery, Alabama. Over the years she has painstakingly shown her dedication to the art of fiction with *The Black Prince and Other Stories, The House on Coliseum Street,* and *The Keepers of the House,* awarded the Pulitzer Prize in 1964. Her most recent collection of short stories is *Nine Women.* This interview was conducted on February 17, 1989, at her home in New Orleans.

During your writing career you have been interviewed a number of times. From those interviews is there anything that you have never been asked that you've wanted to discuss — a subject or pertinent issue interviewers have overlooked?

I don't think so, though my most ghastly experience was an interview on a television publicity tour, where it was perfectly obvious the interviewer had not read the book. The better interviewers had at least read the jacket blurb. Many of them had had two or three lines the staff shoved into their hands, and invariably they asked the exact same questions. But that's probably the demands of a thirty-second or two-minute television interview. That's when interviews go wrong. Then there are the interviews that go right. I did a very nice one that came out in *Publisher's Weekly* a couple of years ago.

When it's obvious the interviewer has not read your books, is it irritating?

Well, you feel like a perfect ass for having gotten yourself into it, but then you try to get out of it with as much grace as is possible. Mostly you just want to get out of the situation. You know it's a mistake. But then everybody has a certain amount of wasted efforts. Once I've done the interview I really don't care about it — I lose interest whether it's my work, or an interview. I don't want to look over my shoulder or look back. You know the old joke that someone is gaining on you so don't look back. I always look ahead to the next book, the next story and project. So I really don't remember too many interviews. Also, I found out to my embarrassment a couple of months ago, I don't remember the details to the plots of my early books. They don't interest me anymore.

By not remembering your earlier plots is there a possibility of rehashing old ground?

It's a logical possibility. Of course, there are so very few possible plots in fiction. In a sense we all rehash plots just because there are too few of them. It seems to me that the writer himself changes enough over the years so even if he goes back to the same location, he is most unlikely to come up with the same treatment. If he does, I'm afraid it is a sign of a writer going into his dotage. The later Faulkner really mocks the early Faulkner. Later Hemingway is a thin echo of the early Hemingway. Certainly, the later Caldwell is almost a bad imitation of good early Caldwell.

Do you think about that — worry you may repeat yourself in imitation only?

Sure. Any writer with a grain of sense worries about it. I choose to deal with it by not looking back. Once I've corrected the galleys I never look at it again. I mean, occasionally I'll go back if someone asks me a question, but I make a practice of never reading what I've written once I finish the galleys, so that it minimizes the temptation to repeat or influence yourself. Writers are always influenced by what they read. I don't particularly want to be influenced by me. The other thing I do is to try very determinedly to keep growing and changing. I don't mean in the sense of improving, but growing and changing intellectually so that I am a different person as I come to each subject. Invariably, a writer's personality gets involved in the subject. After all, the subject filters through your consciousness. So I go out of my way to change the consciousness the material filters through, and having done those two things, I have done all that I can, and I don't worry about it anymore. It's a matter of alertness, artistic integrity. If you do those things and are honest with yourself then you should be fine. Also, it's knowing when to stop writing. Age catches up with everybody. While it's true and, theoretically possible, to be really ancient and still creating extraordinary work, I can't think of any case where that is actually true.

What happens to a writer — the difference from when they were young as opposed to older when their writing has lost that passionate spark?

An imitation is always boring to begin with — it's a flawed concept. Neither Faulkner, Hemingway, nor Caldwell left personal accounts as to what happened to them. I don't believe there is any description. In many cases I think it's failing health. All fields have their time limits, not just writing. It's a truism to say that mathematicians are finished by the time they are age thirty-five.

Could you discuss your early background?

It was comfortable. It was the usual WASP middle-class background. Nothing unusual and nothing special. It was very comfortable and very unruffled. I grew up in New Orleans and in Montgomery, Alabama.

Earlier we discussed education — you had a very formal education. By today's standards your education would be exceptional, if not elite.

My education was a little old-fashioned even in the late thirties and forties when I went to school. It was a very small school in Montgomery where it was expected that Latin would start in the third grade. Greek started in the eighth or ninth grade. It was an unaccredited school, and if I were to go on to any accredited college I had to graduate from an accredited high school, so I came back to New Orleans where there was a great deal of difficultly finding a school. I was not going to give up the Latin or the Greek. Eventually, my father found those subjects in a Catholic school. They routinely taught it. There was a nun, bless her heart, who would take on an extra small class of Greek.

Then luckily at Newcomb I found a classics teacher. By then I was reasonably competent in Latin — I could take it by myself, but with Greek I was still too tentative and needed someone to help me along. After awhile just the pressure of getting credits enough to graduate cancelled that out. Also, I began to see the practical side that the country could support perhaps one new Greek Ph.D. every year. I simply did not like the odds, so I shifted to English, a field with a lot more opportunities. I haven't kept up with Latin or Greek, so short of amusing my children by reading an inscription now and then, I have no use for it.

In today's world are we able to receive as thorough an education as you did?

I don't know. It was perhaps not very practical in the sense that I have not used it, but I can dissect practically any word and tell you where it came from. That isn't very useful. I can get a dictionary to do that. It was not a practical education. No. What Latin and Greek did, because they were so very much dead languages, was supply a form of discipline, of memory training, of emotion training that made me accustomed, like scales of a piano, to working very hard over a fairly long period of time.

Has the study of Latin and Greek benefited your writing?

Probably not. The rhythms are altogether different. I remember doing some translations once, but I could never get anything in English that approached the Latin.

In the last eight to ten years you've returned to the short story, most recently publishing Nine Women.

Yes, I like the short story. It's very demanding. In the short story if you make a mistake every reader will see it. In a novel, the sheer weight of the words tends to cover mistakes. Novels are easier. I like to work with tight precise constructions. A short story is all skin and bones, the shape and construction, holding up the story. The bone structure has to be solid in a short story.

In the eighties the short story has undergone a renaissance, and I was wondering if you decided to go back to the short story because of this?

No, you have to follow your own schedule. There are writers who write to demand, who, when their publisher says they need something they produce it. That isn't the way I do it. I follow my instincts. After a bit of not writing short stories, I suppose I decided I needed to. It's a lot like going home again. Short stories are much more popular and I see more than I did years ago. It fits, perhaps, the reader's lifestyle. That's another word I despise — lifestyle. Though short stories are harder on the writer, they are easier on the reader. A short story is an evening. A novel is a good longtime commitment, and a lot of people today opt for the one-shock experience.

I have this joke I tell my friends — The 1970s was the novel decade and the '80s are the short story decade, and because our attention span continues to decrease, the 1990s will be the decade of the poet. The poem will be for the minute.

That will be the day.

Are short stories better now than thirty or forty years ago?

Yes. The best of today is better than forty or fifty years ago. The technique of writing has improved dramatically. The prose seems more flexible, and the images are more apt, better suited to say what they need to say. The technique is just extraordinary. This is just technique, without technique you can't say anything. You have got to be technically skillful to communicate.

You began your career with the short story, then began writing novels. Which are you most comfortable with?

It doesn't matter to me, because I've been at it so long that I trust my instincts and follow them. I know I started with short stories, and that was because I was frightened by the novel. After all, if I made a mistake in a short story I could toss it out with relatively little loss — your pride is undoubtedly hurt — but a novel is a major investment. It takes a great deal of intellectual arrogance to sit down and write a novel. Many people start with a novel, but they had confidence I didn't have.

How did Nine Women *come about?*

I supposed the title is a little misleading. It should be *Nine Stories about Women.* There are more than nine women in the book — we simply condensed it. I was writing short stories and realized they were all about women, so therefore, nine stories about women. I'd write a short story and put it on the shelf, then write another and put it on the shelf, and then the pile began to look thick enough for a book. I found I had nine stories about women and one which had a male protagonist. I couldn't very well call it *Nine and One.* (*Laughing.*) I pulled that story. It was a little long anyway.

The two stories from Nine Women *that fascinated me are "Housekeeper" and "Hunter."*

"Housekeeper" is based very loosely on a true incident. The plane crash is just made up. I've always wanted to do ghost stories — not quite real stories. Many writers are tempted that way. It's an attempt to expand reality, to being in another level of experience, and it is just plain fun to write ghost stories.

Have you been writing any ghost stories?

Something like that — image making, legendary stories. Oh, yes I did write a ghost story. It's called "We Three."

Yes, I remember that story.

I'm not used to thinking back. "We Three" is about an army widow and her two husbands — the first a dead one and the second a live one.

Do you have any plans to write a ghost story novel?

I don't know. I've just finished the first draft of a new novel, and it is not a ghost story. I do like short stories that have a slight tinge of unreality to them, the elements of mythmaking. I'm not sure you can sustain that for a novel, but I'd really like to try.

After you published a few short stories in Surf *how did your publishing career begin, because you didn't go the route of the small literary magazine?*

Well, I published a few stories in *Surf* and a student magazine — those stories were training exercises. Then I published "The Black Prince" in Albuquerque, and that was it. I've always known a great many people. I joke that my hobby is collecting people. So after I finished seven, eight, or nine stories, I cast around in my list of people I knew, and found a writer who sent me to her agent. And I'm still with the firm, though the agent is long dead. It was just a matter of friends and contacts. It's worked. It was luck.

What were your thoughts when publishing came so easily?

I didn't know any better.

How do you compare your current work to earlier?

I don't. I don't think it helps a writer to think about oneself as a writer. I'm always thinking ahead to the next book, to the next day — always forward. It's the only thing you can do. Looking back is just too darn dangerous.

What was your childhood like?

Very comfortable. My father was an amateur wire sculptor; my mother was a clever painter and a darn good pianist. The house had lots of books. My grandfather was a prize eccentric. One year he was going to emulate the Puritans in their first year, so off he went planting corn with fish, and cats came from fifteen miles around to dig up his garden. I don't know what the Puritans did about their beast problem, but it was a total failure and a smelly failure. Except that it was a house where eccentricity was not only tolerated, but expected, it was alright.

As a child had you ever thought about being a writer?

I remember learning to read very early. One of my grandfather's eccentricities was that children at a young age should be able to pick out the book they want to read. My grandmother didn't agree. I hunted around and came up with a red leather bound book of Shakespeare's songs. My grandfather taught me to read from that, which meant when I finally did get to school I not only could read, I had an awesome Elizabethan vocabulary which must have sounded incredibly odd to the teacher. My grandfather didn't believe in locking up books or restricting books. Period! He said if you were old enough to understand what was in it, you could read it. If you couldn't understand what was in it, it couldn't possibly matter to you. He believed if you could comprehend something you could cope with it. That was for the time a rather unusual attitude. My grandmother had a more formal view.

I have read some critics who mentioned that you have used some family scenes or characters in your books.

Only one. William Howland in *The Keepers of the House,* not only has my grandfather's name, but is patterned after him. There are stories in there that are from my family. I never do autobiography for one simple reason—there is not enough. You run out of material very quickly. That's as close as I've ever come. In the other books, stories, I get ideas from reading newspapers.

Out of your childhood do you have a favorite childhood memory?

It's one of frustration. I was very small, and the first magnolia always bloomed at the top of the tree, and hostesses loved to outdo one another to get the first magnolia. So there was a bounty out for the first magnolia for which they would pay fifty cents. That was a prodigious amount of money back then. All the kids scrambled to the top trying to get the magnolia. I was almost to the top, but had forgotten to calculate the wind. I came bumping down, banging off branches, and breaking my collar bone on the way down.

I'd hate to hear your least favorite.

Isn't that funny? After that I was grounded and I was sitting on the porch in my cast looking at that darn magnolia just glaring at me at the top of the tree. That was rather exciting, and a great adventure. I was forever walking on rooftops. When I was young I remember talks about Japanese troops, and for awhile I thought all things had M's in them, Manchuria, Marco Polo Bridge, Munich. It seemed that all the buzz words had M's. I remember all the violence of the Chinese/Japanese war, the rise of Hitler, and my father urging his family, his distant cousins in Germany to leave. I heard talk about that, but it seemed so far away. My music teacher was a Polish refugee. It was all there, the evidence of a violent world, but somehow I wasn't threatened by it. Even the Sunday when they interrupted the New York Symphony to broadcast the Pearl Harbor news. Even then it had no emotional overtones. Father went off to war, and life became more difficult, but no horrors. People are supposed to grow up with a set of horrors—I just didn't have any, even though the world was violent. One of my earliest memories is of walking under tables and looking up at the chalk marks on the underside, and being very mad that I couldn't read them. Also, drinking my first Coca-Cola out of a silver cup, my baby cup, the way the bubbles felt, tickling me, because I had never met a carbonated drink.

You don't consider yourself a Southern writer . . .

Not the way that word is generally used. I'm a writer who lives in the South, sure. There's nothing wrong with the word, it's the usage I object to.

The critics and scholars tend to categorize writers, because they have to define a writer somehow, either by region or ethnic background seems to be easiest. They also will say "woman writer." You're not pleased with these categories — woman writer or Southern writer.

Both Southern and woman have strong pejorative overtones. There is a natural antipathy between critics-scholars-writers. The scholar has to organize his material, he has to categorize, but once you categorize you do violence to the material you're organizing. It's a catch-22 situation. I have never been thrilled on this insistence on women studies, women writers, and so forth. I'm badly outnumbered on that. At the MLA convention I was impressed by, I won't exactly call it a feminist presence, but the presence of women scholars insisting the issue of "femaleness." There are good writers and bad writers who happen, incidentally, to be male or female. It seems to me that if you are going to lump all women writers into a group, you may as well lump all redheaded writers, or left-handed writers, or writers who have written more than three books. What matters is whether the book is any good. And good books are hard to come by. Anyway, the writer is not important, it's the book. I've often thought books should be published without the author's name — just numbers.

Ten years ago you said you didn't know where writing was headed, and since then, as we have been discussing, the short story has been reborn, so to speak.

Yes, the short story is so much more technically skillful. Again, I'm not sure where writing is going. That's really a critic's question. I'm not widely enough read in American letters to know. I get most of my information about the literary scene from the *Times Literary Supplement,* which is heavily balanced towards the British scene.

You're working on the new novel at this time, but after that where do you see your writing moving? Though you don't look behind you, do you like to look that far ahead?

Nope.

Who are you reading now?

I'm reading a biography of Katherine Mansfield, which is absolutely marvelous. This is an accurate picture of a women who is a more interesting person than short story writer. She was a most interesting woman — intelligent as can be. I'm also reading *Crumbs of Creation* — a very nice book on popular science. I've decided to read poetry by decades, just to organize it, so I'm now reading poetry of the forties. And I'm enjoying it. This sends me to secondhand book shops to rummage around for poetry collections.

Which poets have you enjoyed reading?

Any and all.

After you won the Pulitzer Prize for The Keepers of the House, *how did that affect you?*

I have a theory that nothing dramatic ever happens to me. Period!

Everything is always funny. For example, the local paper called me and said, "What's this about the Pulitzer Prize?" At the time I had many friends who were great practical jokers. I said, "Oh, yes, Daniel, very funny." And I hung up the phone. I sat down and began to think—it's about the right time of the year. I called Alfred Knopf and asked him about the award. He said, "Yeah, it's true, but don't get puffed up over it. It's not the Nobel Prize." That was it. It was over and done with. It really doesn't change things.

I've always lived such a chaotic life, a husband and four children, and I've always said I run a small hotel here. The house is always in chaos, so I didn't notice any significant change in the amount of time I had after I received the award as opposed to before it. In a rainstorm, what's one more thunder? There was really no change.

In mentioning running a small hotel, was it difficult managing a writing career and a family?

Yes, you get very sleepy sometimes. I will admit I once corrected proofs, back in the days when we had those enormously long galley sheets, in the pediatrician's office, because one of the children was getting shots. I just spread the galleys out on the doctor's table and corrected away. This struck the doctor as absolutely fascinating. The pediatrician and the nurses came in to see the galleys—then they were curious about the proofreader's marks. What was perfectly usual to me struck them as exotic as a Japanese scroll. Any writer with children misses a lot of sleep. But it all gets done. I've always been able to work. This morning I was up at four o'clock. I cycle my days backwards and forwards.

Though it is noisy, I do go into a room and shut the door, but I don't have to have quiet. Just so long as people are not talking to me or touching me, I can write. It's totally impossible to keep children, and now grandchildren, and run a house and keep your writing to a schedule. It would be nice if I could, and it would be more productive, but I'm not a writing machine geared only to write. Writing is part of a whole assortment of things I do, and I enjoy it just like I do anything else.

Do you write every day?

Pretty much. It isn't written on tablets of stone that one must write every day. But basically, yes. When I'm on vacation I can go a week or two without writing, but longer vacations now pose a real problem. It used to be that I would take a portable typewriter along. But computers don't travel. For longer vacations I have to figure out ways of renting a computer or somehow having access to a computer. Like so many technological events it's much less convenient. In the last year I've gone completely to the word processor, which means I have practically lost my ability to type. I'm conditioned to the speed of the word processor. After two weeks of not writing, I begin to get frightfully bored with what I am doing, and nothing begins to feel right. Then you know it's time to go back and do something. Writers are so used to the make-believe worlds they live in for so many hours a day that they just can't stand to keep away from that world.

The Black Prince and Other Stories is said by critics to be your best work. Do you agree with this?

It was the best I could do at the time. I couldn't possibly agree with that or else I would not have written anything else. Again, I just don't go back and think about my work.

Of your collective work which do you have the most fondness for as being what you consider the best?

The one I haven't written, yet. (*Laughing.*) Of course. The one that isn't finished, and possibly the one that isn't even thought of yet. To keep writing you have to think there is always something better around the corner. It's always the unborn child.

So, you have not written your best work yet?

No, or else I wouldn't bother. I don't have the money pressure other writers have. I can see if you're being paid by the word there's a great pressure to turn out volumes, but since I don't have that pressure, the one that is coming is the best. Many writers writing strictly for a living don't have that luxury. They often think: what I'm working on may not be my best, but by God it's going to be long. I have to think the best is yet to be written.

What are you working on at this moment? Earlier you mentioned a new novel.

Yes, I have just finished the first draft of a novel. Unfortunately, it's only half on the computer, so I'm having to do the drudgery of putting the rest of it on disk. It's about New Orleans in the 1930s. I haven't got a title, yet, but then it's only a first draft. This will be the first book I've written entirely on the word processor.

Do you see the word processor making a difference in the work?

I don't know, but it's destroying my eyes. I can tell you that. Of course, any mechanical device like the computer has got to have an effect. People swear they can detect when reading the King James Bible went out of fashion — they claimed to see the difference in the English prose style. It's logical to think this way in approaching a text in the computer age. The speed is marvelous, and years of listening to the "ping" on a typewriter end line, the wrap around feature is utterly delightful. Those days of the typewriter, and rewriting an entire page, forced you into a correctness which is good. So perhaps, it will produce a looser way of writing, a little less mannered, and with the price of computers coming down more people can afford them. We'll have to see. I have an Apple, and I kind of went at it backwards. I found the software I liked, then fitted it to the computer. Most software is emphatically not written for writers. And most software, like Wordstar, is very clumsy. In fact, I was just about to give up and have some young friends of mine at Rice write a program for me, when I stumbled upon Microsoft Word Processing. It was written by a human being.

After this novel that you're working on do you have any plans?

After this novel I would love to get my library in order. I think I'll take off a bit after this book. The library is quite good but it has never been cataloged, which means I know where everything is, but I'd like to put it into a standard Dewey system.

How many volumes do you have?

It's around nine thousand. They're mostly classical. I picked up many of the books in the forties as fifty cent books. I have all the early Faulkner. I'll probably look at them and think it's too much of a job, and start work on a new novel instead.

Since you don't like to look behind yourself to see where you have been, where do you see your work moving to?

There are plans that have hung around in the back of my head for years — one of those may pop up into a novel — like the ghost surreal stories. I would like to do something other than naturalistic stories. Then too I've always wanted to write a novel about the academic world. McCarthy's *Groves of Academe* and Randell Jarrell's *Pictures from an Institution* are the only two I know that are halfway decent. It must be a very difficult subject because there are very few. I'd like to write a novel involving sailboats, a sailing novel, because I like the background. Will I write any of them? I don't know. Over the years you collect a heck of a lot of ideas and plans that you stuff in the back of your head, and at certain times they pop up again. Sometimes they merge.

Most writers begin a novel without knowing where they are going and without the ending completely in mind. The story develops as they write it. Is this true for you?

No, because that way you might very well find yourself petering out. I like to have a beginning, middle, and end, and know where I start is going to lead me logically to the end. I want to know that the premise I start with I will develop logically every step of the way, and that my characters will behave true to themselves, to the selves I started with and not have them change on the way. I could write a quick first draft of the novel, perhaps, but I don't need to do that. I'm a strong believer in the logic of fiction. Things have to march according to common sense logic — with consistency. I want to be sure when I start from a point I know exactly where I am going, and go there the simplest most direct way. I know the beginning, middle, and the end, and a good many details in between. There's no way of proofing a novel until you've followed it through, and I'm not going to write a novel and find out that it shifted in the middle. That doesn't mean that characters won't jump in that you didn't expect.

Is there anything I haven't asked you that you would like to discuss?

It seems to me that people will write or won't write apart from what I say or don't say. I'm not even sure how much you can teach writing. It's one of those fields where, thank heaven, there are no rules. There are no rules, just discipline, and it's the only field I know that doesn't require any particular education. In fact, some of the best writers I know are quite dumb, but it doesn't matter. They understand the logic of fiction. There are no rules or requirements, which suits me fine, but it upsets a lot of people. Once you get over the need for rules and restrictions, writing follows. Again, every writer has his own approach, and writers are a motley crew, wildly divergent. I say that with delight, because diversity is fun.

Madison Jones

Madison Jones was born in Nashville, Tennessee, in 1925, and is the author of *The Innocent, Forest of the Night, A Buried Land, An Exile, A Cry of Absence, Passage through Gehenna,* and *Season of the Strangler. An Exile* was made into the 1967 movie *I Walk the Line* starring Gregory Peck and Tuesday Weld. He is a quiet man who chain smokes one cigarette after another, thinking and carefully choosing his words in what must be the same manner that has produced seven powerful novels. This interview was conducted at his house in Auburn, Alabama, on February 22, 1988.

Could you discuss your background?

I'm a Tennessean, born in Nashville. My father was a businessman. When I was about thirteen he bought a farm north of Nashville, where I spent a lot of time. I was educated at a public grammar school, but attended a private high school — a college preparatory school, Wallace. It had about fifty-five students from the seventh grade to the twelfth, and we studied Latin and French. I got a pretty good background from that school, even though I wasn't an earnest student. In my last year I did go elsewhere, because the old man closed the school down. He ran it for fifty years, until he was eighty. I graduated from Montgomery Bell Academy. I started college, then stopped and went to work on the farm. After awhile I decided I wanted to go back to school, but after I graduated I still thought I might want to be a farmer. I decided otherwise and went to graduate school. From there I went to Vanderbilt, and then to the University of Florida, mainly because Andrew Lytle was down there teaching and he had courses in creative writing. I thought after I got an M.A. I could get a teaching job, but I couldn't get a job, so I stayed and did all the Ph.D. work, took the exams, but never wrote the thesis. I did write a novel, but at the time I didn't know they would have accepted the novel for the Ph.D. dissertation. So I never did get the degree.

You recently retired from Auburn after teaching there for thirty-one years. How has that been working out?

146

Very well, so far. I taught there thirty-one years. Being retired gives me more time to do what I want, but I didn't lack time for writing when I taught. I taught one or two courses a quarter. For the last couple of years I taught one course in the fall, two in the winter, and one in the spring. So that was no burden. Nevertheless, it was some interference. I was tired of teaching and I always had wanted to get out of teaching, but there wasn't anything else I could do. I couldn't make enough money writing or doing anything else to support a family. I got married in my second year of graduate school, had a child nine months later, and my children began to multiply after that. We have five. So I stayed in teaching. I always said I would get out of teaching when I could. So at sixty-two I retired, and I'm not sorry.

You've been working on a family memoir.

Yes, but it isn't the kind of thing I would like to publish. It's just for my children. I finished a novel about three weeks ago—finished seriously rewriting a book I had already written, which had not been very successful. I rewrote the book and I am very pleased with what I have done with it—there were some things I should have done in the first place. It's called *Last Things*. As I had it at first it just didn't seem to work; at least some publishers didn't like it. A couple of fine critics, M.L. Rosenthal and Monroe Spears liked it very much. Their opinion helped me stay confident that essentially the book was good. It has a good deal of comedy in the beginning. It's an academic comedy concerning a graduate school professor. It turns very serious later. The professor doesn't remain a major character in the book—he disappears and then reappears at the end. He doesn't play a large part except in a thematic way.

Your books have never really gained a large audience and the acclaim critics say they should have.

No, I am afraid they have not. I wish they had. It would be awfully nice to think there are people out there who are dying to buy my books, but I haven't had that kind of fortune. Maybe things will improve. I'm not really much concerned about that though. I would prefer to sell a lot of books, but I'm more interested in writing good books and having the respect of people who know what they are talking about.

Well, how does this affect you as a writer?

In one way it has probably been a bad thing—that is, I probably would have written more books if I had felt there was a big demand. But on the other hand, I think that for this reason I have never felt much pressure to hurry or to deal with what has a chance of appealing to merely transient interest— themes that are popular at particular times. It's true that I often build a book around subject matter that which may be of contemporary concern—as for instance this book has to do with the narcotics business. That's an important matter in the book, except that's not what the book is about. The narcotics part is merely a plot device to introduce my character into an illegal world.

I wouldn't care if it were something else other than the narcotics business — I'd be just as glad. And maybe more glad, because the market is saturated with those types of plots. This could actually hurt the popularity of the book rather than help it. But it's important to the theme to have the character outside the law. In the past I often used moonshining for the same purpose. So, I'm not writing a book about narcotics for the same reasons that many current books about narcotics are written.

Monroe Spears once said in reference to you that the Tennessee-born novelist's best works seem destined to be "saluted only by the odd and usually obscure reviewer." Do you think your work has gone unnoticed and that possibly you may not receive the attention critics believe you deserve?

I think I should have more attention. I guess every writer does. And I think someday I will. The recent article in the *South Atlantic Review* is a good sign — on *Passage through Gehenna,* which is one of the least noticed of my books. I'm delighted to see an excellent article like this in a prominent journal that tries to print what they consider significant. The *South Atlantic Review* reaches a fairly large reading audience — and a quality audience.

Your work is often compared to that of the Greek tragedians as well as to modern writers such as Faulkner, Flaubert, and Hardy, but still you seem to have been neglected?

I suppose in instances where critics have mentioned the *Greek* tragedians, by and large they don't mean I'm dealing with the same subjects as the Greeks did, but simply that my formal procedure parallels theirs'. Also, my books aspire to be tragedies. And of course, it's Greek tragedy that people remember. Comparatively few Greek comedies have survived in literature. Almost from the start I somehow wanted to write tragedy and Greek tragedies took my eye early. I'm certainly not a scholar of Greek tragedy, but I've long been interested in it. My early efforts in some measure were made in that spirit. Also Thomas Hardy was an early figure I admired, and he comes about as close to writing tragedies, I suppose, as any novelist. I was at one time very interested in Hardy and hoped to write like him. *Return of the Native* is essentially a tragic book and I admire that greatly. I believe *A Cry of Absence* is a tragedy.

Your characters are very much similar to the characters of the Greek tragedies, in that they are flawed, and the character's flaws propel the story and the action.

I hope that's true. My characters' flaws set my stories in action. I believe my technique is to proceed out of the faults and flaws of the main character. In effect I ask myself, "What would be the consequences of a certain kind of flaw in the character, given certain circumstances?" That makes my job at the outset simply to invent the initial circumstances that would set in motion the logical consequences — leading to the others, and on to the ultimate catastrophe. Maybe you could call that a tragic method. Of course tragedy is something that has been rare in modern literature. A lot of books end unhappily or sadly — like Drieser's *An American Tragedy,* which ends most miserably. The trouble in *An American Tragedy* is the lack of an idea of human dignity and free will. Things are just pushed from pillar to post by pure naturalistic circumstance. So it isn't really a moral flaw — it's a failure of adaptation on the character's part. It's society's fault. He follows false values — they mold and ruin him. I hope it's the case that my characters are not just conditioned creatures who do as they must do because of the inevitability of natural laws.

As in A Cry of Absence, An Exile, Season of the Strangler, *and your other novels, your characters are caught up in a microcosm and their mental conflict is confined to a vacuum which explodes, propelling the action forward.*

You always think outward from the central character. The lesser characters are there for the purpose of the central character, and what's false in Cam, in *A Cry of Absence,* derives from the mother. So you don't actually explore how the lesser characters are shaped, you explore it all from the point of view of the mother. It's one of the terrible things that happened to modern literature, and the modern world, that there is this sense of people not really having choices of their being mere victims of conditioning, that this should be habitually accepted and manifested, not only in literature, but in political life and in every other way. This view deprives man of his dignity. His happiness is derived from being adapted perfectly to circumstances that are modified to give happiness — the kind of happiness you'd give a dog that you scrupulously care for. All this has diminished life and diminishes literature.

America, particularly has had, until fairly recently, very little in literature in the way of tragedy. There's Hawthorne and Melville, and then we have the long optimistic period with Whitman and his company, and the whole spirit of American literature until we get to Faulkner, who was a tragic writer. Anyway, there have been few enough of them. Of course — until recently — America's success as a nation has been a contributing cause. There was the idea that we could solve all the problems, that the human problems were just a matter that could be essentially solved by sets of circumstances that we could create — through proper legislation, etc. Supposedly there were no limits to the success we would achieve. That attitude is not one that can very well generate tragedy. Here, of course, is where we find one of the strengths of Southern literature. We have had a much greater sense of the tragic than any other part of the country. We think, or did think, there are things that cannot be solved. Americans generally are fond of the phrase "social problem." The very choice of the word "problem" indicates there is a solution, but in fact, to many things, political and otherwise, there is no solution. So instead of a problem, you have a dilemma — with two choices that are opposed to each other. So you take what you think is the better horn. You win and you lose at the same time. That is at the heart of tragedy — there isn't any satisfactory answer. Many things in life are simply unsolvable.

When did you begin writing A Cry of Absence?

It came out in 1971. I'm not certain about exactly what kicked it off; there is always more than one thing that kicks off a book, a couple of things that come together. There was all the civil rights uproar in the sixties when I began writing it, but that wasn't the reason for writing it, although many people did proceed to write novels about the civil rights movement. I wasn't outwardly engaged in the civil rights movement, but I was very much inwardly engaged — I felt a lot about it. The way that novel came about was that someone told me a story that seemed to fit right in, and suddenly it crystallized. I don't, and I'm certain most writers don't, start out writing a book knowing the whole story. I started out with an idea and two or three main characters, and once things began to work I started thinking of the next steps. I follow my nose once I have forty or fifty pages, follow the book's lead. Occasionally I follow the wrong lead. At a certain point in *A Cry of Absence* I went off on the wrong lead and finally threw that part away, then went back to that juncture and took a different direction. It meant discarding a couple of chapters — it was after Cam's death in the car in the garage.

In the case of *A Buried Land,* I had for a starting place an anecdote told to me about a young man who got a girl pregnant and she died from an abortion, and he tried to conceal it. That connection between flooding the valley and burying the girl was the key to dramatize burying the past, to bury the evil. Generally, our attitude now is that everything in the past was either bad or undeveloped, and the best one can do is forget it. Respect for the past is another feature of Southern literature that has emphatically diminished over the past generation. But I think that distinguished bodies of literature have a sense of the living past in the present, and decent respect for it. Our past had its serious faults, of course, but when they look back on this day from the perspective of a hundred years they're surely going to see a hell of a lot that is seriously wrong with us. Our present attitude toward the past is simply provincial.

In A Cry of Absence, A Buried Land, An Exile, Season of the Strangler, *and your other novels, you treat themes that have to do with small towns, loyalty to the past, and racial tension. Do you see these as particularly Southern themes and will they continue to be Southern themes?*

I hope they have been particularly Southern themes. The shape of things always changes, but a spirit can endure. I hope that virtues apparent in the best of our literary treatment of these themes will survive. But I want to make a point here about *how* these, or any, themes should be treated. If a book is confined to its subject in the sense that it does not transcend the circumstances of the immediate present, then you can be pretty sure it's going to be forgotten in ten or twenty years. Just think about all the books that have been the rage for awhile and counted as serious literature. You must know books formerly praised highly by respected critics that are no longer esteemed at all; you never hear them mentioned anymore. The reason, most likely, is that in spite of their authors' skills as writers, the subjects of the books have ceased to be of interest to readers. That's to say that the authors did not discover in their subjects anything that might have kept them alive and relevant to the future as well as to the present. So they are now dated and essentially tiresome. The Greek tragedies are thousands of years old and still speak to us — despite the strangeness to us of the myths they are based on. Because, at bottom they are about the choices and failings and relationships that are the common property of humanity. Without this kind of dimension, the story or novel doesn't have much chance to survive for long.

Will the Southern myth hold up?

It depends on what you mean by the Southern myth. If you mean the Southern romantic myth — that surely won't, and hasn't. But if you mean the kind of thing we find in Faulkner, that's something else. His myth of the South permeates his fiction, shapes it, and time won't destroy the kind of validity it has. It's more than just history, it's archetypal history. People caught in those kinds of dilemmas that many Southerners were caught in — that's not over with. It will happen again. Faulkner's situations are certainly associated with his myth of the American South, but notice that many countries with no cultural relationship at all to the American South have, still, a great interest in writers like Faulkner — the Japanese, for instance. They have very little in common with the Western world, the South, and yet, Faulkner, is translated into Japanese and admired and read. Obviously, the Japanese feel that Faulkner speaks to them, too.

In A Buried Land, A Cry of Absence, *and* Passage through Gehenna, *all the violence takes place offstage.*

I don't think I can say that I deliberately chose to keep the violence offstage because the Greeks did that. It was more a dramatic consideration. To show the violence would be sensationalism. The Greeks' literature, their tragedies, were not just a public amusement, they were involved with religious rites, the cultural life, and they wanted an audience not just to be excited by action, but to think. They wanted the intellectual response at the same time. And when literature, in whatever form — TV dramas or whatever — present blood-curdling action, people getting their brains beat out, the intellectual response is being lost in the process. It becomes pure sensation. Your emotions and your glands take over. The Greeks didn't want that. That was not the purpose of these very heavy thoughtful dramas. I don't want that kind of response to my work either. Serious writers want a reader's response to have a firm connection with his intelligence. I suppose that the insistence of Eliot and others on this idea is part of the reason that serious literature through most of this century is more difficult, has required more of the reader, than literature of the last century did.

Your novels deal with the changing South in the last thirty years. But with the economic boom the South has had in the last fifteen to twenty years, how does that affect the Southern writer and the southern myths?

I haven't really kept up with the newer Southern writers as much as I should. I've read them here and there, and read about them. Certainly economic and other factors have made a large difference in the newer Southern writing. Important characteristics that we formerly thought of as distinctive commonly are absent or greatly deemphasized. On the whole you don't see much about the past, for instance. You don't find much, that I know of, that conveys the sense of the tragic. All the changes, I suppose, made the differences in our writing pretty well inevitable. Of course, life in the South has greatly changed in the last few decades. The sixties made a kind of watershed. Whether or not you like the kind of noise generated, that decade was the last potent cry of the Old South. I think in the 1970s a new orientation began. There no longer is the passionate feeling there used to be about things Southern, and no longer the consuming interest in preserving traditions. I don't know how much of the Old South is left. I'm afraid that what is left that is identifiable as "Southern" is fairly superficial — a sort of formal nod to what "was." Southerners still have better manners than are common in other parts of the country. Generally, we still have the Southern accent. That may very well last. You'd think it would be completely eroded by TV, but it still holds on. I don't know how much is left. Maybe more than I think there is. There are still lots of good writers, of course, some with most impressive talents. But you know, I'm getting tired of redneck women narrating their stories — sturdy redneck women who are crude and vulgar but nevertheless admirably strong.

With the economic boom the South has seen is it a better place now than it was?

That would depend so much on your personal values. Certain kinds of dissatisfaction and disaffection now exist on a greater scale than they did three decades ago. I think this is especially noticeable in the case of black people, because in important respects integration — I think predictably — has been a failure. Their general situation has improved, but they have also lost something. They have lost, I think, for instance, a certain kind of friendship with the whites and no other kind has appeared to take its place. Economically, of course, both blacks and whites are better off. There's more of almost every material thing, things too obvious to need mentioning, and less of certain kinds of injustice. But your question is hard to answer — for me, at least. I think of things like increased educational opportunities and more widespread literacy. But I'm not sure it means much. After thirty-one years of teaching at a single university — one as good as most — I am unable to see any significant improvement in the quality of the education as liberally handed out. The students have a little more polish — and a certain knowingness they didn't have in the past. But that's about all. There have been, as I see it, some obvious and serious losses. I've mentioned our fading sense of the past. This is a loss of an important dimension of experience. And still more serious, I think, is the drastic decline — at least outside the Fundamentalist churches — of religion worth the name, with the idea of the sacred at its center. It's becoming increasingly difficult for me to see why most of the mainline churches should exist at all. Humanitarian and ethical societies could very well take care of ninety percent of their business.

Have the Southern racial attitudes changed since you wrote The Innocent *back in 1957?*

They're different, and in important respects improved. Blacks now have certain rights that they ought to have, and whites in general, especially the younger ones, are glad they do. But significant gains tend to come with corresponding losses. I've already mentioned the matter of diminished friendship between the races. It's true that there are now personal black-white friendships of a kind that's more or less new in the South; but these tend to be nervous and self-conscious, with too much forbidden ground between the friends. Also, the guarantee of civil rights did not do away with black resentment. In some cases, because of high expectations not fulfilled, nor likely to be fulfilled in the foreseeable future, these guaranteed rights simply exacerbate black resentment. The fact that in integrated schools black students, against expectations, continue to do less well than the whites is one example of this. And black resentment, of course, tends to generate a hostile response among whites.

How has your Southern upbringing influenced your fiction?

An enormous amount. It is the basis of many of my deepest feelings — some of which have been outraged, some of which have been adjusted. I just wrote a long sketch of my grandfather, describing what he was like. I plan to do the same with my other grandparents, because I would like for my children to both know about them and feel some reverence for them. But yes, the positions I hold, political and otherwise are pretty much in the spirit of my family. I have my assumptions and prejudices about the South and other matters. They determine the stance I take as a fiction writer and so, up to a point, the kind of subjects I choose and the way I handle them. I don't think a good writer just picks subjects at will. They are given to him — or maybe forced upon — according to what is in his deepest self. They are related to him and, in a way, once he has articulated them as fiction, explain him to himself. This makes his writing a kind of exploration for him and, I think, militates against the kind of writing that's directed by abstract opinion — that is, a propaganda — style of writing, that is ultimately controlled by a determination to assert something. I like to think that my kind of inherited suppositions about things has been in my favor as a fiction writer.

What was your childhood like?

Good enough. Never any material want. I was born in town and moved away to the suburbs when I was five. There were woods and fields nearby.

Later my father bought a farm. I loved it, and stayed and worked there a lot during my teens. I had a fairly happy childhood, though I was a grieved little boy, morally overscrupulous. I can't say it was a very happy childhood, because I was never carefree enough. It certainly wasn't a bad one, though.

Do you have a favorite childhood memory?

I often think that when you look back on how lovely that time was, when you've been thinking about it, you see that you weren't really happy at the time, but now it is so poignant in your memory. I have a great many poignant memories, but maybe they weren't always pleasant. I think the best way to judge your childhood is by how much you are moved by the memories.

Your family never read the Bible as anything other than the word of God — they never read it as literature. How then did you begin to write, since writing, to your family, wasn't something one did as an occupation?

To them, being a writer was about the same as being a space traveler. (*Laughing.*) My maternal grandmother wrote a little. It was all right for women to do, but it wasn't a serious consideration. The closest I ever came, before I went to college, to considering writing as an occupation was thinking about being a newspaper reporter. In my freshman year at college, my freshman English teacher told me I could write. I think that was when I first began to take it seriously. I left college, then came back into Donald Davidson's creative writing class. After two or three stories he was very encouraging. He was the kind of man who could just overwhelm you, if you were at all sympathetic. He had a lot to do with my decision to write.

A Buried Land *was republished by Second Chance Press in 1987. How do you feel about the book twenty-five years after it was first published?*

I don't have as much feeling for that book as I do others. A good many people think it's my best book. It's the one that is most ideologically fitting to the agrarian tradition. I haven't reread it and I never will. I have gone through and looked at it. As to the books I have retained warmer feelings for, I think *A Cry of Absence* is first. Maybe *A Buried Land* is the one I think the least about. I don't like the hero enough. Not that my other heroes are necessarily admirable people, though I do think that Hester in *A Cry of Absence* is admirable. *A Buried Land* just doesn't have a warm place in my heart.

In A Buried Land *the Tennessee Valley Authority touches and affects everything — the land, people, their lives, futures, their minds, farms, relationships — everything is completely destroyed, buried under, literally and metaphorically. This is occurring more and more throughout the South as it expands under the economic promise. How do you see the threat of these organizations like the TVA and the DOT, and their confiscation of land that has been in families for generations — land that the South, historically, has been loyal to?*

Of course, it's gone so far and happens so often. It's as if your whole family has been raped twenty times — you don't think much about it anymore.

This is the sort of situation that has come to be and you're not likely to get much resistance from the people whose land is being confiscated. I don't think there is any longer the old strong attachment to the land that there was. In the first place not as many people are on the land. They are an awfully small minority. And most of those seem to think more about the money they're going to get in compensation than about their loss. I suppose the farmers that are still around have such a terrible time making a living that giving up their land is made much easier. It's all a sad development — the basis of the Old World just eliminated. I guess it's as strongly stated as anywhere in *Gone with the Wind,* where Margaret Mitchell places such great emphasis on Scarlett's devotion to the land — "As long as there is the land." But that element, that theme, is all but gone.

You were influenced a great deal by the Fugitives, mainly Donald Davidson and Andrew Lytle. What other writers in that group influenced you?

In a small measure Robert Penn Warren, not personally, because I didn't really know him. I only met him a couple of times when I was young. But his books in some measure influenced me. I don't know that any of the other Fugitives influenced me in any significant way. I didn't know any others well, though late in his life Allen Tate and I became friends. I met Ransom a half dozen times.

You were friends with Flannery O'Connor. How did the two of you meet?

She wrote me a letter about my first book, and we corresponded from time to time. I went to see her several times. We became friends. I remember when she sent me a copy of *The Violent Bear It Away,* which at the time I only half understood. Which was the case with a lot of people. *Time* magazine gave it a lousy review. I didn't know how good it was until years later. There's really no way to speculate about what she might have done if she had lived longer. I can't imagine what she might have gone on to. Maybe she would have taken some sort of great leap — into something almost fundamentally different. On the other hand, she might have already said all she had to say before she died. Andrew Lytle was always fond of saying writers don't die until they've done what they have to do. Maybe that's true.

How did you feel about having An Exile *made into the movie* I Walk the Line *with Gregory Peck and Tuesday Weld?*

I felt about it the way most writers feel about movies made out of their books — you sit there and say, "That isn't right, that's not what the book does." I now think it's a much better movie than I used to think it was. You put your novel in someone else's hands and you're always painfully aware of how different the director's treatment is from your idea. They take it and make something, if not completely different, different enough so that you feel your book has been violated.

Did you have a hand in writing the screenplay or working with the movie?

Not a bit. I just sold the rights. I was on the set once while they were filming over in East Tennessee. I just watched them do one scene. I met the actors. It was disappointing. The lead actress was especially wormy looking. I watched them film one scene. They were doing it with great care, and I watched them film the same little scene about twenty times. I couldn't see anything wrong with the first time. (*Laughing.*) They made my villain a victim of poverty, which was to explain his wicked behavior. I had tried to depict him as more than just a poor man who because of circumstances, must do ugly things. I felt the script sentimentalized him.

A Cry of Absence was almost made into a movie. I stayed in Palm Springs, California, and wrote the screenplay. Then some things happened. One thing was that current movies about racial conflict were flopping. That was the main reason the project didn't come off: they didn't want to take a chance on losing money. I was told that they had Patricia Neal for the lead, but the insurance company wouldn't insure her because she had had a stroke. Anyway it never got made. I can buy the screenplay back for $2500, but why would I want it back when I wouldn't know what to do with it. (*Laughing.*)

Donald Justice

Donald Justice was born in Miami, Florida, in 1925. He attended the University of Miami, where he studied musical composition with Carl Ruggles. He received his M.A. from the University of North Carolina and a Ph.D. from the University of Iowa. In 1980, he was awarded the Pulitzer Prize for his *Selected Poems*. His other works include *The Summer Anniversaries, Night Light, Departures,* and *The Sunset Maker*. In addition to his poetry, he edited *The Collected Poems of Weldon Kees*. He returned to Florida in 1982 to teach at the University of Florida. This interview was conducted at his home in Gainesville, Florida, on February 7, 1988.

You've said in the past that you really write for the written page. I found The Sunset Maker *geared more to the spoken word.*

I've always had in mind that poetry in the modern age, that is, for several hundred years now, has been an art for the reader and speaker both. I would be hard pressed to mention a poem of mine which I don't think of as natural speech. There may be a few in which I have tried something else — something like song — something a little more rhetorical or formal in a particular way, but always for a specific purpose. Speech is the basis for most poetry that interests me.

Could you discuss your background?

I was born in Miami in 1925 in the midst of what was then a boom. I lived through the Depression in Miami. I really didn't leave the South until I graduated from college at nineteen. My parents came from south Georgia, my father from a small settlement outside Tifton, my mother from Boston. I went to several graduate schools and ended up a teacher in universities. I've taught at schools all over the country.

You didn't learn to write poetry from any specific teacher or poet. How did you learn to write — on your own?

That's how most people learn to write. It is certainly the way most people have learned throughout history. If they were going to learn to write at all it was not from a master, except perhaps from the poems already written by masters they had chosen; it was from trying out new things on their own. That's the best way to do it, probably the only way. I can't think of a single person who hasn't learned to write on their own. That doesn't mean they may not have had teachers, but the teachers have been books more often than classroom teachers, more than café cohorts and companions. Teachers may serve as examples, models of a sort, for better or worse—encouragers.

In mentioning a writer who you could think of as learning to write from a specific teacher, I tend to think of Robert Lowell, who camped out in Allen Tate's front yard—in the sense that Lowell went to Benfolly for that specific reason—to learn from Tate.

One of the things you do as a young writer, hoping to write better, is to listen to what your elders say, and even to seek them out, but I can't believe that Lowell thought that he was having lessons in the style of Tate, say, and I can't believe Tate thought that either. Nor does Tate propose it in the preparatory note for *Land of Unlikeness,* as I remember. But a man as knowing and as good a poet as Tate would certainly be worth hanging around, and for literary reasons no doubt. But as for learning to write—it's a much more secret, private process. Your example is an interesting one, but it was John Crowe Ransom at Kenyon that Lowell was in classrooms with, and I don't doubt that he must have added to his own sense of literary value and literary tradition from that experience. I don't think you see it in any specific way in his poems—maybe in his general approach to literature, but by the time of *Life Studies* even that much was mostly gone. Just in his early work.

So you would say that the writer taking the initiative to write, coupled with guidance, is the most appropriate method?

Yes. He doesn't have to camp out on somebody's lawn, though that might be an option if the older writer has a lawn and the young writer has a tent. Also, some sense of tradition and literary values counts—it comes from talking to friends, too, those who are not necessarily literary, who may not turn out to be writers at all. Some of the most interesting literary talk in my life occurred in the last two or three years of college and the first two or three years after that with people my age who didn't know any more than I did. Or in many cases knew different things. It was the exchange of fresh thoughts about art, writing, life. All that is very stimulating to a young writer. Maybe if I had had teachers as good as Allen Tate I would have felt that classrooms counted for more. I've been in a lot of classrooms, mind you.

I think university life helps the life of the writer's mind. But it's been hard to see the direct exchange taking place. Whatever benefits these are are more indirect. If some of my students have learned things from me, which I hope they have, I've also learned from them.

It hasn't been exactly a matter of learning to write, it's been more a matter of thinking, of acting—all of which in the end might end as writing. Teachers who try to dictate to their students how the act of writing must be done—and there are some who do this—are betraying the art itself, not to mention human relations.

You actually started out studying music. How did you become interested in poetry?

In the Miami of my time, there just wasn't much cultural life an adolescent interested in the arts could get into. There was a Sunday column in one of the newspapers dealing with poetry, but at a woman's club level. Nevertheless, at the age of fourteen I was grateful for even that. There's not even that much in the *Miami Herald* today, come to think of it. I knew no one else at all remotely interested in poetry, including my teachers. As for music, I did know a few other kids who played instruments, and my best friend was interested in composing. So there was a reinforcement of interest and desire in that direction; and then you could actually hear and play music yourself. I was inclined toward music rather than writing probably because it was more immediate; it was more *there*. I couldn't learn as much as I wanted to about poetry; about anything at all, for that matter, but poetry in particular. There was nobody to tell me what was what—nobody within hundreds of miles— and it took me awhile to find the right books. Just as well, probably. I tried writing, but it was obvious even to me then that I wasn't writing up to my hope and ambition. I was writing well enough in comparison to kids my age, but that was barely enough to keep going on. In college I made a few friends who were crazy about writing—as I was—and that must have been connected with my decision to give up writing music. Basically, I didn't have a good enough ear for musical composition. When I learned how much some people could actually hear I realized I wasn't hearing nearly enough.

At that young age most kids are out playing ball and climbing trees, but to be involved with the arts, didn't you feel alienated?

I had a very good childhood, looking back, still, it was very hard in Miami to find any reinforcement for an interest in the arts. What there was was minimal. School life, playground life was fine. In Miami, there are twelve months of outdoor life. Sports—I did as much of that as I could, but I happen to have a bad leg, so I couldn't do all I wanted. My life was made up of a going back and forth between the inner life and the outer life. Of course, I felt alienated at times, but I think adolescents who aren't interested in the arts feel alienated, too. I was glad to read novels; I was glad to play softball. The one didn't exclude the other. It was good to have something going on inside as well as outside.

When did your interests turn more serious?

By the time I got out of college I was thinking of myself as a writer. That was before I had written very much. (*Laughing.*) It wasn't until my midtwenties that I wrote anything I was willing to keep. I had published some things by then, but they weren't very good. I didn't write much and I still don't write very much.

Who were some of the writers that first drew you to poetry?

Contemporary writers, modern writers at first. The summer between my junior and senior year in high school I read Eliot, and I was going through anthologies of American and British poets. If I found a poem I liked I would go to the Miami Public Library and see what they had by that author. And they did have a fair selection, if not a terrific one. I read what they had. William Carlos Williams, Wallace Stevens, and some early Pound. The poets who seem to have remained important are poets who were all in those anthologies I was going through. There were poets then that I liked who no longer interest me—Carl Sandburg for one. When I was in the ninth or tenth grade I found him exciting. For someone fourteen years old, I guess he is. I really didn't like Frost much then. I have long since grown to see how good he is. But I was attracted then to the writers I thought experimental and modern. I believe that must be a common experience of the young.

Do you still believe there are no major poets writing in the United States today, or have been in the last twenty to twenty-five years?

I must have missed them. I don't think there are. Who are they? I like numerous poems written during that time, but there's nobody to put in the same league with the poets we've been mentioning: Eliot, Pound, Williams, Stevens, Frost, Hardy, Yeats. Those are major poets. Poets since then—poets I like—just don't seem to be of the same rank. I like their work somewhat, but let's be realistic.

So why haven't we produced a major poet since before the late fifties?

I don't know. Bad luck, I suppose. (*Laughing.*) I don't know if any profound analysis of the cultural or historical situation is available which might explain it. Maybe, but I haven't heard it, and I certainly am not about to come up with it myself.

In the same respect, there are poets who are extremely underrated. In the past you've mentioned Weldon Kees and Elder Olson.

Yes, I mentioned them a long time ago. It made little or no difference then and will make none now if I mention them. Too bad. Elder Olson is a good poet no one remembers. He's still alive and writing poems. Weldon Kees—there's a small number of followers; a following has developed over the years, and he is not as undervalued as he once was. I feel better about Kees. On the other hand there's been almost no critical consideration of Kees, and a great deal too much of people who don't belong on the same library shelf with him. So, in that sense, he's still ignored by academic critics, experts on the period who don't know he exists—or mistakenly don't care. Seems he's a poet's poet.

Let me ask you, without making this appear to be a baseball box score, why has his literary standing been so unappreciated? Why has it not happened for him, so to speak?

Well, two of the primary forces behind the shaping of opinion in literary life are the universities and various types of journalism, literary journalism.

Some true literature escapes the notice of these forces. I have some theories about why it does. Aside from the very bad taste of some literary journalists and academic critics, I think both camps tend to like work which they can talk easily about because the ideas involved in the work lie on the surface or because the writer can be said to *represent* something, a school or movement or trend or party. Now Weldon Kees — as a test case — doesn't fit anywhere and therefore you can't write about him easily; you actually have to read and think about the work. That's hard for some people.

Could you discuss why before Night Light *was published in 1967 you felt there was a loosening up of verse in America?*

The sixties. Everybody now seems to know what the sixties represented. What happened to verse was a minor indication of what was happening everywhere. Strangely enough, sometimes, the literature of a society actually reflects what is going on in that society. Part of *Night Light* is written in very strict forms and part in free forms, free verse. So it's both. And in the sixties, the poets of my generation who had grown up trying their best to write in traditional forms were jumping ship. I had all along been trying, as maybe they had, too, to write in free verse as well as the more traditional meters, but I found free verse very difficult. When I did finally manage to write a few poems in free verse that passed my inspection, I was glad to have been able to branch out like that. It had something to do with the pressures and tilt of the times and with what others who were writing, but not a great deal. A number of influential books came out that didn't really influence me, but which did have something to do with the little shifts and swings in the temper of the times. Lowell's *Life Studies* was a most influential example in those days — coming out in the late fifties and swiftly entering the stream of culture like an injection. I never wanted to write like *that* Lowell — but that he had done it did seem to matter to a great many people.

Would you say the whole loosening up begins in the late fifties with the Beats?

It doesn't fail to astonish me that the Beats are still thought important in the history of poetry. To me that's all sociology, or, at best, cultural history. Lowell, though, is something that happened in what I would call "poetry." In what now for a couple of decades has been called lifestyles, the Beats were crucial, but lifestyles are not to be confused with poetry.

I guess you would say that a writer such as Allen Ginsberg hasn't really contributed or changed the tide of poetry?

From my point of view, no. From the point of view of a great many people, yes.

How would describe your poetic style?

I write what I can in whatever way I can. Others have called me a formalist, and I would agree, but I like to think my sense of form is more complicated than people who don't care for a formal sort of poetry consider it to be. When I am going good, I can write in any form I can understand, which of course includes free verse. I like feeling free to do whatever I please. One of the things I please to do — often — is write in very strict forms. Style and form are not of course the same. Style is more a reflection of personality. But as far as form goes, I am open to most things. Some poets narrow their range and learn how to do one or two things well, and then do that over and over again. It's better to be open if you can.

You don't really consider yourself a Southern poet?

I don't consider myself a Southern poet — in that it means being like certain other Southern writers. But there is no way I can avoid being a Southern poet. I write poetry and I'm Southern. It might be that I would escape that fate, given the choice, but I am not given the choice.

What has defined the contemporary Southern poet in the last twenty years, in comparison to the older generation poets such as Tate, Warren, Ransom, and Davidson?

All I prefer to say on that theme is that the contemporary Southern writer needs not to be "gothic" or freaky, despite indications to the contrast — and as for trailing along after the Fugitives-Agrarians, the Southern writer was never under any obligation to accept the mindless and cruel reactionary politics which for too long was taken to be the more or less official Southern position — and was, sadly, in one form or another of certain Southern writers as well as politicians.

"Beyond the Hunting Woods" is really about leaving the South. It states, "And over the hunting woods/ That gentlemen should lose/ Not only the best in view/ But Belle and Ginger too,/ Nor home from the hunting woods/ Ever, ever come?"

It's about the crumbling of what I think of as the Southern "myth."

Your Southern myth, or the Southern myth?

A Southern myth, at least the one I had found in the literature. I was interested in it. I'm still interested in it, but I can't think of it as anything but mythic — the dream of the Fugitive-Agrarians.

If it is on a personal level it is about your leaving the South behind.

Spiritually, yes. I came from the poor South, not the aristocratic South. I believe the Fugitive-Agrarian view of the South came mainly from the aristocratic South, at least from a stock of aristocratic ambitions and desires, despite the inclusion in *I'll Take My Stand* of an essay on the virtues of the yeoman farmer, as I recall it. That South is all dream and hearsay to me. It never fitted with my experience, but it was terribly interesting to me many years ago — to read fine poems growing out of it, and to read also opinionated and narrow-minded essays that also came out of it. In graduate school I wrote my master's thesis on the Fugitives, trying to analyze their thinking as well as their writing. That's the background, you might say of "Beyond the Hunting Woods." It seems to me those gentlemen lost their way and their hunting dogs, too, as the poem says. I don't think they were seeing the South as it existed. As for me, I was living in the Midwest when I wrote that poem, but the South was still on my mind.

Have you read Close Connections?

No. I no longer read about the South.

It's Caroline Gordon's biography, and, of course, it deals with her marriage and divorce from Allen Tate, and the entire Fugitive cooperation. I was amazed at the disruptive life they led. Their lifestyle, the Tates', was maddening at times.

It must have been very hard to sustain the illusion, at least that the Agrarian aristocracy of mind was still possible in the South. Though Allen Tate returned to the South in his later years, he lived in New Jersey, New York, and Minnesota for many years. John Crowe Ransom fled an ungrateful Vanderbilt in the thirties. Robert Penn Warren became a Midwesterner, and eventually a New Englander teaching at Yale. They became more Fugitive than Agrarian. And I think reasonably so, in terms of the life of the South in the thirties and for some long while thereafter. I have no personal knowledge of life in the South in the twenties, but in the thirties it was a very hard life for the people on the little farms and in the small towns.

You mentioned the illusion of aristocracy. In reflecting Close Connections, *the Tates lived an almost aristocratic life, with one exception — they had no money. They entertained friends and writers as though there was an endless supply of goods. Though they were firmly aware of their monetary situation and produced quite a bit of what they lived on on the premises, Benfolly, they nevertheless always appeared to be neck-high with company to entertain.*

It wasn't just Southerners in the case of the Tates, either. They were very friendly with other writers, very helpful, which had to do with the Tates' character and the way literary life was conducted in those days. There were certain groups of writers who were socially very close-knit and the Tates belonged to one or two of those groups.

You studied with non–Southern writers: Robert Lowell, Karl Shapiro, John Berryman, and Yvor Winters.

As for my own teachers, Lowell, Berryman, and Shapiro each taught at the University of Iowa when I was a graduate student there. That's how I came to be in their classes. Winters was a somewhat different story. I went to graduate school at Stanford after my master's degree at North Carolina to see what I could learn, and a very good friend of mine and my wife's had gone out there the year before to study with Winters and instantaneously — yes! — became a much better writer as a result. That was thrilling to me from a distance. So we made the move out there. I sat in on Winters' classes for a year.

Come to think of it, all my teachers were non–Southern. The first poet I met was George Marion O'Donnell. He was Southern and in particular thought of himself as Southerner. He's now forgotten, but he was a very promising young poet in those days and had been a contemporary of Jarrell's at Vanderbilt. He's of what might be called the second generation of Southern intellectuals. He appeared in one of the New Directions volumes — The Five Young American Poets series — I believe in the same one that Jarrell and Berryman were in. I suppose he was the only Southern poet I met for many years.

What did you learn from each one that was uniquely different?

Well, not much to tell the truth. From Winters I learned a more severe regard for the meters than I had earlier been acquainted. It's very hard to be specific about this, but beyond the meters of poetry, I gathered in some sort of sense of poetic structure, attention to detail. I don't think Winters was, in the classroom, a very good teacher, but what he stood for, a very hard-nosed integrity and refinement of taste was important, whether one chose to agree with that taste wholly or not. Berryman was the best classroom teacher by far of those I had. I don't want to be particularly critical of other teachers that I had, but my skepticism about what can be taught specifically in a classroom about writing comes in part from my experience as a student. Partly, too, of course, from my experience as a *teacher*.

In Departures, *there appears to be a remembering of one's childhood which has been lost or reluctantly given up. In "Absences" you write, "Like the memory of scales descending the white keys of a childhood." And in "Presences" you write, "All those I remembered passed through my hands like clouds/ Clouds out of the South, familiar clouds/ But I could not hold onto them, they were drifting away,/ Everything going away in the night again and again."*

Sure, and that becomes more or less the subject of my last book, *The Sunset Maker*. But *south* in "Presences" probably doesn't mean the South we are in right now. Maybe, but I don't think so. I tend to write more about the South in the later poems in *Selected Poems* and definitely in the *Sunset Maker*. A lot of the poems in that book I wrote after moving back to Florida.

Departures, *to me, seems to be a collection of poetry of personal pain.*

Maybe. If it seems so to you, alright. But let's not blur distinctions. It's very different from D. Snodgrass's first book, *Heart's Needle*, for instance, which is openly personal. There was a whole sweep of American poetry during which a great number of poets were writing directly about personal experience, personal feelings — including pain. That was the big subject. *Departures* is ninety percent more impersonal than that. The specific personal references are limited and few, and they are expressed in such a way as to be purified a little of the personal dross. The point is not that it is personal experience. There's a distance. There's a distance on purpose — which is the way I like it. I won't deny the presence of feeling, a feeling which happens to be personal, but, well, there *are* degrees.

In the poem "1971" you were really writing about a confused America. We had just mentioned Night Light *and the loosening up of America preceding and during those times. Did we go from an America that was loosened up to one that was confused about what had just happened?*

Sure, but there has been confusion all along. "1971" — I did not put that one in *Selected Poems,* by the way — was about that point in history. That's the way things seemed then. I wrote it while living in Southern California; no doubt Southern California seemed that way. There is a reference to the Pacific looking like the edge of American civilization. Other poets have felt the same way, other people. The notes to the poem point out that it is based on an old poem by a Hungarian poet, Attila Jozsef, from the early 1930s. So, the world looked pretty much that way to Jozsef in the early thirties. Things are still confused, but now in a different way.

Something we touched briefly before — you wrote a memoir about taking piano lessons in The Sunset Maker. *What was your childhood like growing up in Miami?*

Looking back on it now, I'd say it must have been a very good childhood and growing up in Miami in those days was, if not ideal, about as close as anyone has a right to hope for. My family was poor, but that was alright. My parents were very good to me. I had friends — had a lot of fun and I learned a lot.

I've read where one of your hobbies is gambling.

Used to be, but I don't do that as much anymore. I still like playing cards, shooting dice, going to the racetrack — dog and horse. I used to be willing to play practically any card game I understood the rules of for at least small stakes. But my interest has weakened.

I've just recently taught my wife to play cribbage.

I've played that one for very small stakes. It's an excellent, fast game. You know it was invented in the seventeenth century by a poet — Sir John Suckling.

Generally speaking, in terms of other poets, you've published relatively little, only five books. You've been called a quiet poet.

Well, in fact, I could wish that a number of more prolific poets wrote less — couldn't anyone? I suppose I wish that I could write more, but I can't and I'm not going to complain about it. As for quiet, I would prefer quiet to loud any day. One of the things that drew me to Kees years ago was that he seemed like a very quiet poet. Given the choices quietness has to be a virtue.

How much of what you write do you publish?

I publish most of what I write, most of what I finish. I have a few things around I've finished but don't much care for; and I wouldn't — not yet — try to publish those. Oh, I throw away things, but then I assume even prolific poets throw things away, too.

You spend a great deal of time revising.

Now that is something I would like to change. I would like to revise less.

What is the process for you?

I've finished a few poems the day I started them. I know people usually manage to write poems that way. In fact, I know a guy who wrote over forty poems in one day. I asked him if he had published any of them and he said most had been published. Were they any good? He said sure. Now that is astonishing. I can't imagine doing that myself. I wish I *could* write a poem every day — that would be terrific — but then choose very carefully which ones to publish. It takes longer usually. "Young Girls Growing Up" was a fairly quick poem. It took maybe about three weeks. I was working on other things in the meantime. I got a good start on it and had a pretty fair draft in three or four days. Then it was a question of tightening up the phrasing, finding the right way to end it, and of course what to leave out. I left out a good deal, some of which I am now working over with the idea of making a quite different poem.

You won the Pulitzer Prize in 1980 for Selected Poems. *What does winning as prestigious award as the Pulitzer do for a poet?*

The main thing that happened in my case, I don't know about others, is that colleagues and strangers treated me with more respect without having in any way become better acquainted with me or my work. And I mean for that to sound cynical. I think prizes work like that. That's alright. I'm glad to have got it. It doesn't make you any better or worse as a poet, but it makes it easier for others to take your work seriously — sometimes of course without having to read it — and there's no harm in that. Saves them the labor.

When you look back on Selected Poems *what is the thing you think of in terms of the collection?*

I actually thought about this the other morning walking the dog, which is the time I do a certain amount of thinking. If I had to do it over again, and maybe I will, I would have left out more poems, a great many more.

What do you think is the strongest aspect of Selected Poems?

That some of the poems are good. When friends wrote me letters about the book, one of the things several of them said — and it pleases me — is that they were surprised to see that the poems fitted together, that there was a coherence they hadn't suspected before. I don't know that that's true, really, and I'm a little skeptical, but if it were so, that would be good.

What is it about The Summer Anniversaries, *your first collection published in 1960, that you find fault in?*

They were the first poems I could think of as having accomplished something in the art of verse. But that's pretty much all they did. They seem to me now apprentice work. They were poems in which I showed myself and a handful of others that I could actually write poems. Well, that's something. That's really something. But later on I did it better.

We have discussed the impersonal aspect of your work, but in The Sunset Maker *you write your childhood memoirs about learning to play the piano which is very personal. And with the poems, short stories, and painting on the front cover, it appears to be the embodiment of Donald Justice as an artist.*

Personal in the sense that the poems reflect my interests, but I would point out that the title poem is fiction. The Kafka poem you asked me to read is, so far as I can tell, impersonal. The poems based on Henry James are impersonal. On the other hand, there are poems about my music teachers that are certainly personal. There is a poem about the death of my mother, a couple of poems about a dead friend, and so on. These have personal sources, but by the time they have been made into poems they have taken on a character of impersonality. What's this hang-up over the personal anyhow?

When looking at the collection as an encompassing artistic collage of music, poems, short stories, memoirs, and the painting on the front cover — it brings together the complete artist Donald Justice where you incorporate a lot of childhood subject matter.

The front cover is really an ink drawing, though it's identified as a painting. Certainly the poems are a product of the person, but they are not written in order to put myself on display or to reveal secrets. The concerns of poems go beyond the personal. This isn't to say that they make the poems better as a result of the impersonal. As a matter of fact, I think the higher art is never strictly personal. There are deeper concerns. One might mention a telephone or a street without providing the number or the name.

I feel as though I have left the impression that I'm saying that you are a very personal writer, because I have been asking these questions. I can see, and I agree with you since you are telling me that you do not write personal poetry, but while I've read your poetry over the years I have felt this. I guess this stems from my believing that most poets write, to a large degree, out of personal experience and personal feelings.

Well, let's say that whatever personal experiences and feelings there are in my poems, they don't come out raw. The poet may not always quite understand what he is doing. But the point is never, for me, to present the personal as a case for exhibition. And there is poetry that does that. One fixed opinion I have is that fixed opinions are likely to have many exceptions, so I wouldn't want to say personal experience might damage the poem. It might not. It might even be essential in some cases, but not all.

I'd like to say that the short story in The Sunset Maker, *"The Artificial Moonlight" was extremely interesting and the metaphors for loneliness with the main character being abandoned on the island were very rich. I thought the style was very smooth. Is there a novel coming out of it by any chance?*

I'm glad to hear this because I thought the story was pretty good when I wrote it, and it got into a couple anthologies right away. But the reviews of the book of poems generally put down the prose if they mentioned it at all. Perhaps it's just that poets — or reviewers of poetry — are snobs regarding prose. I wish I *could* write a novel. If I had been able to, I would have done so — would have written a dozen. I still have dim hopes in that direction. I've started several, but the sustained labor seems to be too much for me. The conceiving, too, is hard, the planning out. You mentioned style. When I wrote that story, I certainly liked the style, but now I think it's overwritten. If I write any more fiction the style will be much plainer.

What are you working on now?

A lecture. I'm not writing any poems or fiction at the moment; I look forward to the summer. Teaching can take up a lot of time.

The simple truth of the matter is there is a great deal of hostility to writing and writers in universities. And I have prospered in universities, so I say this from the inside. There is. And that part of it one doesn't need. There often is internal dissension. There's always—I mean that—always a split between the writers and the academics. Sometimes it's unconscious or no more than half-conscious. The others sometimes don't realize the ways in which they are expressing hostility. No doubt there's a bit of envy in it. Many are failed writers themselves. There's an element of snobbery. Well, I still think teaching is an honorable life, a good life. Teaching literature, you're dealing with fine and honorable things.

Well, for the young writer, do you have any advice?

Reading is terribly important. Many young writers seem to read only what's being done now and that's a great way to get started, but I think reading from the past is absolutely essential. I've met young writers whose reading goes back only about one generation. Well, I think the hope for them cannot be strong. Knowing a great deal about literature does no harm. It may not do much direct good, of course. (*Laughing.*) But it's always a great pleasure to learn as much as you can. Always a good piece of advice for a writer is not to believe what anybody tells you. You need to find almost everything out for yourself. Whatever opinions are abroad at any given moment are likely to be wrong. The opinions of the past are likely to be better, and the opinions of the future are likely to be better still—but the opinions of the moment, well. . . .

Terry Kay

Terry Kay grew up in Royston, Georgia. His novels include *The Year the Lights Came On, After Eli,* and *Dark Thirty,* all are set in the North Georgia mountains. In addition to writing novels, he has written feature films and theatrical pieces, and served as the host on "The Southern Voice" — a 1984 public television series on Southern literature. He lives in Lilburn with his wife and children. This interview was conducted on November 2, 1986, at the Blue Ribbon Grill in Tucker, Georgia, where we ate two-handed hamburgers, drank coffee, and talked about writing.

When did you start writing?

I started in journalism in 1959, quite by accident. I was working for an insurance company in Decatur, Georgia, and I had decided to go to graduate school at Duke, but neither my wife nor I could get a job in Durham, North Carolina. I decided to take a year off. She didn't like the insurance job and neither did I. I was the worst insurance salesman in the world. She had a job teaching school, and one morning while I was still in bed she came in to tell me she was leaving for school and said, "When I come home today you better have another job." She was very definitive about it. I was in bed wondering why I was such a failure at the age of twenty-one, when there was a thump on the front door. I went to the door and picked up the *Decatur/DeKalb News,* carried it back to the bed and started reading. I found an ad that said, "Wanted: young man to learn interesting profession." I had no idea what it was and I had no idea why I made the phone call. It was a blind ad for the newspaper. They were looking for somebody to do copyboy work, so I took the job at forty dollars a week, but it didn't take me very long afterwards to realize that I could write as well as anybody on the staff. I just sort of worked my way into the fever of journalism and after two and a half years I left to work for the *Atlanta Journal.* I worked in the sports department for three years, then did film and theatre reviews for eight years.

I was in journalism for about fifteen years. I never thought of myself as a writer; I was a journalist. I really enjoyed journalism. When I left the newspaper, Jim Townsend, who was editor of the *Georgia Magazine,* heard I was leaving and asked if I would be contributing editor to the magazine. I said, "Sure, do you want me to write a movie column?" He said, "Yes, but I also want you to write. You're a writer and you don't know it, so I'm going to teach you." This went on for a number of months where I'd take in a movie column. Then he said to write a story—any story he didn't care. He expressed enough faith in me, so I felt I owed him something. I finally told him I would write a story if it could be half truth and half fiction. One afternoon I sat down and wrote a story called "I was a Teenage Quarterback or the Hoo Doo Voo Doo on Hut Hut." This was about my football experience at Royston High School where I played for a coach who was literally crazy. He was committed to an institution. I knew the story would be turned down, but to my great surprise it was not. It was accepted and ran, becoming one of the most popular pieces the magazine had ever had.

I had met Pat Conroy while doing a story on the filming of *Conrack.* He and I became real good friends and he encouraged me to write. I wrote my first book because Conroy and Jim Townsend got together one afternoon at the Point Restaurant and had a bit more to drink than they should have. They decided to force me to do something, so Pat called his editor at Houghton and Mifflin, Anne Banett, a true heavyweight in the business. She had been Tolkiens' editor. Pat told her that he had read one hundred and fifty pages of a manuscript his friend had written and they should see it. I didn't know any of this until I got a letter from Anne Banett inviting me to submit this manuscript that Pat Conroy had so praised. I didn't have a word written—not a single word. I called Conroy to see what this was all about. I was terrified to write a novel; I didn't even want to write one. We decided I should write some short stories, because Pat didn't remember what he had told her. I wrote back telling her I didn't have anything I was really satisfied with, and could I have some more time. In one month I wrote one hundred and fifty pages, four short stories held together with a very thin transitional line. I wrote her an honest cover letter saying that I wasn't really satisfied with any of them, except one story about getting electricity on the farm. I thought it would make a good book. They agreed and offered me a contract and an advance to write the book. When people ask me how to get published, I don't know how a writer gets published. Mine was pure luck.

That was *The Year the Lights Came On.* It was very successful for a first novel, selling around fifteen thousand copies. That led the way for another contract on my next book, which they did not accept. I rewrote it five times and it's been rejected five times.

In one of the depressions I had, my wife became so distressed with me, she wisely threw me out of the house with a typewriter. She told me to go find some cheap motel and start writing again. I did. And that's how *After Eli* came about. That's how I started writing. My writing wasn't planned at all, it was an accident.

Who are some of the writers whose work has influenced you?

Almost all of writing intimidates me. I can't stand to go in libraries. I find bookstores a horrible experience. I look around at all these books and think God almighty, what am I doing here instead of sitting in front of a typewriter. All writers have an impact. I'm intrigued by their knowledge and their approach to things. I think the writer I most admire, who, if I could emulate I would, which means I couldn't in a million years, but John Steinbeck has had more impact on me than any other writer. Playwrights have had a great amount of influence on me.

Such as?

Arthur Miller, Tennessee Williams, Eugene O'Neill, not because their ability to plot, but the reasons behind action. I'm more influenced by theater than the novel form. So much of the setting I write is a controlled setting. *After Eli* is really a play. It could easily be put into a play. The same with "Lights" and *Dark Thirty.*

I thought Flannery O'Connor might be an influence because she deals a lot with the grotesque — a recurring theme throughout your novels. Has she influenced your work?

No, not very much. Though I admired Flannery O'Connor and think she may be the best of all Georgia writers. I think she created grotesque for the sake of bizarre characters. I did that to a degree in *Dark Thirty,* but only in *Dark Thirty.* What surprised me a hell of a lot were the high school librarians who are horrified over how violent I am. I'm not violent. I don't write violence. What I write you perceive to be violent because of the condition that exists. I contend that my friend William Diehl will have more people killed in three pages of his genre spy novel than I will in everything I write until I die. Bill will blow them up, have eyeballs hanging off the walls, fingers and guts and everything else. Nobody ever thinks anything about it, but when it happens in my stuff people get horrified. The reason is because I write about innocent people being killed. The degree of perception of violence is directly proportional to the degree of innocence of the victim. In film when you want to set up a tense scene, you always throw somebody innocent in it. Always. If you don't, it doesn't mean a damn thing.

In *Dark Thirty,* the whole obvious story, the springboard of the story, is the Alday family murders in Donaldsonville, Georgia. Quite frankly, what the murderers did was a lot more horrifying than what I wrote. The reason I got angry enough to write about the Alday murders was the murder of Jean Buice in the park in Decatur, Georgia. If I had written what really happened to that woman... It was horrendous what really happened, how she was killed. I didn't write that. I didn't write it at all. What I wrote was mild compared to what really happened to these people. When you put it in novel form people get the idea you're making it up. All I'm doing is disguising the truth.

That's all. I think Flannery O'Connor wrote some marvelous characters. She also had the great ability to contrast characters. In writing in any form, poetry, theater, film, short story or the novel, it's nothing more than a continuation of dramatic contrast.

Immediately, I tied the first part of Dark Thirty, *the Slaughter, to the Alday family murders, and since you just mentioned it was the basis for your novel, how do you feel about the retrial proceedings that they want to start after twelve years?*

It's a tragedy they have to go through it. I think they should have anticipated this years ago. I'm surprised the main petition they've got it on is pretrial publicity. If I was arguing the case I would have argued against the prosecuting attorney and the judge being nephew and uncle. That is a more pertinent issue. Frankly, I don't think they've told a very good story about that. I guessed at a lot of the stuff in my book, and I was so accurate it wasn't funny. The preparation of the mob going in and killing those boys (the accused murderers), it was there, it happened. You'll find different sources down there, those who say it never happened, but my God I talked to the guys who had the guns. It was a brutal, horrendous murder. I'm not sure if I believe in capital punishment, except sometimes. The real questions is, what is the difference between justice and vengeance? What I learned in writing *Dark Thirty*, to me it was simple—justice is something that I do, vengeance is something that you do.

So the last scene of the novel—it's not vengeance?

It's justice. Incidentally, that scene is not made up. That's happened all over the country, just nobody's ever written about it. I heard of it, by accident from one of the gentlest men I know. It's called "stump justice." I couldn't believe it, it was the most horrifying thing I'd ever heard. I started checking it out and it's happened all over this country. It's happened in Georgia, South Carolina, New England and out West.

You've sold the movie rights to Dark Thirty.

Yes, and *After Eli*.

You've written for film before, are you writing for either?

I'm doing *After Eli*. I may wind up writing *Dark Thirty*. It's very much a business. When you've got my agent it's very much a business. It's no compromise when you say this is both an "art" and a "business." *Dark Thirty* is with an independent film company, but it's an earnest offer, the terms are very good, and you take the terms.

After Eli is the one I'm pleased with. Columbia Pictures picked it up. Taylor Hackford, the director of *An Officer and a Gentlemen*, bought the property and will direct it either next spring or next summer. They might film it in Georgia. I'm very eager to get into that project.

I try to take a very objective view of what I write. One of the problems that I have is working full-time. I too easily make compromises with the publishers. They want something and I say fine, just get off my back, because I have a pressing job to do across the street. It hurts me, I know it does. I would like someday to say, "You got nothing else to do but write. Boy, go see what you can do with it." I could make a living writing full-time. Honestly. I don't think I want to, not right now. I've responsibilities to my family.

What was your childhood like?

A splendid childhood. It was one of very hard work and discipline. My father was a farmer and a nurseryman who grew trees and shrubbery. I was the eleventh of twelve children. My family, as a whole, is a very gifted family. We worked hard. I read a lot though most of my siblings would not remember me reading, but I did read a great deal as I was growing up. We lived in the country where there was a lot of freedom. It was a joyful childhood.

Do you have a favorite childhood memory?

Though I would not have said so at the time, the thing that is closest to me is working with my father, being with him in the fields. I remember the creeks, the swamps and the fishing. I guess if I zeroed in on one thing, it would be the school. It was a junior high school, nine grades, four classrooms, a tightness of community, the childhood sweetheart. All the stuff that essentially is reflected in *The Year the Lights Came On.*

Is there something that you regard as a least favorite childhood memory?

Work! We never stopped working. I hated digging trees when the ground was half frozen in the winter time. Yet, the result of it has been helpful. It's made me something of a workaholic.

Where do you see the novel going in the future?

The novel is now, and will be more so in the future, affected by the electronic medium, particularly television and film. The language that I so cherish will not be demonstrated in the novel form anymore. I think there will be a cheapness of the language, it will be more of a plotted type of thing. You won't see those lovely, episodic novels we all grew up with and enjoyed so much. I'm not convinced people read very much. We publish a lot of books, but people don't read much. And the people who do read want some sort of instant thrill out of it. People don't care to think when they read. We're seeing the demise of literature and the rise of popular concepts.

Literature is becoming extremely esoteric.

Sure. It distresses me when someone says they read my book overnight. No they didn't. What they did was pick through it. They read the end of chapters, and now they think they know what this book is about. What they've missed was the language, the hours I spent on one sentence. They missed what I wanted to leave you with that says, "Jesus Christ! I see that, or I feel that, or I sense that." It is real sad that people choose to read only Lewis Grizzard, while Phil Williams and Mary Hood remain basically unknown. Grizzard can't compare to them; he can't change the ribbon in my typewriter. I don't mean that arrogantly, I just damn well mean it objectively.

He can't do it. He certainly might have had he dedicated himself, but he didn't. Yet, he's what people are reading.

Dr. Floyd Watkins, professor at Emory University told me, "You have to realize that you and probably a half a dozen or fewer Southern writers working today grew up in the rural South. The rest of them grew up in the suburban South. Therefore, there are not many who are going to carry on the character of the rural South. The best of writing is twenty, twenty-five years in retrospect, which means the topics that were really significant in the South are just now getting to the point where we might address them."

There are two great themes that came out of the 1950s that are as great as any theme of this century, including the Depression. That is the decentralization of the unit system where the family and community I grew up in doesn't exist anymore. It's a great question to address in the South. I also think white Southern writers have never addressed the race question. Hopefully the book I'm working on now does that. I don't know how it's going to come out. I've never had a title for a book before and I told my agent that I had a title for this book. I told him he wasn't going to like it and it's going to sound very racist, but it's not. It's a comment made by the black man in the book. It's called *The Nigger Situation.* He said I simply couldn't use it. "Why not?" I asked. It's still the working title, though they won't use it. I sent him the first one hundred and seven pages, and he called me back saying that's what the title should be. Those are things we have not addressed. Now, after twenty-five years we can address them. It's time to do it. It's okay for us to do it. It's fine to say, alright we grew up thinking we were liberal, and maybe we're not. Maybe there's that residue from the background that's still there, that's almost genetically there.

In your novels, especially with Dark Thirty, *there's the comradeship, the unification of the township and the family; it's a deep underlining in the story.*

Yes, it's very strong. The character I molded Jesse after was my father. That's why I spent a great amount of time in the barn with the history of the tools. There are two things I cannot avoid in my writing. One is family and the other is religion. That's a part of being a Southern writer. All Southerners are very impacted by religion, family, place, and what we call oral history. I don't call it oral history, it's gossip. And it's usually family gossip. I wanted to say in *Dark Thirty,* this was not the matter of a murder, but the matter of killing a culture, killing a whole family. The town suffered.

Will the family theme be prevalent in your next book?

No, ironically. The next novel will have the principle character being a loner, truly separated from his family. He lives in Vermont, where he's been for a number of years as a teacher, a professor of Southern literature at a small private college. And yet the entire action takes place in Atlanta. There is a portion, in the beginning of the book, that very heavily implies the family unity.

I've heard mention of the "Southern renaissance in literature." What do you think about that?

It seems there is a need for some Northern publication, every few years or so, to declare a new renaissance in the South. If the South had never been identified as an indigenous region for writing that would never have happened. I can't think of another part of the country that's considered a "region." There are Western writers and the Western story, but there was only one Steinbeck. The rest of them wrote cowboy stories for the most part. New England to some degree is labeled, but then you hit the big cities, New York and Boston. Maybe it's because we were defeated. There's always been a fascination with the Southern writer. When they edited my first book, *The Year the Lights Came On,* the publishers were afraid to edit it, they didn't want to ruin the southernness. They gave me total authority on the editing. I could veto anything they said. They asked me questions about what something meant. I said, "Do I have to footnote this? This is a plow. It's part of a plow." Editors are afraid of Southern writing because of the great reputation it has gained over the last fifty years. There's always a tendency for someone to come back and say, "Okay, the agrarians are dead and gone, Robert Penn Warren being the exception. There is a new breed." It's amusing to me to see that new breed declared every ten years. My contention is that if you don't make it in the first ten years, you can make it the next. I can still be part of a renaissance if I last long enough.

Is there anything I haven't asked you that you would like to discuss?

For myself I never intended to be a writer. I had many people tell me over the years that I would be a writer. In my own family I wasn't the one who was supposed to be the writer, my brother was. I don't know if there is anything to writing beyond the moment of doing it. By putting it on paper it becomes an experience that I take into myself, and when I do this I add to the capacity that is there. Everyone has that capacity.

Pat Conroy and I were at a forum at a college when someone mentioned a scene from *The Great Santini.* They said, "Mr. Conroy, this was a lovely scene, but it's got nothing at all to do with the book." Pat said, "You're right. It doesn't have anything to do with it. I could take it out and it wouldn't hurt the book at all. But you see, one of the joys of writing, one of the privileges of writing, is that you can say to a single person I care about you, or I hate your guts. And only that person will know it. In this particular scene I wanted to say to this man who coached me as a kid, I love you. That's why I put it in the book." You don't have the opportunity very often to be able to put something in a book that thousands of people will read, and maybe someday translated so that millions of people will see it.

When I wrote my first book I knew one of the main characters would be my childhood sweetheart. I had not talked to her in sixteen years, except to say hello. It was very obvious to everybody in the community that I was writing about her—I told everybody I was. But only she knew the real personal things. When I sent the book in I told the editor I was afraid that the last four or five pages of this book will be considered too much of a soap opera. But quite frankly every word happened exactly that way. Everyone who read it thought it was a sweet soap opera ending to a book. She knew exactly what it was, because I carried the manuscript to her to read before I sent it off. She read the last pages while I sat there, and she began to cry. She said, "How do you remember this? It's been so many years." Only she knew it was that personal. She said, "I didn't think you ever truly loved me or cared for me, because you broke up. But you cannot write this unless you did." I told her, "Just because we didn't run off and get married doesn't mean I didn't care." It was important for me to tell her this is what I felt. I wanted her to understand. Of all the things I've done in writing, that is the one thing I feel most triumphant about.

Marion Montgomery

Marion Montgomery was born in Thomaston, Georgia, in 1925. He began his teaching career at the University of Georgia in 1954. His books include novels, collections of poetry, and criticism: *Dry Lightning, The Wondering of Desire, Darrell, Ye Olde Bluebird, The Gull and Other Georgia Scenes, The Reflective Journey Toward Order: Essays on Dante, Wordsworth, Eliot and Others, Possum, and Other Receits for the Recovery of "Southern" Being,* and a three-volume overview, *The Prophetic Poet and the Spirit of the Age* which includes *Why Flannery O'Connor Stayed Home, Why Poe Drank Liquor,* and *Why Hawthorne Was Melancholy.* He lives in Crawford, Georgia, in a large picturesque antebellum house. This interview was conducted on January 21, 1987, in Montgomery's front sitting room.

Could you tell me when you first took an interest in writing?

That's a difficult one, because as far back as I can remember accurately, I've been interested in writing—from grammar school on. But, then, I suspect it's not unusual, if man, by definition is the creature who uses language, as Aristotle and other people have said. Naturally, if this is true, man will be interested in using language. What I mean is, I don't think an early interest necessarily distinguishes me. I've been interested in writing from grammar school on. I suspect that most children in grammar school are likely to be inclined to be poets, to make up rhymes of one sort or another.

What made you decide to become a scholar of English literature?

I don't know that I am a scholar of English literature. I would not characterize myself as a scholar. I'm, maybe, an amateur scholar with a fascination for the mind and the way the mind works, and with what other minds have said about the way the mind works. I have a curiosity about existence. My colleagues look at me askance, because I seem to have no main interest of study, and so I usually calm them by saying I'm a medievalist, which means I'm interested in all things that one may study. I don't really have a *main* interest. I'm interested in philosophy, history, poetry, fiction, geography, science.

Liberal arts studies.

Fundamentally that. Of course, the liberal arts have their roots in the middle ages.

Which one have you found the most enjoyment from?

Oh, fishing and reading, daydreaming. The point is still the same. You try to live as completely as you can. That involves not setting aside certain things as your favorite. See, to set things aside as your favorite begins to make you a specialist of some sort, and that begins to limit and narrow your options. That's what I shy away from.

You wouldn't want to be considered a specialist in any one category so that you'd be able to take advantage of all areas?

I don't believe being a specialist in one area means an advantage in all areas. But it's really up to somebody else to determine whether you're a specialist or not.

Is there a different point of view one has as a writer as opposed to the same person who is a scholar? And I used the word scholar loosely. We can change that to mean one who is interested in study.

I don't know if it is necessarily a difference in point of view. There may be a difference in the focus, but if you use metaphors like that, it's as if you're talking about a telescope or a camera lens, and the eye that's viewing is not so much changed as the mechanism through which you view. So there's that sort of difference which isn't quite a difference in "point of view."

To write a criticism or to write a poem, obviously, is not the same sort of action, but they are actions out of the same mind. It's the focusing that is likely to be different, the tentative position you take might be different. It doesn't mean that the mind doing the action is necessarily different. That's a point that's overlooked by some people who are puzzled by my writing many different kinds of things. I write poetry, novels, short stories, and criticism.

In 1981 you published The Prophetic Poet and the Spirit of the Age, *a trilogy, which included "Why Flannery O'Connor Stayed Home."*

Yeah. That was the first of three volumes. The other two are "Why Poe Drank" and "Why Hawthorne Was Melancholy." The whole thing is called *The Prophetic Poet and the Spirit of the Age.* I wanted to call it one thing and we ended up calling it another. It was originally called *The Prophetic Poet and the Popular Spirit.*

You were friends with Flannery O'Connor?

Yes. I'd like to think we were pretty good friends.

Could you tell me about your friendship with her?

Not a great deal beyond saying we were interested in the same sorts of things. Some of them are what I've just discussed about art and form. I have some of my roots in Aristotle and St. Thomas Aquinas, and that's where her roots are too in respect to art. We recognized in each other this central interest and concern. The trilogy is a way of advancing an argument which is really as much mine as hers, but it belongs to neither of us. You can't go through the trilogy without discovering that it wasn't just a position Flannery O'Connor held, but that it's a position I'm developing out of a dependence upon many artists and philosophers and theologians.

Many of the letters in The Habit of Being, *Flannery O'Connor's personal letters, are between you and her. They're quite serious and quite comical. Was she an extremely funny woman?*

Oh yes, no question. Very witty. But beyond being merely witty, she had a sense of humor. It's one thing to be witty, it's another to have both wit and humor. It's that combination that she enjoyed in Faulkner's novels.

Back to the title of the trilogy, why did Flannery O'Connor stay home?

It revolves around the question of what it means to be at home and what is involved in the home. It has to do with our whole address to creation through the focus of art and philosophy and theology. She was very comfortable where she was in Milledgeville. There was no necessity for her to live somewhere else, and what she realized was that if she went somewhere else she could well have been at home there and that it would have been essentially the same home she left. The differences in place get exaggerated in the telling of the journey—people turn out to be pretty much people wherever you encounter them.

So even when she was studying at Iowa, or living in New York City, she was basically at home?

I think she was, though she viewed those worlds with a slightly raised eyebrow, and was happy enough to come home. One of the myths of the century in relation to writers is that you have to get away from home to be a writer—you have to go to New York or Paris.

Didn't that start with Hemingway and Sherwood Anderson?

Sure. That whole crowd. What about Faulkner?

He left, but returned to write.

So did Hawthorne. So did Dante.

She attended the State University of Iowa, where she received an M.A. Do you think that upon returning from Iowa there is any specific style or idea she really took on as a result of returning to Georgia?

I don't know that you discover it at the level of style, but she undoubtedly realizes the importance of her using what is immediately at hand for use. She says at one point that if she had tried to write in a voice characteristic of the mid-West, it would have still sounded like Herman Talmadge. In addition to which, look at who taught her at Iowa, Andrew Lytle. She ran into a Southerner out of the South, and she began to realize things about her own environment. But you don't necessarily learn that lesson in a school. I don't know that she was much improved, and she was certainly not corrupted, by going to a writing school. Remember that marvelous thing she said about learning to write in "creative" schools, "There's a kind of writing you can learn to do in schools, it's the kind you then have to teach people not to read."

Would you speculate about Flannery O'Connor's work. Where might it have continued moving had she not died so young?

It's difficult and, finally, fruitless to say. It's not the sort of thing I can talk about with any comfort. I know what we have from her, and I'm thankful for that.

Okay. Not necessarily where she was going, but what did she want to do? Did she talk to you about this?

I think I can answer that reasonably well, though it doesn't have any concreteness. She wanted to keep on doing what she was doing, realizing that she would see more and learn more, not knowing what would come of it. But you see, that's exactly what she was doing from the very beginning. One grows, presumably. She said in response to the question of the nature of good, on the moral level, "good is something under construction." To an artist, art is something under construction, and you're building it. You don't have a blueprint in advance, not in this age. And she recognized this. That sets her aside from somebody like Dante. He had the prospect of an overall blueprint. That's why he could write a poem that's exactly one hundred cantos long. Dante could see the larger form of the *Divine Comedy*, partly because of the world in which he lived and the vision possible to him at that moment. Vision is always in relation to the immediacy of history and nature as you engage it. History and nature opened an order for Dante which allowed him to see the larger form. In our world we're struggling to see order and form. And it's the artist who's going to get caught up in this as it is a structural problem.

Can you think of any writers today who have been able to write with a form?

If so, there's likely to be a deadness about it, depending upon the rigidity of blueprint. There's something arbitrary in approaching art that way.

Would you say we're in a formless age?

No, we're not in a formless age, but we're in an age in which the pressures to discover form are intensified.

What about a writer like A. R. Ammons, especially his poem "Corson's Inlet," which is about wanting no form, to be formless?

Even there, that is a form by definition, in advance of the mind's action. Formlessness is form. The mind that spools forth the formlessness is the center, and therefore can bring a definition to formlessness. It's a contradiction in the aesthetic position. At the moment it's a very popular position, but it's already dying. You can see this if you look at the critical dimensions of this particular aesthetic, which you also find propounded in deconstructionism. That's another species of the same approach. The deconstructionist argues an infinity to the text. That implies a formlessness in the text. This

aberration of mind started in the 1950s with the statement, "God is dead."
Well, this cry turned into the latest criticism: "The author is dead and what
remains is the text with an infinity of possible uses of that text." The text then
becomes a trampoline on which the critic performs the art of criticism.

*Then could Faulkner be considered a deconstructionist, because of his view that the
art was everything and the artist did not matter?*

That's not quite the same thing. With the deconstructionist, what's really
being said is the only thing that matters is myself as the artist. What I make
of this dead text is what is important, and I am the maker of it. What Faulkner
is expressing is a Thomastic idea. St. Thomas says that the artist's responsibility is to the good of the thing made. Now, if that's one's responsibility,
then it removes the artist as being important over his work. That's why the
art does not have as its end moral correction — a correction of the appetites.
That's not its purpose. The artist's concern is not his own or someone else's
rescue. That's somebody else's calling, not the artist's.

Flannery O'Connor's work is full of this sort of insistence. "Art is reason
in making," she says quoting St. Thomas. And the intellect is engaged, using
its best reason in making what is possible or probable, in a thing being made.
What happens to that thing — story or poem — after it's made, who knows? Insofar as the work is good, it is adequate to leave it on its own. But this in itself
is a medieval idea.

If you look at the artistry of the medieval cathedrals, what are the names
you associate with this magnificent art? Obviously, here is magnificence, but
who made it? We don't have any names. The artist is not important. But we
are talking, nevertheless, about a highly sophisticated civilization, not a
primitive one. It wasn't that they were unaware of themselves as artists. They
were extremely aware, but they were more aware of their responsibility to the
good of the thing they're making towards ends beyond themselves. It is
something of this idea meant when Faulkner says the work is important and
not the writer. Of course, it is very difficult to say this and believe it. Because,
we're human. I did, you see, agree to be interviewed.

In 1969, you published a collection of poetry, The Gull and Other Georgia
Scenes. *How important do you think Georgia as a locale is in your work?*

It's what I know and so it's what I use. But in what I accomplish and in
what I want to accomplish, I'm not writing merely local color — I trust. If that
were so, the automatic camera would do the job better. Look at Flannery
O'Connor — she has a peculiar gift for observing the way Georgians on a particular social level and in a particular region say things. She hears those
voices, and uses sentence structure which carries the voice. She's extremely
good at that, but that is not the limit of her interests. That's one way she gets
to what she wants to get at. That's a way to a larger vision. Obviously,
Georgia is important, but it is a position in which and from which to move,
from the sensual level beyond the sensual level.

That can be seen in your novel, Darrell, *where the main character Darrell continuously tries to move on. He's always trying to leave the small town for Atlanta, but he's really never getting there. And we know he isn't going to get to Atlanta. He was doomed to fall short, and ultimately, this leads to his death.*

That's right. But, so long as you realize that he is not at a level of intelligence sufficient to recognize that that's what is happening. If he could grasp that knowledge, he might settle where he was, or he might go back to the country where he would not have to leave home. He, too, would have stayed home.

Darrell and the little girl, Sandra Lee, die together in the motorcycle accident. It is evident that she was the only person he loved, and it was inevitable that she would die anyway, because of the incurable illness. His love for her was very strong, and even though their age difference was so great, symbolically, they died as man and wife.

I think about it as a love story, but one with no sex. It has a suggestiveness, not of Eros, but of Agape. Agape being a more inclusive love. Darrell's fascination with his motorcycle and other things is sort of erotic, but his is an eroticism that gets lifted beyond the sensual.

When the newspaper photographer came to take Sandra Lee's picture in the creek scene, metaphorically, it was a wedding picture being taken of the young bride.

What's going on there is an indictment of the obscenity rampant in our age. The literal meaning of obscenity, the obscene, is that which ought properly be off the scene. The Greeks understood this. For instance, after Oedipus has blinded himself and everyone else is dead, Creon reminds everyone that there are some things so personal and private that they are not appropriately revealed in any public way. That's the very center of why it is outrageous to have certain human conditions of spirit made public. Of course Darrell, who's no Aristotle, senses the obscenity of the invasion of Sandra Lee's privacy. He recognizes the obscenity that dominates the news media.

Look at the obscenity when we had the recent hostage situation. The networks went into a family's home — just like mine here — there's the television. The newspeople knew already that in a few minutes, there would be the pictures of these hostages — members of this family — being suddenly released. What the news media is interested in is the picture of the family's response as it sits innocent of what is about to happen. That's the sort of obscenity that has developed till it ought to be actionable in a court of law. It is ultimately more destructive of community than pornography.

You found the same sort of thing during the Atlanta child murders. A mother had tears running down her cheeks, and somebody stuck a microphone in her face, and asked, "How does it feel to have your little boy killed?" That's obscene. We have reduced and tailored a term like obscene, and now it applies to the sexual act made public. That in itself is obscene. But, for the same reason, not because there's anything wrong with the sexual act, but because it is as personal and private and sacred as grief. Some invasions of grief are more obscene than the sexual act displayed publicly. And that is what Darrell is aware of.

Do you think people today are aware of this obscenity?

Not as angrily aware of it as I think they ought to be. The principle of obscenity is so eroded that the obscene may be practiced for monetary profit with impunity.

Let's change the subject for awhile. What was your childhood like growing up in Georgia?

Probably like that of thousands of other children growing up in middle Georgia on the edges of a small town, between the small town and the mill village — sort of a never-never land. The farm was an obvious presence. I was born in 1925, and the shift was long on the way towards the city. But it would be a long time, the post–Depression, the post-thirties, before we dawned to the fact of our shifting.

As in Darrell, were you as a young man, looking for the place to move to?

I don't know. Maybe so. I think it has been curiosity more than anything that has led me to where I am, which isn't far from where I started. It was a fascination with the fact that things *are,* that anything *is.* And it has grown. The fact that anything exists is arresting at any moment. And perhaps, if we are lucky or graced, at every moment.

The embalmed baby in Darrell is one of those things that "exists." To an extent, it also reminds me of the mummy in O'Connor's Wise Blood.

Yes, but I think they're quite different, in this respect: In *Wise Blood* what's happening with the mummy is that you're getting Hazel Mote's argument of the nature of man-made concrete in a shocking way. If man is what he is by Hazel Mote's definition, then man is in effect this creature, the mummy. It fits every requirement that Hazel makes for his new Jesus. With Darrell, it's almost the fascination of the existence, not that it represents anything, but that it *is.* That it exists. This is the beginning of philosophy — our recognition of our existence. It's the recognition that being *is.* That's the ground of philosophy, which most philosophers have forgotten.

We live in an age where people believe that the life you save may be your own, and that it's a life that exists at a biological level only. If this is the case, then you're shut off from those recognitions, and believe that some people have indeed got where they were going by their own natural will. There's a kind of selfish intensity that is involved within that safety text about saving our lives. The new testament says, "Since before the days of John the Baptist, the kingdom of heaven has been given to the violent, and the violent take it by force." That the kingdom of heaven is given to the violent — the violent bear it away. That's another way to put it. That's pretty rich, because it means that natural will is a very low concept of our being. We might as well be stuffed animals.

Could you discuss your latest book, Concerning Virtue and Modern Shadows of Turning?

It's a series of essays that I gave two or three years ago. It has to do with the question of the nature of virtue, and of course, the modern shadows of turning is a phrase picked up from the Bible, describing God "in whom is no shadow of turning," in whom is constancy. I'm talking about how we shy away from the question of virtue and the complexities in a term like "virtue," which doesn't necessarily have to do with chastity. There are the virtues of art that we have been talking about. The whole complaint is that the importance of virtue is lost from our education with art and literature. Lost from the proper centers of our concern, whether you're dealing with moral issues or intellectual issues, hence the modern use of *turning*, with a suggestion of *returning*. We have lost the orientation of the full light of intellect. When you turn from the light, what you encounter are the shadows. That makes for a pretty good metaphor with which to talk about the problem of modernism. We're concerned for ourselves, with saving our own "life" as on the highway. But that "life" may be just a shadow of ourselves.

Previously, actually many years ago, you were the assistant director of the Georgia Press as well as business manager of the Georgia Review. *Could you discuss some of the problems universities have with publishing?*

Remember, I was involved about thirty years ago, and university presses have changed a lot. I will say this: I don't think they've necessarily changed for the better. They came into existence primarily to accommodate a kind of work that was valuable, but which would return no sufficient financial return to justify commercial publication. What I've seen develop is the commercialization of university presses, and many of them are so huge, you'd think you were dealing with Random House. They've largely lost their primary cause for being.

With the commercialization, have they lost their aesthetic value?

It's tempting, but dangerous to talk in such large generalities. One of the things they have gained is a sense of the making of the "thing." Book production is much more artful now than it was when I was involved. What may be lost is the spirit that's in that body. I think it's the inclination to commercialize that must ultimately hurt the spirit in the book.

As we close in on the twenty-first century, do you think writing will equal or surpass the classic writing that emerged from the thirties, forties, and fifties — as with Fitzgerald, Faulkner, Hemingway, and Warren?

Dante, very wisely, put seers and prophets in one of the lower circles of Hell, where they have their heads turned backwards on their bodies so they see where they've been, and not where they're going. This is their punishment for reading the future as prophets. So you're asking me, again, to risk my soul in hell, and I don't want to do that.

Okay, that's fair. Well, here's another question where you can risk your soul. As we close out the twentieth century, where do you think writing is headed? Do you have any idea?

No. What I see is a considerable struggle for writers, especially young writers to discover whether there's a new form possible or a new subject possible. I think it's as if, at the moment, that we're in sort of a backwash, or calm. When you drift becalmed there's a temptation for self-agitations, a concern to get under way again. That sort of art is not likely to transport anyone. Take a copy of the *American Poetry Review,* and read it. Ask yourself this: If you read the poems of an issue without the biographical notes and the names of the poets, which of those poems could you spot as being by separate poets? There's a terrible sameness to the work. They all use the first person pronoun I, and the discovery of the self in one way or another is the theme. There is a sophistication in diction, but there's a terrible youthful naïveté at the same time. That's almost characteristic of where we stand now in poetry and fiction. One is tempted to call it "workshop" art, almost committee art. What we don't know is who's already sailing ahead. There are so many sails flapping in the wind, it's hard to see who's moving out in front. Of course, that's likely to be true at any period we happen to be born into.

Notice what happens when Faulkner gets the Nobel Prize. It seemed a dead time in letters. Meanwhile, he has done a tremendous body of work, nearly all of which at the time of his prize was out of print. It was as if he was already forgotten. It's almost in retrospect with such participants in the journey of Faulkner that you spot and see the power that was there all along. That's true at every level and time of human action. And you can't see the pattern until you're at an end, perhaps.

Lawrence Naumoff

Twenty years ago Lawrence Naumoff was a promising young writer who received a National Endowment
for the Arts Fellowship, The Carolina Quarterly Fiction
Award, and a Thomas Wolfe Memorial Award. But then
he quit writing. The year 1988 marked the return of
Lawrence Naumoff, with his first novel, *The Night of
the Weeping Women,* from Atlantic Monthly Press. His second novel, *Rootie Kazootie,* was published in 1989 by Farrar,
Straus and Giroux. This interview was conducted on
December 4, 1988, at his writing office in Durham, North
Carolina.

You were born in North Carolina, in Mecklenburg County.
That's right. I had a traditional middle-class upbringing in Charlotte. I
left there after high school and went to Chapel Hill to study English. I never
thought about being a writer until my freshman English teacher, who was a
graduate student, read a paper I'd written and said I needed to be in the
writing program and marched me over to see Jessie Rehder, who ran that
program. It was a stable family with the standard things — camp in the summer, one trip a year with the family, then college. I was ready to get away
from my family as soon as I could. I got married during my junior year in
college. I was so taken with all that goes into writing that I dropped out of
school, but a few years later I went back to finish my work in English and
did receive an A.B.

I started writing for real then, and loved it. I used to publish under the
pseudonym of Peter Nesovich. A little while later, after getting a lot of attention as a writer, both locally and nationally, I quit.

*There is a twelve year gap in your writing career, and on the back of the dust jacket
of* The Night of the Weeping Women, *it says, "In the early 1970s Lawrence
Naumoff was a promising young writer who received a National Endowment for the Arts
Fellowship, The Carolina Quarterly Fiction Award, and a Thomas Wolfe Memorial
Award. Then he stopped writing for ten years 'for the kind of reasons you might write*

about but don't want to talk about.'" That's what I would like to talk about. What were the reasons you stopped writing?

I tried to tell somebody from the *Washington Post,* deciding to be completely honest and tell everyone everything they wanted to know. I have nothing to hide. I told him exactly what happened — everything relating to my wife's family and her and my family and other things. Well, it didn't come out right. I then figured I could better tell everyone what was *not* happening, because I asked the guy at the *Washington Post,* "If I don't tell you, what do you think people will imagine happened during those twelve years?"

That you were in jail.

He said people would figure I had been in an insane asylum or was running from the law. I was not crazy and I was not in an insane asylum. I was not in prison, I was not drunk for the twelve years, I had not had a sex change operation, I wasn't a Hare Krishna. I thought it might be easier to say what it was not than what it was. It's just best not to say what it was. You can't tell anyone. You have to write novels about it. Writers know you take something that is slightly true and dramatize it and exaggerate it. Take *The Night of the Weeping Women* and the next novel, which is coming out next year, and look at both of them. That's the only way I can say what was going on with my life. It takes a year of pouring over the pages to say accurately. So I'm not going to say it. A writer can talk for twenty minutes to a journalist working for a newspaper, telling him the whole thing in perfect perspective and it comes out in one paragraph in the newspaper out of perspective and it has too much emphasis.

With the interview format your words are taken verbatim.

I was married to a terrific woman — married for ten years. She was talented, bright, hardworking, completely devoted to me, completely unselfish, and she took care of me for three or four years completely. She worked and let me write, and she liked doing that. I began to receive some attention for my writing. Then we thought, and I thought especially, that she needed to have her life. I asked what she wanted to do, and she wanted to have a baby. So I worked so she could have a baby. Then she couldn't have a baby. It turned out she had a lot of problems and couldn't have a baby. Everything deteriorated from that point. Although it's fun trying to get a woman pregnant in one sense, if she can't get pregnant it begins to work on you in the most primitive sense to not be able to fulfill that. A lot of trouble and dramatic things happened from that. When she found out she couldn't have a baby she had all sorts of operations. We didn't have much money at the time and no hospital insurance. The middle-class world doesn't know that if you don't work for a company you can't afford hospital insurance. It costs practically as much as the hospital bill. So every time she went into the hospital we had huge hospital bills, and that would set us back monetarily, psychically, and make our life that much more complicated. Young people don't know this, but years can go by, another year and another year, and you're just sort of mired in the middle of all this struggle. A lot of time went by before I was able to get myself clear to start writing again, and also financially stable enough to write again. During that time she was still a good woman and a good wife, but eventually we did separate and get divorced.

What kind of work did you do during this time?

The only jobs available out in the country were farming and carpentry. Of course, you can't farm yourself—it takes too much money. You have to work for someone else. I worked for farmers and I loved it. I loved nothing better in the world than getting on a big John Deere tractor, and I'm a guy who came from a middle-class professional family. When I graduated from high school I couldn't tell the difference between the air cleaner and the generator of a car. I'd get on a John Deere tractor and stay in the field for twelve hours a day. It was just heaven—the most wonderful job I ever had. I drove bulldozers, too. I also became a carpenter and learned to build houses. I don't want to make myself out to be a macho type of a guy, and that's why I left the jobs off the dust jacket, because if you read about somebody who did all that you may think of Harry Crews at a younger age, a tough macho guy. It never effected me that way. I never cut off the sleeves of my shirts to look tough. I farmed and built houses because it was fun and the only work out there.

I built a lot of houses with other "back to the land, counterculture, young, educated types" and nobody knew what they were doing. We built houses that weren't built right. There were no inspections. They stood up, but they were badly built. I had the reputation of a hard worker, and out in the community, Silk Hope, which is twenty-two miles from Chapel Hill, an old builder in the community who built all the houses for all the farmers asked me to come to work for him. I was the only nonnative who worked for him. They built houses from the ground up, and they were well built. We didn't do the masonry, but we did everything else—the framing, trim, cabinets, everything.

There was an old man who worked for the crew named Silas, and he's in my new novel because I loved him—I really loved Silas. He was an old primitive Quaker, not just a Quaker who went to church. He was so primitive that he didn't drive a car until he was fifty-seven years old. In his mind and pacing and approach to people he lived in the nineteenth century. Silas didn't talk much, but I could tell he had a kind soul. He kept watching me, slowly getting to know me, and one day we were eating lunch and he was sitting beside me on a foundation wall. I was eating my sandwiches and he looked over at me and said, "You know what? You eat like you was mad at your food." (*Laughing.*) And he imitated me how I would bite down on it real hard and bite it again real hard. See, Silas got to the core of my whole being by that one observation. I learned an awful lot from these people. Later on I became a licensed general contractor and builder. I never subcontracted the work out, I built everything myself. So, that's how I supported myself from 1978 until Atlantic Monthly Press bought *The Night of the Weeping Women.* And they paid me enough money so I could stop that to write. So that's what I did — I built one house at a time for people in the country, and it helped me with my writing. Writing is like building houses — no matter how hard the job is you have to get some lumber up everyday or the house never will get finished. So that's a typically complex writer's answer to the question of how I supported myself.

When did you begin writing The Night of the Weeping Women, *and how did it come about?*

I kept thinking about this woman I had known, who was brilliant, talented, gorgeous, and as sweet as can be, but who had a terrible self-destructiveness, and who had made a mess of everything. I wondered how anybody who was that wonderful and beautiful could make such a mess of things the way she would. That set in my mind for awhile and finally I decided I had to write about her, and then I wrote the book, which took about eight or nine months. I started it about three years ago. The writing was intense. I put in five days a week, six hours a day. It took a lot out of me and when I went home each day I was dead tired. I've been much more tired from writing than I have from building houses.

The young woman in the book, Sally, cannot have a child and is distinctively similar to your ex-wife. Is your ex-wife the basis for the character?

No. You're supposed to say that this book bears no resemblance to anyone living or dead, and having said that, the most impossible statement anyone could possibly make, because everything bears a resemblance to everybody, it's based on her only in terms of the motivation to write it, and in terms of the sense of how things felt at one point, at one moment. It's not factually based on her. Her father did not lock her mother in the bathroom, nor did he drag her mother behind his camper in a car at seventy miles an hour, nor did her mother jump on top of her father and wrestle him to the ground in the driveway. Those are exaggerations of funny things that occurred to me as I was writing the novel. They probably wanted to do those things, but they didn't because they were civilized, middle-class people. Things felt that way and should feel like that to a person reading the book — desperate, chaotic, at times sweet . . .

How well received has the book been?

The very first review was in *Kirkus,* and the reviewer said, "Avoid this mean, vicious book at all costs." I thought, "Oh my God. People are missing the point of the book." It was supposed to be hilarious and tragic, but redeeming, which I think it is. The next review was in the *Washington Post,* "One of the most endearing books about family life ever penned." That's the way it has essentially been received. It's upset some people a lot — they hated it.

They've gotten me mixed up with the main character. They must have thought I'm the same way. For a first novel it has received a lot of attention and a lot of reviews, was bought by an English publisher, and has just received a major review in the Sunday *London Times*. No one has thought it was boring or dull, but some people didn't understand that a man dragging his wife down the road at seventy miles an hour is just a wonderful metaphor for being trapped in a marriage and dragging each other through the world. They thought it was mean, "THAT MEAN MAN," and they said so.

He isn't the nicest guy in the world.

No, he's a creep, but the other characters get him. They get him good. It's not my job to make sure everybody pays the price for being bad in the world, but I made sure he paid for his actions.

The book received some of the strongest reviews of any book Atlantic Monthly Press published in the spring, except for Raymond Carver's, but they didn't do anything with my book as far as promotion. They had already bought the second novel, and when I saw that they weren't doing as much as I thought they should have with *The Night of the Weeping Women,* though it did better than most first novels do, I asked Atlantic Monthly Press to release the rights to the second book. My editor was upset about that, but he's a gentleman, and a Southerner, so he did. My agent sent the book to Farrar, Straus, and Giroux and they bought it five days after they received it.

What kind of advances are the publishing houses giving?

Nobody ever tells. The first book received twice the money normal first novels go for. But to get that you have to have some leverage. My agent sent five copies of the book out, and two editors sent it back saying they hated it. They didn't just not want to publish it — they hated it. One editor wanted it, but with revisions. Then Doubleday and Atlantic Monthly Press called to say they wanted to buy it immediately. If more than one person wants it and badly, and immediately, you know you have something. If you're lucky you can get yourself in a good position. You don't really get yourself in a good position, the book gets you in a good position. It doesn't really matter who your agent is, or who you are, or how many people you've kissed, known, or fondled your way into their being in your debt, it comes down to whether they like the book or not. The second book received even more money than a second novel would normally receive. It's a much better book than *The Night of the Weeping Women,* and I'm worried that I'll never be able to write another book that good. I'm worried a lot. Something happened while I was writing it, and everyday I was in my office something amazing happened on the page. I'm dying to start another book this winter to see if I can do it again. So even though you might have two editors or three publishers who want the book, the book itself has got to be that good for the advances to be substantial.

The characters in The Night of the Weeping Women *are desperate to escape from their situation; they are literally being strangled in their relationships, and just when it appears like they are going to free themselves, they turn back into the circumstances they are comfortable with.*

A woman who reviewed it in the *New York Times* said, "This book makes suffocation look like more fun than marriage." The older couple is literally strangling each other, and figuratively. That happens a lot in marriage—more than people would like to admit. The younger couple tries not to strangle each other, and they're doing everything they can not to, but the force of that family is strong.

Is your novel an accurate assessment of modern marriage?

Everyone in a marriage starts out in love with each other. There was an "old black man" who lived on some land where I was building a house. He really was someone from long ago, and he had always lived by himself, kind of a bootlegger in that he made berry wine. He always had this twenty gallon container floating with berries. The stuff would make you throw up in two seconds. He and all his friends drank it and they'd end up shooting each other. You had to kill somebody after drinking that stuff. When I remarried I was building a house on land that he lived on—he didn't own it. One day I drove up the driveway with my arm around my new wife, and he came out and said, "I see you got a new wife there. I been married, you know. At first you love 'em so much you want to eat 'em up. After awhile you'll wish somebody would."

So what I'm saying is that everybody starts out in a marriage, most of the time, in some kind of glorious love. You rarely start out in the condition you end up . . . But if you marry someone, remember, you're marrying her, her parents, friends, ex-lovers, future children, everything that ever happened to that woman and is ever going to happen to her. You think you're just marrying her and that beautiful vibrant skin and the way she looks at you with all her hair spread out on the pillow, and all that stuff. That's what you figure you're marrying. But you're marrying all the rest of that stuff, but you don't know it until after you're married. Then it slowly starts coming in.

You get married and move into the house. Then one day she comes driving up in a garbage truck and dumps this whole load of garbage inside the house, and you think where did all that come from. Well, it was just around the corner all the time. You didn't know it, but she had that truck parked around the corner, or he had the truck parked around the corner. You don't really know about the family garbage, and you don't start out that way, or you wouldn't marry them. I don't know if it happens to everybody, but my God, all the people I know are on their second or third marriage. People of my parents' generation didn't accept divorce as easily as we do, but they did move into those "separate bedrooms," or went from the double bed to the single bed. They made provisions, like working late. Working late doesn't mean you're having an affair, it just means you're staying away from home. Or couples take a lot of trips—they have to keep busy, or anesthetize ourselves by drinking a lot, or smoking cigarettes until they're buzzed out. There are social ways to get through a marriage without getting divorced. You can watch television until you're dead. But somewhere in this world there probably are people who marry and everything is wonderful and perfect just like you always thought it would be.

In the book there's an incident where the mother and father hold the daughter down to examine her to see if she's still a virgin, which is a startling scene.

Yeah, that actually happened to somebody I grew up with in Charlotte and I think it happens more than most people like to believe. When I was fifteen a friend of mine had a new Mustang. The Mustang had just come out and it was the most special thing you could have. I don't know what you could compare it to now.

The Space Shuttle?

Yeah, (*laughing*) it was that special. We double-dated in his car and went to a cabin on the river, which back then was a really big thing, because you couldn't get away from your parents back then. Kids grew up under more strict circumstances and parents kept up with them. Anyway, we went to the cabin on the river for a party, but got back real late. Monday morning at school my friend asked if I knew what happened to so and so when she came home? Her parents had been so mad at her that they thought she had gone "all the way" and they held her down to examine her. "Goddamn," I thought, "that's as awful as you could get!"

It's a powerful scene. Her struggle and denial to her parents, face to face, and then finally going limp and giving up was her way of saying that no matter what you do to me you cannot possibly hurt me more than what you've already done, and that things will never be the same. Metaphorically, it is a rape of her spirit.

I remember being exhausted after writing that.

You had been off the writing scene for many years. How did you find an agent and finally get the book published?

I had been kind of well known when I wrote under the name of Peter Nesovich, and a lot of people did a lot to help me get started. Then I quit after having won several awards. When I started back I knew I couldn't call these people and say, "Guess what? I'm back. I'm writing again. How about starting all over again and give me your agent and your editor?" That wouldn't have been right. I had to do it on my own. I went through a list of agents in the library and I wrote letters to a bunch of them. Only one person wrote me back saying she would be glad to look at the book. I sent it, which by the way, wasn't *The Night of the Weeping Women*. I started writing a novel six months before I wrote *The Night of the Weeping Women, Shooting Stars,* which my agent has. I have asked her to destroy it, send it back, but she loves it, and wants to sell it. But she's not going to do it. We're having a struggle, because I'm trying to prevent her from publishing it. She wants me to revise it. But, also, I'm trying not to hurt her feelings. Soon after she had *Shooting Stars* I was zooming on *The Night of the Weeping Women*. For some reason it was not that hard for me to get an agent and it wasn't hard for the book to get published. So I've had a real lucky time of it, because that's not the average case.

Do you have any advice for writers?

Yeah. I've never been able *not* to write. I fought for years not to write, and it ate me up. There was something going on in my head all the time, and I was always avoiding respectable careers that would take me away from writing. I avoided respectability that would put me solidly in the middle class where I couldn't be the kind of writer I wanted to be. My opinion is that if you want to write, you will write, because you can't stop yourself from writing. You're not going to write if you're just sitting around thinking, "God I want to write, but I don't have the right table or my typewriter buzzes too loud, or my husband won't let me write, or I could write if I hadn't had these six children." Well, you shouldn't have had six children if you wanted to write, or you're going to have to do it anyway. That's harsh advice to people who claim they want to write but aren't writing, because you will write if you really want to. You have to or you'll just go mad. You'll go mad with the words rolling around in your head. My advice on money to writers two years ago would have been the same thing everyone told me, "You can write, but if your novel is published, be prepared not to make any money." That's not true. I don't know what the case is for most literary novels, but I've been able to live off the sales of the book. And it's getting better all the time.

What writers have influenced you?

That's a good question that no one has asked me until now. I gave a hint in the section title: "The Family That Exploded." That's supposed to make the reader think of *The Ticket That Exploded*, an early William Burroughs' book. The writers who I've liked the most are early William Burroughs, Paul Bowles, B. Traven, and Charles Bukowski. Put in a little bit of Walker Percy, run them through the screen of suburban life, marriage, family, and work, then you'd have me. They're my favorite writers and I read them all the time.

You mentioned your new novel. What's the title?

It's called *Rootie Kazootie*. I loved writing about the main character and I could not wait to get back to the page to see what she was going to do. She's the wildest woman you could ever write about. She is a sweet, innocent, out of control, wild woman. *Rootie Kazootie* was an old children's television show from the early fifties. It's about two women, Caroline, who is Rootie Kazootie, and the wealthy ex-wife of a doctor. The doctor's ex-wife has a Navajo room. They went out West and she fell in love with the Navajo Indians, because the Indians are so real. She bought every Navajo thing you could buy and had it shipped back to her big house. She has a Navajo room in her house and she goes in that room when she feels bad and then she comes out real — just like the Indians.

Who were your teachers when you studied writing at Chapel Hill?

My first writing teacher was Jessie Rehder and she was an old-time writer and writing teacher who knew a lot of writers from the thirties, and the forties. She wasn't that good of a writer, but she was a wonderful teacher. She was a great big, huge, hulking tragic figure who had lost her looks and gotten fat and drank a lot and couldn't sleep at night, and when she went to sleep she put earplugs in her ears and covered her eyes with a mask, because the world was too much for her and she couldn't let go of it to go to sleep. She wanted her students to succeed so much that she didn't care anything about herself, whereas most writing teachers are still worried about their writing careers. She didn't care about her career. She just wanted you to make it, and so she gave you everything she had. She was wonderful. But she died three years after I met her. She died of a heart attack, which fits because the world was too much for her. After that I studied with Max Steele, Doris Betts, Sylvia Wilkinson, Leon Rooke, and Carolyn Kizer. They were all good.

What was your childhood like?

One of the main memories I have as a child is a bully named Richard. Richard terrorized me for twelve years. He was huge. I was always going to see his brother, who was my age, and Richard always had some kind of sadistic thing he had to do to us. One time he made us take our clothes off and stand outside in the snow. I remember my feet hurting. Another time he made his brother and I sit on a bench outside and he lit firecrackers called "Ladyfingers" and made us sit on them. Once he strung his brother up by his ankles upside down from the steel crossbars that held the clothesline and he left him hanging there. Richard was bad. He was real bad. My main memory of my childhood was avoiding Richard. Going from my house to somewhere else without Richard jumping out of the bushes and chasing me down. He got his comeuppance because he got a football scholarship to a college in Tennessee and lasted only three days before he called his mother on the phone crying and asked her to come pick him up at the bus station. He had run away from school and was in the bathroom at the bus station hiding from the coaches who were looking for him. When it came down to who was really tough Richard got his comeuppance. But then we were in worse shape because he was back home and he didn't have anything to do. Even though he was nineteen years old he was still after us. The last I heard Richard was a private detective.

I had to come home every year, four times a year, with a bad report card. My father did not take it kindly. He did not say, "Well, son. Let's go into the other room and have a little talk." He did the other extreme. He sort of slung me through a series of doors. My grades would be like an A, one B, two C's, a D. No F's until the tenth grade. Then I got two of them. I had a real active childhood. I was in a lot of car wrecks. I got beat up a few times. Charlotte was a rough town. There was the rich section and also a huge working-class section, and people from the working-class section always came over to the rich section to find a group of rich boys to beat up. I wasn't rich, but I lived in that section of town, and I got beat up a few times by some rough people.

What defines the Southern writer?

The Southern writer could be defined as a person who writes essentially the same novel over and over with the same kind of characters that have been written about for the last thirty or forty years, coupled with the same scenes, often with white trash characters in the novel, and lots of family doings in the novel, not just one generation, but multiple generations, and it's humorous. It is an interchangeable novel that anyone of a thousand writers could have written. Or you could define the Southern writer as one who is removed from the Northern commercial world, the world of commerce, and the main cultural thrust of the country. You could define the Southern writer as someone who is removed from all of that, and, therefore, has a little bit more perspective and truth in writing. The Southern writer also has a connection to the land, religion, the heart, and is not afraid to write about those things.

Your characters are very Southern and the setting is in North Carolina, do you consider yourself a Southern writer?

It's true that my characters are Southern, but when you say Southern writer I think of someone who has regional appeal, but does not transcend the region. *The Night of the Weeping Women* has been received favorably in Chicago, St. Louis, London, and Boston as well as in the South, and none of the reviewers have called it a Southern novel or me a Southern writer.

Throughout the book there is a powerful use of dialogue revealing a lot about the characters, especially in the scene where Robert picks up the young girl off the street. Her sexual presence is a pivotal point for the novel and for the character, as Robert is thrown out of that scene to where he is supposed to go, which is back to his wife.

You're a sharp reader, because not everyone caught that. She tells him to go back. She turns him around. Max Steele asked me where she came from, and I had no idea. I was just writing and suddenly I had the greatest character. Max said, "Of course, you don't know where she came from. She represents Robert (the main character's) wife Sally, the way Sally was." She is a pivotal point in the book in showing Robert something about life that he didn't know before he met her. Her dialogue is wonderful and strong, and is filled with nonstop talking, and even though it goes on like mindless chatter, it's not mindless chatter.

The things she says are hilarious, "I've never done it with a Jew before . . ."

(*Laughing.*) "Is it a sin?" Yeah. See, she's completely innocent, saying whatever she thinks. And she wants to know if she's any good. "Am I a good person? Am I pretty? I just don't know. Is there anything about me that's any good? Do you like me at all? Would you like me if I were different? Would you marry me if you weren't married?" Yeah, I think she's as sweet as can be.

When you're not writing what do you like to do?

I need to be writing all the time, but when I'm home and I'm not in my writing office, I spend practically all my time with my son Michael who is nine years old. We have the best time together you could imagine. We ride around, pal around, do anything in the world we can think of. He hasn't gotten old enough to start using me as a foil for the reason life is not the way he wants it to be. I don't know if he will. We're great friends.

I do not party. I never go to parties. I'm notorious for never going to parties. I have almost no social life and don't want a social life. Very rarely do I drink. I will have a beer or two, but I never go out drinking. Drinking makes me feel bad, physically. What do I do? I write, I live in the country on ten acres of land that I mess around with, have fun with my son, and occasionally talk to my wife, and generally, most of the time, I'm happy.

Larry Rubin

Spanning a poetry career of over thirty years, Larry Rubin has published over 800 poems in magazines like *Harper's, Keynon Review, The Nation,* the *New Yorker, Poetry,* the *Saturday Review,* the *Southern Review, Virginia Quarterly Review,* and the *Yale Review.* His three collections of poetry include *The World's Old Way, Lanced in Light,* and *All My Mirrors Lie.* He has taught English at Georgia Tech in Atlanta since 1955, except for four years he spent in Poland, Norway, Germany, and Austria as a Fulbright scholar. This interview was conducted in his Georgia Tech office on December 3, 1987.

You were born in New Jersey and raised in Miami. Could you discuss your background?

We moved from Bayonne to Miami Beach when I was two, so I'm practically a native Floridian, though firmly rooted Southerners in Atlanta have referred to me as a "transplanted Yankee." My father had a drugstore in Bayonne, but I was born four months after the stock market crash of '29 and things looked more promising in South Florida, which was recovering nicely from two disastrous hurricanes: 1926 in Miami and 1928 in Palm Beach. My grandmother had bought some property with a building suitable for a drugstore in Miami after the real estate bust of 1926. So my father rented that building from her. I was practically raised in that drugstore. The first thing I ever learned to read was the "Drink Coca-Cola" sign.

You've said that after living in the South for thirty years you consider yourself a Southern writer. What characterizes a writer as Southern?

I meant that I'm a Southerner by geography. The conventional critical and scholarly view of the Southern writer is of one whose *roots* are Southern and who displays a love of tradition and of the land, one steeped in Southern ideas, customs, dialect, folklore — all of which has been bred into his or her bones. And of course, I can't lay claim to *that* — the whole concept of *heritage* involved here.

With the growth the South is experiencing, with more and more people moving South, how will this affect the Southern writing in the future?

Well, obviously the whole country has been experiencing a sort of cultural homogenization for the past three or four decades, with television as the major contributor, along with air travel and increasing mobility of the population in general. For example, the Southern accent is harder and harder to find, except in small towns and rural areas. Increasing urbanization and similar social forces will probably result in a diminution of the feature of the Southern writer that I mentioned — such as love of land, deep-rooted tradition, regional dialect and so on — that whole Southern heritage that the writers of the region, who are distinctively Southern reflect, is an agricultural one, primarily, and with the fading of that kind of society will come the fading of the writer who reflects that society, or so I suspect. It's a sad loss, I think, but one of the prices of the rise of commerce and industry, and a more cosmopolitan urban culture in the South.

Could you tell me about your childhood? What was it like?

I had an older sister whose death is memorialized in my poems. I was very attached to her. I was very attached to my mother. We had quite an oedipal family. My sister and my father were allies and I was allied with my mother, and in family arguments that was always the lineup. I enjoyed my grammar school education very much. It was a neighborhood school, three blocks away — South Beach Elementary School. We used to get out of school not only for hurricanes, but also for cold weather. In Miami Beach the schools had heat, but it was all one county, Dade County, and a lot of the poorer neighborhoods didn't have heat, so the entire school district had to go one way — open or closed. If they had to close for cold weather, which meant under fifty, the whole county closed. I used to love it. I'd go bicycling, skating, kite-flying on the beach. I'd always hope to see frost. When I was ten there was one day it fell to freezing in late January. I set out an ice cube tray with water on the back porch, but it didn't freeze. Though my science teacher reported that on 41st street where she lived, three miles away, the fountain was frozen with icicles. I was just ecstatic. I hung around the drugstore my father owned reading all the magazines and watching my father fill prescriptions. We had a nice city library that I patronized. One year we went away for the summer and I didn't bring back four Lucy Fitch Perkins Twins books in time and I was told unless the eighty-cent fine was paid, which was an enormous amount of money back then for a kid, I could never take out another book. So I was twenty-three before I got a new library card. (*Laughing.*)

You are Jewish, and a great deal has been written about Jewish writers, and in a large sense they are grouped into a genre much like Southern writers. There's Saul Bellow, Bernard Malamud, Allen Ginsberg. I didn't find much of a Jewish influence in your writing as with other writers. Is this something you steer away from?

Not deliberately. But if you look closely, you can find a number of poems of mine containing Old Testament allusions and values, such as the line "my sons shall weep for Rachel" — a clear inversion of "Rachel weeping for her children" — in "The Unbegotten" and that whole poem "in lower case," where the Jew wonders if God will strike him with a lightning bolt for genuflecting in a cathedral. There are a number of others in my books, and quite a few ethnic poems in *Midstream*, a Jewish magazine in New York City, though none of those are in my books as yet. On the whole, I feel pretty well assimilated; but my Jewish roots are plainly visible in some of my work.

Does being Jewish in the South bring about an alienation? Southerners are often very stubborn when it comes to religion. In their opinion there's only one side to the coin so to speak. Have your experiences presented any problems with this?

Southerners have a stubbornness with religion?

The Fundamentalists.

Oh, yes. There is an intolerance with the Fundamentalists. Eventually all religions will be homogenized with the rest of society. Atlanta has always been more liberal, more tolerant than the rest of the South. As an example of how there is no reason to look upon one religion as superior to another, I told you earlier about my sixth-grade teacher who drew a wagon wheel on the blackboard. He said the hub was God and every spoke was a different religion leading to God. So there's no reason to look down on any one spoke. They all have the same goal, and they all get there eventually.

There was a little Catholic girl in our apartment house when I was a boy, and she said to my sister that people who aren't Catholic are going to Hell. My sister said, "Well, we're Jewish. Does that mean we're going to Hell?" The little girl looked at her and said, "Well if you're a good person, and you really believe in your religion, then maybe you won't go to Hell." (*Laughing.*) She was very broad-minded, unlike some of the people I've met.

I don't know too much about Jewish doctrine because I'm more or less assimilated. I'm not a religious Jew in the sense of devoted adherence to ritual. But religion goes beyond ritual or doctrine. It involves attitudes and traditions and ways of looking at life — and even the food. Americans are becoming more interested in Jewish foods. Jewish food is "in," like bagels. These are people I might call Gastronomic Jews. Jews who are Jewish because they love the food.

As much as I don't want this to be a discussion centered on religion, I would like to know what is the biggest misunderstanding about Jews?

There are a lot of them. There are stereotypes: mercenary, the pawnbroker and the shylock. What did I hear lately? "You can kill a Jew dead, bury him and he'll climb right up out of the grave and sell you the spade." (*Laughing.*) That's funny, but prejudice grows out of that stereotype. I'm terrible at business. The first section of the newspaper I throw out is the business section. (*Laughing.*) The only thing in there that interests me is the foreign exchange, because I like to go to Europe.

Several of your poems suggest that you have a background in classical music such as in All My Mirrors Lie — *"Part One: The Farther Side of Music."*

Oh, yes. That's about Beethoven. I like to think I have a musical background. I studied piano for seven years during my childhood, but that wasn't unusual in a middle-class society where everybody was supposed to be "accomplished." Middle-class mothers made their children study piano. My sister studied piano, too. Also, I like to go to concerts. I'm into classical music. I listen to WGKA and WABE. I think it's one of the great arts, and I think there is a connection between poetry and music. Poetry is musical. Lyrical poetry is the type I write and for that you have to have a musical ear. Edgar Allan Poe was a big musician for poetry; he really showed us the musical possibilities of the English language. Emerson called him that "jingle man," but I think that is very unfair. He pulled out all the stops of alliteration, rhyme and meter, internal rhyme — "Once upon a midnight dreary, while I pondered, weak and weary. . . ." That's all one line. Dreary and weary rhyme within the sentence. He's just such a pleasure to listen to.

Over your career you have published something like five hundred poems. How accurate is this?

It's more than that now. It's something like 800. Within the three books there are about fifty poems per book, but in the magazines I've been publishing approximately twenty to twenty-five poems per year since 1958.

The point I want to get at is that your poems have been published in major magazines and have been included in many anthologies, yet, you only have three books of poetry, The World's Old Way, Lanced in Light, *and* All My Mirrors Lie.

Yeah, I've been trying to get a fourth book published. I have two manuscripts — a fourth and fifth book. I've been circulating them for about seven years, but it's not easy to get books of poetry published. There's a lot of competition. If I wanted to go to a very small press it might be easier. I'm up on the big presses. Since my first three books were published by a big press I'd like to maintain that. I'm very proud that I have three books published, and so I can wait for the manuscript to hit the right editor at the right time. Which I have faith it will do.

By going to a small press aren't your chances of being published greater?

I suspect so. There are a lot of small presses, and I'm just guessing, but I could probably publish with them. I've had several small presses recommended to me — one I made a big mistake with — The American Studies Press which publishes poetry that reflects American society. Mine is much more personal, confessional poetry: love, death, maturation. So that was a mistake. Later I saw that this particular editor doesn't like what you call solipsistic poetry — poetry that turns inward. Confessional poetry is very solipsistic, so he was the wrong man to submit to. (*Laughing.*) In fact, he said I should have it privately printed. I realized that this type of poetry really turned this guy off, and I'm sorry I sent it to him, but I had been given his name by someone. You run into some cul-de-sacs; it's trial and error. You can't weep into a dainty pillow and say nobody loves me. You have to keep sending them out until you hit pay dirt.

What will a large press be able to do for you that a small press would not?

There's a sense of prestige that you get with a large press. It's very satisfying. Also, you feel they will advertise, but that's not necessarily true. The biggest press I had was Harcourt and Brace for my second book, and I don't remember seeing much advertising. A lot of the big presses publish poetry to justify, culturally, their existence. They can feel good about themselves. Harcourt and Brace has become Harcourt Brace Jovanovich, a megacorporation, and I understand they won't publish poetry anymore. They're interested in the bottom line, and poetry just does not contribute to the bottom line.

What are the titles of the books?

I keep changing them. The one circulating is *The Unanswered Calls,* originally called *Journey, Through the Bone.* The fifth manuscript is called *Spawned in Space.*

In your books you have what can be called your "bachelor" poems. You're not married. Have you ever been married?

No.

I see out of your bachelor poems two different attitudes — a sadness and a comfort in being a bachelor.

Well, it has two sides. It boils down to independence versus companionship. The positive side is independence; the negative side is loneliness. It's a trade-off, and you have to decide which is worth more to you. Throughout most of my career, my checkered career, I've felt that in the end independence is worth it. As you get older it becomes a question of the balance sliding. I keep my options open despite the poem "The Bachelor" where it says the author will never get married. I think there are possibilities, other possibilities.

Is marriage possible in the future?

Maybe. One plays it by ear. As you get older the tendency is to get lonelier, and the independence doesn't seem so important as the companionship. The balance tilts the other way. It's a slow process, but there's also a certain sense of inertia; you get accustomed to the independence. I like the Italian word for bachelor — *il escapalo.* The literal meaning is "the one who has escaped." Isn't that marvelous?

In the past have you come close to being married?

No, I don't think so. I'm a slippery fish. (*Laughing.*)

What percentage of your poems do you publish?

It varies. I write a lot more than gets published. I have a big pile that I keep sending out. That backlog, nevertheless, keeps accumulating. I'm satisfied with my acceptance rate. Every time I get an acceptance I type it on a list. That now has thirty pages, line by line, single spaced. It's my chief source. If anybody asks me when or where this poem appeared, I have to search through that. I can remember generally within five years.

In The World's Old Way *there's a poem I absolutely love, and since we are discussing publishing I thought this would be an appropriate time to mention it. The poem is "God Opens His Mail." Need I ask what inspired you to write this?*

That's a favorite of mine. I often read that poem and I tell this at every reading. When I first started writing poetry I used to ask the editors to scribble a note of comment, editorial comment, on the rejection slip, because all I was getting were rejections. Sometimes they would be good enough to say something. Very often they would say they haven't got time for it, or you have some talent but it hasn't been developed, our staff is too limited — something real cold and nasty. I got the idea that if God submitted his universe as a poem to these editors he'd get a nasty letter back. "Dear sir: Your poem interests us somewhat, but we do not find it to be entirely successful." (*Laughing.*) That's the way they talk. I've gotten millions of those. They're overwhelmed with submissions, and it's true they don't have the time to be nice and write, "You're probably a good poet, but we're too full. This is good, but somehow it just doesn't move us." I often have the image of a robot opening my submission and just sticking in a rejection slip.

In that poem, the last lines state, "P.S. Since half the battle is knowing/ Your market, perhaps you would care to subscribe."

That always gets a big laugh.

That's becoming more and more true. In the AWP *listings awhile back there was a magazine asking for submissions, but then went on to say they only publish subscribers.*

They're very honest. Most magazines that are angling for subscriptions aren't that honest. Most send you a subscription blank and you're supposed to draw your own conclusions. That's not right. That SASE is supposed to be for their editorial reply, not business purposes, but those magazines use it for business purposes. They break the rules on your return postage — they advertise and solicit.

It bothers me to subscribe to a magazine for the sole purpose of having my poetry published. It's like a vanity press. I have about a dozen magazines I subscribe to, in fact, I've been published in only a few of the twelve, but they're just twelve magazines I've always enjoyed reading. You can't possibly subscribe to all the magazines being published.

That was my original feeling, but that is not their feeling as I have discovered. Their feeling is that if you are interested enough to send your poems you should be interested enough to support them, because they're doing you a favor by affording an outlet. The fact is that nobody reads poetry, and money is lost, so where is the money going to come from? Let the people who are so concerned with getting published subsidize the magazine. On that basis I subscribe to twenty or thirty places, mostly places that have published my stuff in the past, and a few places where I've never been published. I can rationalize it. I felt the way you did, called it a vanity press. However, I saw that they really meant business; they can't survive unless they have money.

I agree that these publications are expensive to maintain, and I subscribe to a number of magazines, but that runs into a great deal of money. If you take the same amount of money during a three to four year period, you could publish your own book of poems. The question that then arises with these magazines that request that you subscribe before they will publish your work is, are they actually going to publish the best material they receive, or are they just publishing subscribers? I mean, anyone with twenty dollars and a poem can subscribe, submit, and almost know they will be published.

A lot of people who write better than their own contributors may not subscribe, so those people are sent out in the cold. It could be counterproductive.

What I am getting at is, don't you think this is damaging to the magazine, the writer and to the art of poetry?

I'm not sure. That objection you raised a moment ago that some good writers will be shut out shows that it could be damaging to the magazine, but I don't think it's damaging to art itself, because "Art" will be turned out. I'm talking about Art with a capital "A," not scribblers who just want to be published. This is a very complicated issue. It's not damaging to the poet except in his pocketbook; it isn't going to affect the way he writes. It could damage the magazine, but it will not damage Art. I'm sure of that. I began subscribing just to those magazines which had published a lot of my work, gradually I moved to those which published less and less of my work, and now, I also subscribe to a very small handful that have never published me. Like the *Atlantic Monthly* which has never published anything of mine. It's a good magazine, and they came up with an offer, like nine dollars a year for a subscription, so you can't refuse. I took the bait. And they do make good gifts. The *Virginia Quarterly Review* has a Christmas gift subscription rate for five dollars. I took four of them for people who would enjoy the magazine, intellectuals. The *Atlantic* is a marvelous magazine, but so far they've been absolutely closed to me. I was in *Harper's* five times while they were publishing poetry. They've stopped. In fact, it would have been six times but before they had a chance to publish number six it was bought by another outfit. I've been in the *New Yorker* once and in the old *Saturday Review* eight times when John Ciardi was poetry editor. I'm very proud of that. It would have been nine times except they changed format and stopped publishing poetry. That's happened to me about a dozen times, where a poem has been accepted and something happens.

When did you start writing?

I started writing poetry in graduate school at Emory around 1954. I was just talking about this the other day. A classics professor gave a course in the great books, a four-quarter course, but I took only three quarters. He wanted a term paper for each of his courses, and an older student I admired very much had written a poem for his term paper. It was a poem based on the *Bible*. I decided I would write a poem, so I asked the teacher, Joseph Conant, a very fine professor, and he agreed. I based the poems on the *Bible;* one about Abraham, one about Sodom and Gomorrah, and a few others. The Abraham poem was published in the *Emory University Quarterly* after I had graduated. I've always felt those poems were the beginning. I was twenty-three. That same summer I went to my sister's summer camp in North Carolina as a counselor, and there was a beautiful girl, a dancer, and I sort of went for her. I wrote poems to her about her dancing. I still remember her. Somewhere I still have those poems. That was some more juvenilia that got me into poetry. I just felt an increasing need to express myself—the needs of frustrations of a Narcissus type. (*Laughing.*)

Who are the writers who influenced you?

Well, that's easy. The top one is Emily Dickinson. To me, she is my mentor. I have a lot of poems I've written in her style. She's number one. Dylan Thomas to some extent. Shakespeare's sonnets. Woodsworth a great deal. Maybe Keats. I like James Dickey enormously, though I don't think he's influenced me. I started writing before reading him. I admire Anne Sexton. Dickinson, Thomas, Wordsworth, and a touch of Shakespeare—those are the ones who formed my poetic sensibility.

Any other contemporary writers?

Like I said, James Dickey and Anne Sexton, but they really haven't influenced me. A lot of the contemporary writers are so obscure I can't get into them. It's people like Wallace Stevens. I love "Sunday Morning," but a lot of his stuff I can't read. It just doesn't make sense to me. I don't think poetry should be cryptical. I don't think you should have to footnote. I love the "The Love Song of J. Alfred Prufrock" by T.S. Eliot. Much of his earlier stuff is okay as far as I'm concerned.

I'd like to go back and discuss a poem from The World's Old Way: *"For a Poetry Reading to Which No One Came." Is this autobiographical?*

(*Laughing.*) Yes, that's very autobiographical, but it's an exaggeration. There were about five people in the audience. I mentioned James Dickey— this was before he was famous, in fact, he had just had a poem accepted by the *New Yorker,* and he was on the stage with me along with Elizabeth Bartlet, and a young man teaching here at Tech, Carl Selph. The four of us were on the stage at the "Castle" on Fifteenth Street across from the present Arts center. This was 1957 or '58, and in those days poetry readings were not widely attended. They still aren't. There were about a half dozen people in the audience at most.

I've been to poetry readings where I was one of only four people in the audience. I felt embarrassed for the poet. It was very uncomfortable, but they read their work as though the place was jam-packed.

At the Jewish Community Center I gave a reading where my brother-in-law, his second wife, and a girlfriend came to hear me. There were three people. (*Laughing.*) And the organizer came, so that made four. I went through the whole thing. "How many of you are gathered in my name?" (*Laughing.*)

In fact, you once said that you could count your fan letters on both hands and toes.

Once every year or two a stranger will write and say they saw a poem in a magazine.

There's a great proliferation of writing programs and we're seeing more talented writers than ever before.

This is true. The writing programs are bringing a lot of talented writers out of the woodwork. They're also bringing a lot of mediocrity. I don't want to discuss this too much, because I don't want to look like a snob, but there is a very good article, "Arts and the Arts," on this subject in *Commentary* magazine, a Jewish, liberal, intellectual magazine in New York City. The arts turned out to be the mediocrity — "art" with a small "a," as in getting grants for the arts... "Art" with a capital "A" is a rare thing, but the article points out that because of the proliferation of workshops we have people with the slightest creative impulse suddenly donning the robes of talent, and thinking of themselves suitable to apply for these grants. So there are a lot of scribblers around.

It's difficult for the editors of magazines who are inundated by submissions — they have to sift through ninety percent crap. See that box under the desk? That's a good example. That box contains twelve hundred poems that I was the judge of for a contest two or three years ago. I was the sole judge. Ninety percent is crap. But think of all the people who like to think of themselves as poets. They scribble. This is inundating the editors. How do you find the good stuff? You have to sift through the mountains. There were some very good poems here and there. Like one in a hundred. It's tedious, it's very tedious. I didn't realize what was involved when they asked me to do this, but I felt it's part of a service. Actually, I was honored to be the judge. So there are a lot of people who would like to believe they are writers. I'm not saying they are all bad, but the real thing is very rare and it's getting harder to spot. But the prize money is going to some of these people because they are networking. This is what irks me so much! A lot of people scratch each other's backs, not just editors, but people who set themselves up as judges. A lot of grants are awarded through networking. Sometimes it is embarrassingly obvious this is being done. The NEA sends out a list of winners by state and city for these fellowships. Some are up to twenty thousand dollars. About seven years ago, one famous woman (I won't name her, but she's a respected poet), was in charge of handing out the loot from the NEA. She lives in New England. When I got the list of winners there was nobody in the whole Southeastern region. Her hometown had something like a whole page of winners, and they were all women. She was very good to her workshop. This sort of thing goes on. It's literary politics. I think it's corrupt.

With the proliferation of writing programs have we come to expect less of writers?

Well, the common denominator goes down. When I was a college student three percent of the college-age population went to college, now it is fifty percent. As you increase the numbers, the standards go down. There's no way out of it. The answer to your question is a clear yes. My reason for sometimes taking a skeptical view of workshops is that writing is a lonely process, it's not a cooperative social process—just the idea of sitting in a group and saying, I'll tell you what is wrong with your poem. That could be helpful for stimulation. I'm not completely against it, but nobody can teach you to write a poem, you learn yourself. I realize that's a very romantic idea, but the workshop style is highly crafted—and dead.

Are we creating writing programs simply for the economics of paying the salaries of the instructors of the writing programs?

That's a possibility. I've never thought of that.

Here are all these people with their M.F.A. degrees and they need a place to teach, so the system creates a spot for them.

When you put it in those terms I see what you mean. We have to have a market for our products. The proliferation goes on, and it really is like breeding rabbits.

You said that if you make $200 a year publishing poems it's been a good year.

Inflation has not helped the poet. Places that were paying five dollars for a poem twenty years ago are still paying five dollars. It's been a good year. I don't have my list of acceptances, but I've had some good stuff come out. The big item is the University of Arkansas anthology, *The Made Thing,* edited by Leon Stokesbury, that came out in June. I have three poems in it and I feel very proud of that. It's a good anthology.

Did they pay very well?

They didn't pay me a penny. They called me up and told me they were using my poems and would I send them a picture. There wasn't a word about money. It's a university press so they don't have much money. When a place like Scott Foresman asks me to reprint a poem then I ask for fifty dollars. No one has ever said, "In that case we don't want your poem." But I don't ask the smaller presses or the university presses because they don't have that much money. Again, inflation hasn't caught up. I was doing this twenty years ago. I haven't gone up from fifty dollars.

Is there anything I haven't asked you that you would like to discuss?

You've been very thorough. I always want to say other things. When poets get together socially, they don't talk about poetry, they talk about getting published. In Dante's *Divine Comedy*—remember the passage where he is walking in Limbo with Virgil and Homer and the other great ancient poets, saying, "As we walked, we talked about matters that are not suitable here to be discussed, but they were suitable at the time." I know what they talked about. They were saying things like, "How long does it take to get into the *Venice Quarterly?*" (*Laughing.*) Or, "Have you been in the *Rome Review?*" That's what they were talking about. That's practically all poets talk about when they get together — the problems of getting published.

Ferrol Sams

Ferrol Sams was born and raised in Fayetteville, Georgia, where he practices medicine at the Sams Clinic along with his wife and two of their four children. His books include two novels, *Run with the Horsemen* and *The Whisper of the River,* and a collection of short stories, *The Widow's Mite.* This interview was conducted on July 7, 1986, in his office at the Sams Clinic.

Do your books mirror your childhood in Fayetteville and into college?

As much as possible.

Did most of the things that occur in your novels happen to you?

No, not most of them, but some of them.

What was your childhood like?

Well, read *Run with the Horsemen* and there it is. I grew up in Fayette County on a cotton farm about six miles south of town. I lived in a house with my parents and my grandparents, a great uncle, an aunt and her husband and three sisters. We had a big family. My father was county school superintendent.

Did you actually go to the prom like in Run with the Horsemen *with your father's farmhand as a chauffeur?*

I did. At the time it seemed perfectly normal and logical, but as I get older and look back and remember the prom and how I felt that night, I cannot believe I'd done that. There are still folks in town that laugh about that old Chevrolet with the beach towel hung between the front seat and the back seat. And we did drink the cherry smashes.

Are you working on a book now?

Yeah. I've finished a first draft on one that has nothing to do with Porter Osborne. I'm also working on a Porter Osborne sequel with med school and World War II. I don't have a title.

Who are some writers whose work you admire?

Dickens, Chekhov, Thomas Wolfe, Robert Nathan. Narrowing it down to present day, Margaret Mitchell. But right now I'm sick to death of it, because we've about overdone it lately. She's a terrific storyteller.

I saw your comment in The Atlanta Journal and Constitution *about the fiftieth anniversary of* Gone with the Wind.

The paper mixed up my first paragraph with Olive Ann Burns. It made her sound crazy and made mine sound terribly disjointed. She's a good friend of mine and she hasn't called up to complain so I guess it was alright. I think we have some real good writers. I think Pat Conroy is a terrific writer. I love the way he handles the language. Emily Ellison is an Atlanta author who came out last year with *First Light* which I thought was tremendously good writing. Of course, I enjoyed Olive Ann's book. I don't much care for John Irving. I think his characters are flat and it's hard for me to feel I know a character that Irving writes about.

You interrupted your studies at Emory University to serve in the military during World War II. Since the other two books are semiautobiographical, will these experiences be in the next book?

Literally what I did was I flunked out of med school. There was a certain amount of willfulness to it. I flunked out of Emory in my sophomore year and went on active duty overseas. I was an enlisted man in the medics and I got out in 1946. I got back in med school at Emory, and I graduated in 1949 — the rest has been a very conventional story since then. Two years of graduate training and then I came back here in 1951 and I've been practicing medicine ever since.

Are you still a prankster as you were in college?

No. No. I don't have near that energy to waste anymore. I direct the energy better now.

You've received a great deal of praise for your books. Did you ever think that would be the case?

No. Nobody's as amazed at the success of these books as I am. When I was writing them I didn't know whether they would be published, let alone enjoy the popular and critical acclaim they've had. I've been bowled over. It's fantastic.

When did you first start Run with the Horsemen *and what was the motivation behind it?*

I started in September 1978. I'd always wanted to write ever since I finished my first year of college. I always had it in the back of my mind that when I had the time I could be a good writer and would enjoy doing that. All of a sudden I realized that I was in my latter days and if I was ever going to write, I'd better start. I had this idea when I started writing a novel that I would describe events and procedures that are gone.

I wanted my grandchildren to know what life was like when I was younger. As I got into it, I said, "Hey, this is working, I'm enjoying this." I'd start over, tear it up, start over. Finally I got into the full swing of it. I think I sort of taught myself how to write a book. Then about halfway through I learned that I didn't have to stick to the facts. I said, "Hell, I can make this up and I can change names and I can have a good time with this." So I did. Then I got the fever.

I started writing *The Whisper of the River* in March 1982 before *Run with the Horsemen* was published. I hate to tell anybody what sort of time I had being published. It's one of those amazing Cinderella stories. I never sent either manuscript off in the mail. I showed it to Jim Winter who is a friend of mine. He liked it and wanted to show it to a friend of his, Jim Townsend, who was an editor. He liked it and showed it to the publisher of Peachtree Publishers, Helen Elliott. She liked it and took it, and it went.

How long was it from the date they saw it to the time it was published?

A year and a half. When I signed the contract, I asked how long would it take to publish? She said, "Eighteen months." I asked why it takes that long to publish a book? She showed me. I had never heard of a galley or a blue line or anything like that. I just loved watching the process. The publisher does an awful lot of work.

Your writing has been described as "beautiful, rambling images and easy poetry." When you were studying medicine did you study writing?

The only writing course I had was freshman composition at Mercer University. I had a marvelous teacher, fantastic teacher. I think students have the sort of feeling nowadays that professors are more approachable. I don't think young people do this anymore, but I had a sort of hero worship for him at a distance. If he had ever spoken a personal word to me, I would have absolutely curled up and died. I loved working for him.

What was his name?

Fred Jones. He was an authority on Shelley. Once he called me into his office at the end of my freshman course in English and asked me if I had any aspirations to be a professional writer. I told him I wanted to be a doctor. He said, "I don't tell many students this, but I think if you wanted to be, you could write professonally. But you would have to want to be a writer." I have always carried that like a little flame in my heart.

I went in the service and after that I didn't know what had become of him. After I wrote *Run with the Horsemen,* a Mercer boy who lived in Pittsburgh knew me and had read an interview I gave in a medical paper. In the article I said that I would love to get in touch with Dr. Jones and ask him to grade this theme, but that I didn't know what had happened to him. This guy was not a physician, but he worked in a hospital and he saw the article. He knew me and he also knew Mrs. Jones. He carried the article to her and she wrote me a letter. Dr. Jones had been dead about ten years. I sent her a copy of *Run with the Horsemen* and a note. She wrote me back and said she remembered me very well and remembered her husband talking about me.

I'm sixty years old and that just thrilled me to death. She also said, "I don't think you would have any trouble getting an A out of it." You can have so much respect for a teacher like that that there's an awe that goes with it. You're afraid to get to know them as a person, as a human being. You want them to be that superhuman kind of a person. That's the way I felt about Dr. Jones. You know, if he had any faults I didn't want to know about them, because I didn't want my image of him disturbed.

Boston Harbor Jones . . .

Wasn't he a great character?

He's one of the strongest characters in the book and he is supposedly killed at Pearl Harbor, although it isn't specifically stated. Will we find out what happens to him in the next book?

Well, actually that's the way I have started the next book, but my editor has cut that out. He says it's too pat. I should just leave that hanging. I enjoyed writing about what happened to Boston Harbor Jones in Hawaii, but that probably will not see the light of day.

It is commented by a critic that in Whisper of the River *the actions of Porter are predictable and not always as believable as in* Run with the Horsemen. *How do you feel about what this person said?*

I don't get upset with reviewers. They're folks just like we are. I love for anybody to read it and for anybody to like it. This is the real reason to write. Those long lonesome hours and tedious sweat are to be appreciated when they appear in the light of day. You don't write for the money. I don't have any feeling about it one way or another. What does predictability have to do with it. If a character is not predictable he is not a believable character.

The only thing I felt was predictable was when he got jumped in the park. I saw that coming before it happened and I knew what was going to happen when they pulled out the brick and the string, because I had heard a version of a similar story.

(*Laughing.*) I also had heard the story and by God I didn't know what was going to happen. I thought they were going to cut the string.

One thing about writing, most authors say this, is that they like to find out what their characters are going to do next.

This did not happen to me in *Run with the Horsemen,* but in *Whisper of the River* I would be writing, enjoying myself and there were three people that took on a life of their own. I had no conscious knowledge of this. It used to spook me a little bit. I would be writing and all of a sudden Boston Harbor Jones, Tiny Yeoman, or Mrs. Raleigh would pop up. They would just jump in and say all these things I hadn't even thought about. I was obsessed with those three characters. I was crazy about them — I love those three people.

My favorite's Boston. And Mrs. Raleigh's no stranger to suffering.

(*Laughing.*) No stranger to suffering. They would just jump in and take the story line this way. I'd jerk it back and they'd take it away again. Finally I would just relax, give it to them and have a good time. It was fun writing about those three.

It most definitely added another dimension to the book other than just Porter him-self.

Yeah, I agree. There's Boston describing his physical for the Army and he said, "Anytime a doctor puts on a glove you know something bad's fixing to happen." (*Laughing.*) Where in the hell did that come from? I never heard anybody say that. That guy had such a personality.

And his extra finger.

(*Laughing.*) Didn't you love that?

A country doctor from Fayetteville seems to be a rather odd prerequisite for a writer. You've always had an interest in writing, but it doesn't seem to be what a doctor from a small town would do. Have you felt alienated in a sense?

Since I wrote the books I know more writers than I'd ever met in my life. I've enjoyed meeting every one of them. I certainly don't feel alienated from my fellow physicians or my family or friends. I haven't lost any friends from my writing. Writing has been a very fulfilling thing for me. New horizons. New friends. It has opened entirely new opportunities to me.

James Seay

James Seay was born in Panola County, Mississippi, in 1939, and is the author of *Let Not Your Hart, Water Tables,* and *Said There Was Somebody Talking to Him through the Air Conditioner.* He received his undergraduate degree at the University of Mississippi, and an M.A. from the University of Virginia, and now teaches creative writing at the University of North Carolina at Chapel Hill. This interview was conducted on November 6, 1987, on the back deck of his house on a sunny Sunday afternoon.

The question I would like to begin with is to ask you about your background.

I was born in Mississippi and grew up there — Panola County — though I lived in Florida during my high school years. Pahokee, a small town in Palm Beach County. I should mention, though, that about the only thing connecting us with Palm Beach — culturally, economically, whatever — was the county name and a narrow road running through forty miles of swamp. The Everglades were quite literally my backyard. My father was down there draining a swamp to turn into farmland. But Mississippi was home and that's where we returned. I took my undergraduate degree at Ole Miss, though I had gone to Mercer University in Macon, Georgia, for a couple of years and then dropped out for four years. I started writing while I was out of school. Then I decided I wanted to go back and get my undergraduate degree — maybe eventually a graduate degree. After Ole Miss I worked another year then went on to the University of Virginia, where I took a M.A. I was granted permission to proceed for a Ph.D. They had a very fine program, a strict academic program which I was interested in, but I was working on trying to get a collection of poems finished and I realized that if I got into the Ph.D. program I was not likely to finish the book of poems in the time I thought I needed to finish it in. So I got a job at V.M.I. teaching, and was able to finish the collection and Wesleyan took it.

That book of poems would be Let Not Your Hart.

Yes, and it occurs to me that what we've been talking about — my background — has tended to focus on the academic aspect, and while that's quite critical, it probably doesn't say much about the poetry.

Something I enjoyed about your poetry is the locale. Having lived for a number of years in Southaven, Mississippi, I knew in large most of the places you mentioned, like Panola County, Sardis Lake, and Senatobia. It's a great feeling to identify with places a writer feels compelled to write about. When I was sixteen and seventeen, I guess, I had a motorcycle that I rode all over those areas that some of your poetry mentions. Was yours a rural background?

I lived in both — town and country — though we weren't farming people. My mother's people had farmed, and my father's father had owned farms, but he was actually a timber man, cutting and milling timber. You mentioned Southaven; I used to ride with my grandfather to Memphis — on old Highway 51, before the interstate was built — and we passed through Whitehaven. Southaven didn't exist then. Is Whitehaven still there?

Yes, I went back about six months ago, and it's still there. Elvis' Graceland is in Whitehaven. Actually, Whitehaven is more a suburb of Memphis now.

It's interesting how Memphis, which is Tennessee, figures so in the culture, the literature, the whole myth of that part of Mississippi. Faulkner said that the Mississippi Delta begins in the lobby of the Hotel Peabody, which is in Memphis. Actually Faulkner was quoting a writer David Cohn from Mississippi, I think. At any rate, he said that the Delta started in the lobby of the Peabody and went all the way down to Catfish Row in Natchez or Vicksburg.

In fact, the long poem I sent to you, the one dedicated to Barry Hannah, has a section in it that is set in the Peabody. My grandfather used to belong to the Southern Lumberman's Association, and they would meet at the Peabody. It's not clear in the poem whether the experience is autobiographical or fictional, but the speaker talks about going to Memphis with his grandfather to donate live rattlesnakes, as specimens, to the Overton Park Zoo — which is something my grandfather did on occasion — and then visiting the Peabody. The big attraction at the Peabody was the ducks being paraded to the fountain in the lobby for a swim. Then they would be herded off. To the roof, I think. I don't know where they are kept now.

They're still there, around to the side. Since the Peabody was remodeled it looks real nice. They have some sort of an outdoor stage on the roof for bands, and tables and chairs so you can listen and talk and have a drink. Along the side, in the back, they have a big pen with the ducks inside.

It's vague in my mind, but it seems to me that in the old days, at least when my grandfather went there and occasionally my parents, they could go up to roof of the Peabody and dance. There was a supper club, as they call it. It's where you would go to dinner, and it would be a whole evening of dancing as well.

Like in the thirties and forties?

Exactly! There were a lot of those, but you don't see them much anymore, though they are quite common in the Soviet Union. You go out to dinner and spend the whole evening eating and dancing. That's the entire evening. My grandfather would do that and my parents as well.

You've been working on a novel, Spoondrift *for a number of years. Could you discuss this?*

Well, I put it aside to finish up a collection of poems, and right now I don't know when I'll get back to it. I hope I can buy some time in the next two or three years and get to it. Part of it was published in the *Carolina Quarterly* here at the University of North Carolina a few years ago.

The central image is an old hunting camp in Mississippi where the main characters have assembled. They've gravitated from various points of both the regular compass and what we could call a space-time compass. John Wilkes Booth is there, for instance, along with our own contemporaries. Booth is one of those people who refuses to die, you know; for years after his death there were reports of his appearance here and there. One such report, in fact, was from my own home county, Panola. But, of course, at the same time he was reported at a campfire there in Mississippi, some farmer in Texas was claiming Booth had come to his back door asking for food. At any rate, one of the ironies in *Spoondrift* is that these characters at the hunting camp don't hunt. Mainly they sit around the lodge and occupy themselves with television, video games, and such. Ostensibly they're to keep the campfire stoked and to tell stories. The main character, Jim, says that they do, but whether that's part of his fantasy we're not sure. The idea is that he needs to believe that there is a storytelling tradition that continues and at the center of it all is this fire. You gather in a circle around fire and tell stories. That's critical, finally, to civilization — that there be a narrative in your life, that you contribute to that narrative and receive the same from others. At least that's what the protagonist holds.

But finally, in this instance, there's something very wrong with all of this, because you look in the lodge at all these characters and realize they're there more for retreat and therapy than any active engagement of life. The challenge I see is to at least get the main character out of there somehow. There are things there that are important but finally it's not a whole life. At one point they trek off to Memphis to visit Elvis, because they're worried that fame is eating this old Mississippi boy alive. Elvis's main response is to take them all out to dinner at a Japanese restaurant and then on to a skating rink. Can you imagine John Wilkes Booth on roller skates?

With a character like John Wilkes Booth, do they reenact history?

He will allude to having shot Lincoln and obviously that part of the fiction has to do with history in the South, the Civil War, race, and all those things that define so much of Southern culture. Basically, the things we are. But you know, if you get John Wilkes Booth and Elvis Presley in a Japanese restaurant, well . . . — history's getting rather remote. And even more remote when Elvis takes them to the skating rink. I initially had in mind a bear that would travel with them, suggesting Faulkner's bear. He was going to be out there skating. I thought that would be a lot of fun, but then I remembered John Irving's bear in — what was it? *The Hotel New Hampshire.* So I dropped the bear.

Since the main character is named James, and in mentioning that some of it takes place in Panola . . . — is the fantasy with the James character autobiographical, in the sense that it's a situation that you want to put yourself in?

I believe that all writing to varying degrees is autobiographical. But, finally, that's not important. What is important is the thing created. That's not in any way to invalidate your question, because I've asked the same thing of people, but it is to point to the matter of final importance, the created thing. What went into the work is usually of interest to the readers, but it really doesn't account for the experience of the thing itself, the artifice. I'm interested in the general idea, however, in the long poem I mentioned earlier, *Said There Was Somebody Talking to Him through the Air Conditioner,* the speaker, at one point, brings up the matter of the relationship between autobiography and fiction in the narrative impulse. It's a perennial critical question, though finally an inadequate way of understanding a text.

You could have easily, if you didn't want to leave the question open, changed the name from James to just about anything. But you do leave that as a starting point to suggest that James Seay is the main character and it takes place in Mississippi, an area in which you grew up.

True. An interesting and related question has to do with the relationship between the individual artifice and the art itself. It's said, for instance, that all poems are, ultimately, about poetry. Well, fine. But I think it's a sign of decadence when art takes as its subject matter itself — in an explicit, announced way, that is. Generally speaking, I don't have much use for poems that are openly about poetry. Obviously there are exceptions. But when we begin examining the thing itself in itself, we're inviting a self-conscious kind of poetry. The aesthetic equivalent of narcissism, say, the poem listlessly pondering its own image in the pool. But, it's an attraction that is hard to resist. The challenge, as I see it, is to play with that at the edges, or deal with it obliquely. That's how the serpent approached Eve, you know, at least according to Milton — "with tract oblique."

How long have you been working on Spoondrift?

I've been talking and thinking about it for years. I started writing it six or eight years ago. I've written sections, made notes, thought about it, but I put it aside to finish up a collection of poems.

You've published two books of poetry, Let Not Your Hart *in 1970 and* Water Tables *in 1974. And there have been some limited editions of poetry, as well as articles in* Esquire *and other magazines. Do you have a new one coming out?*

Yes, I have a new collection being considered by a publisher now. It's titled *Part of a Story,* and I hope to see it in print in about a year.

You mailed me a copy of the limited edition Said There Was Somebody Talking to Him through the Air Conditioner *to read, and which I greatly enjoyed. Could you discuss the central idea behind this and how it came about?*

Well, it's unlike anything I've ever done, and unlike anything I'll ever do again. It started with a personal experience. I was taking my sons to Mississippi, back to my home. We usually visit at Christmas, but on this occasion we were going back one summer. The World's Fair was going on in Knoxville so we stopped off there for two days. Then we went on to Mississippi and arrived near my sister and brother-in-law's farm very late at night. While driving back in the country there was a man on the side of the road waving me down. I stopped and he asked for help. Said some people had broken into his trailer and were threatening to kill him. He didn't seem drunk, but something about the brief details of his story and his manner made me realize that he was probably imagining things, but I couldn't be sure. I told him I'd come back with help. I went on up to the farm to get my brother-in-law and we went back down after calling the sheriff. It then became obvious, with some other evidence, that the man was very sick. But, in some curious existential way, he was actually living this danger, this threat to his life. It was for him a very affective fiction. So I started thinking about the relationship between that paranoia and fiction. The main difference between him and us is that we can come out of a fiction, we can step out of it at will. In a paranoid "fiction" the person experiencing the fiction is an actual character and cannot leave it at will. And that's the terrible hurt of it. You're caught in a fiction that you can't escape from.

In fact, you write in the poem, "The character he's become says he doesn't want to die, but he's got only one foot in the fiction, / everlasting, the other in the grave of this life."

Yes, and of course this life dies. Fiction never dies. Any world we create is eternal, it goes on, whether it's in a poem, a story or a novel. That struck me as unusual — a person having one foot stuck in a fiction and yet another foot in this life.

I even felt after reading this poem that the narrator was questioning his own ability to differentiate the two, fiction and reality. I thought that could be true.

What he realizes is that the paranoid man wants him in the fiction entirely. But he neither can nor wants to be and realizes that any involvement in this man's fiction is dangerous, because the paranoid man's informing vision is one of violence. The speaker of the poem realizes that and tries to stay out. But still, there's a human call for help. And in growing up, my training was that you try to answer that call as much as possible. That was the dilemma. The poem is a very complicated one. It goes off in all directions. And it's not finally a poem about paranoia. It's about good and bad "fictions."

It's about what the speaker calls, "the mixed texture of belief, how the measures of voices and motions register/ and randomly become a way we think of ourselves, our times and place. . . ." It's about "the voices and motions bidding from both sides of the border to be what we believe."

How would you describe your poetic style?

It changes. To look at my first collection you see a lot of narrative poems, and you see that most of the images in those poems are peculiarly Southern, Deep South. If you look at the second collection you'll see some narrative, but obviously there was an attempt to change, to develop. You don't want to repeat yourself. Some of the poems in *Water Tables* are probably like a lot of other poems that were being written at that time. I would say one of the things that the poetry of that period suffered from was a kind of a self-consciousness. I don't want to say cuteness, because many of the poems are quite serious. In the late sixties, early seventies, there was obviously a lot of turmoil and uncertainty and self-indulgence in the culture and that's reflected in the poetry. And a lot of us really were self-conscious in the poems. I don't think my poems suffered terribly from this, but some poets got rather precious in that self-consciousness, a bit silly. And, truth to tell, I'm afraid I may have tried to be the neo-surrealistic wag at times. I'm all for humor, the comic mode. But I'm talking about another quality of attempted humor or amusement, which I hope we've put behind us. I don't ever want to do it again. I want an honest voice that is aware of the potential for humor and the comic mode, but also knows that that is not enough to carry the total poetry.

What writers were you most influenced by?

Once you're past Shakespeare and Yeats, and Faulkner, when you're young, you're dealing with writers closer to your own generation, and if you grow up in the South and begin reading, you're influenced by Southerners. But you have to get over that. For me it was Robert Penn Warren, James Dickey, Flannery O'Connor, Eudora Welty, Walker Percy, the names you would expect. And, outside the region, James Wright. But then you get over that and you want to be your own person. I don't think any of my poetry is derivative of Dickey or Wright, but certainly their influence informed the way I thought about poetry.

Could you comment on the Southernness of your poetry?

It's your source of imagery, at the beginning at least, and if you continue living in the South, and if it continues to be anything you can identify as peculiarly Southern, then it seems inevitable that some of that will come into your writing as part of its texture. That is, unless you have reason to guard against it in a systematic way, and I don't have reason to do that. Obviously, I'm not interested in local color, I'm not interested in being identified as regional, but you draw on experience. If you live in a place that continues to have identifiable traits, you use them. But that's leaving. Things are becoming homogenized.

*With the homogenization of the South, do you think there's no longer a Southern genre
and that the Southern writer no longer exists?*

You see more and more of that, the homogenization, but, hell, it's still
there. I can drive twenty minutes and find things that you would identify as
exclusively Southern. I can go to Mississippi and find even more things. And
obviously this whole process of cultural transition goes beyond region. You
can go to Moscow and see the Western influence and the ways in which Russian culture is being diluted. You can see in Leningrad, Moscow, or any
metropolitan area things that aren't Russian. So you say they're losing some
of their Russian-ness, but then you turn a corner and there's Mother Russia
looking you right in the face. When I was there it just so happened to coincide
with a congress of heroes. They weren't all heroes — that's a special designation in the Soviet Union. But most of these old men were decorated World
War II veterans and they were coming from all over the Soviet Union, which
consists of various, distinct regions. You could see old Russia in those heroes.
Or you could go out of the city and see women digging potatoes as though
the tractor had never been invented. And then in the next instant some guy
is going to come up and want to buy your blue jeans or an Oxford button-
down shirt. Very specific, "Oxford button-down."

You were invited to the Soviet Union. What was that about?

A group of Mississippi writers was invited as a delegation. I see now that
it was one of the functions of glasnost; things are indeed opening up over
there. That's not the exact translation, "openness," but that's how we know
it. One of our purposes was to meet in Moscow with various journal editors
and their associates. Very formal meetings. We sat at big tables, they brought
in tea and pastries, and then together we discussed our agendas as writers,
editors, what have you. In general they're better informed about recent
American literature than we are about recent Russian work, owing in large
part to the fact that more of our books get translated and exported. I found
myself apologizing often because most of what I know about Russian
literature is based on my reading of their great nineteenth century novels and
poems — and in translation. That's a pretty good foundation — given the
richness of those works — but obviously much had happened in their literature
since then. Sure, I've read Pasternak and Solzhenitsyn, Voznesensky, Yev-
tushenko, Brodsky — all in translation, of course — but I don't think I have a
very comprehensive sense of the larger literary map over there. The present
landscape, I mean. At any rate, I think we accomplished a small degree of
cultural exchange, and I feel good about that. Among the gifts I took to them
was a sheet of the new Faulkner postage stamps, which I distributed here and
there, and they seemed genuinely pleased to have them.

One of the most memorable events for me was our program at Moscow
University. I read some poems — in English and through a translator. We
were in their lecture hall, formally called Theological Hall, though the name

was changed to Communist Hall in 1918. A strange feeling, walking up the marble staircase, past a life-size statue of Lenin, and into that hall, which was literally packed with students and scholars. They sat there for three hours, long after we made our formal presentation, asking question after question, which they wrote on slips of paper and passed to the moderator. Such hunger for news from the West. I have to confess, though, that much of what they wanted to know about was our music and films, rather than our literature.

Could you discuss what it means to be a Southern poet today?

No one wants to be defined as this or that kind of writer, but the culture that produced me seems different in many ways than the culture that produced the writers that are growing out of North Carolina. I'm not prepared right now to articulate what those differences are, but it seems that North Carolina writers are up to something a little different. But surely we share a lot of common ground.

If you're born in the South and you grow up in the South and you write poetry and if all that makes you a Southern poet, fine. If those are the terms, it probably means that you have some sense of all those things that are identified as peculiarly Southern: intense individualism, a sense of the land, of place, an inclination toward romanticism, rhetoric, religiosity, violence, a concern with race, a strong memory of the past — all those things that W.J. Cash identified for us in *The Mind of the South*. Maybe so, but it's more and more difficult to apply those traits exclusively to Southernness. I mean, my first impressions of France were the incredible orderliness and care with which the farmland was tended — seen from the air — and a small but sobering bomb explosion when I entered the baggage claim area of Charles de Gaulle airport.

In the first instance surely there's a sense of land, of place; in the second, my guess is that the intended violence had finally to do with religion, maybe race, and probably a kind of mad-dig rhetoric. That is, the French had just shot down a Libyan bomber over Chad, and the explosion probably was connected to some kind of reprisal. Which takes us into the state of affairs in the Middle East. All of which is to suggest that, except for what Cash said about the gargantuan amounts of whiskey that Southerners are supposed to consume, you could just as well call his book *The Mind of the Mid-East*. And talk about a strong memory of the past; try walking around Moscow or Leningrad without thinking long and hard about history. And of course Cash's list can easily be applied to other regions in the U.S. But, yes, there is still something that could be called "Southern," and I guess what I'm doing right now is trying to avoid the hard-thinking of redefining it. As for your question, it means that I live in an area that has a very compelling history, and the traits I've mentioned do suggest something about the culture, and I have a deep investment in both, but at the same time I'd like to think that in my poems I'm a part of that larger community I mentioned earlier.

Could you discuss what your childhood was like?

My friend Vereen Bell recently wrote the foreword to the reissue of his father's well-known first novel, *Swamp Water,* and in that foreword he said that most Southern men give up their childhood reluctantly, and he thought that his father was no exception. The same is true for him and his friends, he said, and that includes me. He went on to say that we are scattered across various parts of the country, and when we do get together, which we do at least once a year, we tend to act like twelve-year olds.

Do you have a favorite childhood memory?

One of my very favorites is in *Spoondrift,* in a passage which is autobiographical, where I'm hearing the wind through the cedars along with all the other sounds, voices coming to me from my family. My father is away in the war, fighting the Japanese. When you say favorite, that doesn't mean it is all happy. It's a very complex set of emotions that inform that memory. It was a time in my life when my father was away, there were a lot of questions which I couldn't articulate, and if I could I couldn't have begun to find the answers. The wind, the breeze going through the cedars and the pine trees and the sounds of family—that's not going to translate well for an interview. That would be one of my favorite memories. And all of that, of course, has to do with the sense that while there are things missing in your life, you are able to accommodate that absence or loss, because you have a sense of being sheltered—first and foremost by people who love you, and secondly by a natural environment. There is a funeral home across the street, there is death, but one doesn't feel the threat.

Well, turning this around, do you have a least favorite childhood memory?

Sure do. Getting a rock in the eye. But everyone has an assortment of experiences, mostly with family—things that hurt you. Family is very complicated, to state the obvious. Very perplexing. You're not always aware of the perplexity and complexity, when you're growing up and going through it. But then you look back and see things that were going on in your family that strike you as incredibly sad. Or you realize the patterns of misfortune. But most families were going through the same thing, more or less. It's not that there was anything horrible or abusive, but you grow up in a family and there is hurt and misfortune. You can't escape it.

Can you remember back to your very first memory?

I don't know how old I was, not very old, but it was when the Arkabutla dam was being built in Mississippi. We lived there in a tent. My father was working in the construction of the dam, and most of the workers lived in tents, though it wasn't like a tent city. There was a little cove where they were set up. There was a wooden floor in our tent I recall. The grounds were racially segregated, but there were black workers nearby. I think they lived in tents as well. There was a black child I played with and I remember that. Tents, a black child, my father's boat. And other images that wouldn't mean anything—such as an old brown Schlitz beer bottle, then something to do with that black child's mother chasing after me. I guess we got into a fight or something. The idea of living in a tent; it's kind of odd.

Is there anything I haven't asked you that you would like to discuss?

Well, we've been talking of childhood, and I'm working on a poem about an experience in Russia that probably relates in that it plays off the familiar idea of possibly explaining behavior in terms of childhood experience. At least that's one of the ways the poem considers. It's called "Tiffany and Co."

I was recently looking in a Tiffany catalog and wondering why it is I've never bought anything from them. There haven't been a lot of times when I could have bought their things comfortably, but surely there have been times when I could have afforded a little bauble of some sort from Tiffany. It's not like it's a consuming desire, but I like nice things just like the next person. So why no Tiffany in my life? I mean, I've never given it as a gift. How do you explain that, the poem asks. Family background? Childhood experience? Freudian analysis? Socioeconomics? Then I thought of Leningrad and the irony of how I went looking for Fabergé's old jewelry shop on Nevsky Prospect, the main street. Why would I have looked for Fabergé's rather than the café where Lenin met with Bolsheviks, planning for their big day? That is, if you look at my past there are no aristocrats; we're all working people. Tent dweller! (*Laughing.*) I'd have a lot more in common with Lenin's masses than I would with Fabergé or the Czar Nicholas or Alexander. I mean, those jeweled Easter eggs weren't commissioned by serfs.

So I was thinking about that—why go looking for Fabergé's jewelry shop—the location it occupied, that is—rather than going down the street to look for that café, which I intended to do? Understand, that I don't lie awake nights wondering why there is no Tiffany in my life. The poem's finally about money and power, the objects and people that the powerful gather around themselves, and the attraction power and the powerful have for us. It's about levels of engagement. Amusement, entertainment, epiphany. How power, unlike James Bond's regimental gin, the poem says, wants to be stirred not shaken. Stirred by one passion or another. And don't we all? But of course when power allows itself to be stirred on a regular basis and in the process neglects or abuses its claim, it's likely to get shaken. A lot of it is a question of what toys are chosen, so to speak. So why did I gravitate that way, toward Fabergé's?

Bettie Sellers

Bettie Sellers, born in Tampa, Florida, lives in Young
Harris, Georgia, where she teaches English. Her books of
poetry include *Westward from Bald Mountain, Spring Onions
and Cornbread, Morning of the Red-Tailed Hawk, Appalachian
Carols,* and *Liza's Monday.* She has twice won Author of the
Year in Poetry from the Dixie Council of Authors and Jour-
nalists, and Poet of the Year by the American Pen Women.
This interview was conducted in her office at Young Harris
College on November 12, 1986.

When did you start writing?

I wrote my first poem June 11, 1971. Dr. Virginia Spencer Carr was
teaching at a little place called Musemont sponsored by Columbus College.
It was a summer arts camp down on Jekyll Island. My husband was teaching
painting, and they invited me to come along just for the ride. Dr. Carr was
teaching a writing class of seven or eight people, and just for something to
do I wandered in and started writing. I got started and couldn't stop. She was
real big on if you write it, send it out there and see if it sinks or swims. I stayed
down there three weeks and I sent out some of those very first poems. They
were terrible. Two of them were accepted for publication. It was like getting
a nibble in the water, you'll keep fishing all day. I guess I was just waiting
for the right time. I don't know why I never wrote before, because I was born
with a book in my hand and I've been an English teacher for many years, but
it just wasn't time for me to write until I was fairly late in life. Everything I
have written has been done in the last fifteen years. Sometimes I think this
is too much trouble, it's not worth it and then I'll wake up in the middle of
the night and there's a poem sitting on the bedpost grinning at me. You can't
turn them away, they're your children.

Who are some writers whose work has influenced your writing?

From earliest childhood I have always loved the sound of Poe. I was as
big as a minute, maybe ten, when I saw my first Shakespearean play and fell
in love with the sound of his words. Being from a very Methodist family I

memorized acres and acres of the King James Bible. It was the sound of the Elizabethan English I enjoyed. Whitman, Wordsworth, Keats, some parts of W.H. Auden, Thomas Hardy, it's a very broad spectrum. I guess in the last twenty years the ancient Greeks. Other than poetry, the one thing I have made a real study of, and I'm probably more expert on this subject than any other is the Greeks: Homer, the poets, the tragedians, all of those. In fact, right now I'm working on a lecture on Greek women poets I'm going to give in Indiana and Illinois. In the ancient world there were a half a dozen women: Sappho, Corinna, Kassia, Zoe Karelli and Eleni Vakalo. I have found another half dozen twentieth century women poets.

There's a distinct voice that comes out of the mountains, and your poetry has captured that mountain voice. What exactly makes up the mountain voice, whether it is poetry, short stories, folklore or visual art?

It's a very specific setting, the conformation of the hills, the flora, the fauna. The *land, family, religion* and the *oral tradition,* those four facets just about sum it up. For it to work, whether it is visual or verbal, it must be in a setting. You must know where you are. The people are in a way isolated and yet, they're a very microcosmic group. There's a tremendous sense of family in this little valley that's surrounded by the mountains. One of the ways in which I have written not only *Liza's Monday,* and parts of the *Morning of the Red-Tailed Hawk* as well, was by listening to the people. Writing dialogue is hard, but writing colloquial dialogue is even harder, because if you try to transcribe it literally word for word it doesn't sound real. So, what I worked on for about five years was trying to figure out what kind of voice uses an occasional turn of phrase or an occasional word. The people in the hills call the mountain lion "the painter." A few words, a few phrases and the right setting are all needed. In writing *Liza's Monday* some of the people are real, but I put them in imaginary settings that are right in the mountains. When I was writing about certain characters, I made each a house. Some of them live over on Cedar Ridge or they live on the side of Double Knob. I went to those places and said what can they see from here? Those people, places and settings are real. *Liza's Monday* is largely about women in universal situations, the sorts of things that happen to all women. Those women in those situations are as real as I know how to make them. It would be foolish for me to write about New York, I don't know the place. I know how the mountains smell, taste, look, feel and sound. I know this place sounds like the whipoorwill. I know what the sky looks like at night. This is the first place I've ever lived that when I look up all of the sky is there. All of it. It'll scare you to death the first time you look at it, because it's too big. We have students who come here then feel claustrophobic; there's too much sky and it's on top of them. Once in awhile we get a student who has such severe claustrophobia that they can't stay.

Another thing, the mountain people and the mountain writers are very much interested in not discarding the best of the past. There are not any better stories than my grandmother's stories, there's not any better chicken and dumplings than hers. These are my roots. We have kinfolk. These people are fiercely independent and loyal, and mean as a snake to anybody who messes with them. After awhile you learn what kind of people these are, you learn to respect them and love them. I'm not a real mountain person. I'm a transplanted mountain person. What I've done is take the people, the mountain, and the smell in through my skin over the last twenty years, building on the fact that I spent the first eighteen years on a pig farm. I haven't really been happy off the land. These people up here love their land. My great grandfather was a circuit-riding Methodist preacher in these hills, and my maternal grandmother was one of the first students at Young Harris. I grew up down below Griffin, but I grew up on stories of this place. My grandmother was a storyteller. So when I came here it was as though I were coming home to a place that I had never literally been.

The setting in *Liza's Monday* is as accurate as I could make it. The location names have come off the forest service map, the *Book of Appalachian Wildflowers*. The birds, the trees, everything is accurate. The people may be made up, but the setting is absolutely accurate.

I begin almost every reading with a quote from Faulkner, "Beginning with Sartoris, I recognized that my own little postage stamp of earth was worth writing about." I know that's where I come from and that's where Byron Herbert Reece came from. It makes perfectly good sense to me that I will write well only about that which I know well. In something like *Liza's Monday,* I'm reflecting on the last twenty-two years. It's my absorption of the place, my own little postage stamp of earth. So I have two: a little creek in the country down below Griffin, and the other one right here in the Brasstown valley.

Many of the artists in the Appalachians are not natives. What brings them here?

I think you absolutely adore it or you absolutely hate it. Think about it for a minute. I live over on this side of the mountain. It takes me a minute and thirty-seven seconds to get to work in the morning. Yet when I am at home I can't see Young Harris. If I lived in College Park or Stone Mountain, Georgia, just outside Atlanta, I'd spend half my life on the road. Living here gives me another hour or two to read, or to mess with speeches on Greek women poets. I don't know what it is. It's probably the same reasons that I am here. At a small school, though I stay very busy, I'm not as hemmed with "publish or perish." I don't have to worry about that. I'm pretty much free to teach and do my thing. I spend a good time counseling students, but I'm not pressured about publishing. The pace is a little slower. I don't know anybody I want to swap places with.

In your most recent work, Liza's Monday, *would you discuss exactly what you were trying to do and why?*

This is going to sound crazy. One day in January 1981, I woke up at three o'clock in the morning, as I frequently do, and in my mind I said, "Satan is sitting on Double Knob." Double Knob is a mountain nearby. I thought that was a crazy idea, and had no idea where it came from. It wouldn't go away. So I wrote it down in my notebook. That satisfied me and I went back to sleep and four hours later I woke up again. This time I said, "Satan isn't on Double Knob, that bugger has flown off the mountain and is down here by Corn Creek and he's building a playhouse." I wrote it down to get it out of my mind, then it opened up just like a door.

The funny thing about it was that when I got it ready to go to the publisher's, the publisher cut those poems off the front of it. They were the first eight poems. That made an entirely different book out of it. Those eight poems have been published, but not in book form. The concept behind it was that this was such a beautiful valley, but Satan flew by after he got kicked out of Heaven and was on his way to Hell. When he flew overhead he saw this place and said, "Hey look, there's a beautiful place, I'll go down there and build my new kingdom." He flew down here and started building his kingdom out of creek stone, metaphorically, like a child's playhouse. Then he went over to get another stone and he looked in the creek and saw that his beauty was fading. This made him mad and he said, "To Hell with it." And he threw the stones back in the creek and flew off to Hell.

But the significance is that he touched the valley. That was the starting point. The eight-part sequence that is excluded is almost like the Book of Genesis. It's sort of Miltonic. All the people who came to this valley were touched by the things like loss of innocence in the Garden of Eden. I didn't realize it until I put the book together, but these were all things that happened to women. The book is mainly about women: the sadness, sorrow, incest, adultery, deep, deep grief, and relationships. The implication is, of course, in the original concept of the book, that had Satan not touched the valley it would have been a paradise, like the Garden of Eden. I have very mixed feelings in having agreed to publish it without the title poems. I'm not ever going to be entirely happy about that.

What do you think it would have done for the book as opposed to the way it is as Liza's Monday? *Or what has it detracted by not being in there?*

It's made an entirely different book out of it. Without the first eight poems, the title really becomes *The Women of Brasstown*. It took away the metaphysical explanation that Satan had touched the valley causing pain and loneliness. You take that away and you don't really have an explanation and the book becomes *The Woman of Brasstown*. I worked for five years in the other concept of *Satan's Playhouse,* and it literally broke my heart to lose that. I think the truth of the matter is that the publisher was afraid somebody would think it was a book about the occult, because the original title was *Satan's Playhouse.* I'll probably always be sorry I let it be published the way it is.

I find the idea of the occult odd, because there's nothing in Liza's Monday *to suggest that.*

It's not in the title poems either. There's nothing to do with the occult. Of course it'd be a Bible Belt notion. The characters are all somehow real, some are based on people walking around in this valley right now.

Basically, you have religious conflict, ideas that are presented in the Bible, and if anything, they're not of the occult. The poem "A Threat of Black Eyes" has to do with a number of things: lust, jealousy, and going further, revenge. These are all topics which the Bible discusses. There's the possible adultery of the young girl, who as the poem states, "Can't be no more'n sixteen neither, flirting round ever since/ she was less'n ten./ Them black eyes sneaking out'n the ruffles on her bonnet like a pair/ of chickadee's a-courtin' in a budding sycamore./ I swear, ain't no woman's man safe when such/ as that is free to run loose in this valley!"

That whole sequence came from tombstones. There's an old graveyard where they've written little life sketches of the people who've died. That sequence, called "Ellie's Neighbors," is based on tombstones. They were real people and I just took the idea and created the characters.

There is a poem about tombstones, isn't there?

Yes, there is a poem in there about a tombstone and that's a real person too. That's O.V. Lewis' grandmother.

I love "Mary's Apples," "She acts like every stick she owns is the Ark/ of the Covenant — .../ Why, just the other day, I seen her beating Lymon Shockley's/ pig because he sniffed her steps and nosed around her tree./ And then chewed Lymon out — for owning a pig! I swear,/ I just can't get nothin done for watching what she does!"

She lives right here in this valley. She's a terrible gossip. That sequence was such fun because I'd just sit at the typewriter and think what would Ellie say about these people? I became the character. I've written some Ellie poems that are really ugly that I won't show to anybody. I just needed to get them out of my system. When I went to the University of Georgia Semiquincentenery, I wrote an Ellie poem, "Ellie Goes to the Bi-Centennial," and made nasty remarks about the people she saw. It was such fun.

What was your childhood like growing up in rural Georgia?

It was the Depression. We were all born during the time when the banks fell. My father had a wife, two children and no job. He had bought a little fifty-eight acre farm out in the country and he kept us alive by raising chickens, pigs, and vegetables. He sold butter and eggs on the streets of Griffin to make a little cash. There are poems reflecting that in *Spring Onions and Cornbread.* There's one place where I talk about the mortgage hanging like a thundercloud over Septembers. We were never hungry and we were never cold; there just was never any cash money. Fortunately, the way childhood has it, I didn't know we were poor, except that we had to wear hand-me-down dresses and things like that. I didn't know how poor we were until I was grown. But it was a warm, wonderful, stable, rich home; mother's voice reading, good solid grandparents to love you. I don't think of it as being anything other than wonderfully happy. I think the major unhappiness of my childhood was the death of my second brother when I was twelve. He was eight. I watched him die. There's a lot of that in the background of the books, and my own daughter had viral encephalitis when she was fifteen, and those two events are kind of merged in my writing.

At Young Harris approximately fifty percent of our students are from broken homes. I never had to wonder whether my parents loved each other or us. Can you imagine what percentage of children growing up today have to wonder whether their mother or father love each other or love them? We had strong religious faith and strong cultural influences. We didn't have too many things, but I remember we had an old victrola and records, German Lieder and operas. I don't know where they came from, grandmother I guess, maybe the Griffin library where Mrs. Wallace wouldn't let me have but six books a week, because she thought it wasn't good for me. Grandmother made clothes for us, because momma couldn't sew. Momma liked books and things, she didn't like to sew. I enjoyed the warmth of being in a big family with dogs, cats, and pigs. We had trees to climb and creeks to dam up. It was a wonderfully happy childhood. You'll not get any childhood trauma out of me. That just ain't the way it was.

What is your favorite childhood memory?

The blacks that worked for my father and eating under a pecan tree in the backyard, telling stories, singing, and my grandmother coming and saying, "Bettie Cosby you come in this house. You're too big to fool around with the blacks. It's not nice."

That was a terrible step from childhood, at a time when I was free. From that time on I envied my brothers because they could go places, and at my age . . . there were just so many things girls couldn't do. I always wanted to do those things. That was a real pivotal point and it was my recognition of the fences there were around girls. I've spent the rest of my life trying to jump those fences. My mother and my grandmother were ladies, Southern ladies. They might have been poor, but they were still Southern ladies. There was a book ten-feet thick of things you did and did not do. My grandmother would not have approved of some of the things I've written, though I've never put a dirty word in a book, never described anything ugly. She would have thought some of the things I've discussed in *Liza's Monday* were things ladies just don't talk about: adultery, incest and lust. Mercy sakes.

I'll tell you a story. I was nineteen when I had my tonsils out and I pulled a hemorrhage. I was in the hospital and not in very good shape. My mother came to visit, and my boyfriend who I later married had brought me a dozen red roses and a copy of Kahlil Gibran's, *The Prophet,* with the original Gibran illustrations where the people are posed wearing only mist. So mother, who is pretty cool, sees the book and leafs through it. No expression on her face whatsoever, and she finally put it back on the bedside table, and she said, "Bettie, I'm sure this is a very nice book, but I don't think we should let your grandmother see it."

When my brother died I don't think we ever knew what was the matter with him. He had been kind of puny. He went into convulsions, probably some kind of brain tumor. The whole family was just exhausted from looking after him. We had a trained nurse looking after him. She fell asleep and I was watching him. All of a sudden he relaxed, and I thought he was all right. I woke up the nurse. "Mary, Mary, wake up, he's all right." She said, "No, Bettie he's dead." My mother blamed herself for his death, just because she was his mother. She felt there ought to have been something she could have done. So for the next forty years she carried around a load of guilt that you would not have believed, all because he was her child, her responsibility, and she should have been able to save him. That was probably the most influential thing in my life. Because when my daughter was so ill and came so near to dying, my prayer was, "Dear God, let me do everything I can so I don't have to be guilty for the rest of my life." It conditioned my knowledge of guilt and that guilt is destructive. My brother died when I was twelve, and it's the thing that shaped my life. I suspect if people read the whole body of my work, they will feel that nothing else has ever happened in my life at any time that was as influential as his death. The knowledge of what that guilt had done to my mother, and the sheer knowledge that I was not going to let that guilt do that to me.

There certainly is a lot of activity going on in the mountains.

They're bulldozing them down! It's sad. If you look out here at Young Harris mountain you'll see how they're just bulldozing the mountain off. They're building a subdivision. One of these days we're going to have a big rain and that subdivision's going to just slide off down the mountain. It's so ugly. I'm lucky, everything near me is national forest, Chattahoochee National Forest, if they'll just leave it alone. I'll tell you how it is. When I came here twenty-one years ago, Sharp Memorial Church had eighty-nine members. This Sunday the preacher said something about two hundred and sixty. If you sit in the back of the church, you can see that they've all got white hair. There's not a native in the bunch. They spend four, maybe five months here, and the rest of the time in Florida. Some of them do a certain amount of contributing to the neighborhood, but most don't. It's a transient population. There are no children in the schools. The schools are gradually shrinking down to nothing. There are no jobs. There never have been any jobs for young people, so why should they stay.

I have real mixed feelings when they say they'll build a new road or a new subdivision, and it'll make jobs. Maybe for a week or two. It doesn't take long for you to be possessive. I don't want anybody messing with my mountain.

What will happen to the mountains, or rather what will they be like in twenty years?

There will be more subdivisions and more pollution. The more roads they build the more people will think they have to live in Atlanta part of the week and the other half in the mountains. Or part of the year in Florida and part of it here. A lot of the people who are here, originally came from Ohio, Indiana and places like that. They didn't want to get *all* the way to Florida, they didn't want to stay in Florida *all* the time, so this is sort of a half-way house. We will continue to fight to keep the wilderness areas and the national forests, but we're wearing out the earth awful fast.

With all of this, is that mountain flavor, the mountain voice, fading?

I think it's taken on some new light. When I first started writing I was almost apologetic for being a regional writer. It might partly be due to the fact that I have more confidence in myself at this moment, but also it's been a good while since I've needed to be apologetic about the fact that I am either an Appalachian writer or a regional writer. I think, I hope, that there are some other writers out there who don't want the entire world sounding like the six o'clock news. They do recognize that we have to preserve some of the regional flavors. Good grief, do we want everything to be Peter Jennings and Barbara Walters? There's no flavor to it. The language is colorless. Sure it's correct and proper, but it's colorless. The flavor is in the pockets. The Appalachians Studies Conference and the Appalachian Writer's Association are alive and doing very well. There are enough people like me who are willing to fight for that. I don't see it as being as big a movement as the avant-garde movement in New York, but I think there are enough of us to keep it alive. We're back in films. Now I'm working on a film on Reece's life with Gary Moss at Georgia State University. He's doing a four-part series funded by several endowments. The first one was on the Cherokees, the second was on Appalachian folktales, then Gulf folktales and there's one more. There are things going on. Apple Shop up in Kentucky is just one. Being a regional artist has become respectable again. It went through a period when it was not respectable, it was "let's march ahead with the avant-garde." The pendulum is swinging back.

What are you working on now?

I'm working on another book that I'm calling *Wild Ginger*. Recently, I just mailed a chapbook of poems I didn't know what to do with. They're the Greek poems, but there's not enough for a whole book. Since I am fairly expert on the Greeks and love the whole Greek idea, I've been writing Greek poems off and on for about ten years. I'd like to see something done with these poems, but they don't fit in an Appalachian book. I had a reviewer castigate me up and down the pike because there was more than one voice in me. She wanted me to be only the Appalachian country momma. Somehow it was offensive to her that I was a college professor and somewhat of an expert of ancient Bronze Age Greece. The Greek poems are my voice, but they're not like *Liza's Monday*.

It occurred to me while I was studying Greek literature that they never allowed the children to speak. So I did a sequence called "Small Voices from Hades," in which Hector's son and Jason's boys and Heracles' children, who are not specified as to sex, are all murdered for one reason or another, never having been allowed to speak. So they speak from the world of the dead and they speak as children.

Is there anything I haven't asked that you would like to discuss?

I am a person who is very much concerned about the state of the humanities. I believe in the humanities as a broad necessity, not a luxury. I spent ten years as the Chairman of the Humanities Division at Young Harris, and I think of myself as a broad spectrum humanities person; art, music and drama are all part of my life and part of what I try to teach my students, my children and my grandchildren. I think we need more missionaries to keep the humanities alive, because this scientific computer age is a real cold bedfellow. That's my sermon for the day.

Celestine Sibley

Celestine Sibley began her writing career as a cub reporter for a small newspaper in Mobile, Alabama, and has been a reporter/columnist for the *Atlanta Constitution* since 1941, where she has covered everything from art to murder trials. She has written fifteen books, including *For All Seasons, Christmas in Georgia, A Place Called Sweet Apple, Jincey, Mothers Are Always Special,* and after a quarter century *Peachtree Street, U.S.A.* has been revised. Most recently she has written her autobiography, *Turned Funny.* This interview was conducted on February 25, 1987, in her office at the *Atlanta Journal and Constitution.*

Would you discuss your early background, when and where you were born?

I was born in Holly, Florida, and grew up in Mobile County, Alabama. I came to work for the *Constitution* in 1941. A few years later I left to have a baby, and then came back in 1945. I covered all news assignments and did a column on the side two or three days a week. Then they wanted me to do it five days a week. I used to cover legislature and most of the big murder trials, including James Earl Ray. It certainly was one of the most exciting stories of the decade. I think, like many people, that he did it himself.

Some people have suggested it was a conspiracy.

I don't think so. I think he acted on his own. A lot of people don't agree, especially blacks. They think it was a conspiracy. But I think it was just a crazy, pitiful, turned-inward kook. You get a big murder case and people start believing anything. People say that Hitler isn't dead, and that Bobby Kennedy is supposedly still alive. Well, there are many complications. John Kennedy — you know how long that investigation took. People latch onto it with their imaginations, and really work it over, adding to the story. The plain facts support the fact that Ray killed Martin Luther King by himself.

You were there for the trial proceedings?

Yes. The first one he pleaded guilty. After that Mr. McGill and myself came back to Atlanta. Then after Ray had been in jail awhile he appealed, and went to federal court to try and get his plea set aside. By that time Mr. McGill had died. I guess I stayed two weeks covering the story in Memphis. All of us in the press section, the *New York Times, Los Angeles Times, Washington Post,* agreed that he had done it single-handedly. You can ask where did he get the money? Well, he didn't have much money. He lived, when he lived here in Atlanta, in a basement apartment on 14th or 15th Street. And he lived on butter beans in those little frozen bags you put in hot water to thaw. He only lived in a little dingy basement apartment. So he didn't have any money. People wonder how he got to England. I think he could have mooched from his brothers or some other people. I don't think there was any evidence that he had a lot of money. He got himself a gun. I guess that cost a good penny.

So you found murder trials exciting to cover?

I like murder trials. I've covered a lot of them. I think a murder trial is the purest form of drama you'll find. It's contained for one thing. Most stories run all over the place, but on a murder trial, it's straightforward—this is the courtroom, this is the stage, and the actors are playing for keeps. It's a life and death matter.

While you were reporting, you were, of course, taking in the facts and making your own judgments. Have you ever been wrong about the verdict?

I've never had presumed to guess what the verdict was going to be. You have a feeling about innocence and guilt, but you can't say for certain. I would say that the fellow in the Atlanta children murders was guilty.

Wayne Williams.

Yeah, Wayne Williams. He seemed guilty to me. Who knows? I mean, you think you know.

When did you start writing?

When I was eleven years old. The summer I was eleven I wrote a story which was practically plagiarism. I had read a book called *Molly and the Golden West.* I had never been any farther west than Lucedale, Mississippi, but I decided to write one called *Mary Ann and the Golden West.* And I did. I looked up the Pacific Coast and picked Berkeley for Mary Ann to go to. Oh, it was a good book.

When did you first start out in journalism?

I started out working for the *Mobile Press-Register* when I was fifteen years old. I was working on the high school paper when the editor of the *Mobile Press* came to make a speech to us, to talk to the class. He suggested that if anybody wanted to they could come in and work for the experience. And I wanted to. So I went down every Saturday and worked on the paper. When summertime came they offered me a summer job for five dollars a week, which just about covered my car fare and lunch money. When fall came I went back to my Saturday schedule. After I graduated from high school they offered me my summer job again. Then I went to Spring Hill College, and the paper helped me by swapping days off in exchange for swapping hours so I could go to class. They insisted on picking my courses. Spring Hill didn't teach any courses in journalism, but they were heavy in history and English, so that's what they made me take.

So your degree was in which subject?

No, I didn't get a degree. I got married and quit school after two years of college.

You've been around newspapers for many years. How have they changed since you started?

The idea about not letting the facts get in the way—that's not typical. No good reporter says that. We've had some people come and go who have thought that, but thank the Lord they keep going. You owe the public the facts. That's what the whole thing is about. That's the reason for the paper's existence. I'm a dazzled member of the fourth estate—I believe that writing for a newspaper is as important as any job in the world. I think you have a sacred obligation, as they say, to let the people know. And when the people know, they act. You know from studying history, the first thing Hitler did was squelch the papers in Germany. Just countless numbers in Germany had no idea what was going on. So I think it is extremely important to bring the facts to the people.

You asked about the changes in newspapers—they're bigger and have more reporters. These young people are extremely gifted. Most are better educated. It used to be that a man with a flair for writing and an interest could just come in and get a job. Now they are carefully picked. A movie editor is really somebody knowledgeable at it. When I started on the paper, one person would write music, theater, almost anything. But now, the writers are specialists. We have many who have studied foreign languages and go abroad as correspondents. Papers are generally better all the way around.

You were writing for the Constitution *in the early forties, but by then Margaret Mitchell had already left the* Journal. *You've mentioned that you knew her briefly.*

Yes, she had already left by the time I started. She left the *Journal* in 1926. But I did happen to know her, and she was an extremely generous and gracious person, greatly loved by all the newspaper fraternity. Even people on the *Constitution,* who she didn't work with, knew her socially. If she read something you wrote that she liked, she'd drop you a little note or call you up. She was an extremely nice woman. Unfortunately, the note she sent me I didn't keep. Now I wish I had. She liked something I wrote. It was the story that's in *Peachtree Street, U.S.A.* about an old lady who was arrested for throwing rocks at passing schoolchildren. This old woman lived on Bass Street in an old house that didn't have lights or water, and was about to be pulled down by kudzu. When the authorities went in they found she had twenty-five pianos. I went to the jail where they arrested her and when they gave her a bath, they discovered she had under her ragged clothes $10,500. Well, Peggy was very interested in that story. It delighted her because it showed that Atlanta was still small town in its attitudes, that it still accepted some of its characters and eccentrics.

Peggy did stay in touch with people on the paper. She would walk in, sit on your desk and swing her legs, and chat with us about the news. She and I lived in the same general neighborhood and I'd run into her at the grocery store. One time I was up there with my children, my two little girls, and we stopped to talk. They got tried of waiting — you know they wanted to go to the dime store — and they started tugging at my dress. They didn't know who Margaret Mitchell was or care. Peggy looked at them, laughed, and said, "I know how you feel, I used to come up here on Saturday with my mother, and I'd have to swallow my locket to get her to stop talking to people." I guess if she swallowed her locket, her momma would take her home.

Recently, you just rereleased Peachtree Street, U.S.A. *Could you discuss why you brought out the revised book?*

Because Peachtree asked me too. (*Laughing.*) They bought the rights, and felt it was time to reissue it. Atlanta has grown so much and there are so many people now.

It's been twenty-five years since it was first published in 1963. Since then, what do you think the most significant change has been in Atlanta?

Probably growth. Last spring when Peachtree bought the rights from Doubleday, they asked me if I would update it. I said sure, no problem. I should have known, but I didn't realize until I got to work on it that everything in Atlanta has changed except who won the war. It took me all summer to revise the book, and I didn't even try to substitute chapters, except the black chapter which was totally outdated. I didn't attempt to put in any new material, I just tried to correct the obvious changes that have occurred. It took all summer to do that. Everything is different.

So was it almost like writing a new book?

No, not really, because I didn't want to do that. I told them I couldn't do that. But on the other hand, I didn't want it to be an idiot's book with a lot of things that aren't there anymore. So I changed it, and I threw in people like Ted Turner who's kind of on the scene now. New buildings and growth are the major factors. We've lost a lot of things that symbolized Atlanta, like all the railroads. It changes, and that's Atlanta's history. That's the way it's been all of its life. You know that if you turn your back for two weeks they'll build another skyscraper.

When reading your books, For All Seasons *and* Peachtree Street, U.S.A., *one realizes your love for the city. It's brought about a better understanding of the city in many ways, especially historically speaking. But, also, I feel as you made comparisons between Atlanta and the rest of the world that Atlanta is the center of the universe.*

But isn't it? (*Laughing.*) Well, it's home, and I guess whatever you call home is your center. I was reared in a wonderful town south of Georgia, and the Georgia thing that always amused me when I first came to Atlanta was that everyone would tell you where they were from in Georgia and how far that was from Atlanta. You know, "I'm from Tifton and it's 150 miles from Atlanta." They'd say, "Valdosta, Georgia — 300 miles from Atlanta." They don't do that much anymore. They always identified with Atlanta. So it's sort of the center.

My husband worked for the Associated Press, and I got a job working for the *Constitution,* which I read every Sunday all my life. My father thought the *Constitution* was just a splendid newspaper. It was famous all around. It was the *New York Times* of the South. I thought I'd die if I didn't get to work for it and have all those famous editors. So I came up to visit Jim and apply for a job, which I got. I went home for a week to load up the car, tied the baby bed on back, and my mother and I embarked on Saturday night.

My mother grew up in south Georgia and had never been to Atlanta. On that Sunday morning when we got here we had a little apartment waiting in College Park. That morning my mother was up, ready to go out and look at Atlanta — you know, just loving every minute of it. She went that day to the Cyclorama and all kinds of places. In those days people used to come to town a lot on Sunday afternoons and window shop. The stores weren't open, but people could wander around downtown just looking at it, enjoying themselves. We did that a lot. Another thing we did was go out to the airport, which we thought was the biggest thing in the world. It wasn't then, but it is now — just about. Second largest, I guess. We just thought it was magnificent to go out there and park by the fence and watch the planes come and go.

In Peachtree Street, U.S.A., *the story I enjoyed most was the one about the young enlisted man who stopped by the* Constitution *looking for a place to get married, and the staff set everything up for him and got him married off right there.*

He didn't have any money, his girl didn't have any money and he was shipping out the next day. Oh we had a nice party for him.

Have you ever heard from him since?

I don't know, I don't remember. Somebody may have heard, I didn't. Somebody on the staff may have. I don't remember the year either, but it was during the war. At the time we were in that old building next to Rich's. It was an old Victorian building, and it had the first elevator in Atlanta. It was such a slow old thing that when I went to apply for a job, I didn't know it was running so I climbed five flights of stairs. When I got up to Mr. McGill's office I was so out of breath I could hardly tell him that I wanted a job. It was a crowded, dirty, wonderful old building.

What was you childhood like?

It was pretty good. I guess it's all in your point of view. I went to the Bread Loaf Writer's Conference in Vermont one summer, and I wrote a story about a little girl whose mother was kind of crazy. She would stay on the road with her walking from place to place. Well they landed at a country place with some relatives and the child loved it and wanted to stay. But then she heard her mother singing one morning and that was the symbol that she was ready to move on again. The mother was, of course, crazy. Anyway, my instructor, Rachel McKenzie, who taught at Radcliffe, was going over the story with me and she said, "I envy you—your rich background." I nearly fell out of my chair. That doesn't sound rich, does it? I told my mother about it, and she said, "Is that what those people up there consider rich, being hard-up, poor, and homeless." It just depends on how you use your background. Relatively speaking, I had a really rich background.

My little granddaughter asked me one time, "Were you a rich kid?" I said "Oh sure, I was a very rich kid." What she meant by rich was not what I meant by rich. She, of course, meant material possessions. I had a few of those. I had a boat and a horse, some pets. My mother saw that I got all the books I wanted to read. We were eighteen miles from Mobile, but she'd drive to the library once a week, and we'd load the car. I'd practically have all of them read by the time I got back home. It was a good childhood. I learned to swim in a millpond. My father was in the sawmill-turpentine business. We had a beautiful, big millpond. I used to walk to school.

Do you have any brothers and sisters?

No. No brothers or sisters. I never rode the bus to school. Children who get picked up by the school bus, and are transported door to door are underprivileged. If you're a country child you have adventures. I think city children do, too, but country children have special adventures walking home to and from school. We always waded through creeks and climbed trees, and picked flowers. This may have given me an idea for a column.

That brings up one question I had. As a columnist . . .

I'm a reporter-columnist. I don't do much reporting anymore, but I like the title.

As a reporter-columnist, does the well ever dry up?

Oh sure, all the time. Especially when I have somewhere to go, like out of town for some reason, and I have to work ahead. There will be days when you think you know what you want to write about, but nothing happens. Mr. McGill had a sign in his office that said, "Lord, give me an idea for today, and forgive the one I had yesterday." When I was a young reporter I read a book about journalism, and it said the earth was three feet deep and for ideas all you have to do is scratch the surface. I have a lot of trouble digging sometimes.

Well, back to your childhood. Do you have a favorite childhood memory?

I told you I had a rowboat on the millpond. I would take a book and go to the commissary where my father's office was, and I'd get some saltine crackers and silver bell chocolate kisses, then I'd row out a good distance in the millpond. It was peaceful and quiet. I would lay in the bottom of the boat and read. No one would bother me. No one could call me to do anything. On the back of the boat I would spread out my crackers and put a Hershey's kiss on them. The sun would melt them, and then I'd slap them together. I would have delicious sandwiches. I remember once when I was lying in the boat and I had heard this splash in the water. I looked up and saw that a deer had come down to drink, and was wading out in the water a little bit. That's one of my favorite memories, and I think about it a lot. For being such a small thing, it was such a magical moment.

Turning this around, did you have a least favorite childhood memory?

I had a few of those also. One of the most embarrassing things to ever happen to me was when I was twelve years old. I wrote a story about this for *Reader's Digest*. They're bringing out a book called *Country Places* and they asked me to do a chapter.

The school would raise money for various things, and they had a box social. Everybody would fix up a box of food. My mother decorated my shoe box with blue ruffles and crepe paper. Then she killed our rooster who used to go through the yard clucking the strangest sound, "Boob, boob, boob." So my mother named him Boob McNut after a character in the funny pages. She hated that old rooster, because he'd flap his wings and make that crazy noise. So she killed Boob and fried him, which was a bad mistake because he was old and tough. Well, a boy named H.B. Lewis bought my box, and you had to sit with the person who bought your box. So he and I sat together, which was embarrassing for both of us. We sort of sat on the edge of the chair. H.B. was an older man of about fourteen. I thought he was very glamorous until that time when he got into my box and pulled out a drumstick and bit into it and pulled. The skin was so tough it snapped back in his face. Mournfully, I said, "Oh Boob." He thought I was talking about him. He said, "Boob yourself. I want my money back." Well my mother, who had more of a sense of humor than I did, laughed and laughed. I was mortified. I still am when I think about it.

In your writing, who has been the biggest influence?

The biggest writer influence, I suppose, would be John Steinbeck. I think *The Grapes of Wrath* is one of the best books written. In his books, Steinbeck finds interesting things in the disreputable, the dirty, the downtrodden, and writes about them with great humor and great affection. He's specific. A lot of writers deal in generalities. My favorite example is in *The Grapes of Wrath* when the car breaks down on the trip out West. That was really a catastrophe because they didn't have any money, and they didn't know how they were going to move on. They bought a part from some secondhand place, and put it in. Steinbeck doesn't just say a part, he tells you exactly what it was. I've forgotten, but I think it was connecting rod. When you read about the boys in *Sweet Thursday* and *Cannery Row,* you know that

Steinbeck was an expert on marine life. That's the kind of responsibility that all writers should have, not just to latch onto vague generalities — be specific. He's been that kind of an influence.

I've also been lucky with my friends in Atlanta. We used to get together and call ourselves *The Plot Club*. It was no club and there was hardly any plot, but we just started calling it that. Wylly St. Johns, who liked to write almost better than anything else in the world except to read, found a little item in the paper one time that she thought had the germ of a plot in it. Each of us wrote a different story with that as the plot. She wrote a novelette, I wrote a regional love story, Andy Sparks wrote a dog story, and somebody else wrote a television play. We all met at Wylly's. We picked up some sandwiches and beer, and sat on her front porch and read our stuff aloud. Well, we thought it was the greatest thing we ever did. Olive Ann Burns was also a member of *The Plot Club*. We gave each other a lot of praise. That was very encouraging, very stimulating. We did it for a number of years. Of course, the thing grew too much, and there were too many of us to read. The original brew was you couldn't come unless you brought something to read. Then we got to where we had covered dish meals. It was very encouraging.

Wylly was a great encouragement to me. When I sent my first book to Doubleday, I sent thirty pages. The editor wrote back and said she thought it was smart-alecky — something like that. If I would change that she would offer me a contract. Well, I didn't know what she was talking about, but I had lunch with Wylly. She took the manuscript, and pointed out eight words that I could change, and it made it less smart-alecky. The editor was satisfied and the book went.

Wylly was that kind of person. She could put her finger right on your troubles. She helped me with *Children, My Children* when I was having problems with all the flashbacks. She was a valuable friend. She died about two years ago.

What are you working on now?

We use that word loosely. I just did a thirty-page synopsis of *Jincey* for the movie. I have an autobiography that I contracted with Harper & Row to do. It's called *Turned Funny*. I started it about five years ago.

Have you enjoyed writing autobiographical material?

Not especially. Since it's mainly autobiographical material, sometimes it's painful to look back. And then you're not too happy about indecent exposure anyway.

From start to finish about how long did it take you to finish Turned Funny?

Well, of course, you know I work every day, and I wrote other things in the meantime, so I don't really know, but I guess it was on the fire about three or four years.

You mentioned that it was painful to look back sometimes. Did you find it pretty difficult to go back and write about these things?

Sometimes, but sometimes things would flow pretty good. Sometimes I would get stuck.

What was the most difficult part of writing Turned Funny?

I guess the exposure of my life with the painful experiences and how I felt about them—things I don't normally go around telling people.

What types of experiences?

Well, my first marriage. My husband was an alcoholic, and all the troubles that go with alcoholism—abuse, job loss, things like that. It'll all be in the book.

You missed your first deadline with Turned Funny.

I did, and they gave me a new deadline which I made. They gave me more time on it. The new deadline was October 1987, and I made it in well before that. The book will be released September 9, 1988.

How did the initial writing of the book transpire? Did you write a chapter and send it to them, or did you finish the book, then mail it in its entirety?

Larry Ashmead, my editor at Harper & Row, is a longtime friend and editor of twenty years, and the book was his idea. I wrote a few sections then sent them to him to see if he felt like I was doing what he wanted me to do.

How much editing did he do?

Hardly any. The first part he saw—I kind of had the idea *Turned Funny* would be a book about newspaper adventures, stories I had covered, that kind of thing, which I enjoyed doing. Then he wanted me to make it more personal. That's when it began to get more painful. After he got the manuscript he liked it, and the people he sent the proofs to liked it, also. Pat Conroy wrote a blurb for the jacket, and Terry Kay wrote me a wonderful letter about the book, and he's going to review it. So maybe it's better than I think.

While writing Turned Funny, *and remembering back upon your life—you mentioned writing about the painful experiences—were there any stories that stood out in particular?*

The things that are pleasant to remember stand out, but I really think the book should have been funnier, though there were funny experiences that I enjoyed telling. The things I did as a reporter I enjoyed writing about—that writing is a whole lot more funny than the personal stuff.

Is there anything about Turned Funny *that you would like to discuss in particular?*

Do you know where the title comes from? Margaret Mitchell once told me she thought Atlanta had remained a small town because of its tolerance of its oddballs and characters. I grew up with what some people call eccentrics. When someone would refer to another person as crazy my mother used to say she's not eccentric or crazy, she's just "turned funny." Well, I have found that all over the South people use that expression.

They are using a wonderful picture of me on the front cover I think is one of the best things about the book. It is a picture of me when I was eight years old in a costume my mother made for me to be the fairy queen in the third grade. I was too big to be one of the fairies, so they created the role of fairy queen for me. She made me this a crepe paper costume, and the night of the performance she had me fixed up real nice — my hair curled, my cheeks all covered with rouge — everyone thought I looked splendid. She didn't get around to taking my picture for a week or two, and this was the most doleful looking child — stringy hair coming out from her crown. My knees were all scabby and my mother couldn't get them clean so she put some of her silk stockings on me to hide my knees, and they bagged. It's just the funniest thing you ever saw — that picture. That's the best thing about the book, I think.

I've enjoyed talking with you. Is there anything I haven't asked that you would like to discuss?

No, I think you covered the waterfront, honey.

Anne Rivers Siddons

Anne Rivers Siddons is the author of *Fox's Earth, The House Next Door, Heartbreak Hotel, John Chancellor Makes Me Cry, Homeplace,* and *Peachtree Road.* She lives in Atlanta with her husband, and summers in Maine. A warm, gentle woman, she has strong opinions concerning the South and the direction it has taken. But, as easily as she discusses the problems, she relishes in the beauty and style the South has preserved. She laughs often and enjoys talking about Atlanta. This interview was conducted at her home on August 10, 1987, where we drank iced tea as the temperature reached high into the nineties.

Could you discuss your background?

I was born in Fairburn, Georgia. Actually, in Atlanta. I lived in Fairburn until I went away to college at Auburn. I am the fifth generation of my family to live there. I studied art at Auburn and have a degree in commercial art. After graduation I came back to Atlanta and got a job with C&S Bank in their advertising department, thinking I wanted to be an artist. Pretty soon it was obvious I was just going to be a much better writer than I ever could have been an artist. Why I never pursued that I don't know. It just seemed too facile for me to attach much value to it, though I did have a column in the school newspaper and was feature editor. This led the way to writing advertising copy. Then Jim Townsend started *Atlanta Magazine* and I went there in 1964 as one of the first senior editors. I stayed there until 1967, then went to Burton Campbell Advertising. At that point I sort of alternated back and forth between magazines and advertising until I stopped to write full time.

When did you begin writing full time?

I wrote my first book while I was still working for Burton Campbell Advertising, and that was in 1974. I guess I started writing full time in 1976. And that's what I've done since.

You mentioned Auburn and studying art. What area did you study?

I have a degree in illustration, mainly because it is the only degree I could find that didn't require any math. I thought I wanted to be an architect, so I went with that idea. I would have been a good designer, but nothing would have stood up because I flunked structure so many times. It was obvious that I just wasn't ever going to get the math. So I switched to art. I like contemporary illustration.

You wrote for the Auburn Plainsman.

I did. I had a column, then was made feature editor at the same time Paul Hemphill was sports editor. So our friendship goes back that far.

Then your writing just kind of evolved?

Yes, it did evolve. I wish I could say I had a passionate, burning desire since I was young, but I didn't. I loved writing and I finally got it through my thick skull that writing is what I was meant to do; it really is what I did, but more at someone else's bidding. It never seemed to me that being a novelist was attainable, and so I really just fell into it with an enormous stroke of luck. Had it not happened the way it did, I wonder if I would have had the insight or courage to do it.

What brought about writing your first novel?

I received a letter from an editor at Doubleday after an article I had written in a magazine, the old *Georgia* magazine. He said that if I ever wanted to write a book to please get in touch with him. I honestly thought a friend of mine at the *New Yorker* had stolen some Doubleday stationery and was putting me on. So I didn't answer the letter. About two weeks later he called and said, "Are you as rude as you are gifted?" From that a great friendship was born. Then my husband and I went to his twenty-fifth class reunion at Princeton, so from there we went into New York to have lunch with this editor, and out of that lunch came a two-book contract — probably the smallest contract Doubleday ever gave anybody, but I thought it was wonderful. It was a wonderful stroke of luck, and that editor is still my editor today, and a great friend, Larry Ashmead. No doubt about it, I would not be writing if it had not been for Larry, or it would have been much tougher.

You have always lived in the Atlanta area?

Yes, Fairburn and Atlanta. I'm in and out of New York a lot, but I have never lived there. We travel a good bit. We spend our summers in Maine, near Bar Harbor. It's in an old cottage colony; my husband's grandfather built it. I would be there right now if I wasn't halfway through my next book. I plan to be there all next summer. I'll never willingly sit out an Atlanta summer like this again. It's been miserable. I get angry every summer and yell and scream that I'm going to leave Atlanta, but when fall comes it's wonderful and I change my mind. We threaten to move to Maine every summer because I love it so. But I would have to go through a Northern winter. I really do live in Maine, I guess, for four months during the summer.

You are from the South, and you are a Southern writer.

Like it or not I am Southern born and bred.

You're in that same genre of writing along with Pat Conroy, Terry Kay, and so many other good writers.

I guess so. I guess you'd have to call us Southern writers because we write out of the South. I hope what we have to say would transcend a region, but certainly we speak out of the Southern experience because a writer must write about what he is born into and knows. I always will be a Southern writer, though I probably will set a book in Maine someday. I would like to write about that area one day, experience all the generations of that old colony. So I hope any gift I have for transcending the South will work for me in Maine. But there's no doubt all my books are very concerned for Southern people — I would think, now, more of the new South than the old South. I'm getting a little tired of the old South. I think we can pack that baby up.

Could you distinguish between the old South and the new South?

In the old South we had grandma's front porch. In the new South we have the malls and Arby's.

What defines the Southern writer?

Religion is certainly one of the factors, that sense of language of the Old Testament that we all seem to fall back on. Marshall Frady and I talked about this a good deal — he's the son of a preacher and I was the daughter of a Sunday school superintendent — where our first experiences with narrative was the Biblical epic, with all its terror and retribution and revenge, as well as the sweetness and hope of the Bible. Another thing that shapes us, surely, is that sense of storytelling. I'm sure everybody has told you that, but for so long, being a geographically more unsettled area and sort of an economically depressed area, there wasn't much to do but sit around listening to the old folks talk on the porch. And I've done an awful lot of that. There's something else; I guess it was Cash in *The Mind of the South,* Van Woodward said it too, and I really do agree — that one thing the South has going for it is that sense of literally being a conquered people. No other area in the continental United States has ever been occupied by an army. And like it or not, or admit it or not, we were party to a very grave moral and social wrong: slavery. I think there's an underlying petulance of guilt there. We lost the war and we deserved to lose that war. No matter how much I love us and am a Southerner, what we were about was wrong.

It's a deep guilt that results from several things. I don't think it's an overt guilt, but the Southerner has an enormous chip on his shoulder, under that indolence and grace and charm, and he was looked upon by the rest of the country as a pariah, and with good reason. We often think of the great Southern eccentric. The fact is there weren't many during the war, what Walker Percy called, "Our recent long obsession. . . ." We already felt too dissident, we already felt too eccentric, we would not tolerate it, and we especially would not tolerate it from our women. This is a pet peeve of mine and the subject of a very long book I'm involved in. I think the South comes very close to murdering its gifted and dissident women, at least the South of a previous time. Maybe we're not doing it so much now. We're just not that quick to allow that difference, that dissidence, and I think the reason we aren't is because women have too much ambition.

That idea is a central point in Heartbreak Hotel *and* Homeplace *with the civil rights. Ironically, Maggie, in* Heartbreak Hotel, *can only free herself from the old South by becoming involved in the civil rights movement. Ultimately, she frees herself by trying to free someone else.*

It's either been a conscious or unconscious burr under my blanket that the price a Southern woman pays for difference is ostracism. It's not so much anymore, because our young women, who are Maggie's age, the college years, are exposed to so much fresh air from the outside. And that's terrific. They have more choices, but we still do these things—especially in a certain class of Southern women. The old Atlanta families, who would like their daughters to be debutantes, are going to make it tougher on her to be a civil rights worker or a surgeon than to be a wife and volunteer.

They hold the purse strings. And on the opposite end of the spectrum is the uneducated.

Sure. I guess everything goes back to economics. My husband says everything goes back to economics if you trace it back far enough; war, etc. Surely, the Southern women's need to play games in order to maintain her status is simple economic necessity. It served her well to learn to flirt over a fan, it literally kept a roof over her head. Women are pretty adaptable, we can learn to do anything. I've never been very fond of the "belle" syndrome, but I can understand it. It's not as useless a thing as it has been billed—it's a strong survival tool.

Do you consider yourself a feminist, or how would you categorize yourself?

Insofar as I would categorize myself as anything, yes, I am a feminist. And a novelist. But not necessarily a feminist novelist.

There is a strong unifying story in Homeplace *that hits rather hard with the Atlanta area, and to an extent with the South, with new roads being built and widened, new interstates, mainly GA 400 and the Jimmy Carter Presidential Freeway, which the majority of Atlantans oppose. Is* Homeplace *your way of fighting back against the Department of Transportation?*

I guess in one way it is. The Georgia Department of Transportation literally did tear down my family's old homeplace about ten years ago. My father was the last one to be born there. It was one hundred years old, and many generations had lived there. My father is a very good lawyer and he fought it, but you don't win those things—you really don't. So, what can you do? Even though I would not have lived there (I was detached from Fairburn by then), it outraged me far more than I thought it would. It just festered for a long time, and did become central to me. Since then I've come to look a

lot at what is happening to Atlanta and other Southern cities. I toured with
Homeplace and saw how many of the other Southern cities are beginning to
develop the way Atlanta did twenty years ago. I just want to yell "stop!" They
still have time to think about it. I'm not saying don't grow, you will grow, but
please think about the *way* you will grow. It doesn't have to be torn down,
it can be incorporated. Atlanta would rather tear it down than anything else.
This is the only quarrel I have with Andrew Young. I supported him and I
used to sit with him back in the days of the movement back at Paschal's La
Carrousel listening to jazz. I think he's wonderful, but I wish he'd keep his
hands off the trees and old structures. I cannot understand it. He's on record
as saying that it's junk and that he doesn't care about it. If we tear down much
more we might as well be Scranton, Tulsa or Dallas.

So Homeplace *really was autobiographical?*

Yes, *Homeplace* on that level really was. Also, I wanted to talk about the
South as it was going into the days when it turned into the sunbelt. What we
have now cannot last, and I'm not even sure it should, but I don't think it
should go unremarked. There's great drama in transition. The South is
caught in this long transition which really started in 1940 with World War II,
and is as sure an Armageddon for the South as was the Civil War. It just took
fifty years instead of two.

The town Lytton was then based on Fairburn?

More or less. I called it Lytton because I made some things physically
different. *Homeplace* is semiautobiographical in that that did happen to my
family. Unlike Mike Winship, I never had a fight with my father about the
civil rights movement and never moved to New York City. My father and
I are very close, but to a much lesser degree I think he feels a lot like John
Winship, about race, I mean. We don't discuss the issue.

As the book reveals, certainly you're opposed to eminent domain?

I think so. And it sounds like I'm a little old lady brandishing my cane
in the air, but I will never be able to swallow the idea that the state can simply
take a man's property against his will. I just can't swallow that. There has to
be something else we can do. I know they offer compensatory damages, but
their idea of compensatory damages are simply ludicrous. My father still has
about one hundred acres left, but there's no road access. What's he going to
do with that? He can't sell it and he can't develop it. He can't get to his
land.

Throughout your books, mainly Heartbreak Hotel, *you mention a verse or two
from popular songs. Is there any special reason you use this?*

Yes, because that particular era seemed to me to be dominated by music.
I suppose anybody's college experiences are awash in music at that time as
you ever are in your life. But a college campus on a hot summer day in the
late fifties simply cannot be talked about without an underlying beat of rock
music. That's really the way things were.

Who are some of your favorite musical artists?

I'm not a fan of rock music oddly enough, though I've always liked The Eagles, and of course, the Beatles. I like classical music a lot, and I love some old country and western. When I was growing up we didn't think of country and western as being anything but all the music there was. I listened to that, and my father taught all the neighborhood kids to dance to the big band records. I'm a great Beethoven fan. I love baroque music. The beginning of rock, rock 'n' roll, was inescapable on a college campus in the fifties. I always loved jazz, too.

In Heartbreak Hotel *there is the civil rights movement, the building up of mankind, the betterment of mankind.* Homeplace *contrasts this idea with the tearing down of the old life, the old South is dying, physically and emotionally.*

Yes, that's true. I think cities are wonderful. An honest city like New York or Chicago is a delight and a joy to be in, even though they're dirty and abrasive and awful and downright dangerous, too. I hate sanitized cities, and that's what we are getting, with our endless miles of strip–shopping centers and fast foods. It's not city and it's not country. It's not anything. The American preoccupation with malls and quickly available consumer "stuff" is just inimitable to the Southerner. I don't necessarily think the small Southern town is the be-all and end-all in the quality of life, but I hate to see it lost to that. If I thought Atlanta was going to turn into the kind of city that had guts and grit and texture and particularity to it, it wouldn't bother me, but I don't think it will. For one thing, people are never going to live in the heart of Atlanta, and that's what it takes to make a real city. Now we're just a succession of interlocking suburban neighborhoods where people live. How could we live in downtown Atlanta? Where would we live? There is no housing. We will probably have to do something with the heart of Atlanta in the next twenty-five to fifty years, and probably *will* do something. But whatever we do, I'm afraid it will be to accommodate the buying of something—the buying of entertainment, the buying of everything. I don't think it will be to accommodate the *living* of human beings.

In the South, we don't have a tradition of living in the city. The Southerner old enough to afford any kind of good housing—in his forties and fifties—doesn't have the tradition of moving to the city. The young Southerner coming up, now, doesn't know anything but condominiums. The ones who love and cherish real city life will find their way to other cities, and maybe come home and bring a little of it back. To love Atlanta is like an old marriage or a long love—it's a commitment, but it's not necessarily un-qualified love. There are times I hate it, but I am committed to it. There are times I adore it, and there are times when it is exasperating. There's a lot wrong with it. But, somewhat like Harry Truman said, "It's a son-of-a-bitch, but it's our son-of-a-bitch."

Who are your favorite writers?

I've always loved Edith Wharton and Henry James. Herman Melville was a great favorite when I was small. Right now, I'm reading the biography of Katharine Augell White. E.B. White was a wonderful craftsmen with the language. I like John Updike, Cheever, Saul Bellow, Walker Percy. I have a hard time with Faulkner, not because of his convolution, but he needs to just lighten up sometimes. Eudora Welty, Peter Taylor, Pat Conroy certainly are included as my favorites.

Conroy's The Prince of Tides *is an exceptional book. His ability to manipulate the reader with conflict is just overpowering.*

He can tell you about conflict. He's the most conflicted man I've known. The conflict comes very directly out of his own life. Pat writes very close to the bone, and he took an enormous risk with that book, and I admire that. It's not a popular form today to write a great, sprawling book. *The Prince of Tides* goes right back to Thomas Wolfe. Conroy got pretty severely lacerated for it, and I can't imagine how so many critics missed the point with that book. But they did, totally. I think it's an absolutely stunning book. The whole experience is one of incredible density and richness, and everything contributes to it.

There are fads in fiction as anything else, and the reviewers who have come out of that New York, MacDowell Colony, University writers axis are very into the linear, spare, Upper West Side business. They don't know what to do with other kinds of books, so they scorn these great billows and furbelows of density that come out of people like Conroy. It's ridiculous. You can't have fads in writing.

Like Emily Dickinson said — Good writing either raises the hair on the back of your neck or it doesn't.

That's right. And it's always raised out of an honest passion. You can't fake that. You need to talk about whatever is eating on you at the time. I think most serious writers end up, for one reason or another, writing to make sense out of something, to give some order to something that is essentially disorderly, which is life itself.

I always end up choosing out of the many things I thought one day I might write about, something that was never on that list, something that came out of some deep part of me, out of left field, and literally *needed* to be written about. I know Pat works that way.

Out of your childhood is there a favorite memory that you reflect back upon?

I always see myself standing in the French doors into our living room at 5:00 on Christmas morning, and someone has always gotten up before me to light the Christmas tree. It was during the war and we didn't heat much of the house. It was a big house. I remember that first minute of seeing that black night, and there in the background, the tree just blazed with light and warmth, and smelled of pine needles. It was just like coming into heaven from purgatory.

Do you have a least favorite?

Sunday afternoons — 4:00 on Sunday afternoons. I was an only child in a little town. I remember in mid–winter I would wait hopelessly for school to start the next morning. It was a very melancholy time, a very desolate feeling. I don't know quite what it came out of. Certainly, it was a worse feeling than just having to go back to school on Monday morning. There's such an ending feeling to it.

You've been out of town a great deal since Homeplace *was published. Do you enjoy promoting the book?*

Oh, God. I hate it. It's just an exercise in humiliation. But I like meeting bookstore owners. I have never met a book store owner I didn't like. They're funny, eccentric individuals. It's the physical grind that's hard for me. Essentially, it's just on the road, door-to-door selling, which I've never been good at. It's very wearing physically, but you can get some wonderful war stories out of it.

Didn't you do ten cities in as many days?

Yes, more or less. I had some time between a few of them. It was nothing like the huge tour Pat Conroy had with *The Prince of Tides.* I understand I'll have a bigger tour with the next book. I told my editor to take his choice. He could ship me around in a refrigerator boxcar, or let me stay home. But I'll be dead by then. It won't really matter. You miss meals. You eat out of airport vending machines, if you eat. You sleep four hours a day. It's terribly wearing.

I didn't realize the severity of the grind.

I didn't either, but publishers have to get as much mileage out of every city you're in as they can. You'll get up at six to go on a morning radio show, then back to back radio and television all morning, then a book signing, then you'll read, then you're on the plane to a new city, then you start the process over again.

Does your publisher set the schedule?

Yes. It is very flattering to be given a tour, not many writers are. I realize that, and I'm very grateful. It means they've invested something in the book. And if you're going to do it at all I think you should do it cheerfully, without bitching too much. I mean, who can really hate the fact that somebody wants you to be on a television show? It's very flattering, even though no one has read your book, and they mispronounce your name, and only three people come to the autographing. . . . I once put an entire roomful of old ladies to sleep after speaking to them right after lunch. They just went over like Douglas Firs. I thought, "Well they came." I figure if I'm going to do it at all I might as well keep an eye open for the funny things. And I guess touring does sell books or the publishers wouldn't do it.

We discussed having your first novel published. Once the contracts were signed, what kind of process did you have to go through?

I just had to find a way to sit down and do it. I had always worked for somebody else on assignment and all of a sudden I'm at home with a stack of paper and a typewriter. It was ten o'clock in the morning and the house was quiet and I didn't know what to do. I sat down and burst into tears and called my editor. He said, "Oh, God. Not you too." I don't know, I just wrote it. I don't know any other way to do it. The process of writing is like the infantry. There it is, and you have to go through it all by yourself. It is frequently very boring and not terribly exciting. It is lonely. It can't be done with anybody else. When I'm working I'm living almost a minimal life. Sooner or later every scrap of energy will go into the book. We don't go out much. I only see my close writer friends. When it's over it's like coming out into the world again, especially with this last one. I came out of a long siege of writing into a tour around the South. It was like a mouse wondering out of a dark maze into, God, I don't know what. It's a terrible case of culture shock. After the tour I practically came home in a body bag. It's feast or famine. The process of writing is always the same — going up those stairs and sitting down at the typewriter.

What kind of writing schedule do you keep?

I'm usually at my desk by nine-thirty or ten, work through to about two or three, when I stop for a sandwich. Then I come downstairs and do whatever errands need doing. At some point I will read over what I have written and do a great deal of editing. When my husband comes home he usually reads back to me what I've written that day. It really helps to disassociate myself with the work and hear it in my ear. I catch a lot of things that way.

I'm not much on "how to" books, but there's a wonderful book called *About Fiction*. It's about understanding what fiction really is. It's bull that you need to have experienced something first in order to write about it. The great gift is the interior ability to perceive an idea and amplify it without having had the experience. And I don't know where that comes from. It's what makes you a writer. It's a matter of focus. I have a friend who has a lovely way with words. She wants more than anything to be a novelist. What she does with that is going to depend on what she perceives, her perceptions; her way of looking at the world will determine how well she writes. Not her way with words.

People ask me where I get my ideas. Can you give me an idea? This drives me nuts. There's an idea in this room. You ought to be able to get ten novels out of this room if you're in the mode of seeing them. And that doesn't always come to a writer. It's not a matter of getting the idea, but recognizing one when it comes. That's the thing — the ability to see them. That's where other writers can help you. Pat Conroy gave me the idea for the book I'm working on now. We were sitting right here last fall when he said, "You know, of course, what you ought to be doing. It's the big Atlanta book. When are you going to quit fighting it and write it?"

I said, "I can't write it. I'm afraid I would hurt some people." But once I was able to think about the reality of doing the book it came naturally. Pat was right, of course. I do have a viewpoint and a focus, but he could see it and I couldn't. Sometimes other people can see it for you, but it almost takes another writer or somebody with that kind of focus. It's a thing that can develop.

What's your new book about?

It's called *Peachtree Road.* It will be out, I guess, a year from this fall, fall of 1988. It's about fifty years in the life of two old Atlanta families, and parallels the growth of the city. This idea that we talked about earlier, the South crippling and killing its gifted women is at the core of it. A lot of the changes the city has undergone will be in it. This interests me. I don't think you can write about the fortunes of an Atlantan without regret to the city.

Will it upset many people?

Yes, it will upset some people, not because it's going to be a scandalous book, but it's probably going to annoy some of the old Atlantans who would really like to think the city hasn't changed, or that it was ever like parts of the book will reveal. I have a pretty good eye, but it is only Atlanta as *I* perceive it. It may be truth, but it's my truth.

You mentioned you were half through.

Yes, and I'm looking forward to getting rid of the thing. It's going to be a thousand pages long. It's working well. But the capacity for screw-ups is infinite, and I will probably do that somewhere.

I would imagine with a body of work that large and that close to you, it would require precise research and double-checking every fact.

Oh, I have done an enormous amount of research. There are sociological aspects, culture, physical; of course, all that is just backdrop. The city, its history, and other facets have to move along precisely.

I have a distinct advantage because I started with *Atlanta Magazine* covering the city at a time when Atlanta was just moving into its forward push. I was covering the ten years that literally remade the city. It was a wonderful vantage point from which to see the changes as they were made. I'll write about that, and the way the city went on afterwards, but mainly it's about how these four people, two families, were affected, and who would change and who would not; who would survive.

We hear about the tribulations of having a first novel published, but for you it seemed to have fallen into place quite easily. Do you have any advice for the unpublished writer?

I would say the smartest thing you could do if you are serious is to have a completed manuscript, and to involve yourself with a group, if you can find one, of working writers who are publishing. They generally know sources, and out of that somebody is going to know an editor. That's the only way to do it. If you can find yourself an agent that's as good, but they are as hard to come by as an editor. The alliance of a writing group, and most people who are serious about writing will have at one time or another run into them, make it their business to know people. They'll run into them at an autograph party or somewhere. And ask for help. There's no other way to do it. We published writers were all helped. It's just writing and knowing on some level you are a writer. I'm not sure writers are ever certain their writing is mature enough. I'm not. I know that I'm a good writer, but I don't know that any individual book is good. I know that I have a gift, but I also know how easily I can screw up. So I go through it every time. Everyday I look at my husband and ask, did you really mean that, did you really like that, are you sure? What did you mean by that? But did you really...? He'll finally ask me, "How many times is it going to take?" I say, "I guess as long as I live." It's not a very good profession to pursue if you're looking for great ego recognition. But most writers can't do anything else. It's what we were born to be. I can't do anything else. I couldn't begin to operate a computerized cash register.

Lee Smith

Lee Smith was born in Grundy, Virginia, in 1944. Barely out of college she published her first novel, *The Last Day the Dogbushes Bloomed,* and has since published *Oral History, Something in the Wind, Fancy Strut, Black Mountain Breakdown, Family Linen, Fair and Tender Ladies,* and *Calkwalk,* a collection of short stories — winner of two O. Henry Awards. She lives in Chapel Hill and teaches at North Carolina State University in Raleigh. This interview was conducted at her house on November 6, 1987.

Could you discuss your background?

I was born in 1944 in Grundy, Virginia, which is in the mountains of Southwest Virginia. I was an only child of parents who were forty when I was born. I don't think they ever expected to have children. I read a whole lot, the way an only child does. I wrote a lot of little stories to just myself as I was growing up. My father ran a dime store in Grundy, a Ben Franklin, and he still runs it today. He's in his eighties and he still goes to work every day.

Your first novel, The Last Day the Dogbushes Bloomed *was published in 1968, when you were twenty-three.*

I wrote that book when I was a senior in college. I wrote the first draft as an independent study. We could do something like that and get three hours credit. I was just really lucky to get it published. It's the kind of book that if it were happening today I don't think would be published. It's what they call in the trade a "quiet novel." It's sort of a quiet, tasteful, little novel.

How did The Last Day the Dogbushes Bloomed *come about being published?*

There used to be a contest that they don't have any more that was co-sponsored by the Book of the Month Club and the College English Association. It was for college seniors, and I was one of twelve national winners, and they put out an anthology with each of our work in it, which was great. It was my first publication. An editor saw it and liked it, and asked to see the manuscript. So, I was real lucky.

Who were you studying with at that time?

Louis Rubin who teaches here at Chapel Hill. He was my teacher for four years at Hollins College. Richard Dillard, a wonderful writer, was one of my teachers, also. Hollins was a great place to go to school in creative writing. I had a lot of friends who were writing and are still writing. There was a whole lot of interest in it and everybody was very supportive of your writing and you didn't have to feel weird. (*Laughing.*) You know, for girls in the South, at the time I was writing, it wasn't exactly the thing you did. And it wasn't what I was raised to think I should be doing. I was more geared to marry a doctor ... you know what I mean? So this was a very supportive environment.

Of your friends in your group, has anyone gone on to write?

Oh yeah. Annie Dillard, who won a Pulitzer. We had graduate students, too. Henry Taylor, who just won a Pulitzer. (*Laughing.*) This was a wonderful little group. Rosanne Coggeshall, a poet, Ann Jones, who wrote *Tomorrow Is Another Day*, which is a feminist critique of Southern women. Most of the people in the group are still writing, which is real unusual. I feel lucky because with this group I felt I had a base and always thought of myself as writing. I did that before I got married and had kids. I thought of myself as a writer first. I teach a lot of continuing ed-type students, and a lot of the times the women will come in who want to write, but they have always thought of themselves first in these other roles. Then it's really hard. It takes an awful lot of nerve to begin to think of yourself differently at thirty-eight.

What kind of effects did having your first novel published directly out of college have on you?

In one way it was really bad, because it made me think that it was all going to be that easy, and it hasn't been. In fact, I've had two separate careers so to speak. After *The Last Day the Dogbushes Bloomed* was published I wrote the next two books and just sent them to the same publisher and they just published them, but without any publicity or promotion, or anything. I was just sort of sending them up to New York from the deep South, not thinking much about it, not bothering to make a personal contact with people, not pushing myself in any way. Then, when all those books lost money, which they did, I sent the fourth book and they said, "Sorry, honey." And that was it. I hadn't made any contacts, I didn't know anybody.

What was the fourth novel you sent them?

Black Mountain Breakdown. It went to something like eighteen publishers.

Even after you had published three novels?

Yes, because at this point you're a proven loser. If you've published three books and they've all lost money, then from their point of view you're in a much worse position as compared to a first-time novelist that nobody knows.

You should have submitted it under a pseudonym.

(*Laughing.*) No, I didn't even think of that. But I lost my agent, too, at that point. It had been very easy for my agent; I would just send it to him and he'd send it to Harper and Row. That's all he ever had to do, so when this one turned out to be hard to publish he said good-bye. So I didn't have an agent or an editor.

That brings up something I wanted to discuss. There's a publishing gap of about nine years between the third and fourth books. You went from 1973 to '80 or '81.

I guess it's closer to eight years. It seemed long. And I had decided to quit writing because I had always had little Podunky jobs so that I would have time to write. Suddenly it just seemed indulgent because I wasn't getting anything published. So I had applied to Chapel Hill to go back to school in special education, at least I could make some money teaching to support myself.

How did Black Mountain Breakdown *finally get published?*

I came up with an agent, finally, after several disasters. I was determined to make a personal contact so I went to New York to talk to agents. I found a woman I really liked, but she ran off to Tibet to find herself (*laughing*) for her fortieth birthday, and never came back. I mean that was it. So I had to start over again. It was really terrible. But I have a friend, Roy Blount, and he hooked me up with the agent I now have. She sent this book to a lot of places and finally she found an editor, Faith Sale, who liked the book, but she wanted revisions. But then she changed publishing houses, she moved to Putnam. So it was a long time. I was lucky to end up with her, because she's a great editor. It was a whole second career with a major hiatus in between.

Do you go back and read over your older material?

(*Laughing.*) No. The trouble with me is that I'm always pushed for time. I apologize again for it being so hectic around here. I don't have the kind of life I think a writer should have. I have a hectic life with kids strung out all over the place, and I don't have time to go back. I don't keep a journal — that's another thing writers should do. I don't approach it as rationally as I wish I did.

In Black Mountain Breakdown *the main character, Crystal Renee Spangler is pretty much a passive main character, in the sense that she doesn't do anything, and that's a difficult thing to pull off and still keep the book interesting.*

I'm not sure I pulled it off. That's one of your first rules in writing — to not have a passive main character, you want an active one. At the time I wrote that, it was really the only book I ever wrote that I had a theme in mind. It's almost a cautionary tale, because I was at a point in my life where all my friends, women I had grown up with, were suddenly floundering, because we were following someone else's idea of who we ought to be or what we ought to do. I decided to write a book about this tendency that women, particularly Southern women in my generation, have to be passive. I have Crystal modeling herself upon her mother's idea, then there are the various men, and so on, with the result that she doesn't have enough of an identity herself.

I'll tell you one thing about that book that I shouldn't admit, but I will. In the original version there was no rape. My idea was that certain kinds of women can be that passive just by the way they're brought up. There is a scene where she goes into the toolshed with Deever and he says something to her, just to scare her and make her think her daddy's weird. In the original version he didn't rape her. It went to so many publishers, and finally, when Faith Sale did want to publish it, she suggested the rape. So I put it in, because I really wanted the book to be published (*laughing*) because at that time I didn't want to go back to school in special education.

As a result, the rape provides Crystal with more motivation for her actions being passive.

Yes, it does. I think it was a good idea. An idea of repression works real well. Another thing I was doing at that time was reading a book on family therapy and it said that what is a quirk in one generation will become a neurosis in another generation, then it might become a psychosis in the third. I was thinking of the staying at home and holding up. I had that in mind. Do you know what a breakdown is in banjo? It's the same refrain played over and over again, but it's augmented each time. So it was the family and the country music. That was my idea. No one ever got it, so I'm delighted to have a chance to tell you that.

When I've talked to people about your work, the novel everyone seems to identify you with is Oral History, *which was very critically acclaimed and has sold well. Do you see this as your best work?*

I do. But it's real weird. I wrote it very fast, and never revised it. It's because it's the material I love the most; it's where I'm from, I mean, that really is the way I grew up hearing language like the language in that book. Though I tried to use the older turns of phrase in the beginning sections. That really approximates the way I grew up and all these stories I would get different people to tell me. I like the material, but it's really weird, because it almost feels like I didn't write the book. These things that you hear about that are so striking — like if you have an ugly daughter then you put her out in the first spring rain to get beautiful. So that makes a great scene, but it's not like I thought that up. Or the hog killing. So, the book was almost conceived of as a series — set pieces bringing to life my favorite little bits of lore. I just lucked out. I never had a notion that it would hold together as a novel, and maybe it doesn't, maybe the format allowed it to get away with some things.

What are you working on?

A new novel. It's fun, because it's the same kind of material as *Oral History*. It's an epistolary, one woman's letters over her life. It's about writing more than anything else. She was born in 1900.

This is The Letters from Home.*?*

Yeah, but I changed the title to *Fair and Tender Ladies,* because she writes to her sisters, daughter and granddaughter, so it's about her letters to other women.

You've been working on this for about three years now.

Yeah. It's the longest I've ever worked on anything. I'm through, but I haven't typed it. I'm in there typing now. I write in longhand, which is not as impractical for me as you would think, because it means I can do it anywhere. That is important.

You teach writing and are involved with editors and publishers . . . How difficult is it for a first novel to be published?

It just depends on the novel. I mean, I've heard the horror stories, but I've seen manuscripts that I thought were excellent which have not yet been published. On the other hand, most of my students who have written good novels — the novels are coming out. If they're good, there's still a big demand for good fiction. The difference is when my first novel came out they were publishing eighty percent more fiction, serious fiction, than they are now. It's just that the market for serious fiction has declined so horribly that they really can expect a lot of rejections, and no matter how good their novel is, they can expect to have it turned down a number of times, unfortunately.

I think people are of two minds about the proliferation of the MFA programs and writing in the university. I think it's helpful for the young writer. They can get feedback on their work, they can get readers and they can talk to people about writing, because the actual publishing has just gotten to be so hard. It used to be people were sitting in a log cabin out in America writing novels, then they'd send them to New York and they'd be published. Now, it's more of finding a community of like-minded writers and finding feedback and encouragement from that as well as from publishing and not publishing your material. Also, you have to think of yourself as a writer if you are a person who is writing, not necessarily if you're being published.

Does the sense of a community hold true for the established writer also?

I think it does, and that's why so many writers are attached in some capacity to one school or another, and why they like to go around giving readings. It used to be that a publisher would publish your good work along with your bad work, and they would nurture a young writer and watch the young writer grow. They don't do that any more. It's too expensive. An exception to that rule is Algonquin Books here in Chapel Hill. What they do is find young, promising writers and they edit them quite a lot and help them. They'll read a manuscript and think how it could be, and urge them that way, nurturing them in the way the old editors used to do in the New York houses, but who no longer do.

Shannon Ravenel is the fiction editor. She's really good. In fact, I sent my first novel to her first when she was at Houghton Mifflin. She was young then, I was young, too. She didn't take *The Last Day the Dogbushes Bloomed.* She didn't publish it, but she sent me a three page single-spaced comment on why she wouldn't publish it and what she thought was wrong with it. I rewrote it according to everything she said, then the next person did take it.

That's why I believe that since Faith Sale has become my editor my writing has improved, because she questions everything. She doesn't stop if something is just okay, she wonders if it would be better if you did so and so. It makes a huge difference. With the first three books, I was literally sitting in the deep South sending them to New York, and they would just publish them. I never had an editor who would talk to me about them and suggest changes.

As a writer what has been the biggest drawback?

Like most writers, I've never been able to make a living writing. I do it for the love of writing, but it is a shame.

You've reached a great deal of success with your novels, they're selling very well and I've talked with some book dealers who say they're pushing your books.

I'm breaking even now. In order to write *Oral History* and *Family Linen* I took a semester off from teaching. Putnam paid me what I would have made teaching. By the time the book came out I had already spent the money on living expenses. I know it's possible to make a living because there are people with movie deals and big paperback deals. My books have gotten good reviews and are certainly selling. At first, it was like working for the company store; Faith took me on, but I was never paying back my advances. Then *Oral History* did well and it paid for the other books, the ones that lost money.

Your writing deals with people caught up in soap operas and Phil Donahue. How would you describe your writing style? Is it the new South?

I don't know. I guess. New South—yeah, I guess so. I've been living in a university community for a long time and teaching on the college level for five years now, and I could no more write an academic novel than fly to the moon. I just couldn't do it.

Your main characters are women. . . .

I think my characters are too much alike, which is one reason this new novel is so different. The work I've done in the last ten years, particularly with the short stories and *Family Linen,* the women tend to fall into two groups: They're epitomized by the two women in the story *Calkwalk* where one woman, Stella, has shallow-oriented values. She's the one who sells make-up. Florrie is natural, she loves children and she's sloppy and she's an artist in her own kind of feckless fashion. There's a beautician character in *Family Linen* who is like her. It seems to me that I have these two types of women that appear in various disguises. So now, I'm tired of them. You do something for awhile before you figure out what you're up to, and I do think I have this polarizing of two sets of characteristics that are found in women in the South today.

Much different than say Faulkner's women?

Yeah. That's one reason that with the novel I'm on now that I've gone back to early 1900s in the mountains, because it is possible to write about somebody who is more like a Faulkner-type character, which is a pure, unadulterated person.

What is it that motivates your characters to do what they do? Like in Family Linen, *burying the body in the well.*

That was out of the newspaper. That was real. There was a murder down near Lumberton. Actually, it was worse. I toned it down for *Family Linen.* It started with this middle-aged woman who had headaches, so she went to the shrink. He hypnotized her and it turned out that when she was three or four she had seen her mother kill her father and cut him up. But the mother had put him down the outhouse in the real story. I couldn't deal with the outhouse so I made it be a well. She's still alive — the woman who had the headaches. In the real story she just called the FBI and turned her mother in. She didn't give her mother a chance to say "Boo." And all these years her mother had been head of the Episcopal Altar Guild. It was amazing. I get a lot of stuff out of real life.

Calkwalk *was the first material of yours that I read years ago, and naturally I thought you were a short-fiction writer. I then realized you had several novels to your credit. I was wondering how the short stories came about.*

Well, I like the short stories better than anything else, but it's just really hard to write short stories. For one thing, you have to put as much energy into them as you do a novel. I like writing short stories better than anything else, but they're hard to place, they're hard to sell. Mine are particularly hard to sell, because they're not really arty, they're not really literary and there's nowhere they can go. I like to write about domestic things, like parents and children and families, and so that makes them not literary enough for many places. But, yet, they're not pabulum, so they can't be published in the *Ladies' Home Journal* or other places that publish shlock. They're not sophisticated enough for the *New Yorker,* so they fall in between. I like to write short stories, but if I can get an advance on a novel, I'll write one. The stories are very iffy.

Do you see another collection coming together anytime soon?

Probably so. I've done a fair number.

Previously, you were married to poet James Seay.

He gave a reading at Hollins College when I was there. (*Laughing.*) Actually, the first time I met him I was a go-go girl as a matter of fact. We had a very long reading and in between we had this entertainment, which was just English majors. We had this rock band called the Virginia Wolves. This is in Roanoke, and I was a go-go girl with the Virginia Wolves when Jim came to give a reading.

I'm interested to know what happened to the other Virginia Wolves?

Hummm. One of them went on to be a real singer and another one is a moviemaker. Jim and I met and started going out when I was a senior and then got married at the end of my senior year.

What was it like being married to another writer?

It was good. One thing I had liked about college was this community of writers and support, and in my marriage that continued, because Jim was always teaching wherever we lived at various universities. He taught at the University of Alabama and at Vanderbilt. He was always teaching creative writing and had his students around visiting and other writers were around. That keeps you enthusiastic. It's very difficult to work in a vacuum. It's a hard balance, because you don't want to be talking about it too much with other people or have too much partying going on. It's stimulating to have a certain amount of contact with writers and writing in general. Being married to Jim really afforded me that. I was working on newspapers, and had I not been married to him, I would have been out of that atmosphere.

Where do you see your writing in ten or fifteen years? Or where would you like it to be?

I have no idea. I don't have the slightest idea. I'm really unable to focus on anything other than what I'm working on. I sort have a short novel about the sixties I'm dying to write next. It's very different than what I'm working on now. I might even quit at some point. I'll just write as long as it fascinates me.

If you weren't writing what would you be doing?

I've always wanted to work with emotionally disturbed children. I've taught now at all levels, and I might want to go back to work with emotionally disturbed or handicapped children. But right now, I'm still fascinated with writing.

You started writing when you were a child and had always wanted to be a writer. When did you know that you could be a writer and that you were a writer?

I don't know that you ever know that. Every time you start writing something you're just in a panic, you're just terrified. You never really know that. I mean, it could fall through. I've figured it out now that when people ask me what I am I'll say I'm a writer. Like on an airplane when someone asks what you do, I'll say I'm a writer. But that's very recent. I used to say I did any old thing to not say I was a writer.

You put a lot of stock in the creative writing workshop. How does the writer best benefit from the workshop as opposed to individual instruction from a teacher?

Well, the instructor is only one person. You might benefit from individual instruction or the instructor might not get what you're saying. But, if you have a workshop and if there's a consensus, which usually there is, you can pretty well trust it. I don't believe you can trust your own reaction to your work. You need readers to see what they think.

Even an established writer?

Yeah. I have three or four people who read my work, but it's not like a workshop. My editor and agent are two people I let see my work, and a couple of friends. I listen real hard to what they say, because if there's a consensus about something that needs to be changed, then I think you should listen.

What do you look for in your student's work?

An original mind and a sense of language. I mean, they can plot like crazy and it will still be really pedestrian. The other stuff you can learn, but you can't learn those two things.

What mistakes do you see occurring most often in their work?

An unwillingness to revise. I think you have to decide if you are writing to express yourself or whether you're writing to create as good a story as you can possibly come up with. There's a big difference. Writing for self-expression is different from writing to learn a craft. You have to get tougher.

You worked a for a number of years with the Tuscaloosa News. *How important was the newspaper work to you?*

Newswriting gives you a chance to go up to a total stranger and ask real personal questions. You hear all these great things. I'm still writing stories based on things that happened at the *Tuscaloosa News*—just people I would interview in situations I would have to write about. I got to walk into somebody's house that I would never get to get into. I think if you were in the police force it would be the same way. It's just an entrée into these other people's lives.

What was your childhood like?

I was by myself a lot because I was an only child and I was sort of sickly and imaginative. I was always having pneumonia and reading long novels. My family was a family of storytellers, particularly my Uncle Vern, my father and grandfather.

Is your work autobiographical?

No. I don't think it is. Although, in *Black Mountain Breakdown* all the minor characters are. Like the teachers in the hospital really were my teachers, and my father did read some poetry to me. I really was Miss Grundy High and won some luggage. The details are autobiographical, but the plot and the main characters are not. I don't like to fictionalize real events. I either write nonfiction, which I like to write, or it's fiction. I don't like a combination of the two.

Of the characters in your books, who would you say is most like Lee Smith?

Richard Burlage in *Oral History*. I would like to say I am more like Candy in *Family Linen,* but I'm not. A lot of these characters I create because I want to be like them, but I won't ever be.

Do you have a favorite childhood memory?

It is Easter. Now when you buy Easter baskets in the dime store they come already done up, but they didn't used to, and so before Easter my daddy would have two nights where everybody who worked in the store would go home late. He had big boxes of the cellophane straw and big boxes of candy and baskets and they'd make their own baskets and wrap and tie them. I used to just love that. One of my favorite memories is of climbing down into this huge container of pink cellophane straw and falling asleep. I remember looking up through the pink cellophane straw. It was great.

I would imagine you must conduct a great deal of research for your material?

Yes, I do. Particularly *Oral History*. In the book I'm writing now I have notebooks full of what mountain life was like during the Depression or 1920, the Unionization, and what it most affected. I do other weird stuff. For *Family Linen* I went to a hypnotist. I got myself hypnotized. I learned how they did it so I could use the scene. Then I worked in the Kroger Plaza Beauty Coiffure for three weeks to learn all I needed to know about beauticians. I'm always going to doctors about illnesses I want my characters to have.

Is there anything I haven't asked you that you would like to discuss?

No. I do apologize for being late. I have to tell you about where I was. This is ironic. My older son keeps forgetting crucial things, so we went out to buy him a notebook and a pegboard to carry around so he would stop forgetting his appointments, and then I came home and you were sitting in the driveway. That's the way my life goes. (*Laughing.*) It's really embarrassing.

John Stone

John Stone was born in 1936 in Mississippi, and is professor of medicine and community health (emergency medicine), and associate dean and director of admissions of the
Emory University School of Medicine. His three books of
poetry are *The Smell of Matches, In All This Rain,* and *Renaming the Streets* for which he received the 1985 literary prize of
the Mississippi Institute of Arts and Letters. This interview
was conducted in his Emory office on October 6, 1986.

When did you start writing?

As far as I remember it was in high school in Jackson, Mississippi. It was
probably before high school, but I remember a poem I wrote that an eleventh
grade teacher identified as a "poem." That was a mercy I'll always be grateful
for. I had no idea what it was, but she called it a poem. That was very important. In high school, when someone says what you've done has some merit,
it means a lot. Then I went on to edit the high school literary magazine, and
for that matter, the college literary magazine. Both were important in giving
me the idea that there was something interesting, something to be gotten from
the best words in the best order.

*Did you ever think you would receive the distinction, the prominence, that you
have?*

No, not really. Certainly, any distinction I've achieved I didn't expect.
One never hopes to achieve any distinction when one writes poetry. It's such
an esoteric art, and yet there is a small band of us for whom it is the only art,
the critical art, the art by which all others are measured. So, a writer hopes
to say it right to that small band or a portion of that small band. First, you
write for yourself and then to a perfect reader, who you hope or imagine is
out there. You try to say it as well as you can.

*You're quoted as saying "As a young man you wanted to be a poet, but you had to
make a living." You also mentioned on the phone the other day that you reserve the weekends
for writing. Well, as a doctor you've probably found that security in your life. Do you
anticipate a time when you will write full time?*

I think that would be hard for me to do. I get such a kick out of medicine and in some ways medicine is the source of the poetry. The best way I can think of it is to use an analogy that I've used before — the physician is paid to look and listen, so is the writer. When both are doing their jobs well they observe the details. What the physician is listening to are short stories or poems. That's a very important observation to me. It really reinforces my idea that poetry consists, for me, in the human encounter, it comes out of the human encounter. It'd be hard to imagine myself doing something completely people-less. I have to be involved with people. The problem, as you've suggested, is to find the time. I sneak in some in the early morning hours or late afternoons, or weekends, sometime when the phone isn't ringing — then hope for the best. That's one of the reasons poetry is easier than prose: it can be done in brief bursts of time. Recently, I've tried writing short stories. Poetry is like needlepoint that NFL tackles and women do, it's something you can take out and do a few stitches at a time, if it doesn't work, you can tear it out and start over.

Have you always wanted to be a poet?

I think so. Another pivotal experience I had in high school was the same teacher had us recite soliloquies from *Macbeth* in front of the class. I liked the palpability, the touching, the feel of the words in my mouth. I like to *say* things. That's one of the things that constitutes my kind of poetry. Everything I've written is meant to be read out loud. It's to be said in the mouth, felt in the larynx, the vocal chords, and the throat muscles. From a purely technical point of view, I've learned a lot of things since writing the poems "Death" and "The Truck." But I think "Death" is better written on the page with "explanations" about how it should be read or "performed" than "The Truck." Nevertheless, because there are certain technical tricks in "The Truck," the reader has to read the poem more than once in order to understand it. The lines tend to run together; it's an enjambment. I like that about the poem. Line breaks are awfully difficult and idiosyncratic. I had someone ask me about the line breaks in "The Truck," which are very idiosyncratic, but the effect is meant to make the reader read it several times and *participate* in the poem.

Have you always wanted to be a doctor?

Yes, but I'm not sure precisely why. I remember when I was growing up in Mississippi, an uncle and my paternal grandfather were doctors. People would say that I was a lot like my uncle, because we both liked to read. There was a feeling then, as there ought to be now, that a physician ought to be a scholar. They should be interested in the written word. There was this commonality between my uncle and me. I'm not quite sure why I was fascinated with medicine, but I was certainly interested in the way the body works.

You received the 1985 Literary Award from the Mississippi Institute of Arts and Letters, for your third volume of poetry Renaming the Streets, *an award also held by Walker Percy and Ellen Gilchrist. What was your reaction to winning the award?*

Sheer humility and absolute surprise. It's a wondrous thing to be recognized, but to be recognized by one's own state is even more wondrous. To have the previous winners to be such eminences in literature is really humbling. One always hopes one's most recent work is one's best. I've been very gratified with the reception accorded *Renaming the Streets*.

What are you working on now?

I'm working on two manuscripts, a book of poems and a book of short stories. The fiction has been a lot of fun. In high school and college I was educated in a scientific way, then in medicine — and when I finished I had to go back an reeducate myself with Edwin Arlington Robinson, Emily Dickinson and Whitman to understand American poetry. Now, I have to do the same thing with the short story. I've gone back to read Hemingway, James Joyce, Faulkner and Raymond Carver, so as to understand how the short story is written. It's so different. Tess Gallagher said in the *New York Times Book Review*, "The ego is so involved in poetry and it's less involved in the short story, so you can let yourself go." I think she's absolutely right. I remember distinctly the first time in a short story I felt free to write what I wanted. I realized I could say or do anything I wanted. It didn't have to have happened. To an extent, the same thing occurs with poetry, it did with the poem "Rosemary" for example. There are real fictional elements in much of the poetry, but its reassuring to know that if I want this guy to jump out of an airplane without a parachute, he can do it. It's very freeing. Yet, there are commonalities; the short story is brief and it has to end right just as a poem does. As Paul Valery said, "The sole purpose of the poem is to prepare the reader for the climax."

How far along are you with both collections?

I've written about twelve poems I'm satisfied with and about six or seven short stories. Recently, the short stories have been coming faster than the poetry.

What is it that interests you to write about people who cannot or do not direct their own lives?

Take for example my poem "Robinson Crusoe" in which Sisyphus is mentioned: Which of us doesn't have his own big stone to roll up his own hill? In the poem, even the cardiologist, which you'd think is a glamorous profession, if there ever was one, is bored. It's possible for every life to be boring, except in the life of the mind; only to the extent that our minds are alive and kept alive are we truly alive. That's what I believe. It's possible to be a bus driver or a cab driver and still be having a hell of a time. Frost said, "My aim in life is to unite my vocation and avocation as my two eyes make one in sight." The excitement of making the vocation and the avocation one is what keeps us alive and prevents life from becoming dreadfully dull. One of the greatest joys in life is the joy of conversation. It's one thing I miss most and one reason I like to talk to people from English departments: they can be some of the best conversationalists. They've thought deeply about life, and they've read deeply. Instantly, we talk in a frame of reference that I am interested in.

That brings up a quote of yours, "Any two people talking are lonely." Is the world that lonely?

I think the world is infinitely lonely. In our deepest thoughts we're all alone. And finally, we are all going to die alone. This is why Edward Hopper is so right about the world in his painting "Early Sunday Morning," which is the first poem in *Renaming the Streets*. Its title is from the painting by Edward Hopper. He was right about life when he painted this scene in the thirties. Originally, he painted somebody, a single figure, in one of the upstairs windows, then he painted them out. This painting, like my poem "Rosemary," is about the loneliness of the world. "As important as what is happening, is what is not." I think one of the central reasons that brings people to a physician is loneliness. It's certainly one of the reasons people write poetry. Loneliness is one of the prime movers of all art.

What was your childhood like growing up in Mississippi?

It was very happy. I was born in Jackson, Mississippi, and lived there until I was five. At that time we moved to east Texas (a town called Palestine) until I was fifteen. We moved back to Mississippi and I went to high school in Jackson, and then to college. I have a brother who is twenty months younger than I, and a sister ten years younger. We had just a great time growing up in small towns, lots of friends and there was never a lack for things to do. My father worked for a glass plant. He died when I was eighteen, and it took me twenty years to write a poem about him. One of the poems about my father is "Losing the Voice." There's another poem, "Autopsy in the Form of an Elegy," from the first book *The Smell of Matches*.

To have one's father die at any age is bad enough, but at eighteen, it can be devastating. I suddenly became the man of the household. It changed my life. At the time I was planning to go to Davidson College, but then I decided to stay home with my mother. I went to Millsaps College in Jackson. That was a great turn of events, because there I met Miller Williams, the poet from Arkansas, one of the two poets to whom *Renaming the Streets* is dedicated. My conversations with him were very important, and led in a roundabout way to my going to Breadloaf to the writer's conference, where both Miller Williams and John Ciardi taught poetry.

What is one of your favorite childhood memories?

I've been thinking about that lately. One of the recurring aims of childhood is to hide, to be invisible, especially to grown-ups. I'm going to start a short story about such hiding. One of the great things about growing up in Palestine, Texas, was that my father was the production manager for this big glass plant (Knox Glass). In one end of the warehouse they stored boxes full of bottles, stacked from ground to ceiling. Just way up. One of the great memories was going there on the weekend and building forts in those boxes. My brother and I could hide behind the boxes and listen to adult conversations. God knows how much damage we did to the inventory. That was really something. I think hiding from the adult world as long as you can has leaped over into my adult life in writing poetry.

What's your least favorite childhood memory?

It probably came after childhood. I finally realized that as a child we always had a white dog, a Spitz. They were called Whitey, Whitey Jr., Duke, Duke Jr. And to me, as naive as I was, they were all the same dog. But now, looking back, they were all different dogs. That means they died, something that's hard for any child to cope with. I was told they were run over by cars. I remember wondering with fascination and horror what death was like. I realize now that those four dogs melded into one dog in my mind, but they were really four different dogs.

At some point they were separated?

Yes. They became four distinct dogs that were now all dead. But there were a lot of great times. I remember visiting my physician grandfather in Tremont, Mississippi, near the Tupelo area. There were Stones all over the place. Talk about roots. You really got an idea of what it meant to be a "Stone." That was nice. I got to know my grandfather a bit before he died. I got to know him enough to remember the medicinal smell, the tobacco smell, his great sense of humor and gift for storytelling. We'd sit on his knee and he'd tell stories about rabbits sliding down a hill on one ear. That may be a genetic reason why I'm turning towards shorts stories. Who knows?

How do you feel about the changes the South is undergoing in respect to technology and so forth?

I think it's depressing. The old way is deteriorating rapidly, especially in the big cities. There will always be small conclaves and smaller towns, and to that extent they have it all over us for the next decade or quarter century, or until the whole state is a megalopolis. We will lose something as we get melded into one. I've been in Atlanta twenty years and I think we have lost a bit of the old gentility. In return we may get some energy, some vitality that we can use. We may learn some new speech patterns, and that's not always bad. We may lose a little of our storytelling. We may have to enlarge our myths. We will certainly have to change our attitudes about things from women to jobs to society in general — the traditional things Southerners have always thought they understood very well.

There is nothing wrong with technology in itself. It's what we do with it. Of course, we have the same problems in medicine. As long as technology is used by human beings it's alright. It's when technology becomes the focus that we're in trouble. If we ever let a machine spit out data and tell the patient, "Here's the answer," then we're in real deep trouble in medicine or any other area.

Do you think there's a Southern renaissance taking place in writing?

Yeah, I do think so. The vector is pointed south as people pour in. The sunbelt is the recipient of a lot of vitality and energy. The art has always been here, but now what's happening is there is a recognition of it. There is a renaissance in Southern art, folk art, realistic art and art going back to the Civil War. For decades artists here couldn't interest the New York art critics, but now there's a recognition that a regional art is very important for its own sake. Certainly the renaissance of Southern writing is unbelievable. It outweighs the rest of the country.

As some of your poems have suggested, is there someone trapped inside everybody who is trying desperately to get out? Writers do it through writing, but not everyone is able to escape. Does everyone have the ability to escape?

Good question. When I ask an audience how many people have written poetry, almost everyone, if they're honest will raise their hand. We've all tried to write at some time. There's something inside of us trying to make sense. I think people should try to write. There is an awful lot of writing that is salutary though it stops far short of being art. That's why I never discourage people from writing. It helps them tremendously, though it may not be great art. But what about the person who can't seem to find anything that's "self-actualizing"? We've screwed up the jargon so much with words like "self-actualization" that people feel they must "self-actualize." But what about that person who just cannot make that contribution? It must be terrible. It's very hard to step outside of one's self, to blend with some other person and to understand that we're all waiting for the message in the bottle.

Yes, and with the popularity of computers and the advent of video we no longer have to go outside of the house to be entertained. Where there's no interaction, there's no threat.

Yes. This is why I believe in what Virginia Woolf said, "A Beethoven quartet really is the truth about the world." Whatever you think she meant by that remark, I think the Beethoven quartets she talked about were the late quartets written at a time when he was completely deaf, totally isolated from the world, when he was trying to maintain contact with a world that was rapidly failing and fading from him. And isolation is made worse by technology, made worse by a lack of commonality, education and cultural background, or even lack of care by which we preserve language.

Sometimes you teach a course, Literature and Medicine. *What is the one thing you most try to convey?*

I try to get the students, medical or otherwise, to think metaphorically, but also to develop a language to test the human situation. Humanists have a better understanding of the language than scientists, so I get them to explore, by literature, an *in vitro* situation before they get to the *in vivo* situation. When they have read about the plague and know what the problems of the plague are, the lack of communication, people dying everywhere, quarantine, etc. — when they know these things, the *in vitro*, then they'll be able to handle them better when they get to the *in vivo* situation with a patient. They know instinctively, as anyone who as read about the plague does, how a patient with AIDS or any disease feels. I always think there are some ethical issues raised in literature that are much easier to discuss from the point of literature than from cases out of medicine. It's much easier to discuss a novel than it is to discuss our lives, but the truth is, when we have a group of medical students talking about a novel, they end up talking about their lives.

Contrary to what you've previously said, from your work, do we know the person John Stone?

More and more, I think. It depends on how long the writer lives. Flannery O'Connor said, "How do I know what I think until I see what I write." I'm just discovering who I am, and what a revelation it is. Every new story, every new poem is a new understanding of myself.

Because you are a cardiologist and a poet, I would like to know, not just in a physical sense, but also in an emotional sense, what makes for a strong heart?

(*A lengthy pause.*) That's a very interesting question. Probably pain in small doses. The reason I say that is because life is painful. Physicians know that. Any sensitive person knows that. I'm working on a short story that deals with holding pain in your arms. It's about holding a baby in one's arms, but actually the character is holding pain. Pain in some ways functions as an antidote, like a poison that builds up a gradual tolerance. Some people are crushed by a big pain and never get over it, but if they can have a small pain, the death of a dog or a series of dogs, then they'll be able to live in the world and stay more nearly sane.

Is there anything I haven't asked you that you'd like to discuss?

The most frustrating thing in anyone's life is time. I'm very surprised we haven't been interrupted more, and the only reason we haven't been is because my secretary has been holding the calls. But I do feel, as I probably told you on the phone, that finding the time to write is difficult. There's a favorite cartoon of mine which shows a man who looks very much like John Ciardi, very big and robust, leaning up against a wall smoking a cigarette. There's another guy standing in front of him who says, "Gee, I wish I had time to be a writer." I think there are always pockets of time one can find. No matter how busy you are, whether you're Wallace Stevens, William Carlos Williams, John Stone or a graduate student, there is time. You can find time to write, to do what one wants to do. The key phrase is, what one *needs* to do.

James Whitehead

James Whitehead was born in St. Louis, Missouri, and grew up in Mississippi. He teaches creative writing and literature at the University of Arkansas, Fayetteville. His collections of poetry include *Domains* (1966), *Local Men* (1979), and a chapbook, *Actual Size* (1985). He has published a novel, *Joiner* (1971). This interview was conducted at his home in Fayetteville, Arkansas, on February 15, 1989.

I'd like to ask you about "Floaters" from your first book of poems, Domains, *as well as your other river-dragging poems.*

In *Local Men* and *Domains* there are several river-dragging poems. "The Young Deputy" is the most horrifying one. I don't think I saw more river-draggings than other people, but having grown up on the Mississippi River and the Pearl River in Jackson, Mississippi, I was exposed to them — enough.

You mentioned on the phone a few weeks ago about the lack of attention writers receive west of the Mississippi.

That was a very specific reference to a couple of anthologies published in the Carolinas. Some good young poets were left out. I am most pleased when Arkansas is included in the South as opposed to the Southwest or Midwest, and when young Arkansas poets appear in the anthologies — the Southern anthologies. Arkansas is a Southern state, not that we want to make too much of an issue about it.

Could you discuss your background?

My parents are from the Ozarks. My father was born in the eastern Ozarks, and my mother was born in Springfield, Missouri. My father's mother was from Van Buren, Arkansas — she died at 105 years of age in 1985. She was a lovely person right up to the end. She really was a Southerner, a heavy-duty Southerner. Though my father wasn't born south of the Mason-Dixon line, he is a Southerner. My mother is more Midwestern. Both of them went to the University of Missouri, then moved to Mississippi in 1939 or '40 when I was three. We spent a few years there, then the war came and we followed my father around the country until he went to Europe, where he was heavily involved in combat and liberated a death camp. For the most part I grew up in Mississippi. I went to Vanderbilt where I received a B.A. in Philosophy and an M.A. in English. Afterwards, I moved back to Mississippi to teach at Millsaps College for three years. Then I went to the University of Iowa to work on an M.F.A.; then I came to the University of Arkansas in 1965. I played football from the fifth grade through college, and I was always a reader. I married the most beautiful woman of her generation. Our seven children are excellent people.

When did you begin writing?

I was very much involved in the church when I was young and I wrote small things for the church. I was a kid preacher and wrote a lot of sermons. The concerns of religion and languages, theological and philosophical questions, persist up to this very day, but church didn't last very long. I wrote a short story in high school. I started writing poetry and fiction soon after I started college. It's an old line, but the interest in language came from an interest in conversation. My father's family is very big, and when World War II was going on we spent a lot of time, in large numbers, in the family home, in southeast Missouri — south of St. Louis. Everybody talked and told stories. I liked that and the literary part of the church service. The first serious reading I did for pleasure was the King James Bible.

What writers influenced you early on?

Which writers do you say influenced you early on if you were influenced by the King James Bible? (*Laughing.*) I read the usual things as I went through school. I read Shakespeare and I love him. In school we read the romantic poets: Keats, Wordsworth, Shelley . . . — the standards. Growing up in my generation, particularly in the South and at Vanderbilt, the initiation into Faulkner, Hemingway, Thomas Wolfe, Katherine Ann Porter, Frost, Eliot, Yeats, was always terribly exciting as it was happening, and it still is exciting.

I see your vast library. Who are you reading now?

It is vast. I've got a lot of books. I've been rereading the collected stories of John Cheever — that big red paperback collection of short stories is superb. Cheever's collected stories and Eudora Welty's collected stories set the standard. I'm also reading along with my Form and Theory class — Yeats, Hardy, Hopkins, Browning, Whitman, Ransom. The contemporary work I read every day is the work of my students, members of the program. That's very contemporary. I've recently read a book of fiction by John William Carrington, a friend recently dead, *All My Trials.* I've been rereading the poetry of Harry Hulmes.

How would you describe your poetry?

I usually don't. It's not in my nature to describe my work. I try to write poetry that I feel comfortable with and that I enjoy reading and look forward to sending to a magazine I like. I want it to be poetry that will be enjoyed by certain individuals I admire.

It's been ten years since you have published Local Men, *your last book of poems. Are you working on a new manuscript?*

I published a chapbook in 1985, *Actual Size,* by the Friends of the Library of North Texas State University. In that black book underneath the bone, the vertebra on the desk, there's a manuscript I'm working on. I also have two novels that I will go back to. *Actual Size* is probably the best title I've ever come up with, and I would love to use it on the full volume that it will be a part of, but I don't know how I'm going to manage using it twice. Miller Williams and I went to Plains, Georgia, for Jimmy Carter's homecoming. That trip got the new book started.

I've written two novels I haven't finished. I should have finished them a long time ago and mailed them off. As soon as I finish this collection of poems I'm going back to the novels. One is about a textbook salesman trying to raise the children of his girlfriend, and the other is about the owner of a professional football team who teases his players.

In the twenty-three years since you published your first book of poems, you have published a novel and two collections of poems, and the chapbook. Though you are work-ing on two novels and a collection of poems, you haven't been as prolific as other writers.

That's right. I guess I'm lucky that all three of my books are in print. That's my good fortune.

You mentioned including Arkansas in the South and not the Midwest or Southwest. I've always considered it the South.

Yes, that's a personal preference I have. We debate a lot about what we are, and I think we really are Southerners. *Southern Magazine* is published in Little Rock, and I think that says something. My home states are Arkansas and Mississippi—deeply troubled places. But not so troubled as, say, Virginia.

Does it bother you, as it does some writers, to be considered a Southern writer, mainly because they believe it places them within regional confines?

I don't see any problem in being collected among a group of writers of a region. It doesn't limit a poet to be an Irish poet. I don't know why it should limit writers because they are an Arkansas or Mississippi writer. I grew up in the South and I write about this part of the country. It's perfectly normal to group writers according to region. Southern culture and Southern identity, states by state, can be useful and interesting. It's a way of keeping us from becoming a poorly homogenized country. And of course, we don't want that to happen. America the various. O.K.?

Is the South becoming homogenized?

Yes and no. Everyone has television. However, the resiliency of certain regional customs and distinctions is rather amazing. Outside the major population centers, the small town and rural town cultures survive. People in media really don't understand how various the entire United States really is. It's amazing. The most unrecorded part of this country is the Middle West. There are very interesting cultures in Iowa, Minnesota, Wisconsin, Nebraska, North and South Dakota, Kansas, Montana, Colorado, outside of Denver and the ski slopes. Those places are different from one another and different of us. They don't get much press, probably very much to their advantage. The press coverage in the United States is crippling to much of the best of what is going on. They get it wrong in almost every way you can get it wrong.

It appears that the media coverage is concerned only with the metropolitan area, except, in the event of a small town tragedy, such as a plane crash or mass murder of a family, then the town is news for a week. And also the media has a mentality which goes something like: How will these people cope with this tragedy in their life—people who don't know about the real world? Meaning of course, the metropolitan world.

Yes, but there are some nice exceptions. For years the *New York Times* has run the essays of Roy Reed who lives in Hogeye, Arkansas. He has a book called *Looking for Hogeye*. He still writes feature stories for the *New York Times*, reporting on small towns and the events in the lives of individuals. I suspect New Yorkers consider this local color, but that's their problem. What's local? What's color?

In your earlier books your concerns deal with racial problems and racial tensions.

That's pretty inevitable for my generation, and it still is the major problem. We're in a different generation of the problem now, but dealing with it and creating a viable, multiracial, multicultural nation is still the biggest project we've got.

Have the solutions to the racial problems worked out the way everyone thought?

I don't think everyone thought the same thing. People who were against integration are horrified that it has done so well, and those who were starry-eyed idealists are bitterly disappointed. This country is not free. Opportunity is not what it ought to be, but in reality, we've made more progress than I had expected.

Those were your concerns early on in your work. What are your concerns now?

I was once on the Amazon. I care about what I felt then. Rivers! Hard rain. The thing that has moved me to write all this time is a primitive religious respect for the natural world. That's an old-fashioned way of saying the fear of God. Since I'm not churched anymore I don't put it that way, but looking out the window on a cold rainy day in Arkansas moves me, and then I fill that space up with human beings in conflict. It may be a great weakness in my character that my first impulse was to be a landscape painter. My father's an engineer who paints and draws very well, but I didn't get an education in art. I can draw. When I travel I keep a sketch pad. Last summer I drew pictures in Boliva, the high and the low of it. I am moved by mortal souls confronting immortal nature or God, or whatever you want to call it. *Joiner,* which is supposed to be about race and football, is just as much about pine forests and swamps and God. It goes back and forth between people and nature and the Almighty Other.

Growing up and living in Jackson, Mississippi, were you aware of Eudora Welty and Margaret Walker, and what were your thoughts early on about them and writing?

Sure, I was aware of Miss Welty all my life, and I became aware of Margaret Walker when I was in college. Or maybe I heard about Walker when I was teaching at Millsaps. I read Walker when I went to Iowa, but I hadn't read her prior to that time. I had read Welty just enough to know I didn't want to read her. She was too good. After I was thirty, I went back and read her work rather carefully. I was stunned by it. She is overall the best living writer in the English-speaking world.

The question has been raised that university writing programs are a breeding ground for workshop poetry and fiction.

Well, I think you have to read the material coming out of the programs. Is Barry Hannah a standard workshop writer? Frank Stanford? Or is Ellen Gilchrist a standard workshop writer? I think not. These are people who have worked in Fayetteville. Leon Stokesbury and C.D. Wright are not cut out of any workshop mold. There are a dozen others I could name. Steve Stern. Over the years we have encouraged a somewhat confrontational style of workshop. Miller Williams and I have done this, and Michael Heffernon and Heather Ross Miller do this, too. So does Bill Harrison. You don't want writers becoming cozy. You have to work out of a community of respect and question each other intensely. There are creative writing programs and minor poets who really do want a protégé relationship with their students— that is to say they progressively wish for their students to imitate them. I'd say that that is not the way to do it.

Anyone you will name?

Certainly not. There are pitfalls, pitfalls in any kind of patronage, but the artist always lives in some sort of patronage relationship. The freelance writer works to a certain extent at the will of his or her agent and editor in the marketplace. During the Renaissance the writers wrote for the Duke, Duchess, the aristocrats, and historically, and the Duke and Duchess made demands. The artist has to satisfy the tastes of the community in some way. In the twentieth century, by the middle of it, writers—many of them— worked for Deans rather than Dukes. I believe that the writing programs offer important opportunities to young writers. I've worked with the Associated Writing Program from the very beginning, and I think writing programs are good for young writers, and they're very good for English departments and the universities. I wouldn't be doing it if I didn't feel that way.

Playing devil's advocate—you mentioned several writers who have come out of the writing program at Arkansas, but for every one of those writers there are probably ten who have not achieved a level of skill or developed their talents. This is true for other writing programs, too.

You realize that that is a very high percentage and we do better than that. We've only had a couple hundred graduates from our writing program. It is small and it has been here twenty years. What happened to the other people? They edit for publishers, write for politicians, work for newspapers, teach in colleges and high schools, and some have gone off to do other things. Most of those who have not achieved published books and some reputation have stayed in the world of letters and writing and publishing.

So even the student who was a terrific writer, who didn't go on to greater writing achievements, has still kept the energy of writing and works within the field.

Yes, I think a great many of them have.

What are some of the major problems facing M.F.A. programs?

Keeping assistantships, fellowships available for the students, making sure the academic side of the department allows the fine arts side sufficient freedom and autonomy. That's about it.

Is there a line down the hall between the academics and fine arts?

I'm sorry about the line being drawn. I don't like for that to be the case, but there is a difference, and it's inevitable. To presume to be a creator of literature is a tremendous vanity, and it requires a tremendous amount of confidence, and we try to inspire that confidence in our students.

When a student comes to the M.F.A. program what is the one thing you try to install in them?

We don't try to *install* anything in them, but we try to help them become the best writer they can. We encourage them to read carefully and widely. That's about 99 percent of it.

What is the single most important aspect a student should possess when they come into a writing program in order to succeed?

Talent. (*Laughing.*) After that—energy, more talent, and will. If you don't have talent the will won't get you anywhere. Will and energy aren't quite the same thing. The *want to* isn't necessarily the physical ability to do it.

Have you ever told a student they would never become a writer?

We've told any number of people that their interest in literature probably will lead them to work in scholarship or journalism. After awhile most people figure it out for themselves.

Switching the subject, what was your childhood like?

My father was an engineer and my mother was a social worker. I did the usual things—went to church, played football, was encouraged to read and think. I played the clarinet. I stayed close to my grandparents. I was introduced to the conflicts that were all over the society at the time. The conflicts sort of crept upon you. I learned about girls. I had a good childhood. In fact, I had a wonderful childhood. I overreacted about things the way kids do. It was nice. I've talked to people who really didn't like the things that happened to them in their childhood. That is sad.

How old were you when you preached in the church?

I was eighteen, nineteen, twenty. It wasn't full-time, just supply pastor with youth groups, rarely a church sermon.

When you were writing the sermons, did you know then that you wanted to be a writer?

No. I wanted to do right, find out what things meant, make sense of everything. I wanted to go to Heaven. I was trying to avoid Hell.

You played football at Vanderbilt. Did you think about playing professionally?

Yeah, but I got hurt in college. I had offers from pro teams — they had me fill out the forms, but I was never drafted. The coach at San Francisco back then wanted me to try out. I was playing third-and second-string at Vanderbilt on a one-platoon system. He thought I could make it in the pros if I just played offense on a two-platoon system, but by that time I was already working towards going to graduate school in English or philosophical theology. I gave football a lot of thought that summer, but the arm was so bad. I had arm-tackled a guy and I tore my arm loose from the socket. It had been damaged before and I played several games with a novocaine shot to deaden the pain. That's not a very nice thing to do to your body, because you don't know you're being hurt when you're shot up, and it grinds everything up. That's why it's all messed up now, the arm.

Out of your childhood do you have a favorite childhood memory?

In *Joiner* there are places where Sonny steps back and looks around and writes about his mother and father from a distance, and he writes about the land with a sense of awe and passion. That's the sort of thing I remember from my childhood — going to the river, going to the woods, fishing, and being on the Pascagoula River fishing with my father on December 7, 1941.

What about the least favorite aspects of childhood?

There were times when we moved so often. We are a nation of people who move. Wars move us around, and we go where the money and jobs are. Companies move us. That was a bad part of my childhood. I moved from St. Louis; to Memphis; to Hattiesburg; to Watertown; to New York; to Carthage, New York; to Phenix City, Alabama; to Columbus, Georgia; to Joplin and Springfield, Missouri; to St. Louis; and back to Hattiesburg; up to Jackson, Mississippi, and that was all before I was in the sixth grade.

How did Joiner *come about?*

I wrote a short story while I was at Iowa back in 1963 and I finished it in 1970 — seven years later. I knew there was more in the short story. I wrote five drafts of the novel. I'm a slow worker. I'm not a slow worker. I write as fast as anybody. I write everyday, but I draft after draft. That's a mistake I've often made. These computer people may have the right idea. To correct two hundred words I will rewrite five thousand. That's very inefficient.

Is that something you would like to change about your writing?

I'd like to write better. I'd like to be quick about it.

If you could change anything in publishing what would it be?

I've been lucky with my editors and publishers, but there should be more good publishers, more well-read, sensitive, and intelligent editors. They should process the manuscripts more rapidly, pay you more, and they should keep everybody in print longer. Almost any element of the business needs improvement, but given the fact that we are a semiliterate nation, because we are so completely dominated by television, I suppose we're pretty fortunate to have what we have.

Do you have any advice for writers?

Write. Read. Talk about it. Enjoy it.

Miller Williams

Miller Williams, born in 1930 in Hoxie, Arkansas, and son of a Methodist minister, earned a bachelor's degree in biology from Arkansas State College and a master's in zoology and anthropology from the University of Arkansas at Fayetteville, where he is also professor of English and foreign languages. He is the author of more than twenty books, most recently, *Patterns of Poetry: An Encyclopedia of Forms* and *Imperfect Love,* his ninth collection of poetry. Williams is the director of the University of Arkansas Press, and among his many awards, he has received the Prix de Rome, given by the American Academy of Arts and Letters. This interview was conducted at his Arkansas Press office on February 15, 1989.

I asked you to read "One Day a Woman," the first poem in your most recent collection of poems, Imperfect Love, *because it's a fear people have of letting go and not coming down.*

It's an inversion of what is supposed to be our first primitive fear — the first fear a baby expresses is the fear of falling. This suggests the fear of falling upward. The poem began to develop in my mind when I saw a painting depicting the rapture, with beings coming up from graveyards, rising from buses and cars, planes and buildings, planes crashing because pilots and co-pilots were raptured at this moment, and I began to wonder what would happen if the rapture began, not all at once, but with a person here and a person there. That was the impulse, but the poem is not about the rapture. It's about whatever it stirs in the reader. A lot of people have responded to it; they ask me to read my rapture poem. That's the association they've brought to it.

You didn't start out to be a poet — you actually began as a professor of biology and a researcher.

Yes, I didn't start out to work professionally in the field of poetry. I knew when I was in the sixth grade that I wanted to write poetry seriously, but I didn't intend to enter the field of letters professionally. I was going to major somewhere in the humanities when I entered college. In those days, in a small liberal arts college, Hendrix, all freshman were given "profiles," psychological examinations. The school psychologist called me in during the first semester and said I was going to embarrass my family if I tried to go into any field that depended heavily on the use of language, because my imagination and mental process were clearly oriented toward the spatial, and not to language. He said the scientific data, at a time when psychologists began to think of themselves as scientists, was undeniable, irrefutable, and indicated I should go into the sciences. I was raised to take scientific data very seriously and respect authority, so I changed my major to chemistry and biology. I received a bachelor's, a master's in zoology, and almost my doctorate, but I realized I was not very happy doing that. I enjoyed it, and I still read scientific publications, and I'm still enchanted with the sciences, but I wasn't helping to shape my field. I was good at interpreting a textbook for the students, but I wasn't a creative scientist. I copublished a couple of papers, but I was not the creative partner in the research. It always seemed to me that a college professor, as opposed to a high school teacher, ought to help shape and direct the field he or she works in. And I wasn't. One day I became disenchanted enough to ask my department head if she could find a replacement for me for the rest of the semester. I left and went to Sears and got a job selling refrigerators and entered their executive training program. I felt a lot more honest. After awhile, on the basis of my publications, L.S.U. asked me to join their English department. I did. Then Loyola asked me to join at a higher rank and, later, the University of Arkansas asked me to come up here as professor of English and foreign languages. That's the sojourn.

It appears as though the psychologist was very wrong.

I think he was wrong, yeah.

In what ways has science helped shape your writing?

It has certainly flavored it. It has affected the texture of it — there's no question about that. There are images, metaphors, and arguments in my poetry that are straight out of the laboratory, and some are dramatic situations with speakers who are scientists, who live in the context of the scientific world. There are metaphors I would not have used had I not been trained in the sciences. The poem "Entropy" deals directly with a scientific concept. I've always been fascinated by the relationship between the humanities and the sciences — the fact that the basic equation in mechanics is physics, $F = MA$, Force equals Mass times Acceleration, means it's easier to get two people to shut up than a hundred. It's also easier to get two people to move than a hundred. Because the mass is greater. In chemistry, when we have two equations in equilibrium, and force is applied to one side or the other and maintained constantly, the equilibrium shifts in response to that force, and a new equilibrium is established. It is virtually impossible to go back to the previous equilibrium. When there is an equilibrium between the sexes or the races, and a force is applied to one side, it shifts, and like it or not on the part of some people, it's virtually impossible to reestablish the old equilibrium. It's gone, and a new equilibrium is established. These are just two examples of what we think of as scientific principles that are also simple principles behind the behavior of groups, individuals, and inanimate objects. This sort of thing intrigues me and it works into my poetry.

Though this is after the fact, do you believe you would be where you are today with your writing had you not studied science and had directly pursued the humanities?

I wouldn't be sitting at this desk at this time. When you change anything in a chain of events, the further you get from it the greater the effect of that change becomes. That's a fact I learned as a scientist, but it works in the humanities and human behavior, also, so I don't know what might have happened if I had studied something else. I think I would be a writer. I don't know if my reputation would be greater or less, but the poetry would be very different. I believe it would probably be softer. My training in the sciences has made me impatient with fuzziness. I don't like mysticism. I prefer the concrete world. I like Federico Garcia Lorca's description of the poet as "the professor of the five senses." Our senses respond to the material. I also like what John Crowe Ransom said, that the components of a poem are the furniture of this world. I like to be able to bark my chin on a chair. I don't like abstraction. And you'll notice, even while we talk, one reason I take awhile to get to my point is that I keep looking for Eliot's objective correlative — I want something I can knock on as an example to the abstract point I'm trying to make.

When L.S.U. asked you to teach, did you encounter any resistance from others in the English department? There's always talk about the line drawn down the middle of the hall between the academics and the writers, and since your background was in science, and not the humanities, though you were widely read and published, was there any resentment?

There was some resistance to having writers there. In a music department you may have ten composers and one music historian, and in the art department you'll have ten visual artists and one art historian. In an English department there are ten in literary history and criticism, and maybe, not always, one creative artist. I wrote an article for a literary journal in which I discussed the necessary marriage between the creative writers and the critics and literary historians, and how students are being shortchanged if they can't be around a creative artist. L.S.U. had a reputation for not keeping creative writers. John William Corrington and I were there at the same time and left together to go to Loyola for that reason.

Besides working at Sears you've had a number of jobs from working at Montgomery Ward, to a stockcar driver, to being a movie house projectionist. How have those played into your work?

Everything one does colors everything else one does. The more kinds of lives one has had, the more varied the experiences in one's life, the more richly textured one's art will be. Whatever faults my poetry may have, I don't think anyone can ever call it a hothouse flower. It hasn't been produced in a conservatory. I will insist that my poems have the feel of the human speech about them, with dirt under their fingernails, and sometimes, the smell of an armpit.

Were the jobs out of necessity or desire?

Sears, Montgomery Ward, and Harcourt Brace were necessities. Stockcar driving and working on a shrimp boat were because I was young, invincible, invulnerable, a little stupid, and certain that I was immortal.

What type of early formal education did you have?

I never attended a school outside of Arkansas until graduate school, but my father didn't trust elementary and secondary school systems. So after we went to school for the assigned hours we would meet in his study, or sometimes in our living room, and study what he didn't want us to miss. For a week we might study the Bible, then the next week classical mythology, then Latin, then Shakespeare for two weeks, then we'd start over with the Bible. That went on from the first grade until I graduated from high school — sometimes we'd study Greek plays instead of Shakespeare — so I had a prep school education tacked onto my grade school and secondary school educations. I went to undergraduate school at Arkansas State College in Jonesboro. I came to the University of Arkansas at Fayetteville for my master's in zoology, then attended Ole Miss Med School, not in the M.D. program, but the Ph.D. program. By that time I had family responsibilities — a wife and three children. I almost finished the Ph.D. program when I realized I had spent fifteen years in the wrong field. In the long run that's not to say it was wrong. I like what I learned in the scientific community and what the scientific training has done to me as a person, and to my poetry.

When did you begin writing?

The first poem I remember writing, and my first published poem, was in the sixth grade. It was about Santa Claus and it was published in the school newspaper. I was praised for it, and one tends to do what one is praised for. If I had received that kind of praise for what I was trying to do on the piano, clarinet, and saxophone, I'm sure I would have been a musician. But we're all Pavlovian enough that we go for the reward. I don't want to sound totally behaviorist, but when people ask why I write, or why I keep writing, part of the answer is that we do what we are rewarded for. Most serious writers would write no matter what opposition they met, and that's certainly true of me — I write because I write — but the early encouragement helped a hell of a lot.

You live in the South and have been anthologized in many collections such as, most recently, A Modern Southern Reader *and* The Made Thing. *Critics and scholars have categorized you as a Southern writer, a term you do not like.*

I don't like the term because of the way in which it's usually understood. I like being from the South and I like the Southern sense of language, metaphor, and narrative. I like what that has done to my poetry. I don't like the suggestion that somehow my concerns in my poetry are Southern. My concerns are universal. They may be expressed through Southern characters. William Faulkner, Eudora Welty, Robert Penn Warren, and Flannery O'Connor were not Southern writers, though you can't take a Southern literature class without studying them; but you can't take an American literature class without studying them, either. It would be awful for one's concerns to be the South in an art form. That suggests a local colorist. National textbooks and anthologies that include my poetry do so not because it's Southern poetry.

You don't mind the term "Southern writer," it's just misunderstood?

It's misunderstood willfully by many people, because there are those who have difficulty believing that one can have a national import without living on one of the coasts. This brings to mind a phrase from the Bible when a Philistine said of Jesus, whom he had just heard of, "Can any good thing come out of Nazareth?" I don't want to appear to have the role of Jesus, but the analogy is nontheless fair. Can any good thing come out of Hoxie, Arkansas, or Jackson, Mississippi, or Millageville, Georgia?

How long have you been the director of the University of Arkansas Press?

The press was founded in the spring of 1980, so nine years now. In our first year we published two titles and had a staff of two, including the director. In 1990, we'll do thirty-four titles, at least, and we have a staff of twenty-one. We're growing by two to four titles per year. It's a successful operation.

Publishing has not seen the best of years lately as expenses increase and the audience decreases. The major publishing houses are no longer publishing, or have reduced the amount of poetry they publish, because they can't make any money from it, so they have handed the responsibility down to the university presses. In that the University of Arkansas Press is successful, does the press make money?

We're not quite in the black, but we're not expected to be because we publish works that the commercial houses have declared unprofitable. We publish them for reasons other than monetary. We publish them because we believe they ought to be available to people either in the scholarly field or people who live by poetry and fiction. However, our stipend, state support, is relatively small. We do have that small cushion. And we do make money from our poetry, but not much. And off our fiction. With scholarly monographs we have a little more trouble getting our investment back. We may publish a book needed by eight hundred people in the English-speaking world, but they have to have it; that's the mission of a university press. Even so, we're awfully close to being self-supporting because we do a good job of acquiring titles and of putting books together and marketing them. I'm very proud of our staff.

The fact that we make a little money off our poetry and fiction is not to chastise the commercial houses too much for not publishing it, I guess, because we can survive making just a little bit of money. They cannot. They could publish it as a pro-bono thing and not expect a return, because it's the right thing to do. And some do.

We also publish midlist fiction — good fiction that doesn't have a clearly defined market. Commercial houses know the market for genre fiction — science fiction, western, romance — and if the material has a good handle on a genre they can depend on a steady audience for that author's work. You see Louis L'Amour and not the book. Then there are the blockbuster authors who have discovered a formula a great many readers find satisfying. Then there are some serious quality writers who have such a reputation that people will buy their works, sometimes to have on the coffee table — John Updike, Kurt Vonnegut. In the middle of all this are many fine writers who are turning out novels and short stories that I believe will be read in three hundred years. They are usually understated, lyrical, probing, and demanding on the reader. The commercial houses have almost totally shut them out. These so-called midlist authors are turning to university presses.

Arkansas published Ellen Gilchrist's first collection of short stories, In the Land of Dreamy Dreams. *When you decided to publish this book did you have any idea as to the success it would have?*

No. It was the feature fiction review almost immediately in *Publisher's Weekly*. And bookstores buy the book in the outlined, blocked review. Very soon after that the *Washington Post* gave it almost a half page. Those are the two things that helped it take off. Other journals, seeing those reviews, also reviewed it. It was a big success, a quick success. We were a very young press, and not prepared for that kind of sales; we had an awfully hard time keeping the bookstores supplied with the paperback. We did manage to catch up, though the back orders sat around for a while. We grew up very quickly with that book. We knew the book was good, but we didn't know other people would see how good it was so quickly. It was brought to me by a mutual friend of ours. I knew Ellen's poetry, but I didn't know she was writing fiction. I took the manuscript home to read and my wife picked it up. Before I read it I asked my wife what she thought, and she said, "This is what Flannery O'Connor would write if she were Dorothy Parker. You've got to publish this." When I read it, I saw how astute her comment was. *In the Land of Dreamy Dreams* has all the Gothic, Southern tone, and setting of Flannery O'Connor, but with the wry wit, slightly tilted hat, almost smartass sting of Dorothy Parker. It's a beautiful marriage of the two.

Arkansas will publish nearly thirty-four books in 1990. What subjects do you consider?

We have only one proscription — we are not interested in books that demand an exotic vocabulary on the part of the reader. This doesn't mean books from technology necessarily. A manuscript in protolinguistics, which is technically in the humanities, might require an exotic vocabulary — that is, a special dictionary of the field — to read it. That considered, we're interested in any work on any subject of interest to the educated generalist. We publish in history, political and social theory, essays, biography, interviews, memoirs and letters, literary criticism, fiction, poetry, art and architecture, music, though not music in itself, but material about music and musicians, folklore, science and natural history, reference, theatre, satire and humor, film, psychology, and we're getting ready to publish our first cookbook.

If you could change any one thing about publishing, what would it be?

The way books are marketed. Books find their way into bookstores through title-by-title negotiation between a bookstore traveler — the field representative — and a store manager. This is not done in any other field that I know of. When you see bread at Safeway, you're looking at bakery products that were brought in by delivery men who simply put them in the store. Tomorrow he takes up what isn't sold and replaces it with fresh bread. It's his business to keep the right assortment on the shelves. The bakery and the store share in the profit. It's the same with magazines. When the vendor goes into a bookstore or drugstore or newsstand, he doesn't say to the manager, "You really ought to carry three copies of *Time* this week." He puts them on the shelf and if they don't sell he comes back and gets them. It saves time off everyone's part. If we could go into a bookstore and, given a limited space, could decide what goes on that space, pick up what doesn't sell and leave some other books the way magazine vendors and dairy vendors do, it would save a lot of time and reduce the cost of books. It's extremely expensive to pay someone to go to a bookstore to sit and talk to a manager for twenty minutes while the new book list is touted. As a book representative you have to say, "Okay, I've got thirty new books and only time to talk about three. What are they going to be?" A lot of good work is lost. It's a nineteenth-century system, and I don't know how we can change it except within Arkansas.

The University Press of Arkansas is in a position to offer the bookstore owner in Arkansas a different deal. Most of the independent bookstores have joined into a contractual relationship with us under which we send them a cloth and paperback copy of every book we publish. We don't have to get in touch with the bookstore managers or spend time talking to them, nor do they have to take time out of their day. They just get the books. Their incentive for doing this is considerable. With the conventional arrangement, the bookstore managers have a certain amount of time in which a book can be returned, so they are always preoccupied with watching the calendar. If a manager has five copies of a book and knows that after tomorrow they can't be returned, they're going to send them back. That's self-defeating on the part of everyone. And the bookstore pays the postage both ways. Under our arrangement with Arkansas bookstores we pay the postage both ways —

we can afford to because we save so much money. We just send them the books. They can return any book, no questions asked, and we pay the postage, two years after the book's publication date. So instead of having a time in which they can return the book with other publishers, they only have a lead time during which time they cannot return the book. They are obliged to keep them, not for two years, but two years after the book's actual publishing date, then we'll pay the postage back to us. If the book's publication date is 1986, they can turn around and send the books back next week. It's a marvelous deal. They can relax.

It appears the publishing houses have been doing it backwards.

We think so, but we can't do this outside of Arkansas, because a third of our titles are Arkansas and regional studies. A bookstore in Minneapolis is not likely to want them, but we do have big bookstores in far parts of the nation who can even sell a copy of the *Inaugural Addresses of the Governors of Arkansas,* so they've joined the program and receive two copies of everything.

I would like to ask what your childhood was like.

It was rich, good, full, poor—we were poor. How poor were you? (*Laughing.*) We were poor by anybody's standards. I lived in a small town in the hills of Arkansas where my father was a Methodist minister. I got beat up a lot just on general principles because I was the preacher's kid. I learned that to survive, you either stand the pain or run. I learned to take care of myself. Although we didn't have much money, some of it was always spent on books and records. The arts were an important part of my childhood. There was a great respect for learning. My mother had eleven children—six grew to adulthood, and I was pretty near middle of those who lived. My parents were card-carrying liberals. My father was a civil rights worker involved in the founding of the Southern Tenants Farming Union. He was a conscientious objector in World World I, a pluralistic socialist, a true populist. From as early as I can remember there were union organizers and black and white civil rights workers in our home usually with the blinds drawn. I liked to read, and all my brothers and sisters read most of what was around the house. As poor as we were, I'm astounded that my father managed to have so many books. I was raised in a sane and loving family.

From your childhood do you have a favorite memory?

I remember my father swimming with me on his back in the Black River when I was five. I used to pick the lower bolls of cotton while the grown-ups picked upper bolls so they wouldn't have to get down on their knees. That made me feel very important. The first time I rode a horse with a saddle made me feel grown-up the way city boys might feel when they first wear long pants instead of shorts. I remember my father teaching me to drive, and childhood as a seamless continuum of pleasure and pain. Childhood and adolescence is so many years of hell, but there's a richness in it. I remember adolescence mostly, of course, in sexual terms, because that's the biggest thing happening to adolescents—dealing with sexuality, and I won't detail those memories.

Is there a least favorite memory?

Once I climbed a tree that was even with the top of the church—two and a half stories high. I worked my way out on the limb, which gave as I walked some twenty-five feet from the trunk of the tree. I skittered off to the peak of the church roof. When I let go of the limb it popped back up again. There I was, unable to reach the tree branch and unable to attract anyone's attention. I thought I was never going to finish my fourteenth year. I called and called until I attracted my father's attention. I wanted him to get a ladder or call the fire department, but he wouldn't. He insisted on teaching me that actions have consequences. My choices were to stay on the church roof until I fell asleep and fell off or stand up on the peak of the roof and reach up until I could get my fingers around the limb and pull it down, which is what I had to do. I gained some wisdom from the experience and my father, I suppose, was right. He was sometimes a hard master.

Basements to houses, stores, churches, and school used to have access from outside through a hole with steps leading down. Covering that grave-like opening were two cast-iron doors. I was trying to get such a door open one time using a shovel as a lever. While I was pushing down on the handle my hand slipped, which threw the handle of the shovel into my forehead. I remember running, screaming, and passing out, then I came to with a concussion. That's the greatest pain I have ever felt, because I didn't pass out immediately—I ran toward oblivion. When anyone says pain to me, just the word brings that memory to mind. When I came around, my father thought the punishment I had suffered was sufficient. He was perfectly capable of adding punishment onto pain, but he didn't. I had learned again, more firmly, that actions do have consequences.

Do you have any advice for writers?

Read. Read. Read. If someone is serious about tennis he watches Bjorn Borg, Ivan Lendl, Billie Jean King, and all the other great players. You'll see painters with their easels set up in a gallery, going up to a painting with a magnifying glass to see a brush stroke, then duplicating it. And yet, somehow, people who want to write think it comes a priori. Maybe they are afraid of being influenced. Everyone's first book is an anthology of influences. It can't be otherwise. I'm astounded by young people wanting to write and don't know X.J. Kennedy's work, or Maxine Kumin's. Sometimes they don't know Howard Nemorov's work or Richard Wilbur's. They know Robert Frost because they had to read him more often in school. I've had them say, "I don't want to write like him. I don't want to be influenced. I want to be my own person." Where poetry is concerned, and for what this council is worth, I advise young poets to avoid obfuscation, to recognize that clarity is the soul of elegance, obfuscation is easy, and therefore suspect. Just as important for a young poet to learn is that the line is the unit of structure and function in a poem, and that a poem coheres when the line is a unit in three ways at once—a unit of sense, syntax, and rhythm.

Outside of writing what are some things you like to do?

Travel, which I do a great deal of. I like to play cribbage. John Ciardi and I played cribbage constantly when we were together. In fact, one of my favorite lines is from one of his letters written when I was taking life a bit seriously and in some pain. He wrote, "Life is only a game, Miller. It's not as if it were cribbage." Isn't that just marvelous?

Philip Lee Williams

Philip Lee Williams was born in Athens, Georgia, and raised in Madison. His novels include *The Heart of a Distant Forest,* winner of the 1986 Townsend Prize, *All the Western Stars, Slow Dance in Autumn,* and *Song of Daniel.* He is a graduate of the University of Georgia, beginning as a music major, changing after one quarter to pursue journalism. The first interview was conducted on December 19, 1985, and the second on March 21, 1987, at Williams' home in Athens.

Your classical background has a lot to do with the "Prelude" which appeared in the Chattahoochee Review *in spring 1985 and is from your unpublished novel* The Inner Kingdom.

Right. Well, I've written several books. That's my favorite and it will probably never be published, not in my lifetime. It's real avant-garde. My agent won't handle it. The whole thing is set at a school of music. "Prelude," which I'm real happy the *Chattahoochee Review* used, is sort of a prologue to that. It's quite a long novel.

When did you start writing?

I started out as a poet. I had a lot of poetry published before I had fiction published, in maybe twenty magazines. Actually, I started composing before writing, thinking I was going to be a composer, starting at fourteen. I quit composing after I wrote several very large orchestral pieces to which I still have the manuscripts as family curios. I started writing poetry when I was fifteen or sixteen. I wrote a novella when I was twenty-two, then sort of threw it away. I didn't write any other fiction until I was twenty-seven, when I wrote a very long, very bad novel.

You also wrote an unpublished novel about the South in the Civil Rights era?

Yeah. That's a novel about growing up in the South in the sixties. I wrote it a couple of years ago. What I was trying to do was make an absolutely accurate picture of what life was like without it being a book that hinged on a tremendously strong narrative as in suspense. I did what I wanted to do basically. I've tinkered with it, but haven't gotten to where I want it. In the meantime, I've written two other novels. One is a detective novel set in Atlanta, called *Slow Dance in Autumn*. I'm fond of it, sort of the way you're fond of an ugly dog. It's something I like, but I don't have any delusion that it's wonderful. I finished a new book called *All the Western Stars*. It's a story, again, which involves some old people. It's about these two old guys in their late sixties who leave a nursing home in central Georgia and hitchhike out to Texas to become cowboys. It's a real bizarre premise, but works out quite well. The title is from Tennyson's poem "Ulysses." Tennyson is also sort of out of fashion, but I've always had a weak spot for him.

What inspires you to write?

I think that most writers who have written a good deal will tell you that writing is really more routine than inspiration. If you sit around waiting on inspiration, you'll probably do a lot of sitting around and waiting. I write every day, seven days a week. I get in there and wrestle and fight with it.

Who are some writers whose work you admire?

If I had to pick a group of people whose work I admire most, it would have to be Ezra Pound, T.S. Eliot, James Joyce, and their latter-day forebears like Thomas Pynchon, John Barth and that crowd, some Hemingway. I'm fond of Saul Bellow. I think poets have influenced me as much as novelists.

What was life like as a child, growing up in the country?

I had an extraordinarily happy childhood. Writers are supposed to talk like Eugene O'Neill in dramatic terms about how tough their childhood was and how that is the genesis for their writing. But, in fact, I had a very calm, quiet, pleasant, happy childhood. I have a brother eighteen months older and a sister nine years younger. We went out in the woods and fields a lot. I'd go out by myself or with my brother or a friend and enjoy the solitude. That's the kind of thing you really can't get in town. I'm not sure you can get it there now. Times were really different in the mid 1950s than they are now. Where I lived in town you could go a mile in any direction and there'd be country. That's one reason why I have a real affinity for agricultural things.

When you were growing up, what were you most interested in and what did you want to do?

That's funny you should ask that because I remember when I was in second grade our teacher asked us what we wanted to do when we grew up. I remember, because I swore to myself I'd remember. I told her two things: an archaeologist, because my family had a great interest in history and archaeology, and I wanted to be in the artillery in the army. But you have to remember this was around 1958. We had recently beaten the Nazis.

The Heart of a Distant Forest *reads like poetry.*

What I was trying to do was create a mosaic like Chinese written characters. Basically it's where these crystal images are strung together like lanterns in order to create a big image, little images that represent ideas that you bring together as a whole. I was trying to use that kind of mosaic technique, little bits and flashes. Which is one of the reasons I used the journal, to show a whole picture without telling everything you need to know.

The title from The Heart of a Distant Forest *comes from James Dickey's poem "The Lifeguard."*

I've always liked his work. I had trouble finding a title for the book and went to his work and found it quickly. I don't know of another book, another novel, so far, that has come from a line of a Dickey poem. It may be the first. *The James Dickey Newsletter* asked me to write an essay about the selection of the title.

How well was The Heart of a Distant Forest *received?*

Very well. It was a critical success, there's no doubt about that. It didn't set the woods on fire as far as sales are concerned. I was an unknown novelist from Georgia, and I didn't live in Atlanta. Frankly, I just didn't go out trying to push and sell it, though I did a lot of autographings. Also, the publisher didn't advertise very much and you can't blame them. It was the first book by an unknown.

Was it difficult getting your first novel published?

Actually it wasn't. It was a lot easier than people who've been rejected three million times want to hear me say. I wrote the book several years ago, basically for Linda. I took all the things I was interested in, put them in the blender, put it on stir and here's what I was going to write about. Then I threw it in the drawer for over a year. Later, I received a letter in the mail from Peachtree Publishers on how they had published more material by Georgia journalists than anyone else. Their editor-in-chief at the time liked it, but they weren't publishing much fiction. He suggested I send it to an agent/friend of his in New York. She liked it, called me up and said she'd work for me. It was almost bought by everyone who saw it.

The book has a great appeal. As a reader you are content that Andrew feels good about dying.

The ongoing struggle between life and death, even though the protagonist at the end is apparently near death, makes it a positive, upbeat book. I wanted to write a book that wasn't tragic, but sort of sad with elements of a power that would make you feel good about the continuity of life and that death wasn't necessarily a rotten break. Which I don't think it is.

It is for a few characters in the book. The one that sticks in my mind is where a dying man entrusts his brothers to buy him a headstone and instead they sell his body to a medical school.

Well, they deserve it. That story is one of the few instances where I have used something that was told to me. I changed the names to protect the guilty. I'm told that actually happened.

How does the character of Andrew mirror you?

The fact that I made him a retired junior college history professor is slightly ironic, in that I'm an amateur historian. I think an intermediate step between being an amateur and a professional historian is someone who teaches at a junior college. Basically, what I did was take what I knew and made myself a little smarter, but not real smart.

There's a great line which reveals the humor: "An elderly woman humped in the pew a few seats from me trembled slightly for the rest of the service, but I could not tell if it was from moral outrage or Parkinson's disease."

I like that line, too. You'd like my new book, it's got some really good lines. I'm good at snappy comebacks.

My favorite is where you quote Thomas Jefferson, "I find as I grow older that I love those most whom I loved first."

I think so, too. Well, maybe I'm a little closer to Andrew than I admit. I really believe that quote. I'm a fairly outgoing, country-type boy from middle Georgia who drinks beer while watching football. I'm not a willowy aesthete going around with my pen in the air looking at butterflies. That ain't me at all. I can see how people might get the opinion if they misread the book, which you didn't, which some people have done—misread it as an idyll, rather than a serious piece of fiction.

Could there be a continuation with Willie Sullivan progressing into adulthood or maybe Andrew's early years?

It's really funny you should ask that question, because the book was out in hardback when a woman asked me when I was going to write the sequel? I had no idea anybody was ever going to print it. Why would I write a sequel to something I never thought would be published? It never crossed my mind and hasn't very often since. If I write anything it'll be a reflection that Willie would make on Andrew.

Let's talk about what it takes to be a writer.

If you want to write, a writer has to work. Raymond Andrews said he wanted to start out writing a best-selling poem. That's not going to work, there's no time involved, but he was kidding, of course. Do two things: take classes, if you have good teachers. But first and foremost, read, read, read. Read anything you can get your hands on. Read the classics, contemporary material, fiction, poetry, criticism, history, the Bible, everything. Make sure you know about art, music, sports. Make sure you have a big frame of reference. If you have a shallow frame of reference, you ain't gonna write fiction. It's just that simple. You need to know a great deal about everything. Pay careful attention, listen to conversations, how people talk, the words they use, the sound of their voice, types of people. That's great training. You have to be involved in life. You can't sit in your study and write. It won't have a ring of truth to it. Write every day! If you don't passionately care about writing and if it doesn't mean almost more to you than anything else, then don't ever think you're going to get far. It's not something you do on Sunday afternoons.

It's something you live with, you put blood into, you get rewards and pain, suffering, but ultimately it's worth it.

Where do you go from here?

Just keep writing. I don't have any great career plan, no master plan. I'm not going to be world famous by the time I'm fifty. The stuff I write is never going to make me rich and it ain't going to make me famous. I got a lot of attention in a small way for *The Heart of a Distant Forest.* The little bit of fame part is fun to a certain extent, and any writer who says it's not is lying. A lot of fame that's attached itself to best-sellers and writers is something I would absolutely hate. I value my privacy and my family life. We're extremely private. When the time comes to publish my next book I'll come to Atlanta and do all the autographings I did for this book, be visible for awhile, then vanish. I'd like to master the short story, which Mary Hood has done. I'd like to get back to poetry and write more plays, but my primary interest is in the novel. If I could ever make a ton of money, I'd probably do something like run a fishing camp, have my own TV fishing show.

The Phil Williams Fishing Show?

That's it.

*   *   *

You just mentioned three books that have been accepted for publication.

We might have talked a little about this before, I don't remember. The first one is called *All the Western Stars.* It's coming in March 1988. The second one is the detective novel, *Slow Dance in Autumn,* which will come out in the fall of 1988, which we're doing as a paperback-original series. So, we'll probably come out with one of those every fall I hope. The third one I don't think we've talked about, and I don't think I'd written it the last time we talked. It's called *Darkness.* It'll come out in the spring of 1989, and is set in 1920 in Branton, same town where *The Heart of a Distant Forest* is set. It's about a young drifter who is has mustered out of World War I and is drifting around the country. He stops in Branton and wrangles a job with a very wealthy family. The mother of this family, who's in her fifties, has recently started a private asylum for people with emotional problems from losing their farms because of the boll weevil. The boll weevil, in 1920, was tearing the South to shreds. There was no way to stop it. At the same time, this young man, while he's working for this family, falls in love with their daughter, who is a very sheltered, protected young girl who's never been away from home. The complications that result from this madhouse in the county builds to a climax involving this young man, the girl, her brother and her parents. It's set mainly in this large mansion in Branton, and the other part is set in the madhouse on the outskirts of town.

What are you writing now?

I've just finished another novel tentatively called *Final Heat.* Again, it's set in Branton. I'm writing about what I know, obviously. It's set in contemporary time, and is about two families, one of which is very wealthy and whose daughter is home from college for the summer. She's a real amoral, ne'er-do-well, who doesn't care what she does next; she just wants to have fun and be excited. She has a relationship with a young man who lives and runs a store outside of town in a poorer area. He is incredibly frustrated and can't stand the fact that he's trapped running this store. His father has become senile and lives at home with his dim-witted brother. This boy decides to rob an old lady in town. The young woman is excited by the idea, decides to go with him, and while they are there, they accidentally kill the old lady. The ramifications that result, the plot shifts, build up into a steamy, involved, violent book.

Have things stayed pretty much on course for what your writing?

It's been a little bit slower than I thought at first. After *The Heart of a Distant Forest* came out I thought things would happen faster than they did, but it's taken a lot of shaking down, both with my writing and in New York, too. I had a lot of trouble dealing with publishers in New York. The kind of fiction I write is not best-seller material. I'm trying to write the best I can, but the stories I want to tell are not Judith Krantz. In New York, now, in order to break even, because of the high overhead, you have to sell nine, ten thousand copies of a book. That doesn't sound like a lot, but it is when they're sixteen, seventeen dollars a clip. And they don't promote books well. Most publishers publish it, throw it out there — if it gets good reviews and does well, then you'll sell a few thousand. If they don't, you're gone. *The Heart of a Distant Forest* has really hung on. It's still in print in hardback, and it's still selling in paperback, which is strange since the book has been out two years in paperback and three in hardback. It's done well. I think winning the Townsend Prize last year had something to do with that. I think my career has gone pretty much where I wanted it to go. The magazine articles are a lot of extra work that I really don't have time for, but they pay well. It's kind of hard not to do it. The "dirt roads" piece in *Southern Magazine* bought me an electric guitar and amp. So I wrote the piece and sold it. That kind of thing is nice when you don't have the money to do it otherwise. I think now my career is going to take off with the deal with Peachtree Publishers. I'm very excited about that. I don't know too many writers who can sell three books in one day.

You mentioned your guitar. What kind of music are you interested in?

Country. I write country songs and enjoy playing them. I play the piano, too. I got interested in country music about five or six years ago, and I'd always been a medium rock and roller, never into the heavy rock stuff. Just regular rock and roll. Country music is another thing I'm going to do one of these days when I'm ready. It's odd, but I primarily listen to country and classical music.

You mentioned before that you had an interest the short story, have you worked any more on that?

I have a short story coming out in *Confrontation* called "Hoping to Glimpse His Face," which is a very wild, violent story. I've only written about thirty short stories. I haven't gotten back to them yet. I like writing novels because I like long projects. I don't like finishing something in two weeks. I've got poems coming out in various magazines such as *Cumberland Review*, *The Kentucky Poetry Review*, *Poem* and *Riverside Quarterly*.

That was one of my next questions. You primarily started out as a poet.

Yeah, I did. And I really dropped it for a long time. I didn't start writing fiction until I was in my late twenties, twenty-seven or eight. I've been writing poetry since I was sixteen and getting published before I got out of college. A little here and there.

If I had gone on with my poetry career, I could have published a good deal by now. I'd like to get back to poetry. In fact, there was a period of about four months in 1986 where all I did was write poetry. Out of that bunch that I sent out, about fifteen have been accepted. There's a book-length manuscript from that which publishers are considering. I've also got a one-act play called *Fancy* that's being considered by theater groups. Right now I'm writing the follow-up to the detective story.

That's Slow Dance in Autumn.

It'll be the same guy, told in first person. It'll be just a regular detective series. He's a hardboiled detective, former AAA baseball player who now runs an agency in Atlanta. His name in Hank Prince. Prince, oddly enough, is a family name on my father's side, and I think Hank Prince sounds like a detective.

What has having a successful novel done for you?

Well it's been successful in terms of critical acclaim. I've not made that much money off it at all. When you say "successful novel," people think you've gotten rich. My advance for *The Heart of a Distant Forest* was $2500, which is about as low as an advance as you can get. And I've made a few thousand dollars on it, but not much. It's sold around 25,000 copies now in paperback. That part of it is fine, but I've got a full-time job. I'd like to make a trillion dollars in the writing business as I think any writer would. The success of the novel has done a lot for me. Winning the Townsend Prize has gotten me magazine work, tons of speaking engagements, which I generally do, whether I get paid or not, simply on the idea that it will help sell the next book. I've done so many speeches that I'm pretty sure my next book will sell, and Peachtree feels the same way because I have been visible. I haven't been hiding over here.

Is that just in the United States?

It's coming out in Sweden in two weeks. I got a letter from my Swedish publisher this week. They're ready to go, and want to know when my next book is coming out, because they want to publish it. It was picked up by a Swedish book club, too, which expects to sell a thousand copies there. It's done a lot of very nice things for me. It's put me in a position to get my work published.

There's a change in attitude since the last time we spoke. You were set against public speaking and promotion of your work.

It's still not something I would do if there were not a reason. Maybe I have changed a little bit. I feel that if somebody thinks enough of my work to ask me to come talk to them about it... — you just don't turn your back on any reader. Any writer is grateful for a reader. I'm the featured writer at the Macon Book Club in April, and they're going to have 200 people there. The Atlanta Pen Women have a large group in May. Two weeks ago I spoke to a book club in Gainesville where there were nine people, so I figure everyone of those people might read my book and want to meet me and want to know what I'm doing. That's good for me. Occasionally, it gets to be a little tiring, and you do give the same speech over and over, but the attention is nice.

Did you expect to win the Townsend Prize?

I didn't know a thing about it — I was totally floored. I wasn't going to go, but I did decide to, because most of the nominees are friends of mine. But, really, I wanted to see the Ritz-Carlton. I'm from Madison, Georgia; I wanted to see this beautiful hotel. For me being in Buckhead is ridiculous; hell, I grew up on a dirt road. I thought I would go, enjoy myself, and relax. All week long my wife, Linda, kept asking if I had something written in case I won. I said I'm not going to win, why should I bother? When Celestine Sibley, a previous winner, started reading from my book, I had two thoughts running through my mind: I won. The other was, oh hell! I'm going to have to stand up in front four hundred people and not sound like a total idiot. So I was floored and thrilled to death. As it turned out, Linda knew about it ahead of time. Linda had people calling her to make sure I was at the awards. She knew I had won two weeks ahead of time, and so she told my parents and her parents, and they were all there. I thought they went because I was nominated. That was a great day for me.

Where do you see your writing headed?

I would like to write as well as I can, and as much as I can. I doubt if I'll ever write a novel that's not set around Georgia. This place is what I know. I want to get the detective series going. I know I'm going to catch a lot of heat from serious writers and my colleagues about that being sort of worthless, but I don't think it is at all. It's like taking a breath from serious fiction. It's not serious in any sense of the word. It's a lark, it's fun. It will sell, and people will like it. But they will be interspersed among what I'm really doing as an artist. I want to write books that will last, and I hope to have a long association with Peachtree.

I just want to do the best I can. You can't worry about sales or the respect of the critics. When you start thinking about those things while you're writing, it just dries you up. The only thing you can do is come to it fresh and do something different. Somebody will tell you if you're slipping: the public or sales or your wife.

Is there anything I haven't asked you that you'd like to discuss?

Oh, I don't know. I seriously would like to sell some songs. That's relaxation. That's my jigsaw puzzle. Maybe perfect my fifteen-foot jump shot. It's pretty good right now.

Did I tell you how I started that first detective novel, *Slow Dance in Autumn?* Linda and Brandon were going to the beach, Panama City, and I couldn't go, because I had injured my back. The day they left my back hurt so badly I could hardly walk, and I was hobbling. I didn't want to take a pill or anything so I started drinking bourbon. This is at eleven o'clock in the morning. It took me twenty minutes to take my typewriter from the living room outside to the deck. I was walking like Tim Conway. Finally, I got out there and set the typewriter on the picnic table, set the bottle next to the typewriter, put the paper in, and typed "Evan Williams Black Label Sour Mash Bourbon Whiskey is the best in the world and I should know." That's the first sentence in the novel. I sat there and wrote forty pages of the novel in one day. The last fifteen pages didn't make any sense, because I'd been drinking all day. I had to throw them away. A few weeks later I pulled everything out and realized it was pretty good, and maybe I ought to write this book. That was the only thing I had ever written while I was drinking — kids don't try this at home — and now it'll be a continuing series. It's also the last thing I'll write while drinking. As I drank, I got smarter and smarter. By about five o'clock in the afternoon I was damn near a genius.

Stuart Woods

Stuart Woods was born in Manchester, Georgia, in 1938. He earned a degree from the University of Georgia in 1959, then moved to New York City in 1960, where he lived throughout the decade. *Chiefs,* his first novel, was made into a television movie, and *Deep Lie* made the *New York Times Best Seller List.* His other books are *Under the Lake, White Cargo, A Romantic's Guide to the Country Inns and Restaurants of Britain and Ireland, Grass Roots,* and *Blue Water, Green Skipper.* This interview was conducted at Woods' Atlanta home on April 2, 1987.

Could you discuss your background?

I was born in Manchester, Georgia, in January 1938. I went to grammar school and high school there. I went to the University of Georgia and graduated from there in 1959. I spent about a year afterwards waiting to go into the service, then went into the Air National Guard. A few months after that I moved to New York City. I had been working in advertising for about a year when I was recalled into the Air Force for ten months during the Berlin Crisis when they built the wall in 1961. After that I came back to New York, and spent all of the sixties in New York. Then, I moved to London, having received a job in advertising. I was there for three years. After that I decided it was time to write *Chiefs,* my first novel, which had been in my mind for a long time. I moved to Ireland to write the book because it was cheaper and prettier there, and I could work two days a week for an advertising agency in Dublin while I lived on the west coast in County Galway. That's when I discovered sailing, and that made the writing sort of go to hell for awhile. I inherited a little money from my grandfather, so I moved to County Cork, where I had a boat built. I used that to sail in a single-handed trans–Atlantic race in 1976. When I finished that I came back to assist my mother with selling my late grandfather's business, and I also worked on Jimmy Carter's campaign that fall as his advance man in Plains, Georgia.

My first book was about my sailing experience called *Blue Water, Green*

Skipper. The second was *A Romantic's Guide to the Country Inns and Restaurants of Britain and Ireland.* I finished *Chiefs* in 1980, and it was published in 1981, then *Run Before the Wind* came two years later. *Under the Lake* should have come two years after that, in 1985, but my publisher, W.W. Norton, wanted to publish *Deep Lie* first and postpone *Under the Lake,* which I reluctantly agreed to. Later, I decided to leave that publisher, and I bought *Under the Lake* back, and I sold it to Simon and Schuster, as part of a two book contract.

Why did he change the order of publication?

He thought *Deep Lie* would be a more commercial book, that it was more topical. It was the first book I had written that seemed to fit into a genre. My books don't seem to fit that easily into a genre — although it wasn't a conventional spy-thriller. So, I agreed to that, and later regretted it, but now I don't know that I do regret it because I think Simon and Schuster will do a much better job of marketing the book. I just finished a book called *White Cargo* that will be out in 1988 by Simon and Schuster. I'm also working on an original six-hour screenplay for CBS about three generations of a Southern political family.

What is Under the Lake *about?*

It's a psychological thriller with supernatural overtones. It's the first time I've dealt in that area. The publishers seem to have high hopes for it.

Each one of your novels has had a very different subject matter.

Yes, they have, and that sometimes troubles my publishers. They said it would be better from a publishing point of view if the readers knew what to expect from book to book. It would be easier to build a readership, but I don't like covering the same ground twice. I might use the same locale, and I do use some of the same characters again. But all my books have been very different, and I'd like to keep it that way. I'd prefer the readers to simply see my name on the book and believe they'll get a good read out of it.

Since you mentioned using some characters again, Will Lee is in Deep Lie *as he was in* Chiefs, *and the town Delano sort of makes a cameo appearance.*

Yes, that's true. The protagonist in *Under the Lake* is the reporter from *Chiefs,* John Howell, the *New York Times'* reporter. Will Lee makes a brief appearance in *White Cargo* — he has one scene. I'm thinking of running him for the Senate.

When did you start writing?

Well, I've wanted to write since I was small. My mother taught me to read the year before I went to school, and I became a voracious reader as a child. From that time on I wanted to write, although people kept talking me out of it on the grounds that it was impossible to make a living, or at least a very good one. It wasn't bad advice; it's not easy to make a living as a writer. The average writer in this country makes about five thousand dollars a year.

When I got out of college I went to New York looking for a magazine job and couldn't find one, but I found one in advertising. That turned out to be very good. I was fortunate in working for some people who were very good writers themselves, who were very demanding. I exhibited some talent for it. I learned to write a good sentence, then a good paragraph, eventually a good page. If you can write a good page then you can make the leap. I never wrote very many short stories. I wrote a few in college. I took a short story course one quarter, that was the last time I wrote one. I didn't want to after that. They were very bad, but I sent them off to the *New Yorker* and the *Saturday Evening Post,* and I got rejection slips back very quickly. As a matter of fact, that's what propelled me to go to New York. I was trying to write in Atlanta, and I got a rejection slip from the *New Yorker,* so I sold my car, bought a one-way ticket to New York, and never looked back.

What did you study at the University of Georgia?

Sociology — not for any terribly logical reason. I took a couple of sociology courses as electives, and I had a wonderful professor, Raymond Payne, who later became the head of the department. I enjoyed studying under him so much that I decided to major in it. I rationalized reasons for it being a good choice of a major. It was a good major. I had a liberal arts background, and it taught me about the society I live in — the way it functions. I don't regret that. Although, I think if I had to do it over, I would study English literature.

Could you tell me about Manchester, Georgia, the small town you grew up in?

It's a lovely little town, and it's fairly well described in *Chiefs.* Delano is a lot like Manchester. It had four or five thousand people when I was growing up — it still does. It was prettier than most Georgia towns, snuggled next to a high mountain ridge. It's near Warm Springs where Franklin Roosevelt's "Little White House" was. I had an idyllic youth in lot of ways. I was the all-American boy. Once, I took a friend, the architect Henry Jova, from Atlanta to Manchester to look at some property. As we were driving down Third Street where I was born, he said, "Isn't this the street where Andy Hardy used to live?" That's what it's like.

Was Manchester the blueprint for Delano?

Yes, it was very similar to Delano, the town in *Chiefs,* though I took great pains not to make it Manchester.

So, were any other parts of Chiefs *autobiographical?*

Well, the first two police chiefs were based on real people. The first one was based on my maternal grandfather, a cotton farmer who lost his farm to the boll weevil and became the chief of police, for lack of any other work. The second section of the book is based on some incidents that happened following World War II. But I only used a suggestion of what went on. The third part is entirely fictional. It was not an autobiographical book in that sense, the only truly autobiographical chapter is when the character Billy Lee spends a Saturday afternoon trotting around the town. He visits the livery stable and some other places. That's right out of my childhood.

That brings up the question about your childhood. What was it like?

Just idyllic. The all–American childhood, but I was not a very good athlete. My folks divorced when I was two, and we lived with my grandparents until I was six. Those are my earliest memories — at my grandparents house. Then my mother remarried. We always lived on the same street. I was born on Third Sreet, and my mother still lives there, just farther down the street. It was and is a delightful town.

Do you have any favorite memory of the town that sticks out in your mind?

The livery stable is a favorite memory. I think that's why I used it in the book. I had the usual anxieties as a child, and as a teenager. I would have like to have been a better athlete. I wasn't terribly good. I was a second- or third-string football player for a couple of years. I played on the tennis team. I was in the band. In fact, when I was still in high school I formed a band of musicians who were my parents age, and we played at a little roadhouse on Friday nights called Gil's. There's a scene at such a roadhouse in the second book of *Chiefs* where Sonny Butts has a fight with a sailor. Gil's was the model for the roadhouse.

There are a number of similarities between the character Will Lee and yourself, mainly, Delano being Manchester, his political involvement, and in Deep Lie *his interest in sailing. Is Will Lee an extension of yourself?*

I don't think so, although I share some things with him. But I share *something* with all my characters, even the worst ones.

Your books have sold very well.

Yes. *Deep Lie* was the first one to actually make the *New York Times Best Seller List.* I've done much better than any writer has the right to expect, or the right to hope. I certainly can't complain.

Do you have any numbers on the amount of books you've sold?

I really don't know. It would run into the millions, because *Reader's Digest* has condensed two of the books, and they generally sell about two million copies each time. *Chiefs* has sold, probably, a half million books in paperback. My books have never sold large numbers in hardback — most novels don't. I hope they will as things go along.

You mentioned the difficulty a writer has making a living — is that your living now? Do you do anything else?

It has been for quite some time. When I first got out of college I was supposed to go into the Air Force for three years, but the starting date wasn't for several months, so I got a job working for a man named Ham Stockton, at the now defunct Parks-Chambers. Ham now has his own clothing stores in Atlanta called H. Stockton. I stayed there until I went into the service. I came out and got the job at Rich's. Then I went to New York, and after that it was all advertising — then writing.

Do you think the variety of jobs you've had has helped your writing?

Yes. I advise young people who want to write to get out and experience life. It's very difficult for young people, say in their twenties, to write good fiction. Occasionally, someone will come along who can write, but I think you have to have some experience in living. I always advise young people who are serious about writing to get a job that requires them to write every day — newspaper, advertising, magazine, public relations — anything that requires them to express an idea in print. Advertising is particularly good, because you have so much more latitude than, say, writing for a newspaper. Almost everything you work on is different, so your imagination is in constant demand.

In an author's note in Deep Lie, *you say you have driven from the office of the President of the United States, the Director of Central Intelligence and all his employees, representatives from Georgia in the United States Senate, the Prime Minister of Sweden, his Minister of Defense . . . insomuch that you use their titles and offices. In all your novels you make a strong note that this is fiction and of your imagination, and anyone who interprets this as his own life story is misinformed or crazy. Do you need such a strong disclaimer?*

That's always been a question against libel if you claim your characters are fictional. Of course, if someone can prove you've depicted him untruthfully in literature, then they have a reason for a libel suit. It's difficult to prove libel in the United States. It's much easier in England. I don't normally base characters on real people, although I have on a couple of occasions. Hugh Holmes, the banker in *Chiefs,* was based on James S. Peters, a state senator and banker. But the character was not him and it was not meant to be a thinly disguised version. Recently, there was a libel suit where a man wrote a novel in which he apparently used his former girlfriend for a character — simply changed her name. She sued him, and demonstrated that the character was very much like herself in many ways, but still she lost. I was very worried when *Chiefs* came out that someone in my hometown might think he had been portrayed unfavorably in the book, when in fact I hadn't. I actually took out libel insurance for *Chiefs.*

You mentioned that it's much easier to be sued for libel in England than the United States?

There's a difference in the law, and I don't entirely understand it. The guidebook I wrote was not published in England, because I had said something disparaging about the food in one of the inns. They threatened to sue for libel. The publisher capitulated, and pulped all the books, much to my annoyance.

Wasn't that just a critic's opinion?

Yes, but that's difficult in England. Publishers are just much more fearful of libel, and so they comply. Their newspapers are regularly sued for libel, and regularly lose.

In Deep Lie, *you mention the many people who assisted and lent information to you. You have a large background on the CIA and KGB's internal functions. How much research did you have to do?*

Deep Lie was the first book I ever did any research on. I went to Sweden twice, to the Soviet Union, and Finland. I talked to people who were former CIA people. I avoided mentioning their names. My knowledge of how the CIA works is slim. I made some assumptions based on what I have heard, what I had been told by my sources, and what I felt was probably true. I characterized the "company," and later I received a letter from one of my sources who said I had done a pretty good job, and that I was extremely close. I assumed there was internal dissension in the CIA, office politics . . . I went to get some background and to soak up the atmosphere. In the book, I had scenes in both Moscow and Leningrad. It was extremely helpful to go there.

While you were in Russia did you interview any KGB?

I met with some people who were thought by some to be KGB, you never quite know for sure. I met some Soviet writers, who had a lot of knowledge about the KGB. I also met for some time with Dr. Georgi Arbatov who is the head of the Institute of U.S.A. and Canadian Studies of the Soviet Academy of Sciences. As such he was the principal advisor to the Kremlin on Western affairs. The *Reader's Digest* thinks he is KGB. You hear all sorts of things about people, but you never know. Before going to the Soviet Union I had never met a Russian, even though I'm well traveled. The Soviet people are friendly, warm . . . They're somewhat chaffed by the rigid ideology they have to live with. You can't have open arguments with these people because they have to take a line, especially if they have any official capacity. I had a marvelous time there. My feet never touched the ground, I was on the move constantly. I greatly enjoyed it, and I'd like to go back, but I'm not sure I'd be able to, because they don't like to issue visas to people who've written what they consider bad things about them.

You met with some Soviet writers . . . In the sense that they are writing, how censored are they, or did they even discuss that?

Well, of course there's a long list of suppressed books up to and including *Dr. Zhivago*. I think Soviet writers are self-censoring in that they know what will and what won't get published, what will and won't bring grief. All publishing is controlled by the government. They have a writers' union, which publishes to an extent, but to be a member you have to be "okay." You can't be a dissident and be in the writers' union. There's a writing establishment in the Soviet Union that does not exist in the United States. There is no controlling organization which controls writers' work in this country. There is over there. In the Soviet Union, some of the more established writers will take a jab or two at the government as they become bolder.

The people I met were anxious to defend their way of doing things, and arguments became quite heated at times. The Soviets are still very emotional about World War II, which they call the Great Patriotic War. I met a man in Leningrad who began to lecture me on how they had suffered during the war. I had to stop him and assure him that I understood. He said there was a place not far from where we spoke, where a quarter of a million people are buried in a mass grave. I told him that the Vietnam War was very painful for our country, that many officers had returned to write about their horrifying experiences. I asked him why no Soviet officers had written about their experiences in Afghanistan. He said, "I cannot imagine such a thing happening." He implied that no patriotic Russian would write a novel critical of the military. Of course, he's right. No one who values his position in the Soviet society would do so. It would never be published for one thing, and he might lose his job or his apartment. He might be imprisoned or sent to a mental hospital. What they regard as a lack of patriotism is grounds for being committed as insane. There is no word in Russian for emigration. The word used for emigrant is traitor. I had dinner with a man who was a Refusenik, Jewish or half Jewish. He was an artist. He had requested permission to emigrate and had been refused. Hence, "Refusenik." Now, he has no work, and must live on his girlfriend's earnings.

I'm curious to find out if you know, as in Deep Lie, *whether or not an invasion of Sweden is possible under those circumstances?*

No one knows. I've talked to people who thought the Soviets were totally capable of it. But they probably couldn't get away with it. I took my thesis for *Deep Lie* from Vice-Admiral Bengt Schumack, who at that time was the head of the Swedish Navy. He said, "A foreign power is preparing for war with Sweden." That was his explanation for the Soviet submarine in Swedish waters. Nobody really knows what the Soviets were doing there, and that's what made it such an interesting proposition for a novel.

Did the Swedish government have any theories as to why it happened?

Well, everyone had theories, but no one knew. The Prime Minister confessed to me that he really didn't know. He figured it was training for something. The question then arises, training for what? And since Sweden is determinedly neutral, the United States would not come to their defense. The closest neighbor, Norway, is a NATO country—conceivably Norway might go in and assist. We wouldn't fight World War III to save Sweden, and that's what it would amount to.

As in the book, do they have the civil defense you described?

Yes. Every Swedish male is an effective militiaman. They still have the draft, and each man has an assignment and a place to go in case of a national emergency. They take that very seriously, though some of it is very creaky. Their antisubmarine warfare was embarrassingly inadequate—they couldn't catch or kill a Soviet submarine. The only one they found was the one that ran itself aground.

When researching Deep Lie, *were you given any confidential material?*

Well, I think people voiced opinions based on information that was confidential. I wasn't told any "secrets," I don't think.

I see you have a fairly sophisticated set-up here. How important is your word processor to you?

Oh, it's extremely important. It's made my life much easier. It's not any easier to write, but it's much, much easier to make changes. I just spent a couple of days making changes in an outline for the miniseries, and that would have taken me a couple of weeks if I had had to retype it, or send it to a typist. The laser printer prints at eight pages a minute.

Do you have a certain schedule you try to keep to when writing?

Generally, I write two hours in the morning and two in the afternoon. Four hours a day is about all the fiction I can write and still be coherent. I can write nonfiction for longer than that.

What inspires you to write?

The story; I've always liked a good story and telling it. The inspiration is mostly hard work. Deadlines inspire me more than anything else.

Do you have any advice for writers?

Finish what you start. You'll never sell anything if it's not finished. It's amazing how many people don't understand that. So many people will say to me that they have this great idea for a book, and want to know what they should do. I tell them to write it, which ought to be self-evident. Writing is hard work, and people who are dilettantes discover that they don't want to finish.

When you've finished the manuscript and sent it to your editor, how much editing do they do?

Well, it depends. *Chiefs* had very few changes made in it. Chapter three became chapter one, and I may have cut half of one scene, and the rest was just tiny stuff. *Under the Lake* probably had more editing than any other book, because it was edited by two houses. First, by Norton, and then by Simon and Schuster. There has been really very little done to the books, and the finished products are very close to the first draft. I learned in advertising that I didn't like rewriting, so I write carefully the first time. When I got the word processor I started to write with a little more abandon. I am more practiced than before, so I've learned that I don't have to labor over a paragraph, that if I simply write it as it comes to me, it will probably be as good as any other way I could have written it. I have some faith in that.

Do you find most of their comments valuable?

Yes, but I reserve the right not to accept them. I am at least equal to my editor, and maybe superior, because I know what I'm doing, and why I'm doing it, and he or she may not understand it as well as I do. If we have a disagreement and I feel strongly about it, I'll refuse to change it. I sent *Under the Lake* to my editor at Simon and Schuster, who was interested in seeing anything I had ready. After the deal was finalized, I asked her to send me notes on the book. Well, the book has a supernatural premise, and she said there's just one thing they wanted me to change; they wanted me to omit the supernatural things. I said, "Are you kidding, it's the glue that holds the story together." They were very serious about it. Other people made the same pitch to me, but I had to dig my heels in and refuse. I didn't flatly say no. I was grateful for the advice, but gave them my reasons why I didn't want to change it. They said it was my book and if that's how I feel then that's how it will be. I think it would have been a terrible mistake to change the book. But still, these are highly paid professionals who have been very successful.

Could you discuss in detail what happened with the Fastnet Race?

An unforcasted and extremely violent storm struck the fleet of 300 yachts. Fifteen competitors and four people on an observing boat were lost. My publisher's yacht, *Toscana*, managed very well with no damage. We were very fortunate.

What has the success of your books done for you?

It's made me independent. It's given me a pleasant lifestyle. It's nice to get up and not have to drive to work. My wife has to do that. I get up and come downstairs. It's nice to have control of my own schedule. If I want to take a week off, I do it. That's a valuable commodity in life. I live a more stress-free existence than most people, and it's nice to get recognition for the books.

Index